D. R.
Grenfell

SOCIALIST,
WELSHMAN,
INTERNATIONALIST

D. R. Grenfell

SOCIALIST, WELSHMAN, INTERNATIONALIST

ROBERT SMITH

Cover design: Y Lolfa
Cover image: *D. R. Grenfell* by Ernst Neuschul,
Gorseinon Institute

Photographs: D. R. Grenfell Papers, West Glamorgan Archives

ISBN: 978 1 80099 714 1

Published and printed in Wales
on paper from well-maintained forests by
Y Lolfa Cyf., Talybont, Ceredigion SY24 5HE
website www.ylolfa.com
e-mail ylolfa@ylolfa.com
tel 01970 832 304

Contents

Introduction

FOR 37 YEARS, D. R. Grenfell served as Labour Member of Parliament for the Gower constituency and attained the status of Father of the House of Commons. Today, he is remembered fleetingly, if at all, in historical and biographical works. Yet at the height of his powers he was at the heart of Labour's work as a parliamentarian, campaigner and policy maker, and played a pivotal part in shaping Labour's gradual recovery from near annihilation in the 1931 election. The work in which he was involved was often unglamorous – but essential in creating the environment in which Labour triumphed during the years of the Attlee government.

His own journey has elements of the heroic, the story of the pit boy who ended his days at the heart of the British Establishment as Father of the House of Commons, or even as the Welsh firebrand who refused a peerage. But to conceive of his life solely in those terms is to ignore key aspects of D. R.'s contribution at Welsh, British and international levels. He was a man whose public life was spent focusing on issues like the mining industry, control of the economy, the role of the State in society, international relations and the status of Wales in Britain. He approached these issues as a man of the Left, and not only in his early years as a product of the South Wales Miners' Federation (SWMF) during and immediately after the First World War. D. R. was part of the rise of the Labour Party from 1918 to 1959 as it became the majority party of Wales, articulating the aspirations of Welsh people.

They were years in which people looked to Labour to forge a better course and secure social justice for them and their families by harnessing economic power to the benefit of working people. This was not the product of abstract economic theory: it represented an articulate and intellectually coherent analysis of economic power in south Wales in a period of industrial strength in the Edwardian period in particular. Huge wealth was being created by coal and metal manufacturing, but its benefits were not being enjoyed by those responsible for its production. That basic premise formed the foundations of Socialist thought in south Wales, and was the starting point for the creation of alternative concepts of how the economy should be organised in a way that would uplift the society that had been moulded by industrialisation.

These matters were at the heart of the discussions of the Gorseinon Independent Labour Party (ILP) branch which D. R. had joined before the First World War. Their members developed a critique of the failings of the capitalist system, both in terms of how it existed and the direction in which it was heading, alongside a view of a fairer alternative. This was linked to an understanding of the way a different economic order would lead to the social, cultural and moral emancipation of both men and women who would be enabled to fulfil their full potential. Gorseinon ILP branch was by no means alone in this, but it was a fine example of this phenomenon.

As an MP the battle was increasingly about the survival of that industrial community in the face of economic dereliction. Wales lost half a million people in the space of 25 years amid an official view that believed in transference of 'surplus' population irrespective of social or national claims. This and the rights of the victims of economic factors over which they had no control were to prove central to D. R.'s work as a parliamentarian during the 1920s and 1930s.

By the time the Labour government was elected in 1945, he was already a marginalised figure, unfairly blamed for mistakes made during the war years and out of favour with the most prominent leaders of the British Labour movement. As a wartime minister he had seen at first hand the impact of a run-down coal industry, something that imperilled Britain's war effort and risked the country's ability to produce the materials required for victory. As will be shown in the relevant chapters, lessons learned during the war could have averted some of the crises that beset the Attlee government, but the warnings were not heeded.

This book will hopefully shed light on a period in history and augment existing research into more well-known Labour figures from Wales. Foremost among them, quite rightly, stand Aneurin Bevan and Jim Griffiths, as well as the valuable work on S. O. Davies which provided an inspiration when it was published in the grim summer of 1983 when the very future of the Labour Party was being discussed. Other works on Ness Edwards, Daniel Hopkin, and Cledwyn Hughes, for instance, examine their lives in the context of many of the events that are described in this work.

Such works exist alongside the rich and varied research undertaken into Welsh history over the last 40 years which has set the kind of political issues dealt with in this work in a much broader context. This has deepened our understanding of the society D. R. represented and the people to and for whom he spoke, both in his own constituency and in other parts of Wales. These have focused on the social and economic, questions of language, culture and identity, and especially of gender. They are essential elements in understanding the world in which D. R. lived and worked and the world view which he espoused. D. R. and those with whom he worked in parliament were put there by people who looked to them to articulate their political hopes and aspirations. Any appreciation of a political figure like D. R. is impossible without an understanding of the political culture of those whose support he enjoyed.

This is a book about D. R. the politician and public figure. I was fortunate to know some of the Grenfell family, brother

Ivor Grenfell's children Bryn and Ann in particular. I also met his brother Mansel's daughter but never had the chance to include Eileen, D. R.'s daughter, in my research. Whenever I met a family member the conversation always turned to D. R. the politician. That is reflected in this present work. There is little information about the Grenfell family, the lives they led, and the relationship between D. R. and those closest to him. That is a weakness in that it means that a fully rounded picture is impossible. Occasionally I present the few snippets of oral testimony mainly from Bryn and Ann, supplemented by documentary evidence. I also have recollections gained through my father whose family lived at Bryn Gwili and Y Bwthyn, Swansea Road, Kingsbridge, Gorseinon, close to the Grenfells after they had moved to Stafford Common. The Richards family who lived a few doors away (and whose uncle, John Griffiths, had married D. R.'s sister) provided further insights and a great deal more beside, for which I am eternally grateful.

It is also a book about a male MP who emerged from the male environment of the mining industry and the SWMF, and who worked in an overwhelmingly male parliament and an international Socialist movement that was led by men. This does not detract from the way D. R. worked with prominent women, especially on issues of international relief, possibly to a greater extent than many of his fellow Labour MPs at this time.

This is not, of course, a detached work by an impartial chronicler, free from any bias. In accordance with local government practice, I must declare a prejudicial interest. I am, and have been, an active member of the Labour Party since a teenager, serving as a local party official and both town and county councillor. That is the starting point from which I come to examine D. R.'s life, and the conclusions I draw need to be understood in that light. Hopefully this book will contribute to the discussion of questions about the role and purpose of the

Labour Party in Wales, its relationship with the wider Labour movement, and the lessons to be learned from history.

Reference is made to well-known figures like Ramsay MacDonald, Philip Snowden, J. H. Thomas, Clement Attlee, Sir Stafford Cripps, Hugh Dalton, Herbert Morrison, Sir Walter Citrine, Aneurin Bevan, Jim Griffiths, and the legion of others without much, if any, explanation of their lives and careers. A bit more detail is provided on other, less well-known figures.

The first two chapters focus on D. R.'s rise to prominence in his home community, where industrialisation came later than in most parts of south Wales. His role as Miners' Agent for the Western District is explored in the third chapter which places his work in the context of the more militant and politicised outlook taken by the men he represented before, during and after the Great War. His election to parliament and early work as an MP clearly on the Socialist Left of the Labour Party is then considered, along with his frustration both at the role of the Trades Union Congress (TUC) leadership and that of the Miners' Federation of Great Britain (MFGB) before and during the General Strike. Excluded from both of Ramsay MacDonald's governments, D. R. championed the miners' cause and earned widespread respect in his own constituency which greatly helped him to survive the debacle of 1931 when MPs in safer seats were defeated. Thereafter, the focus of the following four chapters is on D. R.'s contribution for nearly a decade as one of Labour's leaders at a UK level, where he worked tirelessly to rebuild the party both in parliament and in the country. As the years progressed he played an increasingly important role internationally, exposing the menace of fascism and helping its victims to escape persecution, culminating in his work in Prague in the aftermath of the Munich Agreement.

His entry into government and the challenges he faced in ensuring the mining industry was in a position to support the war effort are considered in chapters 11 and 12. Chapter 13 looks at the part he played as an opposition member once again during the second half of the war. His sometimes fractious relationship with the Labour leadership during the Attlee government, as D. R. sought to champion causes with which he had been associated throughout his political life, are examined in chapters 14 and 15. The attention then turns to his final years in parliament when he became, for five years, the MP with the longest continuous service.

Throughout the book I use the initials D. R. to refer to him, and that is for personal reasons. In his hinterland in Gorseinon he was never known as Grenfell. Neither was he ever known as Dai in our household, as Liz, my grandmother's sister, made clear to me. Whatever might be the practice elsewhere it was D. R. for my family in Bryn Gwili and Y Bwthyn, and it is as 'D. R.' that he is presented in this book.

Acknowledgements

DURING THE TIME I have been engaged on this research I have received valuable assistance from Kim Collis and his colleagues at the West Glamorgan Archives where the D. R. Grenfell papers are held, and from Siân Williams and her colleagues at the South Wales Miners' Library in Swansea. Staff at the National Archives in Kew, the National Library of Wales in Aberystwyth, the Bodleian Library in Oxford, the Joseph Priestley Library at Bradford University, the archives of the London School of Economics, Churchill College Cambridge, and the British Library in London, enabled me to access a wealth of material on which to base this work.

I should like to express particular thanks to Professor Deian Hopkin and Dr James Phillips for reading a first draft of the text and for their extremely valuable comments. I thank them both for their interest and for giving so generously of their time. I am indebted to Dr Gerald Gabb who has shown a keen interest in the work and generously shared his own research into Swansea's history.

The book has appeared thanks to the assistance of Lefi Gruffudd and his colleagues at Gwasg y Lolfa, and to the patient and meticulous editing by Eirian Jones for which I am eternally grateful.

I would like to thank West Glamorgan Archives for permission to reproduce photographs held in the D. R. Grenfell papers, and to the committee of the Gorseinon Institute for allowing the use of a copy of a painting of D. R. in their possession for the front cover.

Fellow members of Llafur, the Welsh People's History

Society, have shown a great deal of patience as I enthused about this subject. I thank my friends and colleagues in Gower Constituency Labour Party, and my fellow councillors on both Llwchwr Town Council and the City and County of Swansea, both now and over the years. They are people who have made their own contribution as the mainstay of community life and as local political leaders in this neighbourhood. They stand in D. R.'s proud tradition and I am grateful to them for their insights, their friendship and support over many decades.

The same is true of members at Libanus, Gorseinon, and Brynteg, Gorseinon, both now closed, and my friends at Penuel Newydd, Loughor, who have been a great source of support to me. I am glad that the first opportunity to disseminate the outcomes of the research came thanks to the sisterhood at Penuel Newydd and I hope that the book does not disappoint.

Colleagues at the National Foundation for Educational Research (NFER) provided great camaraderie as my attention turned from history to the policy priorities of the education system in the twenty-first century. Particular thanks go to those who worked at its Welsh office located at various times in Llansamlet, Townhill and Llanelli.

My wife, Ann, showed great patience while I disappeared to research and write this book and I thank her for allowing me the time to do so. Her parents provided much practical help that released me to pursue this interest, and I thank my late father-in-law especially for the important part he played when my son, Alun, was enjoying his formative years. Alun's passion for geography and geology meant it was in those subjects that he pursued his own studies, with outstanding success. But I am glad that he has retained a lively interest in history as well as in his own field and he has taken a close interest in this work.

My parents encouraged me to complete this work and I thank my late father, J. Beverley Smith, for his recollections of D. R. and the Grenfell family. He could testify at first hand the respect that existed for D. R. in his constituency and had fond recollections of the Grenfells as neighbours. He was able to read a draft of this book but did not live to see it appear in published form. I dedicate the book to his memory.

Abbreviations

ASLEF	Associated Society of Locomotive Engineers and Firemen
BISAKTA	British Iron, Steel and Kindred Trades Association
BTC	British Transport Commission
CBC	County Borough Council
CLP	Constituency Labour Party
CPC	Coal Production Council
DORA	Defence of the Realm Act
EWO	Essential Works Order
IFTU	International Federation of Trade Unions
ILO	International Labour Office
ILP	Independent Labour Party
KC	King's Counsel
LSI	Labour and Socialist International
MFGB	Miners' Federation of Great Britain
MRC	Medical Research Council
NCB	National Coal Board
NCF	No Conscription Fellowship
NCL	National Council of Labour
NEC	National Executive Committee
NIDCW	National Industrial Development Council of Wales and Monmouthshire
NUDAW	National Union of Distributive and Allied Workers
NUM	National Union of Mineworkers
NUR	National Union of Railwaymen
NWMU	North Wales Mineworkers' Union

PAC	Public Assistance Committee
PLP	Parliamentary Labour Party
RDC	Rural District Council
SCM	Students' Christian Movement
SEG	Socialist European Group of the Labour Party
SOE	Special Operations Executive
SWMF	South Wales Miners' Federation
TGWU	Transport and General Workers' Union
TSC	Timber Supply Committee
TSMA	Tin and Sheet Millmen's Association
TUC	Trades Union Congress
UAB	Unemployment Assistance Board
UDC	Union of Democratic Control
UDC	Urban District Council
UNO	United Nations Organisation
WAC	Welsh Advisory Council of the British Broadcasting Corporation
WCL	Welsh Council of Labour
WEA	Workers' Educational Association
WPP	Welsh Parliamentary Party
WTB	Welsh Tourist Board

CHAPTER 1

A Boy from Penyrheol

DAVID RHYS GRENFELL was born on 16 June 1881, in Penyrheol, a small hamlet in the parish of Llandeilo Talybont, some three miles from the main settlement of Pontarddulais and close to Rhyd-y-mardy, a rapidly-expanding locality that was developing as the commercial centre that was, within a few short years, renamed Gorseinon. Penyrheol was one destination among many in the Grenfell family's nomadic journey during the nineteenth century. Their ancestors originated in St Jude's, Cornwall, from where D. R.'s great-grandparents had moved to the village of Lancriwed, and it was there that John Grenfell was born. In common with many of his compatriots, John left the rural isolation of Cornwall in search of work, and by the 1840s he had reached south-west Wales where he met and married a local girl, Hannah. During the early years of their marriage they lived in a succession of the frontier industrial communities that were emerging in south Wales, eventually settling for a time in the iron town of Blaenavon, Monmouthshire, where their youngest son, William, was born on 16 August 1858. The Grenfells then turned westwards once again, and returned to Loughor, where William, 'Billy Bach y Sais' (a nickname that belied his Cornish origins), spent his youth and married Ann Williams, who's family's own journey had taken them from Cwmavon, then to the Swansea Valley via Aberavon, before they too settled in Loughor. Ann was a woman of firm political and religious convictions whose views stemmed from the early struggles of industrial communities and the radicalism of the protest movements of rural Wales. From her, D. R. and his siblings learned of the Merthyr Rising, the Rebecca Riots, the evictions of Liberal tenant farmers in 1868, and the struggles of early trade unionists across the coalfield.[1]

Once married, William and Ann began their own journey that took in several of the industrialising villages along the banks of the River Llwchwr, beginning their married life in Llangennech, on the Carmarthenshire side of the border, where their eldest son, William John, was born in 1878, followed by Anna Jane, their daughter, two years later. By 1881, however, they had returned to the Glamorgan side of the River Llwchwr to Penyrheol, where four more children were born – David Rhys in 1881, Maud in 1885, Mansel Thomas in 1884, and Ivor Martin in 1887. A fifth brother, Emlyn George, born in May 1893, died aged seven months on New Year's Day 1894.

The area in which they settled, the small village of Penyrheol, formed part of the low-lying, but undulating landscape between the River Llwchwr which separated it from Carmarthenshire and the River Llan (also referred to as the Lliw Eithaf) in the direction of Swansea and bounded by Cefn Drum and Mynydd y Gwair to the north, while Cefn Stylle provided a natural separation from the Gower peninsula to the south. The neighbourhood was at the heart of the rapid expansion of the steel and tinplate industry and coal mining in south-west Wales in the middle decades of the nineteenth century, which saw Gowerton (Ffos Felen), Loughor, Gorseinon (Rhyd-y-mardy) and Pontarddulais emerge as thrusting industrial communities that absorbed a massive amount of in-migration throughout the last quarter of the nineteenth century, especially during the 1890s and then into the 1900s. Industrialisation in the area occurred somewhat later than in the neighbouring areas of Llanelli and Swansea, but the effect was dramatic, especially after the extension of the railway from Gorseinon through Gowerton and along the Clyne valley to Swansea Victoria station in 1866. This meant that the area's industrial output could be conveyed easily to Swansea's docks where a ready market could be accessed both in Britain and, more importantly, across all parts of the world.[2]

The original Mountain Colliery was sunk in Gorseinon, along with the Birch Rock in Pontarddulais, the Grovesend Colliery, the Bishwell in Ffosfelen, and the Broadoak Colliery in Loughor. However, coal mining was not the only major employer given the importance of steel and tinplate manufacturing, a state of affairs that was common across the western part of the coalfield where both sectors coexisted. In Gorseinon the Lewis family saved the fledgling Gorseinon Tinplate Works from bankruptcy when they acquired it in 1885, and expanded it into a flourishing business that was part of an interconnected industrial complex extending from Kingsbridge to Gorseinon that included modern works like the Mardy and Bryngwyn. The Grovesend Steel and Tinplate Company (originally the Grovesend Tinplate Co.) soon developed, first a tinplate works and then a steelworks at Gorseinon, as well as similar plants elsewhere in the region. The Fairwood Tinplate Works and Elba Steelworks were opened in Gowerton, while in Pontarddulais the Cambria, Teilo and Clayton Works became operational in the same period.[3] Within a short period of time, several local collieries were also acquired by the steel and tinplate manufacturers in a form of vertical combination (where steel and tinplate manufacturers owned colliery undertakings) that became increasingly the norm (along with lateral combination whereby colliery companies amalgamated) in the second decade of the twentieth century.

The Grovesend Steel and Tinplate Co. was a Swansea-based firm with extensive interests across the western part of south Wales, while the works in Gowerton, managed by John Cecil Davies, were part of the Baldwin industrial empire. The Lewis family, the original pioneers of the tinplate industry in Gorseinon, had much closer links with the community.

William Lewis hailed from Llan-dy-fân in Carmarthenshire, and for years operated the mill at Melin Llan, in Penllergaer, before purchasing farms in the Rhyd-y-mardy area. These included the land on which the original Gorseinon Tinplate Works had been built. When its owners became bankrupt, the whole edifice passed to the Lewis family who were able to make a commercial success of the venture. William Lewis remained in Gorseinon throughout his life as did two of his sons, Thomas and Rufus, who exercised day-to-day control over the works and emerged as Gorseinon's great philanthropic benefactors, along with a third brother who lived in Blackpill. They were related through marriage to the Glasbrook family of Llangyfelach, owners of the Garngoch collieries, and familiar faces in the local area.

The Lewis brothers were joined by dozens of small businessmen who seized the opportunity to set up shops and other outlets in the hundred or so premises along High Street, Gorseinon, and in neighbouring Pontarddulais, both of which emerged as important commercial centres in the 1890s and 1900s. They included grocers like David Jones, Crown Stores, who arrived from Llan-egwad in Carmarthenshire, and Timothy Jones from Llan-non, Cardiganshire, Joshua Evans, Hong Kong Stores from Rhydcymerau, and Tyrynys Thomas, a pharmacist from Llanelli, all of whom took advantage of the young community that was coming together in response to the expansion of the coal, steel and tinplate industries. The locality also provided a fertile market for the operation of enterprises like the Gowerton Gas Co. and GEC (Gorseinon Electric Company, responsible for making Gorseinon the first high street in Britain to be lit by electricity), while the Pontarddulais Co-operative Society grew from small premises in Hope St, Pontarddulais, to a position of dominance in retail trade within a few years of its establishment. A similar spirit of voluntary community self-help was evident in the work of the friendly societies, who between them had more than 3,000 members by the time the National Insurance Act became operational in 1911, and the creation of public benefit organisations such as the Gorseinon Building Society, together with a plethora of associations such as the Gorseinon Mutual Aid Society and the Gorseinon Nursing Association as well as local branches of national friendly societies.

This expansion was made possible by an explosion of population in Gorseinon and the surrounding areas. The total number of individuals enumerated in Llandeilo Talybont had increased from 1,410 in 1841 to 4,634 in 1891, while the borough of Loughor increased to 2,084 in the same period. Thereafter, the population grew at an even more astonishing pace as the population of Llandeilo Talybont, predominantly centred in Pontarddulais and Gorseinon, almost doubled to more than 10,000 by 1911, and a similar pattern was seen in Loughor and in Gowerton. Most of the migration into the area came from neighbouring Carmarthenshire, especially from Llanelli and its surrounding villages, creating a locality that was dominated by young families. Most of the inhabitants were Welsh speaking, and this was certainly the case in Penyrheol and the surrounding neighbourhood where more than 600 people were enumerated in the 1891 census. Of these, nearly 70 per cent were recorded as speaking Welsh only, while only a dozen could only speak English. The rest, like the Grenfell family, were bilingual. Billy Bach y Sais had clearly acquired a fluency in Welsh, even though his first language was English.

Responsibility for building regulation alongside public health and other regulatory functions after 1894 rested with the Llangyfelach Rural District Council (RDC), later the Swansea RDC which was dominated by the Liberal shopocracy that was only challenged by the arrival of Labour councillors after 1913. The fledging Labour movement had, however, established a greater presence on the parish councils, particularly in Llandeilo Talybont, where candidates nominated by the Trades and Labour Council gained a majority for the first time in 1901. The rapid expansion of the area also resulted in the creation of public bodies tasked with meeting its needs, and this included the Llandeilo Talybont School Board, established shortly after the passing of the 1870 Education Act, which opened schools in Pontarddulais and Penyrheol as immediate priorities. However, as is clear from the correspondence with the Education Department in London, the Liberal elite who exercised power in Llandeilo Talybont were only beginning to build enough elementary schools, and much of that under duress, with officials repeatedly showing their exasperation by the lack of progress. The same could be said of the Llangyfelach RDC whose inactivity in improving the standard of public health was a constant source of comment by Dr Trafford Mitchell, the council's Medical Officer of Health, who continually berated his employers in his annual reports. Moreover, the RDC ignored the need for new housing to accommodate the influx of people, and the fact that this was only partly met by the speculative builders whose fortunes were made constructing the semi-detached houses and small terraces which predominated in the area in the 1890s and 1900s. A glance at the census data from 1891, 1901 and 1911 highlights the magnitude of the overcrowding problem that affected the area and it was this, and not the issue of slum dwellings, that was the main problem in the locality in the Edwardian period.[4]

The Nonconformist denominations and the Established Church were keen to respond to the locality's spiritual needs by building chapels and churches, mainly for Welsh-speaking congregations. The original causes at Brynteg and those of the Baptists at Penuel, Loughor, and Moriah, the Calvinistic Methodist chapel in the same village, provided the nucleus for new congregations in Gorseinon itself. The Calvinistic Methodists opened Libanus close to the boundary of the two settlements and its members were subsequently responsible for the building of an impressive edifice on Mason's Road. Members of Penuel were released to establish a new cause at Seion in the centre of Gorseinon. The Congregationalists followed suit, releasing members from Brynteg to enable the creation of Ebenezer on the Penllergaer side of the River Lliw where it was anticipated that much of the future of Gorseinon would be located. The Anglicans, for their part, benefited from the patronage of the Lewis family who built a Welsh-language church, Trinity, on the High Street (supplied by electricity from GEC in which they had a controlling interest) and they were also generous benefactors of the larger St Catherine's church on Alexandra Road. The philanthropy of the Lewis family was also in evidence in the building of Gorseinon Institute, opened in 1906 on Lime Street, as a meeting place and recreational facility which boasted a library, snooker room, and several committee rooms as well as a main auditorium. Managed by an elected committee supported by subscriptions collected from local workmen, the Institute became a focus for the area's secular social and cultural life and became the meeting place for the fledging Labour movement.

Gorseinon and its surroundings formed an important part of the Western Division of Glamorgan (increasingly referred to as the Gower Division) which contained the industrial villages around Swansea as well as the Swansea Valley and parts of the Amman Valley at one end and the fishing port of Oystermouth and the Gower peninsula at the other. Formed in consequence of the changes instigated by the Reform Act of 1885, it was represented by a Liberal for the first 20 years of its existence. This continuity masked important differences in the nature of the Liberal representation. Its first Member of Parliament had been the industrialist Frank Ash Yeo, a former Mayor of Swansea, who personified the kind of man often selected by the Liberal Party as their torchbearers in Victorian Wales. His death in 1888 exposed the tensions that were already evident within Welsh Liberalism. Efforts by the Liberal hierarchy in London to impose the prominent barrister Horace Davey as its candidate provoked a local rebellion within the Liberal association, centred on the loose Labour association that was one of its affiliates. Their chosen man was David Randell, a Llanelli solicitor who acted on behalf of local workmen and was the official solicitor to several local trade unions. Efforts by Liberals to persuade Randell to withdraw proved futile and merely prompted local trade unionists to threaten to support his candidature in opposition to that of the official Liberal, if necessary. Davey withdrew, leaving the field to Randell who faced a formidable challenge from John Dillwyn-Llewelyn, owner of the Penllergaer Estate and a prominent local industrialist, standing in the Conservative interest in the by-election held at the end of March 1888.[5]

Randell's selection in Gower came within three years of the revolt in the Scottish Highlands that led to the election of Crofters' Party candidates (in preference to official Liberals) as a clear sign of the need for a new urgency in the implementation of radical policies. These themes were at the centre of Randell's campaign that dwelt on land reform, disestablishment and the other cornerstones of Welsh Liberalism at its most radical. Not surprisingly, William Abraham (Mabon) was prominent on his platform and he proudly read messages of support from the Crofters' Party and from Irish nationalists in a campaign that alarmed the moderate element within local Liberal ranks. The outcome was much closer than anticipated, a fact that was interpreted as a warning to the more radical elements in the Liberal Party about what could happen if the party selected men of Randell's ilk, but it also exposed the fault lines within the Liberal coalition in Wales.

These fault lines were exposed again in the Gower constituency at the turn of the century when the selection of a local industrialist as Randell's successor prompted John Hodge, of the British Steel Smelters' Association, later a government minister, to stand as an independent Labour candidate. Officially, the miners threw their weight behind the Liberal, and Hodge was handicapped by being an English-speaking outsider in a strongly Welsh-speaking constituency, but his defeat by a few hundred votes reinforced the view that Gower was moving away from the Liberals.

The Grenfells witnessed these stirring events, and their second son would speak proudly of his neighbours in Penyrheol where it could be said, 'there was not a single Tory in the village'. The cottage where they lived stood at the outskirts of the cluster of houses that constituted Penyrheol at the time. It was recalled by D. R. with mixed feelings:

> I remember the house in which I spent my early years. I
> would not like to have to go back to live in it although I have
> a kind of affection for the house and the place in which it
> stood. There was a large garden attached to it and, in spite of
> the wretched house, the green food from the garden helped
> us to maintain our health and to survive the wretchedness of
> the hovel. The house was dark, miserable and gloomy, and
> not a ray of sunlight found its way into the rooms; but living
> in that house gave us a taste for the outdoors which helped us
> afterwards as boys and girls. We had to live outside because
> the house was so wretched.[6]

Whatever the living conditions, the Grenfells were part of the fabric of the society that was emerging in Gorseinon and the surrounding area. William Grenfell was a member of the Western Miners' Association and a founder member of the Pontarddulais Co-operative Society. But the main focus of his life was Brynteg Independent chapel, defined in its constitution as an Independent Calvinist cause, with a history that could be traced to the early years of dissent in the locality. Brynteg was affiliated to the Annibynwyr, a loose union of wholly autonomous chapels that were self-governing and, crucially, free to determine their own doctrinal standpoints. Brynteg's minister, the Rev. John Stephens, was not only an outstanding evangelical preacher but also a prominent figure in the radical politics of nineteenth-century Wales, and a member of the Llandeilo Talybont School Board that grasped control of elementary education from the Anglican Church, and a determined advocate of Welsh disestablishment.[7] This was the dominant issue of Welsh Victorian Liberalism and one that united the various Nonconformist denominations in common cause. However, this outward unity across the chapels masked important differences in terms of doctrinal teaching and, more significantly, on the question of church governance. On the latter question the Annibynwyr and the Welsh Baptists were agreed: authority was vested completely within each individual congregation, each one taking its own decisions without deference to any other worldly authority, with the minister as the servant and certainly not the master of his members. This strong democratic ethos and spirit of self-reliance required and nurtured organic leadership within the chapels themselves, and William Grenfell was one such leader as a deacon at Brynteg and an official of its Sunday school who led theological discussions, prayer meetings, visited the sick and interceded with public authorities on behalf of his fellow members. Brynmor Grenfell recalled: 'The family were members of Brynteg Chapel where the foundations for personal service to the community was established in the children from an early age. The need to speak one's mind with scant regard for the "status quo" became a way of life.'[8]

This was doubtless encouraged in the Sunday school class led by John Jones, Pencefnarda, a deacon at Brynteg whose members included David Rhys and his siblings.[9] There are no formal records of the discussions he led, very few were ever kept, but the 1890s were years which saw the questioning of the Calvinist doctrines that had historically held sway in Welsh chapels, a process which was soon reflected most strongly in the various denominational academies and colleges. The fact that the Annibynwyr had no formal denominational creed gave added impetus to such discussions in those chapels, although members were formally obliged to adhere to each individual congregation's doctrinal standpoint. None of the Grenfell brothers became members of any congregation. As an adult, David Rhys occasionally attended chapel services both in Gorseinon and in London, but could never be seen as a tribune of Welsh Nonconformity. He remained on very good terms with John Jones, Pencefnarda, who became one of his staunchest supporters during early political battles in Gower. The fact that he was not a practising Christian did not affect the steadfast support that he enjoyed from members of the chapel congregations and his own willingness to take up many of the causes they espoused during 37 years as Gower's MP.

When David Rhys was two years and ten months old he followed his brother William John to Penyrheol Elementary School. He was taught first by Elizabeth Hughes, a former pupil teacher, who was recalled by D. R. for her unusually kind and gentle way with the children. She became a certificated teacher while David Rhys was at the school.

David Rhys was then taught by the school's headmaster, Thomas Jones, also known by his bardic name 'Alaw Defynog', a certificated teacher who had arrived at Penyrheol from Gwernogle in rural Carmarthenshire to take charge of the newly-built board school. A renowned poet, musician, and chapel deacon, he made an immense contribution to the cultural life of the locality, particularly as a conductor. His entries in the school log book testify to the challenges faced in the early years of universal elementary education in Wales. The impact of the weather, yearly meetings and outings held by local chapels, local fairs (especially the main ones at Loughor and Llangyfelach), helping with the harvest, as well as outbreaks of epidemics such as whooping cough, often affected attendance.

English was the language of instruction at Penyrheol Elementary School when David Rhys attended, and the anglicised ambience was reflected in the school's choice of songs which, in the year of David Rhys' entry, included

'Watches and Clocks', 'Wake Up Mary' and 'The Pendulum' for the infants, and the Irish air 'The Harp That Once Threw Sarah's Bells' and 'Hail To The Chief' for the junior classes, along with 'Llandovery' and 'All Through The Night' with Welsh words thrown in for good measure. What sense the children of Penyrheol could make of these songs, especially in the infant class, given their linguistic background is not known. However, Thomas Jones was among those in the teaching profession who called on the education authorities to recognise the impact this had on the school's work. The annual inspectors' reports on the school often referred to the task facing the school – 'difficulty with vernacular in remote districts like this' was one such phrase. This was echoed by Thomas Jones who noted that many children 'cannot comprehend the most easy questions owing to their scanty knowledge of English' and that children experienced 'great difficulty in arithmetic owing to inadequate knowledge of the English language'. By the time the school was inspected in 1888 it was reported that, 'An endeavour is being made at present to cultivate the intelligence of the pupil using the Welsh language as a medium', a task for which Thomas Jones was very well suited.

There are very few references to individual children in Thomas Jones' log book and it was not his practice to regularly record any misdemeanours on the part of those he taught. There is, however, one reference to David Rhys and three others being 'reprimanded for insolency and bad conduct' at the age of 11, but otherwise his time at Penyrheol Elementary School passed without comment in the headteacher's account. What is clear is that whatever happened that day, David Rhys made a lasting impression on Alaw Defynog for whom he retained the greatest respect (as an adult he was instrumental in organising a testimonial evening for him to mark his retirement), and his former headteacher was fulsome in his praise in later years.

Outside the school, the Grenfell boys showed early signs of enterprise by running a horse and cart round delivering produce from Llanelli's midweek market to homes in Gorseinon and its vicinity. By then it was clear that David Rhys' period in school and his only formal instruction was coming to an end. The Welsh Intermediate Education Act, the much-vaunted educational ladder of opportunity on which the Liberals held such hopes, had been passed when David Rhys was eight years old. But any such hopes for advancement were seriously lacking in the reality of Penyrheol in the 1890s. The task of creating the area's intermediate school, eventually located at Gowerton to serve the peninsula as well as the area around Loughor, Gorseinon and Pontarddulais, had only just begun. William John had been encouraged by Thomas Jones to take up the position of pupil teacher at the school, where he might have joined several others who made the journey to full certification as a teacher under his tutelage. This was not to be, and William John left school destined not for the colliery like his father but to the local tinplate works where his grandfather worked. David Rhys followed his father and, at the age of 12½, entered the mining industry where he was to earn his living for the best part of the next 30 years.

CHAPTER 2

The Making
of a Miners' Leader

DAVID RHYS BEGAN his working life stationed at the main door at level No. 8 slope at the original Mountain Colliery, where he was given the responsibility of ensuring that the air current was kept in circulation. He recalled his early experiences describing how, 'I was left alone with my little lamp alight and a sea of darkness around me, and nothing else except the soughing of the air current through the canvas flap over the notch through which the rope passes in jerky spasms as the brakes were put on, or raised in the engine-house, to regulate the speed of the train of ten tubs speeding down the slope of the pit bottom 800 yards away.' He recalled the working conditions, 'the pit was not very gassy, and naked lights were in general use in the workings and roadways. I did not dislike the work, but I knew that rats were dangerous, and I always kept a small heap of stones and a stick for self-defence, in case they were bold enough to attack me.' After 18 months he left to work at Garngoch No. 1 Colliery where, he recalled, working conditions were extremely poor. There he met 'Friend', a larger-than-life character who took a supportive interest in the young lad from Penyrheol and was in turn hero-worshipped by the boy.[1] David Rhys was among those who carried his body to Loughor where he was laid to rest after being killed in an accident underground.

The Grenfells then embarked on two ventures of their own, taking a license on small mines in Stafford Common, along with some neighbours. The practice of issuing licenses was used by colliery owners to work the coal in mines that were on the verge of exhaustion, but which could be operated economically for a small profit. The first of these ventures proved fairly successful, but the second was beset by difficulties from the start. As a result, David Rhys took an apprenticeship with a blacksmith in the neighbouring village of Ffosfelen, by then beginning to be known as Gowerton where he remained until the outbreak of the South African Boer War. The conflict generated a renewed demand for coal that enabled him to secure work with the Loughor Colliery Co. at Cae Duke where he was to remain for the next three years. Hard work and sheer grit meant the Grenfells were eventually able to move to more modern accommodation than that available at the cottage in Penyrheol, first at a terraced house in Belgrave Road, Upper Loughor, and then at Penhafod, a larger house with an extensive garden in Stafford Common, where a small cluster of houses were built in the first decade of the twentieth century adjacent to the main road between Loughor and Swansea.

Loughor and the surrounding area were to gain worldwide attention from the autumn of 1904. For years, many Nonconformist leaders had complained that spiritual matters were being lost as ministers devoted more time to politics and because their theologists sought to move away from strict Calvinist doctrine. This feeling was evident most strongly among the Calvinistic Methodists whose rigid doctrine and organisational structures set them slightly apart from the other denominations. Many of their leaders became convinced of the need to reinforce established teaching and concentrate on matters of the spirit. Among those who championed this standpoint was the Rev. Joseph Jenkins, principal of the Calvinistic Methodist preparatory college at Newcastle Emlyn, where Evan Roberts, a miner from Loughor, and Sidney

Evans, a shopworker at Crown Stores in Gorseinon, enrolled as students in September 1904. Both Evan Roberts and Sidney Evans were faithful members of their respective chapels, recognised as spiritual leaders in their own community, although neither initially planned to enter the Christian ministry (Evan Roberts was an active trade unionist while working in the collieries around Loughor, while Sidney Evans was intent on setting up in business on his own accord). On arrival in Newcastle Emlyn, however, both men experienced an intense spiritual awakening and a feeling that this needed to be shared with the congregations that had nurtured them. This prompted them to return home where they took part in deeply spiritual prayer meetings held at Libanus (where Sidney Evans was a member) and later at Moriah (Evan Roberts' chapel), and then at Brynteg, in late autumn 1904. At Brynteg, the chapel was full to capacity as Evan Roberts conveyed the full intensity of his spirituality. Worshippers shook uncontrollably in the pews under its influence. Local courts heard few cases, the public houses emptied, and some of the roughest and coarsest elements in the neighbourhood mended their ways. Within a few weeks, the Revival's influence had spread like wildfire throughout the coalfield and into mid and north Wales.[2]

David Rhys did not witness those stirring events, although he knew enough about them through his family at Brynteg. The industrial slump immediately after the end of the Boer War forced many in the Gorseinon and Loughor areas to contemplate whether their future might lay elsewhere. South Africa, Australia, New Zealand and Canada were among the destinations to which several local men, especially young bachelors with no family ties, considered. They included David Rhys and his eldest brother, William John, who became aware of the opportunities for experienced miners in Nova Scotia and persuaded a close friend, David Williams of Pontybrenin, to join them. Their path to the new world did not go smoothly (David Rhys was almost prevented from leaving), but eventually they headed for Liverpool where they embarked on a sea voyage on the Allan Line's *Siberia*, making their way to Cape Breton. D. R. remembered the voyage, describing:

> This was a good time of the year to go. We found we had a very mixed body of Europeans for travelling company. We were made up of small lots of Welsh, Scots, Geordies, Midlanders and Cockneys, with a few European miners and other workers to make up the company. Our voyage started badly. We were struck by a bad Atlantic gale off the coast of Ireland. Almost all the continentals were seasick.[3]

Eventually they landed at St John's, Newfoundland, where they rested until taking a further voyage to Halifax and then proceeded by rail for the last hundred miles to the Chignecto mines in Nova Scotia. D. R. later wrote:

> We got to Canada at the best time of the year. The Indian summer was well in. It was the right time for seeing the Canadian woodland in the Eastern Provinces. There is no better picture. The maple leaves are in fine colour. The general condition of the land, the numerous rivers are long, the warm sun, the blue sky, do not give the slightest hint of the coming of winter.[4]

But any sense of romance was soon dispelled as the grim reality of life on an unregulated industrial frontier dawned on David Rhys and his fellow Welshmen:

> … conditions which I would not recommend any boy or young man in this country to undergo. Certainly I would not send anyone unless he had, at the end of his journey, as I had, the best friend a man has in Canada or elsewhere – a pound in his pocket that enables him to resist the exploitation so often imposed on a man who has been sent from home. I had some bargaining power when I went there, because I

had a few pounds left and was able to refuse the first half-dozen jobs that were offered to me. Yet for two months no kind of bed did I have at all, and it was only after very severe hardship that I found myself able to sleep once more in bed like a Christian.[5]

They arrived at the town of Chignecto before heading for the pit village where William John became an overman at the colliery, while David Rhys and David Williams worked at the coalface.[6] Chignecto was a small frontier town, enjoying the facilities of a school, a court, and a Methodist minister who called on a fortnightly basis. A rich mix of Belgians, Germans, Flemish, Czechs and Russians, many of whom did not speak a word of English, lived and worked side by side. For David Rhys this resulted in a daily immersion in other languages as the men desperately sought to communicate amid the dangers of the primitive conditions in which they worked. Thus, he came to discover his talent for acquiring languages that was to continue throughout his life, acquiring further French and adding German and a smattering of Italian to be able to communicate effectively with his workmates to explain working practices and to deal with problems and disputes.

Within weeks, the Welshmen had established themselves at the heart of the men's activity at the colliery, and later boasted that the three boys from Gorseinon were the only ones in the mine who could speak Welsh and hence formed the intelligentsia which ran the camp. William John became chairman of the social committee and David Rhys was elected vice chairman of the Provincial Workers' Association branch, with John McLinnon, a one-eyed, Gaelic-speaking Scotsman as its secretary.

When the colliery was not working, David Rhys and his two compatriots obtained work from the roadmaster for duties when the camp was snowed in, helping to clear snowdrifts that prevented the mail or essential goods from being delivered. What little respite they had was greatly valued: 'Sunday was a real day of rest. We took walks and paid visits to our friends. Occasionally we went for rides in sleighs or "buggies".' During the summer, they would take picnics to the Maple forests where they could indulge in maple sugar molasses, a luxury that played an important part of the diets of the rural people.

*

David Rhys returned to Gorseinon with the experience gained from his time in Nova Scotia, finding work at the Mountain Colliery which was recruiting men to begin production in the four-foot seam, a new development which commentators predicted would make it one of the largest and most profitable undertakings in the western portion of the south Wales coalfield.[7] His spare time was taken up by study at the Board of Education evening classes held at Gorseinon Elementary School where he pursued courses in mining surveying and principles of mining, which enabled him to obtain the necessary certification to work as a colliery under-manager, with the added accolade of having secured the third highest mark in the county.[8] The following year he took a step further and gained the first-class certificate, enabling him to qualify as a colliery manager.[9] In the midst of all this activity, he and his longstanding fiancé, Beatrice Morgan, who lived in the Brynteg area, close to Penyrheol, were married. Beatrice was herself no stranger to travel. Born in Gorseinon, her parents John and Emma Morgan had sought a new life in the state of Victoria, Australia, where two of her siblings were born, before returning home when her father began work at the Mountain Colliery.

The young couple took a lease on a six-roomed terraced house at 74 Brighton Road in the centre of Gorseinon, and it was there that their daughter, Eileen, was born on 23 February 1907. With Gorseinon and the surrounding area enjoying a period of industrial boom, opportunities would doubtless open for a man like D. R. Grenfell. The family had reason to be confident.

One thing was also clear, the voters of Britain were about to reject the Conservative government that had been swept to power amid the jingoism of the 'khaki election' in the autumn of 1900, but whose reactionary policies, in particular over the control of education, caused outrage in many parts of Britain, but especially in Nonconformist Wales. The Liberals' hold on the Gower constituency, however, was challenged by the Western District Miners' Agent, John Williams, standing as an independent Labour (though not ILP) candidate. A Welsh-speaking, Baptist lay preacher close to Mabon, John Williams was the personification of a trade union moderate whose strength lay in his work on compensation cases.[10] He could count on the support of a significant body of Nonconformist voters impressed by his determined espousal of the cause of Welsh disestablishment, and he toured the constituency denouncing the privileges of the Church and demanding that its endowments be put to the benefit of society as a whole. This placed him much closer to that which united radical Liberals across Wales than with the Socialist creed that ILP propagandists had been preaching to receptive audiences across the constituency for over a decade. His appeal was sufficiently broad for him to take the seat, which he won by the narrow margin of 319 votes over the Liberals' T. J. Williams.[11]

Electoral victory led to a redoubling of Labour's efforts in the constituency, both to strengthen organisational structures and promote Socialist thought. Active Trade and Labour Councils at Pontardawe, Ystradgynlais, Gorseinon, Pontarddulais, Llansamlet and Fforestfach created an electoral machinery that enabled their nominees to gain seats on Glamorgan County Council, the three Rural District Councils in the constituency, as well as on Boards of Guardians and parish councils.[12] They ran tireless campaigns to expose the inadequacies of Liberal administration in local government,[13] focusing on overcrowded homes, inadequate water supplies and drainage, and poor housing conditions.[14] Such work coincided with regular visits from prominent Labour and trade union leaders to the area, and large annual processions which became gala occasions during which the crowds flocked to hear national speakers like Keir Hardie, Tom Mann, Ramsay MacDonald, Bruce Glasier, Philip Snowden and Agnes Brown.[15]

These great festivals were undoubtedly important inspirational occasions, but Labour's most important missionary work took place in the programme of activities sustained by ILP branches in the locality each month throughout the years leading up to the Great War. The ILP branch in Gorseinon was a particularly fine example of the phenomenal movement that nurtured Socialist thought across Wales in that crucial formative period. It was fortunate that it had, in a man of the calibre of William Evans (Llanerch), a leader of exceptional talent who was able to bridge the disparate influences that shaped the emergent communities in Gorseinon, Loughor, and the surrounding areas. A prominent figure in the British Steel Smelters' Association, William Evans was a deacon and Sunday school teacher at Seion Baptist chapel, who saw the Labour movement as a moral as well as political force whose success rested on a combination of practical responses to local, national and international issues, with an almost spiritual sense of moral purpose concerned with all aspects of the human condition.[16] This was reflected in the topics debated at the ILP's monthly meetings in Gorseinon which grappled with themes as diverse as industrial efficiency, international trade, democratic diplomacy, the international brotherhood of the working class, the temperance question, women's emancipation, and the role of the family under Socialism, among others. While religious faith was a matter of individual conviction, the Gorseinon branch included several avowed atheists and agnostics alongside committed Christians who saw the Labour movement as a vehicle for them to fulfil their responsibilities in this world.[17] D. R. (as he was increasingly called), William John (who also came to be known by his initials) and Mansel, in particular, immersed themselves in the world of the ILP during these years as they developed the articles of faith that were to sustain them for the rest of their lives.

Practically, too, the brothers threw themselves into the daily work of representing their fellow workers, in D. R.'s case through the militant miners' lodge at the Mountain Colliery.[18] There he was exposed personally to the reality of raw capitalism in the coal industry as the men paid the price for the business failure of the Swansea Navigation Coal Co., which had over-reached itself and was unable to shoulder the heavy burden of the massive capital outlay of at least £150,000 which had been necessary to start and then expand production. In February 1909, matters came to a head when the company filed for voluntary winding-up and was eventually sold for £26,000 to the Gellihir Colliery Co., and then to Swansea Navigation Collieries Ltd, a wholly-owned subsidiary of Richard Thomas & Co., one of the main steel and tinplate manufacturers in south Wales.[19] Thus the Mountain Colliery was brought into the structure of a 'vertical' company combination. As will be seen later, the far-reaching impact of these changes was a vital factor in the economic and industrial context of the succeeding decades.[20]

It was to D. R. more than anyone that his fellow-miners looked as a leader at this time of adversity, the articulate speaker with a persuasive argument and a manager's certificate who could negotiate with officials with the facts at his fingertips. As far as D. R. was concerned, wages and conditions had to be defended and safety in the mine was paramount, irrespective of who owned or managed the colliery, and the men should not be the ones made to suffer because of the heavy debts the colliery had incurred.[21] Throughout 1907 and 1908 he was at the forefront of events as the men downed tools over a succession of grievances, primarily safety issues.[22] Barely six months after the colliery restarted under new owners in 1909, there was further trouble, leading the men to give notice of strike action to secure three objectives, clearly defined by D. R.: to maintain the established standard rates and customs, limit Sunday working to essential maintenance, and restrict the use of sub-contractors at the colliery.[23] The dispute lasted throughout the winter and the eventual compromise agreement placated neither side.

Given the deep sense of grievance at the Mountain Colliery, it was no surprise that it was one of only two lodges in the Western District (the other was Birch Rock at Pontarddulais where the miners were locked out in a dispute over the working of double shifts) which voted against the extension of the Conciliation Board Agreement in the coalfield-wide ballot in April 1910, and demanded that the SWMF adopt a more assertive policy.[24] Elsewhere in the locality, discontent also festered. Production at the Broadoak Colliery in Loughor was stopped for ten months over the question of night working, and at Tirdonkin Colliery the failure to reinstate men who had been involved in a previous dispute led to strike action.[25] The truculent approach adopted by the management at Thomas Williams & Co. (whose managing director Evan Williams would feature prominently in subsequent years as a representative of the Mining Association) led to a succession of disputes at the Brynlliw and Grovesend collieries. The discontent within the rank and file of the SWMF, clearly evident in 1909–10, and which intensified subsequently, was reflected in the unofficial reform committee's book, *The Miners' Next Step*, but, in the context of the Western District, was reflected more in the emergence of a younger, more forceful leadership manifested in the election of D. R., along with Caradoc Jones of Pontarddulais, W. H. Davies of Penclawdd, and W. J. Jones (known by his bardic name, Gwilym Bedw) of Birchgrove to the district executive.[26] What they had seen in their own collieries was enough to persuade them that it was empty to talk of conciliation and of the common interest of owners and coal owners when those who owned the mines in south Wales refused to join their counterparts in other parts of Britain to discuss the question of a minimum wage. Furthermore, men like Herbert Asquith could not be trusted after they, as Liberal ministers, failed to include a national level of wages in the Minimum Wage Act.

A similarly militant industrial outlook was also emerging among the steel and tinplate works in the locality. One of the most acrimonious episodes to occur happened in the Mardy works in Gorseinon in the spring of 1913.[27] Matters came to a head on 24 May when a skirmish between the police and the strikers on a piece of waste-ground in Brighton Road was only stopped after D. R., together with Oliver Harris, David Jones and Montague Jones, intervened to calm the situation. Matters remained tense for the rest of the day due to the pent-up anger felt towards the police on account of their aggressive attitude towards the strikers that morning and during previous disputes. As D. R. walked from Gorseinon Institute towards Brighton Road just after 10pm, he met a crowd outside Seion Baptist chapel which had gathered to watch the police carry a man arrested for drunkenness by the railway station. When the policemen reached Gorseinon square, a man by the name of George Morgan, who had been with his wife buying chips from a street trader outside the West End Hotel, darted to catch hold of his child who had run, suddenly, into the road. George Morgan's actions were those of a father fearful of an accident, but the policemen standing close by gave him a beating with their truncheons, the severity of which did lasting damage to his health. A crowd of around 2,000 people then gathered around the square and along High Street, Alexandra Road, and the vicinity of the police station in Pontarddulais Road. In the melee, the arrested man escaped from the police but, instead, the police seized his brother who had come to his aid. After an altercation had taken place between some of the officers and vociferous residents angry at the way George Morgan had been treated, the police filed out and charged down Pontarddulais Road, clearing it of people before proceeding up along Alexandra Road to disperse the remaining crowd.

Within days more than a dozen men, including D. R., Oliver Harris and Edward Martin of Loughor, received summonses for their alleged part in the disturbance. The charges against the three of them were dropped almost immediately, but proceedings were brought against ten other men.[28] It was clear that this was not a normal case of drunken disorder as claimed by the authorities. D. R. and William Evans (Llanerch) arranged the defence of the accused men, meeting the costs from their own pockets, while John Williams MP demanded a public inquiry into the police's actions on the night of 24 May.[29] On 1 July, nine Gorseinon men appeared before Swansea magistrates, with the police describing the situation that evening as 'tumultuous and riotous' in which 'a reign of terror' had been instigated by an intimidating crowd.[30] Officers had been assaulted, they alleged, stones had been thrown at the police station, and the leaders had made clear they were determined to get the arrested men out of custody.[31]

When the trial started, it was clear that D. R. had been a marked man that evening and was accused by Sergeant Apsey of being a 'big agitator and one of the men's spokesmen in disputes, and he had a lot of influence over the men'. When asked by the barrister, 'Do you suggest that Mr Grenfell was urging them on to throw stones?', his reply was, 'No, his presence was keeping others there in my opinion.'[32] When D. R. entered the witness box he insisted that the police action that evening was not a single occurrence, and that the 'riot' had arisen due to the pressure that had been building in the locality. The *Cambrian* newspaper reported:

> David Rees Grenfell, of Gorseinon, a collier, said he held a first-class certificate as a colliery manager. He had taken part

in ambulance classes and was on good terms with the police. While he was talking to a friend on the night in question, his attention was called to a crowd outside the Zion Baptist Chapel in High-street. He saw some policemen coming through the crowd carrying a man. There was no booing or stone-throwing or bottle-throwing, and he did not see the police hustled in any way.

There was nothing threatening in the attitude of the crowd he insisted and the police were looking for a fight that evening:

'Why do you suggest they should want to smash some people?' he was asked.

'Because they had become excited, sir, after the arrest,' he replied.

'Is it your experience of the police of Gorseinon that when they become excited they smash people?' he was asked again.

'They have a bad reputation,' he responded.

'Do you mean that they have a reputation for taking up people who are drunk and disorderly?'

'And treating them roughly sir,' said D. R.

When asked by the judge, 'Did you really think that five policemen were going to charge the people, most of them children? Did you really mean that?'

D. R. was adamant, 'Yes, my lord.'

George Morgan was acquitted, largely because of the testimony of Dr Trafford Mitchell, the doctor who had treated him that evening who attested both to the severity of his injuries and to his upstanding character. The others were found guilty, resulting in five of them receiving sentences of between six weeks and six months' imprisonment, while the remaining three were bound over.

Within days, D. R. addressed a mass meeting outside the Mountain Colliery, where he denounced the attitude of the police that night, in particular their foul language towards the crowd. Thereafter, he joined William Evans (Llanerch), Oliver Harris, the local chemist Tyrynys Thomas (who had treated many of the wounded in his pharmacy), and several other prominent figures from the business community on a defence committee which organised events in support of the men and their families. As far as D. R. was concerned, the incident demonstrated one thing clearly: any notion of equality before the law was a complete fallacy judging by the treatment meted out to the people in Gorseinon at the Glamorgan Assizes presided over, as it had been, by the former Liberal MP, Lord Tennyson.

*

In the meantime, far more dangerous pressures were growing across continental Europe as the dominant imperial powers vied with each other for dominance economically and politically. Throughout these years D. R., along with the majority of the leaders of the Labour movement in the western part of the coalfield, subscribed to an uncompromising anti-militarist stance, placing their faith in the international brotherhood of the working class, led by the Socialist movement, as a means of defeating war.[33] When the Western District's lodges met in August 1914, delegates endorsed the call for united action by the working people of Europe to prevent an imperialist war. The workers, said Caradoc Jones of Pontarddulais, needed to prevent war for their own sake, and he expressed his firm belief that the organised workers of Russia, Serbia and Austria would be intelligent enough to do so as well.[34] At the same meeting, D. R. paid tribute to the assassinated French Socialist leader Jean Jaurès, 'as Socialists they abhorred the deed by which a man who had done so much good for his country, and no harm, had been shot. They despised the method of the friends of war when used against the friends of peace.'[35]

Within weeks the mood had changed as the British working

class responded not to the internationalist appeals of the Socialist pioneer Keir Hardie but to the national call to arms against reactionary Prussia, for its militarism and barbaric conduct towards neighbouring nations. What was needed was a swift, decisive victory that would restore diplomatic order and the international equilibrium. In no time, trade union leaders joined capitalist employers in recruiting campaigns, while Labour MPs accepted insignificant government posts in return for their loyalty. Dilution of labour, a temporary suspension of craft distinctions in workplaces, and other controls on the freedom of individuals to change jobs, were accepted along with the Defence of the Realm Act (DORA) and then the Military Service Act which extended the State's ability to direct the life of ordinary people even further. In the Gower constituency, Labour leaders put aside their differences with their Liberal and Conservative opponents to appear on recruiting platforms and urge young men to enlist in the forces.[36] When the Socialist and trades union leader Ben Tillett called on his fellow workers to respond to the national call at a meeting in Pontarddulais in November 1915,[37] he was echoed by local leaders like Matthew Griffiths and Ivor Gwynne, General Secretary of the tinplate workers' union, the Tin and Sheet Millmen's Association (TSMA), who cited the rights of small nations in justification of the war.[38] They joined industrialists, small businessmen, and ministers of religion to canvass the area alongside Anglican clergy asking for recruits.[39] A meeting of the Free Church Council in Loughor in the spring of 1915 heard the Rev. D. H. Thomas, Ebenezer, Gorseinon, criticise ministers who were not giving their full support to the war effort, and his views were supported by the Rev. L. Richards of Gowerton and the Rev. D. M. Davies, Waunarlwydd, who believed he was speaking for his Saviour when he declared that he would be serving his country in its hour of need.[40] The Rev. John Williams, Brynsiencyn, was clad in khaki wearing a minister's collar when he preached at Libanus a few years later.[41] Not surprisingly, perhaps, the minister who showed the greatest zeal for recruitment was the Rev. M. J. Jones, Seion, Gorseinon, whose virulent opposition to the doctrine of Socialism had led to the resignation of the majority of his deacons before the war and a very public dispute with William Evans (Llanerch) in particular.[42] This uncompromising support for the nation's struggle intensified after the arrival of Belgian refugees who gave vivid accounts of German atrocities. This strengthened the community's resolve in support of the war effort. Countless committees were formed to organise home comforts, food parcels, and raise funds to help pay for the war, both in towns and villages and in workplaces and places of worship – War Savings, Bomb Weeks, Tank Weeks, and 'Victory Soon' campaigns became part of the fabric of life.[43]

For those in the mining industry, the war had an immediate impact as men found themselves unemployed following the loss of overseas markets.[44] As might be expected, the coal owners responded with schemes to reduce costs in the industry, which mostly involved the repeal of the Eight Hours Act (Coal Mines Regulation Act, 1908). Miners thrown out of work drifted to the recruiting stations and joined the colours. Those who remained in the industry were subjected to a range of measures that affected their freedom of movement and rights at work. They were required to register with labour exchanges and warned that they could be transferred to other collieries, not necessarily in south Wales.[45] While remaining silent on whether Labour should support the war, D. R. led protests at the western miners' monthly meetings about their leaders' acceptance of such terms for the duration of the war. Miners transferred to other areas had not been paid the minimum wage, they had been given work that local men were refusing to do, the miners were not adequately represented on the local pensions committees that were administering relief programmes, and the Prince of Wales Fund, supported by voluntary contributions and a levy on workers' wages, was failing in its task of providing temporary assistance to the unemployed.[46] The number of people applying for relief, he insisted, was low, not because help was not needed but because families would not subject themselves to the kind of questioning which the local committees were using when interviewing applicants.[47]

Throughout this period, D. R. was aware of the tension among the miners of the Western District on the issue of the war and its demands on the working class. A large section was, of course, fully supportive of the national effort, and regarded a willingness to respond to the call to serve in the Forces as a public duty. This may well have been the attitude of the majority, but others were equally convinced of the fundamental wrongs of the 'combing-out process', the government's demands on the working class, and its conduct of the war. Like James Winstone and others within the SWMF leadership, D. R. was convinced that the conflict stemmed from the failures of the capitalist system and the evils of secret diplomacy. He believed it was the Labour's movement's duty to understand the causes of the war and prevent any recurrence.[48]

Mansel Grenfell was more outspoken and was at the forefront of the work of the No Conscription Fellowship (NCF) in the locality since its establishment in November 1914. He served as chairman both of the Gorseinon branch and the coordinating body for south-west Wales. Its membership was drawn largely from the ranks of the ILP, although significantly it also drew support from local trades union organisations, and the Gorseinon Peace Council. Furthermore, the Trades and Labour Councils in both Gorseinon and Pontarddulais were affiliated to the Union of Democratic Control (UDC), which demanded open diplomacy and democratic scrutiny of international relations.[49] Mansel was among the organisers of large anti-war demonstrations in Ammanford, Llanelli and Swansea, which saw local leaders such as the Rev. T. E. Nicholas (Niclas y Glais) and the Tumble miners' leader, T.

Gibbon Davies, share platforms with Labour national figures Tom Mann, George Lansbury, and others, who as Christian Socialists denounced both the instrument of war and the political failures that had caused it.[50] Fenner Brockway, a leader of the NCF, was a regular visitor to Gorseinon throughout 1915 where Mansel and other local leaders of the anti-conscription NCF led discussion groups at the Institute on topics such as political liberty. These became the focus of attention for the local police, alarmed at the seditious materials that were being distributed.[51] Many, including Mansel himself, and William Evans (Gorseinon), Oliver Harris, Sid Lewis, Albert Lewis and W. J. Roberts, were active trade unionists in the steel and tinplate industry. They were joined by other comrades from the ILP, such as E. A. Martin, a tailor from Loughor, W. I. Thomas, a Gorseinon cabinet maker whose shop contained a Socialist bookstall, and Dan Harry, a teacher from Loughor.[52] They drew support from some religious leaders: the Rev. J. Morgan Jones attracted congregations that had not been seen since the Revival when he preached at Tabernacle and then at Libanus on anti-war themes. Similar numbers heard George Lansbury at St Catherine's church where the vicar, the Rev. Richard Jones (a regular attendee at NCF meetings), questioned the righteousness of the government's position.[53]

CHAPTER 3

The Miners' Agent

IN FEBRUARY 1916, William Morgan, the Miners' Agent for the Western District, died aged 57 after a long illness.[1] His life story personified the development of trade unionism in the coal industry in the Swansea Valley, and he was described by *Llais Llafur* as 'a fine type of labour leader, cultured man of more than average insight, though unassuming and avoiding the limelight', whose moderation, fairness and integrity had won the respect of employers and miners alike.[2] Tom Richards, first General Secretary of the SWMF, was equally fulsome, paying tribute to the man who had 'laboured honestly and sincerely for many years in the promotion of everything that he believed tended to uplift his fellow workmen to a higher and a better plane of industrial and social life'.[3] On the day of his funeral the cortege made its way from his home in Swansea to the chapel in Alltwen where the service was led by the prominent Socialist minister, the Rev. D. Eurof Walters, while John Williams MP gave the eulogy.[4] As the mourners headed home, attention turned to the question of who would succeed to the most important position in the affairs of the Western District miners and, through it, a key role in the work of the SWMF more broadly.

From the outset, it was clear that D. R., by virtue of his position as the miners' leader in one of the largest collieries in the area, would be one of the strongest candidates, notwithstanding that others with more formal experience would also be seeking election.[5] Within days his chances were helped by the decision to elect both an agent and sub-agent, something which was long overdue in the minds of many prominent figures in the Western District who had maintained for years that the job was more than one man could do. A total of 25 candidates were nominated, of whom four polled more than half of the votes in the first-round ballot – D. J. Williams of Clydach, the District Treasurer, with 2,000 votes; D. R., who polled 1,840; W. J. Jones (Gwilym Bedw), who had 1,360 votes; and W. Henry Davies of Penclawdd, who secured a total of 1,185.[6] These names appeared on the ballot paper for the second round of voting in April 1916. When the final vote was declared at the Elysium Hall in Swansea, D. R. triumphed, polling 3,797 votes, with D. J. Williams on 3,337, W. H. Davies 3,026 and W. J. Jones 2,930.[7] Immediately there were protests, primarily from lodges that had wanted a separate ballot for the two posts and others unhappy with the shortlist that had been presented. But the outcome was clear and heralded a new era for the Western District with D. R. as its agent and D. J. Williams as his deputy.[8]

His victory was welcomed by the most avowedly Socialist sections of the Labour movement in the area, notably his old friends in the Gorseinon ILP whose correspondent, 'Chum' (Oliver Harris), declared in the *Merthyr Pioneer*:

The ILP in the district is delighted to hear of the success of Mr. David R. Grenfell, who has been appointed Agent for the Western Miners. The miners have the right man in the right place; a man not easily moved; a, man for the workers in reality, not half-heartedly. When one thinks of the opportunities offered to 'D. R.' as colliery manager, etc., all of which he has refused, though possessing the first-class certificate as colliery manager, one can realise the benefits of having such a man as D. R. Grenfell for workers' agent.

He concluded with the stark and accurate prophecy, '[I] predict him to be within seven years "D. R. Grenfell, MP.'"[9]

At the end of May, D. R.'s election was marked at an induction meeting in Gorseinon where he pledged to be a very different leader to those who stood in the tradition of Lib-Lab moderates. Chum's report for the *Merthyr Pioneer* quoted him:

> There were certain legal cases that a Miners' Agent had to deal with, but there was something more. Agents should assist the rank and file in their desire to better their conditions; to improve life and to attain to that beauty and joy in life that the capitalist class enjoys. To secure those benefits we must get into one body... For many years he had tried to show the workers that the wealth of the country was in the hands of a few and that this was absolutely wrong. The legal machinery was in the hands of the employers. So the worker believes! But legally no. Comrades, all, yes all was in the hands of the workers if they desired it. But to carry this through in a successful manner they must put aside class jealousies. They could not achieve this unless they banded together. The Federations of three Unions would be settled very soon, which would exert great pressure in fact, such pressure that it must have the desired effect on the legislators, etc. As regards myself, I shall not be satisfied with this Federation until there be an International Federation. When this is achieved, what is happening on the Continent at the present will never occur again. The worker will not be led by the man on the top, but shall have all the power to decide; therefore, I conclude by asking you to awake, that the state of things as you found them be left better for your having been.[10]

As he commenced his duties he was under no illusions about the responsibility the role entailed. He would be serving a district that extended from the outskirts of Neath in the east to Pembrey in the west, taking in the whole of Swansea and Llanelli as far as the boundary with the Anthracite Area.

The district contained around 45 working collieries in which around 14,000 men were employed, who together produced an annual output of two million tons of coal. His first task would be to address the organisational weaknesses which he, along with Caradoc Jones, Gwilym Bedw and W. H. Davies, had complained about in meetings for years. He persuaded the executive to abandon the practice whereby the agent's home was used as an office and took a lease on a suite in Chappell Chambers in Castle Street, Swansea.[11] He did, however, abide by the requirement that either the agent or sub-agent should live in Swansea itself, moving his family from 74 Brighton Road and taking a lease on Ardwyn in Carnglas Road, Sketty, where he was to remain for the rest of his life.[12] The new agent clearly intended to run a professional operation on behalf of the western miners and his determination to be at the centre of the SWMF was also made clear when he replaced John Williams MP on the central executive of the Federation.[13] Practically, he also realised what was required. He needed to master the geology of each part of the district, the difficulties encountered working each seam, and the complex array of wage agreements and terms and conditions that operated in the different collieries. He also began to attend a depressingly long list of coroners' inquests, cross-examining witnesses and establishing grounds for compensation claims.[14]

At the same time, he had to contend with an unprecedented level of government control on the lives of working people as it used the legislative provisions of the DORA to direct workers and restrict individual freedom. Miners across south Wales were certainly in a militant mood, angry because of their worsening economic position caused by rising prices, and infuriated by the clear evidence of profiteering by the colliery companies.[15] Nowhere was this more evident than in the Western District. Men at the Birch Rock Colliery (where a voluntary levy of 6d. per week had been instigated by the men to support the war effort), had longstanding grievances about the way the colliery was run, which intensified during 1915 and 1916. Disputes at the Mountain Colliery continued, while at Tirdonkin attempts by Lord Glantawe to break the Union through the use of workmen brought in from elsewhere led to strike action which later spread to the Garngoch collieries.

D. R. also faced the task of ensuring that miners' interests were represented during the 'combing-out process', implemented in response to the Military Service Act, whereby miners released for the colours were selected. The work had initially been undertaken by the Collieries Recruiting Court, which adopted the seniority principle, thus providing exemption for those who had worked in the industry for the longest time. However, the task of selecting men had subsequently been given to the mining tribunal for the Anthracite and Western Areas, which included three conflicting interests, those of the owners assiduously promoted by colliery managers, members elected by miners' lodges, and representatives of the military authorities.[16] By the time that D. R. was in post, the military tribunal had already started its work under the chairmanship of Col. Pearson, the District Inspector of Mines, whose background clearly disposed him towards the demands of the military authorities, represented for much of the period by Capt. Harold Williams.

Col. Pearson made no attempt to disguise the fact that he regarded the miners as slackers looking for shelter in the mines while others were doing their duty on the battlefield, and this became obvious in his first encounter with D. R. at a hearing that considered the position of a checkweigher at Cefngolau Colliery in Gowerton.[17] D. R. maintained that the man should be exempt from military service on the grounds that he was an elected official of the miners. This argument made no impression on Col. Pearson who demanded that, as a man of military service age, his work was needed for the war effort.

Col. Pearson: 'There is no doubt that this man is exempted, but for that work you do not want a man with his full faculties. For weighing purposes, a man with one arm, one eye or one leg could do the work. It applies to the weighers as well as the checkweighers.'

D. R.: 'He has to do other things besides weighing... I am of military age myself.'

Col. Pearson: 'The same thing may apply to a Miners' Agent, sir.'

D. R.: 'Very well, we will fight that.'

Col. Pearson: 'We want fighting men in the army.'[18]

Some months later D. R. represented a miner from Grovesend who, it was alleged, had not worked in the industry for the required period. D. R. knew the man and told the tribunal, 'He worked alongside me.' Col. Pearson: 'You worked underground?' D. R.: 'Yes.' Col. Pearson: 'I thought you'd always had a soft job.'[19]

At the same time, D. R. became involved in arguments over alleged absenteeism, making detailed investigations into individual cases to establish the facts. One such incident occurred in August 1916 when he managed to disprove allegations that 11 out of 45 men had been absent from the Acorn Colliery, establishing that there were only three cases of preventable absenteeism. Likewise, at the Mountain Colliery he proved that some of those reported absent were on the compensation list. For D. R., the remedy lay not in prosecution but in the establishment of colliery committees that would vest authority in the men themselves and prevent victimisation by officials determined to remove marked men.[20]

At the MFGB conference in May 1916, D. R. was among those who voted to oppose the Military Service Bill, and demanded total opposition to the principle of conscription.[21] Throughout, D. R. was true to his belief that the miners and those employed in other industries should be guided by their consciences and not be forced to enlist for military service.[22]

Such ideas, however, were far from the reality of government regulations which reflected their standpoint that a nation's need for fuel was the only ground on which miners should be exempted from military service. Moreover, the authorities were increasingly desperate to find more men to send to battle. From the beginning of 1917, D. R. realised that the supposed involvement of the union in the machinery of the State was a fallacy as the mining tribunals began to revoke exemption certificates without any reference to him as the Miners' Agent or to anyone else in the SWMF.[23] He therefore recognised the anger that was provoked by the government's proposal for a further comb-out, designed to recruit an additional 20,000 men from the mining industry by removing the exemptions on men aged 18 to 25 and establishing a quota system to bring each colliery to the average for the district in which it was situated. When the MFGB Executive reached a compromise with the government over the way the scheme would be operated, it faced immediate criticism within the SWMF, including the western miners who demanded a national strike, and bitterly resented the failure to prevent a further combing-out process.[24]

The situation in the westernmost part of the south Wales coalfield was complicated further by the way the government set the quota of tonnage to be mined in each colliery under the terms of the control scheme. Both the SWMF and the local colliery companies believed that the quota scheme favoured collieries in the Cardiff area at the expense of those in Swansea and the Anthracite Area.[25] As a result, of the 7,500 men organised in the Western District lodges in February 1917, 2,000 were working half-time, 2,500 were on two-thirds time, and 1,000 were working occasional days, a position that remained unresolved for most of the year, and a similar situation prevailed in the Anthracite Area.[26] Although the coal controller agreed to increase the tonnage allocated to the collieries in the west, D. R. understood what the implications were: several companies had already given notice to the men, thereby reducing the capacity for coal production, and any new scheme would be based on output that had already contracted.[27] This, in turn, would affect the future viability of the collieries in that part of the coalfield and prevent them from playing their part in the war effort, while the men who worked in them were faced with the demands of the Military Service Act.

Matters intensified after November 1916 when workers in the tinplate industry were denied exemption from military service and subjected to a system of combing-out that differed significantly from that used in the mining industry, in that it gave managers autonomy to decide who was no longer required in each works. This coincided with a decision by the government to centralise tinplate production in the English Midlands, interpreted in south-west Wales as a deliberate attempt to undermine the area because of its militant industrial and political reputation.[28] It was not surprising that the men at the forefront of anti-war activities were among the first victims of the combing-out process in Gorseinon.[29]

Of even greater personal immediacy, on 14 March 1917 Mansel Grenfell was arrested and placed under the military authorities after he refused to enlist. He was subsequently brought before a court-martial which he used to denounce the war on the grounds that he was an internationalist Socialist who rejected all forms of militarism, irrespective of nationality. War was, he insisted, a consequence of the capitalist system, a form of institutionalised murder perpetrated by a ruling elite in their own interests. Other close comrades from Gorseinon also appeared before the military tribunals; Albert Lewis told the military tribunal that as an opponent of the government he could not, in conscience, do anything that served its interests and he refused to give a guarantee that he would not distribute anti-war literature, as to do so would be to deny the political principles that were central to his life.[30] Oliver Harris cited both his deep Christian faith and his political views in claiming exemption.[31] The military authorities were also confronted with other opponents of the war from the Gorseinon and Loughor area, including the sharp logic of Dan Harry, and from W. I. Thomas and Edward Martin, who cited Lloyd George's opposition to the Boer War in defence of his rights.[32] Throughout, D. R. was totally steadfast in his personal support for Mansel, visiting him during his period of imprisonment and fierce in defence of his character and the sincerity of his stance.

More broadly, as has been pointed out by several historians of the period in Wales, the Russian Revolution led to a significant hardening of the political opposition to the war on internationalist and class-based lines.[33] Nowhere was this more evident than among the ranks of the miners in the Western District. Its monthly meeting resolved to be represented at the Leeds Convention in June 1917, organised by the ILP and the British Socialist Party to try to expediate the end of the war, and sent D. R. as their delegate. He joined delegates who declared their solidarity with the Russian Revolution and expressed their hope that it would bring the war to a speedier conclusion. The Leeds Convention also supported international negotiations, called for a British charter of liberties and the establishment of a Council of Workers' and Soldiers' delegates.[34] This motion was endorsed by the Western District at its meeting in June 1917 when they joined the Merthyr Tydfil and Dowlais districts who had also taken the same position.[35] In this, the Western District reflected the views expressed at countless local meetings across south Wales that testified to the way that the decisions of the Leeds Convention reflected a widely held view within those communities.

The Swansea Labour Association invited delegates to a conference of soldiers' and workers' delegates at the Elysium Hall in Swansea, to be held on 29 July 1917. This gathering failed to proceed after an angry mob, initiated by the Swansea branch of the Naval and Military Pensions and Welfare League, who had convened a counter-demonstration the previous day, broke into the hall and attacked those present.[36] D. R. was not there that day and was therefore spared the violence meted out to many prominent Labour leaders in attendance. He had travelled to Glasgow five days earlier to take part in the MFGB conference and then visit D. J. Williams, formerly of Gwaun-cae-gurwen but by then a checkweigher in Fife, before returning to Swansea on 31 July.[37] But, despite the evidence of a pro-war feeling in Swansea, his views remained firm. He successfully sought the western miners' nomination to stand in the election of the Welsh delegate to the Central Provisional Committee of the National Soldiers' and Workers' Council which met in the third week of October 1917, although he failed to be elected. More immediately, he attended the SWMF conference in August 1917, which considered the government's proposals to introduce a combing-out scheme within the mining industry that proposed that 4,000 men, aged 18 to 25, be called to military service. D. R.'s opposition to the policy stood in sharp contrast to the views of the MFGB leadership and many within the SWMF, as was evident when the comb-out proposal was put to a ballot of all members in November 1917, and was endorsed by a majority of three to one across the whole coalfield. However, the vote indicated significant opposition to the comb-out in the Western District along with the Anthracite Area, Merthyr Tydfil and Dowlais. This broadened the nature of the political opposition to the war from the highly politicised ranks of the ILP (and related organisations such as the NCF) which as far as the Western District was concerned was reflected in resolutions that were passed throughout 1917 denouncing war profiteering and declaring support for the Stockholm conference.[38] The following year the district resolved unanimously to support the Garngoch No. 1 lodge in protesting against the disenfranchisement of conscientious objectors and issued a protest against Bertrand Russell's imprisonment.[39]

*

As D. R. reflected on the political scene as 1918 progressed, he knew that changes in his own locality could well determine how Labour would fare in the area for years to come. The extension of the Swansea County Borough Council (CBC) that year meant it subsumed parts of the Swansea RDC like Llansamlet, Tirdeunaw, Fforestfach, Waunarlwydd, and Sketty, together with parts of Treboeth and Morriston and the whole of the Oystermouth Urban District Council (UDC).[40] The changes to local government structures coincided with the redistribution of parliamentary constituencies, by which the Pontardawe RDC area was placed in the new Neath constituency. The changes created a Gower constituency consisting mainly of the westernmost areas of Glamorgan, but still including those wards that had been transferred into the county borough. Under most appraisals the change was likely to harm Labour's chances, because the party's strong areas were now to be included with Neath. This calculation had to be balanced against the impact of changes to the franchise, especially the inclusion of women over 30, which added nearly 30,000 voters to the electoral roll, almost double the number at the time of the previous election in 1910.

As the election drew near, D. R. agreed to serve as John Williams' agent in the campaign, but not before several lodges in the Western District had broken ranks and nominated him as the Labour candidate.[41] It is not known whether D. R. himself instigated the challenge but the message was clear: a body of opinion in the Labour movement in Gower were looking for an alternative to John Williams and saw D. R. Grenfell as his natural successor. Even so, notwithstanding any differences over the question of the candidate, Labour in the constituency was united in its determination to fight as an independent political party. John Williams therefore had no choice but to tell local Liberals that he would be a Labour candidate 'pure and simple', even though he had already received a letter from the government Chief Whip, the Rev. Towyn Jones, MP for East Carmarthenshire, declaring that Lloyd George did not want him to be opposed.[42] Labour's insistence that John Williams should stand under its banner without any other association gave the Gower Liberal Association an opportunity to challenge whatever intention Lloyd George and Towyn Jones had in mind. They selected D. H. Williams, Secretary of the Gower Liberal Association, a native of Three Crosses who had begun his working life as a pupil teacher before entering the Borough Training College in London and returning to the area, first as headmaster of D. R.'s alma mater, Penyrheol Board School, before moving to a similar position in Neath.[43] In many ways his political programme hankered back to the Liberal social policies of the Victorian era, imbued with a strong faith in the ability of the education system to solve the nation's social problems by means of an 'educated democracy'. But D. H. Williams was also prepared to fight dirty. He continually sought to pander to the anti-German mood with references to Labour pacifists and the power wielded by anti-war agitators like Ramsay MacDonald and Phillip Snowden.[44]

John Williams was in no mood to show mercy towards the Germans, promising that, if he represented Labour at the Peace Conference, he would make them pay the utmost penny in war indemnities.[45] On the home front he emphasised the need for a massive housing programme and called for strict restrictions on profiteering as part of a broader programme that encompassed leasehold enfranchisement and nationalisation of the railways. 'When our men returned from the field of battle… they should and must have the country's first claim, and a living wage worthy of their great sacrifice during the war's eventful period paid them.' These were, however, mere side issues in John Williams' campaign, which focused far more on the issue of Welsh disestablishment as he regaled his audiences with tales of how he had led the Welsh MPs into the lobbies singing 'Hen Wlad fy Nhadau' during a vote on the question in 1914.[46] He was supported by some of the denizens of Welsh Nonconformity – the Baptists in particular – led by the Rev. Gomer Lewis of Swansea. 'Gomer' was a true representative of nineteenth-century Welsh radicalism, having been involved in the farmers' agitation in Cardiganshire in the 1860s and a witness to the eviction of Liberal tenant farmers in the aftermath of the 1868 election. By 1918 he saw the chance of realising his lifelong battle for Welsh disestablishment while also proclaiming a social gospel directly concerned with tackling poverty, poor living conditions and inequality. On the eve of the poll, Gomer called for 'Victory for John Williams, victory for the Labour Party and victory for social justice', and proclaimed that 'God will see where you have put the cross. Do not disappoint God. I have taken the matter up with God and I do know he is on our side. Do not lose the chance of voting for the right man and the right social gospel tomorrow. Do not disappoint me. Do not disappoint John Williams and make certain you are on God's side in this most urgent occasion tomorrow.'[47]

Gomer's proclamations of divine intent were reflected in the outcome which returned John Williams with a majority of 1,756 over D. H. Williams. Elsewhere in Wales, Labour performed abysmally, winning ten out of the 36 seats. John Williams returned to the House of Commons to face the impregnable power of the 473 members who were pledged to support Lloyd George's coalition government, and sat somewhat uneasily as one of the 59 Labour members who shared the opposition benches with two dozen independent Liberals.

An overwhelming electoral mandate for the Coalition could not overcome the fact that nearly three-quarters of the new MPs were Conservatives or Unionists, and internal divisions meant the government soon found itself lurching from crisis to crisis as it sought to negotiate a permanent peace settlement, while dealing with the challenges of a new political system in Soviet Russia (whose existence was anathema to most on the government benches) and honouring the commitment to Home Rule for Ireland (which many of them found equally abhorrent).[48] Meanwhile, the impact of wartime inflation, continued food rationing, and the eventual collapse of the export markets for shipbuilding, coal, cotton, steel and tinplate created mass unemployment on a scale and duration never seen before.

Labour's defeat engendered a robust response from the movement throughout Wales as the party's leading figures wasted no time in launching a propaganda offensive. D. R. played a full part in its work, addressing meetings across south Wales calling for the nationalisation of the coal industry and the railways and urgent action to deal with housing and public health conditions.[49] His central message was that the working class should assert its demands through both political and industrial spheres. By the spring of 1919 he was again at the forefront of Labour campaigns in Gower, leading the efforts that won them the Llandeilo Talybont seat on the Glamorgan County Council with a candidate who had been a leading opponent of the war, and enabled the party to make significant progress in the first elections to the more compact Swansea RDC a few weeks later.[50] D. R.'s efforts on the Gower peninsula, however, were less successful. Outside the populous mining villages of north Gower, in particular Penclawdd and Llanmorlais, his message fell on deaf ears, while in Swansea itself an uneasy coalition of 'Independents', consisting of Liberals and Conservatives, retained a small majority. However, Labour polled strongly in the wards transferred from the RDC in 1919, and by the following year held eight of the ten seats in those areas.

The ILP remained the intellectual powerhouse of the

Labour movement, nowhere more so than in Gorseinon and its surroundings. Dan Harry had returned to the area and took charge of the branch during the years immediately following the Great War. D. R., having moved to Sketty, was unable to take as active a role as he had done when residing in Gorseinon, and Mansel was by now living in mid Wales. Both kept in touch with the branch and its activities, which included visits from renowned speakers such as Walton Newbold, the Rev. G. W. Sorenson, Gordon Lang, and prominent Welsh ILPers, in particular S. O. Davies.[51] The desire to consider all aspects of human existence continued and was seen in regular local appearances at ILP events in Gorseinon and Pontarddulais by the musician D. Vaughan Thomas and the educationist Helen Woodhouse, while a large and appreciative audience listened as the Estonian violinist Eduard Sõrmus recognised the support he had received in the locality by performing at an event in Gorseinon.[52] The vast majority of the Gorseinon ILP viewed Communist affiliation to the Labour Party as a natural and welcome step, and supported joining the Third International as a means of securing the vast resources of the Soviet Union in the struggle for Socialism. On the latter point, the branch stood among a handful which retained that standpoint after it had been rejected by the majority within the ILP.[53] There is insufficient evidence to come to any firm conclusion about D. R.'s involvement, if any, in these discussions in Gorseinon, and he subsequently refused to countenance any notion of collaboration with the Third International or the CPGB. His move to the Swansea suburbs may have been prompted by a necessity to live close to the Western District office, but it undoubtedly meant that he was not at the centre of discussions which may well have placed him in a difficult position had he remained in Gorseinon.

*

D. R. lived life to the full, undertaking his duties as the Miners' Agent, his work on the SWMF Executive, and as one of its delegates to successive MFGB conferences. There he bore witness to the MFGB's bitter struggles with the employers and with Lloyd George's government, and its battles within the broader trade union movement as it sought support for concerted industrial action in support of the miners' own claims and those of other workers throughout 1919 and 1920.[54] In his own area he actively promoted the Miners' Programme published in January 1919, which demanded wage increases, the introduction of a six-hour working day, and joint control of the industry by workmen and State.[55] But he was under no illusion about the challenge that faced the miners. When the government appointed the Sankey Commission to examine the industry, it was clear that it had been frightened by the militancy being shown by the miners, especially in south Wales where the SWMF voted by 117,302 to 38,261 in favour of industrial action.[56] D. R. listened as the MFGB conference endorsed its interim proposals to reduce the working day by one hour, with a promise that it would be reduced by a further hour within two years, accompanied by a wage increase for all adult miners of 2s. per day, as well as a commitment to a degree of worker involvement in the ways the collieries were run.[57] He knew that a government dominated by the Tories could not be trusted to fulfil the Sankey proposals. D. R. was dismissive of the government's alternative (limited to state management of royalties and coal deposits, welfare benefits, but allowing for the creation of pit committees, and worker representation on company boards), warning that it would not provide a lasting solution and predicting that any worker involvement would be by-passed by the creation of trusts or other conglomerates to replace individual companies.[58] The powers that the government intended to take were no more than those already enjoyed by the coal controllers, and nothing in their proposals would remove the antagonism between capital and labour in the industry.

D. R. continued to regard the working-class struggle in Britain in the light of international experience, and he roundly condemned the British government's actions abroad, in particular their attempts to overthrow the workers' government in Russia. His view was endorsed by the western miners at their monthly meeting in January 1919, which roundly condemned British 'interference with internal affairs in Russia'. The following month the district endorsed a resolution from Garngoch No. 1 calling for a campaign of political education on the actions of the British ruling class and their allies against proletarian movements across the whole of Europe, Russia in particular.[59] It went on to condemn the deportation of violinist Eduard Sõrmus. The call for a change in international policy was reiterated the following spring when D. R. presided on one of the platforms at the annual May Day gathering in Swansea in 1919, which declared that, 'in accordance with the declared policy of the Allies in regard to the right of self-determination of all countries, that all military and political intervention in Russia, or any other country, be stopped forthwith, and that arrangements be made immediately for the withdrawal of British troops from Russian soil,' going on to welcome the establishment of the League of Nations as a means of ending war and settling international differences.[60]

Further evidence that the miners in the Western District were in a militant frame of mind was shown by a series of disputes at the Ashburnam, Pentre, Killan and Dulas collieries in 1919 and at the Broadoak, Cape and Cae Duke collieries in the first months of 1920.[61] In March the men at the Mountain took strike action that lasted for over a month. There were also prolonged problems at the Garngoch collieries and at Tirdonkin.[62] D. R. sat as a delegate at the MFGB conferences in January where he reiterated his support for nationalisation and a unified wage rise for all those working in the mining industry.[63] This he insisted, in speeches that month, was the only way of advancing the workers in the industry. Private ownership had failed to organise efficient production or ensure safe working conditions and this situation would continue as long as coal was seen as a commodity in the interest of profit making. Only when the mines were nationalised would all concerned with the industry be able to work collaboratively for the ultimate good of all.[64] The western miners, he insisted, would support industrial action in support of nationalisation, if required to do so, and when the MFGB proceeded to ballot on the government's offer his confidence was confirmed when the Western District Executive voted to recommend refusal of the government's offer and repeated its support for an advance of three shillings.[65]

Matters were put to the test again at the end of September when the MFGB demanded an increase of two shillings on the basis of the existing output, with a further increase based on output in response to the impact of inflation.[66] The fact that the miners rejected the Mining Association's counter-offer (with over 90 per cent of the SWMF members against acceptance) came as no surprise to D. R. given the men's longstanding opposition to any scheme that linked wages questions to output. Within weeks he was again at the heart of discussions within the SWMF Executive Council after a large majority was secured in a ballot for strike action to start on 16 October 1920, this time reinforced by a commitment from the National Union of Railwaymen (NUR) to take action in support of the miners. Little wonder then that when the MFGB agreed to the Datum Line agreement (whereby the Mining Association agreed to an advance in wages provided that output reached an agreed quota) and advised its member to return to work, D. R. was among the large majority in the SWMF who rejected the agreement in total.[67]

By the end of the year the SWMF demanded that the MFGB should campaign for measures to stimulate the economy, including a resumption of trade with Russia and Central Europe, a maintenance wage of 40 shillings a week to every housebuilder, and a programme of public works in order to stimulate Britain's ailing economy. The Western District was in the vanguard, 'condemning the inactivity of leaders in not calling a national strike of the Federation to compel the Government to make peace in Central Europe and Russia, the absence of which was the cause of the present unemployment'.[68] These demands were rejected by the MFGB Executive which instead called for a new board to regulate wages and profit and a '1921 standard' wage rate, alongside an agreement that future wage advances be paid on a flat-rate basis, and for surplus income in the industry to be shared between workers and owners, combined with the creation of a national profits pool. The complexity of the proposals brought forward by the MFGB Executive, including the question of establishing a National Wages Board, and the difficulty of securing a way forward that would be acceptable to all sections within it, was clear from the discussions at the special conference held on 18 March 1921. At that conference D. R. argued against any proposal for a National Wages Board, believing it would bind the men to a settlement that the owners could manipulate to the miners' disadvantage. A National Wages Board, he believed, could result in conditions being imposed that reduced rather than increased the men's wages, as no-one expected the existing rates to be sustained.[69]

The notion of guaranteed minimum profits was a very dangerous principle. 'They will be able to prevent our wages rising until they have recouped themselves. That is not a new principle. We had it in the south Wales agreement in 1914... we must not commit ourselves to principles of this kind.'

In any event, he knew that the Mining Association's continued refusal to abandon the practice of separate district negotiations and their rejection of a National Profits Pool meant a confrontation was inevitable. When the owners issued notices ending all existing contracts as from 31 March 1921 immediately following decontrol, no-one was in any doubt that their intention was to initiate wage cuts and longer working hours. From 1 April the miners were locked out and troops were dispatched to the coalfields under the Emergency Powers Act passed five months previously.

D. R. oversaw arrangements in the Western District where he could be certain of the determination and loyalty of the men and their families. They had reason to expect the support of the Triple Alliance (the agreement by the miners, dockers and railway workers to take united action in support of each other), but on Black Friday, 15 April 1921, D. R. knew the miners would have to battle alone. A flow of indignant messages flooded into the Western District office from lodges furious with the other unions and with the role played by the MFGB secretary, Frank Hodges, over the previous days.[70] D. R. addressed large gatherings at the Llanelli May Day rally and at mass meetings in Pontarddulais and Loughor, culminating in a demonstration in Swansea on the afternoon of 7 May.[71] On 15 May he addressed a mass meeting at the Brighton Hall in Gorseinon – one of the largest political meetings seen in the area – and received the full support of all trade unions represented at the gathering.[72] Amid the suffering, D. R. could at least point to the strength of the community's support for the miners across all sections of the workforce. For the next two months he worked tirelessly to organise relief, as food and other support was put in place through local distress committees in the main centres of population.[73] Concerts and drama productions were held to raise money, including a production of *Rybeca* by bard and theologian, the Rev. J. Gwili Jenkins, at Pontarddulais, and work for strikers was organised through the influence of Labour councillors on the local authorities.[74]

Despite the suffering the miners were in no mood to compromise. In June 1921 the SWMF rejected the owners' terms by a substantial majority. More than four-fifths of the men at Graig Merthyr rejected the settlement, a similar result was recorded at Grovesend, while at the Mountain Colliery nine out of every ten miner was against it.[75] In the end, however, the outcome was one of bitter disappointment for D. R. and those for whom he spoke. The MFGB agreed to terms which granted the industry a government subsidy of £10 million along with a 20 per cent advance on a new standard wage, but there was no progress on the questions relating to the organisation of the industry. The agreement also introduced district ascertainments, based on a calculation of standard which meant that, in south Wales, wages per shift were reduced to half what they were in 1920–21. In the Western District there was significant resentment at the terms and D. R. predicted further problems for the industry: the owners were not honouring the agreement and the men remained dissatisfied with their attitude.[76]

Outstanding issues remained at the Mountain, at the Garngoch collieries, and at Tirdonkin which had occupied much of D. R.'s attention for most of the previous year. There were recurring disputes over issues such as arrangements for emergency services following accidents, the re-employment of injured men, as well as price lists and working conditions.[77] Many of the problems stemmed from the change of management and the financial burden of paying dividends on unsustainably inflated capital. Glasbrook Bros, owners of the Garngoch collieries, were bought by the Grovesend Steel and Tinplate Co. in 1918, and the Tirdonkin Colliery had been sold to Lewis, Stephens & Co.[78] The outcome of the relentless drive for profit that ensued was under-investment, cost-cutting, poor safety practices, and constant efforts to increase hours of work and to reduce pay.

The local disputes remained unresolved and this meant men at Tirdonkin and Garngoch continued to be locked out after the end of the national dispute in 1921. In order to force the issue, an angry meeting decided to escalate the dispute by withdrawing the safety men. Meanwhile, the tense atmosphere was inflamed by a circular from the Ministry of Labour instructing local authorities not to employ strikers in relief schemes.[79] This provoked a furious response from the Labour leaders in Gorseinon, who called a protest meeting on Loughor Common which began peacefully with an address by W. J. Roberts, a man who went on to give a lifetime's service to his community.[80] Local feeling was riled further when D. R. brought news of the outcome of a court judgment on the Pentre case, where the judge decided against W. J. Richards and his wife, whose son had been killed while shot-firing was taking place at the colliery the previous February, during which the judge accused the men giving evidence against the company of perjury. For D. R. it was 'a blatant case of class bias'.[81]

There was no violence or unruly behaviour of any sort at the mass meeting on Loughor Common, and those assembled included some of the most highly respected men and women in the locality. However, around 100 police officers on horseback, drawn in from outside the area, insisted on dispersing the crowd into the surrounding streets. Within days, an angry crowd gathered at Mynydd Cadle, some three miles from Gorseinon, and decided to march to the various local collieries to demand that the enginemen, stokers and firemen stop work.[82] They failed to do so and the following day 800 people marched to Tirdonkin, with women in the vanguard, where they were attacked by police officers guarding the colliery at the behest of the manager.[83] A total of 4,000 men remained locked out throughout the summer with no sign of settlement, until eventually an agreement was reached whereby the Garngoch men returned to work in accordance with the national agreement at the end of August, while those at Tirdonkin were forced back at the start of September.[84] Matters continued to be tense at both collieries for the following years, resulting in recurring strike action.[85] Elsewhere, conditions across the

Western District deteriorated further as hundreds of miners found themselves unemployed, and those who were in work could barely earn the minimum wage.[86]

*

When John Williams MP announced that he would not be seeking re-election, ostensibly due to declining health, some suspected that his increasing alienation from parliamentary colleagues, the miners' MPs in particular, was also a factor. Various names were mentioned as possible candidates including the Fabian Sidney Webb and the economist Sir Leo Chiozza Money, but in the event no candidate from outside the area was able to muster any significant support. D. R. secured the overwhelming support of the SWMF lodges in the constituency before facing two other local candidates in the final selection. One was Walter Samuel, a 39-year-old barrister, who had left school at the age of eleven and started work as a miner until an injury prompted him to start attending night school and he eventually qualified as a barrister. He had been an active lodge official and an ILP propagandist and was heavily involved with the Swansea Labour Association. The other was Ifor Hael Gwynne, the 54-year-old leader of the south Wales tinplate workers, who had the kudos of being a longstanding councillor in Swansea and a prominent figure in the TUC. Ifor Gwynne had sought Labour's nomination for Neath for the 1918 election, but had been defeated there by the miners' nominee, William Jenkins, and had subsequently contested Pembrokeshire against the Coalition candidate, without success. He had the support of the steel and tinplate unions, was determined to increase their voice in parliament and was resentful of the miners' monopoly on parliamentary representation in south Wales. In common with most trade union leaders, Ifor Gwynne had supported the war effort and took a prominent part in recruitment campaigns. Even so, he was politically well to the left of his union leadership (now British Iron, Steel and Kindred Trades Association (BISAKTA) after the TSMA had amalgamated with other unions in the steel and tinplate industry) and others of the Lib-Lab tradition, and efforts to portray him in the mould of John Williams were wide of the mark.

D. R.'s strength, of course, lay in the organisation of the SWMF and the fact that he enjoyed the support of the ILP element in the constituency, both as a member in his own right and also as Mansel Grenfell's brother. This was sufficient to ensure victory in a ballot of members affiliated to the Gower Labour Association. On the first ballot D. R. polled 2,920, with Walter Samuel on 1,611, and Ifor Gwynne receiving 1,216.[87] There was no need for a second round. D. R. was to add the work of nursing the Gower parliamentary constituency to his other tasks over the coming year.

CHAPTER 4

A Man of Extreme Views

THE DEATH OF John Williams aged 61 in the summer of 1922 meant D. R. faced his first electoral test in a by-election, to be held on 20 July of that year.[1] The *Western Mail* predicted imminent doom for Labour in Gower, in the words of its London correspondent who alleged that, 'The Labour Party in London do not expect to hold the seat and undoubtedly this conveys a truthful impression not only as heard in London but in the constituency itself.[2] Mr D. H. Williams, as a supporter of the coalition and a man of moderate and certainly not Socialistic views would probably more adequately "carry on" the principles of the late member, Mr John Williams, in his representation of the constituency than would Mr D. R. Grenfell the miners' agent who is certainly a man of extreme views and does not hesitate to express them and whose only likeness to Mr Williams is that he was once a miner.'[3] Moreover, the 'London Correspondent' was convinced that D. H. Williams enjoyed the support of 'sober-minded workers', while D. R.'s appeal was confined to 'colliers and the extremists'.[4]

This was certainly the message which D. H. Williams hoped to promote as he sought to portray himself as the 'genuine working-man's representative', in contrast to his Socialist opponent. At Birchgrove he declared, 'As for the legitimate purposes for which the Trade Union is established, [I am] as strong a Trade Unionist as any man. But I object to the rise of Trade Unionism for political purposes.' While

Labour proclaimed themselves the party of peace, they were all too ready to support class war.[5] The prospect of imminent revolution was never far from the thoughts of his platform supporters. Dan Thomas, a Liberal and a senior figure in the coal industry prominent in London Welsh circles, warned of the likely 'displacement' of commerce and industry with credit going to the wind if Labour won. J. A. Seddon, a former Labour MP who now sat as a supporter of the Coalition, accused D. R. of hiding his Communist and ILP sympathies.[6] Thomas Williams accused Labour of running away from its responsibilities for ex-servicemen, while the Rev. Robert Lewis at Kingsbridge said that it would be 'political suicide' to put in a Socialist government.[7] D. H. Williams, of course, could also count on formal support from the Conservatives, as leading Tories like Sir John Llewellyn and Roger Beck appeared on public platforms, while Austen Chamberlain wrote a personal appeal to the electors, repeating the message of imminent revolution, professing that the election was about the 'protection of Parliamentary institutions against "direct action" and Sovietism, defence of individual enterprise against nationalisation of industry, and resistance to the socialisation of the State'.[8]

D. R.'s campaign had already made headway in the months since his selection, which he had spent on the stump addressing public meetings across the constituency with the support of old comrades like the Rev. T. E. Nicholas and John James, the anthracite miners' leader from Cwm-gors. A prominent place was found on his platform for John Jones, Pencefnarda, who delighted in extolling his former pupil's virtues.[9] Even so, there was a grain of truth in the *Western Mail*'s reports of concern within the Labour leadership in London who recognised the need for an energetic campaign to counter a united front of Liberals and Conservatives, leading them to deploy the party's leading platform speakers to bolster the local efforts. The former party leader Ramsay MacDonald, speaking in Gowerton, did not mince his words in lambasting the government. The coalition government could not unsay the promises made in 1918.[10] Another former MP, George Lansbury, was given a warm reception at Sketty, where he denounced those who believed that Labour stood for revolution, insisting that, 'Prosperity would not come by perpetuating wars and hatred, but the peace and truth for which men and women were wishing the whole world over could only come by a new and better understanding between humanity in this country and others, and by abandonment of the spirit of vengeance.'[11] A religious society like Wales would never be able to accept a foreign policy designed to bankrupt Germany.[12] Arthur Henderson, Labour's leader during the First World War, denounced the Coalition's desperate tactics and told an audience at Gorseinon Institute that the government's latest statement on policy was nothing but a 'cynical, dangerous, undemocratic class device'.[13] The Rev. Gordon Lang accused the government of 'callous' treatment of the working class in the country by deploying the army to resolve industrial disputes.[14]

The arrival of Scottish trade unionist Robert Smilie during the final weeks of the campaign provided a further injection of energy and indicated that Labour was not going to moderate its appeal. He declared himself tired of 'milk and water' Socialism and proclaimed himself a rebel who would remain a rebel while the decaying living conditions continued.[15] Throughout the campaign, D. R. insisted on putting forward a positive vision of international and domestic issues.[16] He placed a strong emphasis on the need to end the use of war as a means to resolve international disputes, arguing for international cooperation and calling for the establishment of an organisation of working people to secure this aim.[17] He rounded on those who claimed Labour's social reforms were unaffordable. An additional tax, through a capital levy, on a small number of people would release £350 million used to pay the interest on the national debt which could then be diverted to social expenditure; it was simply a matter of asking for a fair contribution from those with the means to pay.[18]

As polling day drew nearer, the local press joined in the attack. The *South Wales Daily Post* denounced the capital levy, denigrating the background of MPs who had risen from the ranks of the trade unions, and deploring Labour's commitment to nationalisation. On polling day itself it declared that, 'the gravity of the case against the Labour Party lies in the circumstance that it contemplates hazy but immense and hazardous changes in the system by which the country earns its bread and butter, as well as in its inclination to take a most pessimistic view of the country's financial condition, and so formulate upon the basis of that pessimism a policy of the most grandiose projects, involving the necessity for finding a revenue inconceivable in its dimensions.'[19] The Conservative *Western Mail* confidently predicted that D. H. Williams would win, claiming that John Williams' hold on Gower was personal and not political, and declared that the Gower electors faced a choice between 'a policy of trade enterprise and a policy of trade hindrance'.[20]

On the eve of poll, the paper became even more strident, and commended D. H. Williams as being as good a Labour candidate as D. R. Grenfell, but not a Socialist bound to support experimentation and ventures marked by interference and peril. The only answer was to keep to the beaten track of endeavour. The miners' decision to support affiliation to the Third International (Communist International/Comitern) threatened a Soviet-style takeover. 'This is political labourism as understood by South Wales: the men and women of the Gower Division will decide to have none of it.'[21] D. R., the paper insisted, might give the appearance of being a quiet and inoffensive advocate of gradual change rather than revolution, but he had been associated with those who had pursued a policy of disruption and political agitation in the police and the army, while his supporters had been engaged in a policy of intimidation, threatening free speech by breaking up his opponent's meetings.

Such attacks were answered in robust terms, not least by the *Daily Herald* which was gaining circulation in the Gower constituency as elsewhere in Wales, which leapt to D. R.'s defence:

D. R. Grenfell, the Labour candidate, stands for the right of Labour – that is, the bulk of the community – to run the country in the interests of the majority. His opponent merely asks for another blank cheque to run it in the interests of the money-laden minority, as represented by the plunder band which makes up the motley Coalition... The workers of Gower and of Pontypridd (where Mardy Jones has excellent prospects of carrying the Labour flag to victory) are sick of the old party cries. To the Coalition carpet-baggers with their electioneering promises of 'what the Government will do if you return us to Parliament', they are putting the deadly question, 'Why the blazes haven't you done it?' And the answer is, if the Government candidates dared give it is, 'because the capitalists who find the cash to keep the old parties in being will not permit our doing it'. Only one party in Westminster is free to govern in the interest of the working masses, and that is the Labour Party. Because the electors of South Wales are aware of this, the Labour candidate will top the poll in Gower and Pontypridd.[22]

Throughout the campaign, D. R. had remained confident of victory but avoided complacency, an attitude that was justified by the result which saw the Labour majority double as a substantially higher voter turnout gave D. R. 13,296 votes to D. H. Williams' 9,841. In his victory speech he attributed his success to the 'general tendency of the country against the Coalition's policies and the fact that more and more people were coming to understand what Labour stood for.' Any attempt to discredit the Labour Party, as had been tried in

Gower, was unlikely to succeed. He thanked those who had attacked him on personal lines for increasing his support, and thanked the ladies in particular for their help.[23]

The Labour press were ecstatic at the result and highlighted the role women played in the campaign. 'Well done Grenfell' was the lead article in the *Daily Herald*:

> Our Gower comrades have delivered a smashing blow against the Coalition. By a majority of over 3,400, D. R. Grenfell has held the seat for Labour. This is a fine personal triumph for him, and a splendid tribute to the magnificent work of his friends in the district. They have demonstrated that enthusiasm and hard work are able to conquer money and lies… From start to finish the Coalitionists relied on abuse and mendacity as their chief weapons. They trotted out all the old bogies. They described Grenfell and his friends as cut-throats, revolutionists, atheists, and everything else which the ladies and gentlemen from London thought good enough or bad enough – to frighten the simple, honest men and women electors… The women in the Gower Division flocked to hear the Labour message, and as a result have once again routed the Coalition.[24]

D. R. immediately made his way to London where he was introduced as a new member of the House of Commons by Tom Griffiths, MP for Pontypool, and Morgan Jones, recently elected as MP for Caerphilly and an old comrade of Mansel's from the NCF.[25] Within days, Gower's new member was greeted by ecstatic Labour supporters as he arrived in Pontypridd to speak in support of Mardy Jones' by-election campaign. He was carried shoulder-high in a chair bearing the placard 'Gower's Reply to the Attack on Labour' as he made his way to the town's Park Cinema, accompanied by the Ynyshir drum and fife band. There he told the assembled crowd that he owed his victory to the way voters had refused to be misled by an underhand and dishonest Coalition campaign.[26] The Prime

Minister's political actions had alienated his traditional base of support, while his conduct in office meant he was mired in one shabby scandal after another. The government's policy in Ireland, arguments over German reparations, the diplomatic status of Soviet Russia, as well as industrial and financial problems, meant that its days were numbered. Within a fortnight T. I. Mardy Jones joined him in parliament, adding Pontypridd to Labour's tally of seats.

D. R. threw himself into Labour's campaigning work in south-west Wales where seats close to Gower, such as Neath, Swansea West, Llanelli and Carmarthen, were clearly within the party's grasp. This test came within three months of his election. D. R. faced another contest this time as a result of the Conservative MPs' decision, taken at the Carlton Club on 19 October, to fight the next election as an independent party, precipitating Lloyd George's resignation and subsequent dissolution of parliament.[27]

D. R. insisted that the infighting that had brought about the election, carried on in the privileged surroundings of London's clublands, made no difference to the voters of Gower. The Liberals and Tories did not differ on any of the major issues facing the country. Their record in government had left the richest in society twice as wealthy as they had been in 1914, while the poor were equally worse off. Nearly nine-tenths of the wealth of the nation was owned by a tenth of the population, while 60 per cent of the people owned just two per cent. The rich never earned the opulence they enjoyed and it was time for the dispossessed to move forward from the drudgeries of life and ask those who benefited to the tune of four million pounds during the war to share what they had gained through other peoples' labour.[28]

Turnout in Gower was nearly 75 per cent, little different from the by-election the previous July. D. R. polled 13,388, almost identical to the number of votes he received four months earlier, but the Liberal, Fred Davies, added more than 1,500 votes to his party's tally to reach 11,302, reducing the Labour majority to just over 2,000. Elsewhere there were signs of Labour progress, as Swansea East, Llanelli, Neath and Aberavon returned Labour MPs, creating a solid block for the party in western south Wales. Across Britain, Labour polled more than four million votes which secured the return of an unprecedented 140 MPs.[29] Such momentous progress immediately prompted the *Daily Herald* to celebrate by producing the *Herald Book of Labour Members* containing short biographies of each member. Of Gower's member its author said:

> David Rhys Grenfell reminds me of Moses. Like that leader of Israel, he chose rather to suffer affliction with his own people than to enjoy the pleasures of sin for a season – those pleasures being, in Mr Grenfell's case, the emoluments with which a colliery manager is rewarded for acting with his employers against his fellow-workers.

> By labour in the pit from the age of 12, by study in the Glamorgan County Technical Classes (where he gained honours in mining and mine surveying, and certificates in geology and mathematics), and finally by taking, at the age of 24, a first-class colliery manager's certificate, he was fully qualified to be a boss' man.

> He had one disqualification – a conscience of his own, a conscience informed and stimulated by the teachings of a Radical mother, and the reading of Tolstoy and all the books on economics he could get hold of. So, he made his choice, and his fellow-miners later on made him their Moses.

> In 1916, when he was 35 years of age, and had worked at every underground pit job from door-boy upwards, he was appointed Miners' Agent for the Western District of South Wales. He is now a member of the South Wales Miners'

Executive and advisory agent for his district.

These appointments, like his return to Parliament by a majority of 3,300 at the Gower by-election in July 1922, and his re-election in November, were the results of steady, patient, and exceptionally efficient work for the miners of his district. He left himself no time for sports, but he, naturally enough, became, many years ago, a Co-operator and a Rechabite.

During two years in Nova Scotia he worked with French miners, and learnt their language as an addition to English, and, of course, his native Welsh, in which he delights to address his compatriots.

A correspondent who has worked with D. R. writes to tell me of the way men flocked to him with the compensation and other troubles, of the patience and sympathy with which he heard them, of his wonderful memory for their names, faces, and individual problems, and the technical knowledge and mastery of facts and figures which he devoted to helping them as counsellor and negotiator. My own encounters with him in your Lobby and recollection and re-reading of his maiden speech in the mines debate last November confirm my correspondent's eulogy. Mr Grenfell has won his way as an unusually well-equipped Miners' Agent, and he is winning his way in Parliament. He is fluent, but not oratorical. There is nothing showy about him. He is too modest to display his capacity until occasion calls for their exercise.[30]

D. R., for his part, threw himself into parliamentary work with vigour. He was one of 14 MPs, mainly the Clydesiders (the group of Socialist MPs elected in Glasgow and surrounding areas) and Welsh Labour MPs with Nonconformist backgrounds, who supported Edwin Scrymgeour's efforts to control the liquor trade through a Prohibition Bill.[31] He became a member of the Betting Tax Committee and, along with Morgan Jones, Isaac Foot and C. W. Wilson, attended a horse racing event where he 'found more to amuse than to admire', and was appointed to parliamentary committees examining minute details of government policy on issues as diverse as the quality of house coal, the criteria determining a widow's pension, the method of undertaking income tax assessments, the administration of the national insurance system, naval policy, and the welfare of ordinary service personnel.[32]

Naturally, however, his main focus was on the crisis confronting Britain's coal mining industry. He knew at first hand the dire situation created by the failure to implement the Sankey recommendations and the conditions that existed across the coalfields: miners were paid the bare minimum allowed by law, unemployment had soared, and victimisation was rife.[33] Matters were at their worst in south Wales where the profit-sharing scheme introduced by the government on the initiative of Austin Hopkinson, MP for Mossley, in an effort to improve relations between the owners and the men, was a delusion in the circumstances facing the industry. In December 1922 he told the House of Commons:

> The so-called profit-sharing scheme in the coalfields at the present time is a misnomer, because for the last 12 months no profits have been available for sharing. This is the amusing device described by the Hon. Member for Mossley to fool the people employed in the mining industry, and the people not employed in it. This is the incentive by which the workers in that industry carry all the loss, save a very small proportion of loss carried by some owners in some of the districts.[34]

He contrasted the position of the industry with that of 1914, when 'the conditions of life for the mining workers were tolerable', and a much higher standard of living was enjoyed by most miners. The selling price of coal had increased dramatically during the first years of the war but there had been no impact on wages until 1915, because they were still set at the rate agreed in 1910. Moreover, the men's endeavours to obtain wages that took account of the increased cost of living had been shattered by the subsequent fall in prices. He challenged his opponents to defend the reduction, in real terms, that would be inflicted on the miners:

> I ask any fair-minded man whether he would have been prepared to accept the 1914 standard of wages, with the cost of living 130 to 140 per cent higher than in 1914. The miners refused the terms. After 13 weeks' stoppage, terms were imposed upon them, and those terms mean that the minimum wages in the coal field are not 43 per cent higher than the wages of 1914, but 20 per cent above those of 1914... The 43 per cent represents the additional wages cost to the industry, partly due to the Seven Hours Act. The cost of living to-day is 80 per cent above the pre-war level, and last year, on an average, it was 105 per cent above the pre-war level.

He went on to set the political climate in south Wales in the context of the circumstances facing mining communities. 'The politics of the Rhondda Valley are the politics of the miners who have been so badly treated by the Government and by capitalist interests in this country.' Men were working harder than ever, while 60,000 were unemployed and an additional 100,000 only partly employed. The message was clear, private enterprise did not provide a proper standard of living for the miners and their families.

As he made his case, he was in no doubt that a well-delivered, cogent argument could not overcome the reality of a hostile government majority, but an unexpected turn of events provided yet another opportunity to convince the electors. When the Tory leadership passed from Bonar Law to Stanley Baldwin in May 1923, it reopened the question of tariff reform, and prompted the new Prime Minister to seek a fresh mandate. Britain faced yet another general election, which for D. R. meant a third contest in 18 months. Once again he faced the combined forces of both Liberals and Conservatives, who this time united behind Mrs Lillian Folland, wife of the managing director of the Grovesend Steel and Tinplate Co., a social reformer determined to win over women voters in the constituency whom she was convinced would reject Labour's doctrinaire capital levy policy and respond positively to her message of industrial peace and conciliation.[35] Fanciful as it might seem, she looked forward to Liberal unity and a government once again led by the former Liberal premier H. H. Asquith, and containing Lloyd George and Lord Grey, which would secure industrial reconciliation and guarantee world peace by bringing the United States into the League of Nations. D. R. might have wondered whether the League of Nations could have mediated between H. H. Asquith and Lloyd George and, in any case, he was convinced that, for the voters of Gower, unemployment rather than the capital levy was the main issue confronting the country.

D. R.'s platform promised a combination of measures to stimulate growth, with a programme of public works that included long-needed schemes to construct the Channel Tunnel and to build a new road bridge over the river Severn.[36] The Liberals, he maintained, had lost any semblance of affinity for the working class, and their behaviour in the House of Commons was personified by Sir Alfred Mond, MP for Swansea West, a man who had never advocated the same policy for more than six months at a time, and only a vote for Labour would usher a change of policy by a British government.[37]

His message evidently resonated with the public yet again. D. R. added more than a thousand votes to his tally, polling 14,771 to Mrs Folland's 10,219.[38] Overall, however, there was little change on the voting pattern seen at the previous year's election, as the Conservatives took 5.2 million votes, Labour 4.2 million, while the combined Liberal vote stood at 4.1 million. Even so, the impact on parliamentary seats was significant:

258 Conservatives, 191 Labour members and 158 Liberals. No party had a majority, none could form a government without the support of the Liberals, and Britain faced the prospect of another general election very soon. Asquith's calculations, that a Labour government without a majority would be sure to fall to his electoral advantage, opened the way for Ramsay MacDonald to enter 10 Downing Street in the third week of January 1924 as the first ever Labour Prime Minister. His overriding aim was to use the opportunity to demonstrate that Labour could be trusted to govern, and any expectation that he would lead a full-blooded Socialist government were disabused when the ministerial appointments were announced.[39] He himself took the role of Foreign Secretary, while Philip Snowden, the ILP propagandist and pamphleteer, as Chancellor of the Exchequer quickly showed that he lacked any appetite to challenge Treasury orthodoxy. The appointment of a Glasgow MP, John Wheatley, as Minister of Health was seen as a token consolation to the ILP and the Left, but there was no room in the government for any of the other Red Clydesiders, nor George Lansbury, nor D. R. Grenfell. Only one of D. R.'s closest colleagues was given a place, Rhys Davies, MP for Westhougton but originally from Llangennech, became Parliamentary Secretary to the Home Office where his duties included responsibility for workmen's compensation.[40]

MacDonald's obvious caution quickly led to murmurings within Labour's ranks, not least within the SWMF who pressurised the MFGB Executive to approach the Parliamentary Labour Party (PLP) to demand that nationalisation of the mines and minerals be part of the government's immediate programme. D. R. was in no doubt that these were urgent priorities, but it was abundantly clear that MacDonald was not prepared to risk a confrontation with the powerful vested interests represented by the coal owners, especially in the circumstances in which Labour had entered government for the first time.[41] Instead, he proceeded to implement a cautious programme for government, but one that was not without merit. It recognised the Soviet Union, sought to reduce German reparations to a level the country could pay, and promoted a policy of disarmament and arbitration to resolve international disputes. Charles Trevelyan, as Secretary for Education, sought to expand secondary and technical education with the aim of raising the school leaving age to 15 and broadening the curriculum. The Housing Act 1924 promoted by John Wheatley provided better coordination of the housing programme with higher building standards, and sought closer collaboration between local authorities and the building industry to end profiteering and speculative development.[42] Rhys Davies also enjoyed a triumph at the Home Office where he secured a change to the regulations to extend compensation to workers in the steel and tinplate industry suffering from the effect of heat on the eye. Appropriately, it was a decision that brought immediate benefit to scores of families in south-west Wales.

D. R. knew that the government's paralysis on the question of the future of the coal industry meant it was unable to address the central issue facing Britain's mining communities. The industry had been given a temporary boost by an increase in coal exports in 1923, caused by abnormal circumstances on the Continent. This had been sufficient for the SWMF to demand a withdrawal from the 1921 agreement and for a new minimum wage to be set. In December 1923 the MFGB had followed suit, and gave notice to terminate the wages agreement. Tom Shaw, the Minister for Labour, supported by Emanuel Shinwell as Secretary for Mines, resorted to analysis, the practice adopted by previous governments to deal with such thorny issues, and appointed a Court of Inquiry, chaired by Lord Buckmaster, a Lord of Appeal and former Lord Chancellor. Once again, the cream of Britain's legal profession recognised the miners' case and recommended changes to the formula agreed in 1921, as well as reform of the profit-sharing system.[43]

In the meantime, the government's precarious position

was made worse by an unexpected crisis when the Attorney General, Sir Patrick Hastings, reversed his decision to prosecute the prominent Communist J. R. Campbell under the Incitement to Mutiny Act. The facts of the case showed clearly that the case against Campbell should never have been brought, but such niceties counted for little in the toxic political circumstances in which the Labour government operated. The Liberals combined with the Tories, this time to pass a motion of censure on the government. MacDonald called an election for 29 October.[44]

This time, D. R. faced a London barrister, E. T. Nethercoat, standing as a Unionist with the support of local Liberals like Fred Davies.[45] Nethercoat's cack-handed campaign – he demanded State subsidies for agriculture but not for other parts of the economy – and a series of gaffes that highlighted his own inexperience, did nothing for his chances.[46] He did, however, benefit from the Tories' national campaign which dwelt extensively on the theme of Socialist extremism and insinuations that Labour were in league with the Communists, a choice 'between the Socialist policy of revolution and disruption and the policy of stability combined with sane and steady progress'.[47]

Unbowed, D. R. went on the offensive, defiantly defending the Labour government's actions in relation to the Campbell case and insisting that the so-called communist conspiracy was nothing but a Tory fabrication. The *Workers' Weekly*, he insisted, was an insignificant paper that carried no weight, the Campbell case had no bearing on any aspect of government policy, certainly not the decision to recognise the Soviet government and to begin to develop new trading arrangements with it. Furthermore, the Liberals' support for the Conservatives' censure motion was a prelude to renewed cooperation between the two parties in a coalition 'composed of the most reactionary political elements in this country to prevent the onward march of the Labour Party'.[48] But the Tories proved adept at exploiting fears of the 'red bogey' and their tactics were boosted further when the *Daily Mail* published a forged letter from the head of the Comintern, Grigory Zinoviev, purportedly instructing the Communist Party of Great Britain to engage in sedition and predicting that Labour's trade deal with the Soviet Union would radicalise the British working class. Across the UK, the Labour vote increased by a million to reach 5.2 million, but the Conservative total increased by 2.1 million. In Gower, D. R. again increased his vote, polling 15,374 and securing a majority of 3,858, but he faced the disheartening reality of five years on the opposition benches facing a Tory government with an overall majority of more than 200.

Despite this disappointment, he resumed his work focusing on the mining industry and, in particular, issues relating to safety and working practices, matters that were placed in sharp focus by two separate events in his own constituency. The first occurred on 26 September 1924 when an explosion at Brynlais Colliery in Llanmorlais took the lives of four men.[49] A total of 25 charges were subsequently brought against officials of the company over breaches of the Coal Mines Act, mainly relating to their failure to ensure that sufficiently trained men were on duty, that there was insufficient ventilation, poor record keeping, defects to the roof and sides of the colliery, and charges related to the use of explosives. The company, for its part, sought to avoid liability by attributing the problems to the carelessness of individual officials and, by the time the matter went to court at the beginning of 1925, the company had gone into liquidation.[50]

The second case occurred on 27 November 1924, two months after the explosion at Brynlais, this time at the Killan Colliery in Dunvant where five men drowned following an inrush of water.[51] Allegations about conditions at the mine soon reached D. R. who was, in any case, aware of longstanding safety concerns at the colliery which had taken up much of his time as Miners' Agent. Before the inquest began, he insisted on going below ground, accompanied by Captain Sims Rees, the Senior Inspector of Mines, and four others, one of whom was the manager, to view the conditions. The investigating party found that black damp and debris prevented a proper inspection of the area where the deaths occurred, but D. R. was able to make a preliminary investigation which provided vital evidence to the SWMF solicitor, Sir Walter Nicholas. The inquest, held at Ebenezer Chapel in Dunvant, heard evidence that 'not a very large amount of water' had accumulated at the No. 4 level, an area of the colliery which had been abandoned for over a decade. However, witnesses admitted that some working places had been driven considerably nearer to the No. 4 level than the 40-yard distance stipulated in the Coal Mines Act. These revelations added to the tense atmosphere at the inquest, as D. R. intervened continuously as the company's solicitor, Edward Harris, sought to lead witnesses, resulting in several sharp exchanges between the two men ('Breeze at Pit Inquest' was the headline in the *Daily Herald*).[52] Even so, the outcome of the case was inconclusive: the jury failed to reach a verdict on two of the three questions posed by the Coroner and the case was then adjourned *sine die*, although Walter Nicholas insisted that that was not the end of the matter as far as the SWMF was concerned.[53]

Neither was it the end of the matter for D. R. as he redoubled his work to effect a revision of the mine safety regulations and related issues in the House of Commons. The situation at Killan was undoubtedly in his mind when he warned about the danger of mining close to old workings. Speaking from the heart, he described the conditions in which the miners worked and their reliance on the State to regulate the industry to provide at least a measure of safety:

> I have worked in mines where there has been a fear of old workings. I have gone home to sleep and have wakened, having almost experienced the actual inundation in

anticipation of a possible terrible event. These things happen. They haunt the lives of our men, harass their days and nights. I ask the Minister not to be put off by excuses from anyone responsible for a mine where men are possessed by fear in this way.

He challenged the Secretary for Mines to observe a miner at work in the bowels of the earth. Their lives depended on the regulations for which the Mines Department were responsible:

These men down there in the darkness may have a limited range of vision, but, thank God! they have an extended range of thought, with a concern for their families, for their duties as citizens. They risk their lives and give service to the community, and they should be given the fullest protection which the Secretary for Mines is able to give to them.[54]

He also demanded that the regulations be updated in light of new working practices, in particular the introduction of machines working underground. A key question was that of miners' phthisis among men who used compressed-air machines for rock-drilling. After the Mines Department reported the outcomes of a preliminary investigation into the issue, based primarily on the views of colliery officials, he called for a much broader survey to establish a firmer evidence base that should be extended to include the testimony of the men and that of medical professionals.[55]

Meanwhile, Britain's coal industry was heading for another crisis as the impact of the return to the Gold Standard was felt across the mining areas, with the most bitter consequences evident in the districts reliant on exports, south Wales in particular. The coal owners restated their standard response to such situations, an increase in the working day and reduced wages. For D. R. this rigid, predictable and unthinking solution reinforced the case for nationalisation being the only way to make progress on a much broader understanding of the changes needed to operate the industry on a sound basis, and he supported the MFGB demand for an investigation into questions around the efficiency of the industry, including arrangements for production, sales, pattern of ownership, multiplicity of directorships, foreign competition, alternative sources of power and the issues of under-consumption. The British coal mining industry would never be in a position to regain international markets lost to Germany and Poland without a fundamental change both in the industry itself and in British economic policy to stimulate exports.

These battlelines were revealed as plainly as they could be when the Mining Association gave notice, at the end of June 1925, that they intended to terminate the National Wages Agreement. D. R. watched as it became clear that the owners would face the determined opposition, not only of the MFGB but also the united ranks of Britain's trade unions rank and file, who recognised that defeat for the miners would jeopardise the position of organised labour movement as a whole.[56]

He was also wise enough to not be duped by the Prime Minister's consummate cunning in offering a nine months' subsidy while yet another inquiry, this time chaired by the former Liberal cabinet minister, Sir Herbert Samuel, was conducted into the operation of the mining industry. Red Friday, 31 July 1925, had demonstrated the power of collective action but, for D. R., the Prime Minister's response was a blatant, calculated and cynical political move that gave the government the best part of a year to marshal the power of the State to defeat the miners. He echoed the *Daily Herald* as it warned, 'By solidarity, the Labour movement has so far achieved striking success in the miners' struggle for a living wage and human conditions; but the battle is not yet won, and the coming weeks will call for unremitting vigilance and unity.'[57] At the MFGB delegate conference on 19 August 1925, D. R. joined those who warned of what lay ahead. The miners, he reminded delegates, had been given promises; the owners had got exactly what they wanted from the government. 'Does not the agreement itself suggest that the owners have got what they asked for, 13 per cent of the profits of the industry after other costs have been met? I think it is quite clear that the owners have succeeded in getting all they asked for. Have they not got from the Government everything they asked for? They have got it from the Government instead of the workmen.'[58]

The government now had time to stock-pile coal supplies, prepare the ground for a general strike, and embark on a deliberate campaign to convince the British public they were facing imminent revolution. The Labour movement should not underestimate the magnitude of the confrontation that would face it when the Samuel Commission published its report.

At the start of autumn, D. R. fulfilled a commitment he had made to the Merthyr Tydfil MP, Dick Wallhead, by joining a parliamentary delegation to Soviet Russia which spent a month from 3 September visiting the country and discussing with ministers and government officials opportunities to increase future trade.[59] The tour started in Riga before meeting representatives of the Soviet Presidium in Moscow, and proceeding to Leningrad, Nizhny Novgorod, Kharkov, the coal mining region in the Donets Basin, Rostov-on-Don, Grozny, the oil producing area of Baku and the surrounding countryside, before returning to Moscow where Wallhead led further discussions with government representatives.[60] For D. R., the visit served as proof that the Soviet government was determined upon a programme of unprecedented economic regeneration, and that it enjoyed the support of the people in doing so.[61] On returning home, he was fulsome in his praise, telling audiences in Britain of the achievements of the Soviet government. He enthused about how they had expanded the area of land under cultivation and were using more scientific methods of farming; a large number of new electric power stations had been built, and productivity had been increased.[62]

For D. R., 'The Soviet Government is as secure as any

government in the world... there is universal support of the Soviet in the country and foolish prejudice against the country should be dropped. If Russia is allowed to work out her own salvation and not be boycotted, she will make greater commercial strides than have ever yet been made by any country.' Communism was the only alternative Tsarism and there had clearly been a revolution in people's minds.[63] Above all, the potential of Soviet Russia as a market for British goods was incalculable. He joined other members of the delegation in publishing a report on the visit which demanded a change in government policy towards the Soviet government, declaring, 'In our judgement it will be an economic disaster for Great Britain if our rulers continue a political and economic policy that undoubtedly tends to exclude British goods from a great present and potential market, and the embargo on Anglo-Russian trade should be removed immediately.'[64]

Later, he linked the demand for restoration of full trading with Soviet Russia with the strategy for broader economic recovery in Britain, and blamed the policy for the problems facing the British coal industry. Speaking in parliament, he deplored the lack of confidence that the business community in Britain showed about trading with Russia, which he attributed firmly to the absence of political leadership on the issue. The government should realise that economic recovery was only possible if new markets were sought and this meant extending credit to the Russian government as would be done to any other country, and give a guarantee that it would not break off commercial relations.[65]

> Russia offers to us the best market for manufactured goods that can be found anywhere in the world, and her economy is such and her ambition for the reconstruction of our country is so earnest that if properly handled we should be able to sell a larger quantity of goods to Russia than we are now sending to all the Dominions of our Empire.[66]

This was a theme which he pursued repeatedly in the following years, advocating a policy of increased trade with Russia as a contribution to economic recovery, and deploring the attempts by governing elites to thwart the Soviet road to recovery.[67]

CHAPTER 5

The People in the Villages were Wonderful

THROUGHOUT THE WINTER of 1925–26, D. R. watched with foreboding as government ministers procrastinated over the future of the coal industry while secretly preparing for a full confrontation with organised labour the following spring. Nowhere was the tension within Britain's mining communities felt more clearly than in south-west Wales, where the miners had been embroiled in a bitter confrontation with coal owners in the Anthracite Area the previous summer. The dispute centred on the protection of established custom and practice in the employment of the men (the 'seniority rule' that protected those with the longest service), but it reflected deeper underlying issues stemming from the unsustainable financial burden being carried by the industry due to changes in ownership in the previous 15 years, as former independent small firms were bought at inflated prices, principally by two companies – the Amalgamated Anthracite Colliery Co. and the United Anthracite Co. Matters reached a crescendo in August when 200 men, including several respected miners' leaders, were arrested and brought before the courts.[1] The sentences handed to the men, mostly pillars of their communities who enjoyed enormous local support, fanned the burning hatred towards the government and courts throughout the Anthracite Area and more generally across south-west Wales. As the leaders of the Anthracite Area dispute languished in Swansea Prison at the start of 1926, demonstrations were held three times a week outside the gates demanding their release.[2] D. R. joined in the agitation for their release, attending a huge gathering organised by the SWMF at the Cory Hall in Cardiff, and then accompanying Tom Richards, S. O. Davies and John James of the SWMF and Dr J. H. Williams, MP for Llanelli, and the Rhondda East MP, Dai Watts-Morgan, to meet the Home Secretary, William Joynson-Hicks, demanding that the case be reviewed. Their arguments, that the men in question had acted from industrial rather than criminal motivations, cut no ice with the Home Secretary, who refused to intervene in the cases of the 14 men still imprisoned, and showed an indifference which further inflamed the situation in south-west Wales.[3]

Concurrently, D. R. continued the miners' battle on the floor of the House of Commons, warning of the impending disaster in the industry if the government acceded to the owners' proposals and supported moves to reduce wages.[4] D. R. demanded a programme that would eliminate waste, with 'sound capitalisation' of industry and equitable distribution of profits in order to raise living standards for all:

It is only when Hon. Members opposite and those responsible for the industrial life of this country recognise that all the people of this country have a right to the enjoyment, not of fur coats at 128 guineas, but of good food, good clothing, proper houses, and a higher standard of life all round – it is only then that the industries of this country will be able to produce, and find a ready demand for, the goods they can produce.[5]

This was not going to come from a Conservative government and neither could its ministers be trusted to place the men's welfare at the forefront of their response to the Samuel Commission's report. When the report was published, its conclusions were not wholly inimical to the longstanding arguments advanced by the MFGB and its affiliates. Samuel recognised the inefficiencies caused by the way the mining industry was structured, acknowledged that small mines should be amalgamated into more efficient units, conceded the need for pithead baths, and concurred with the case for nationalisation. But, on the crucial and immediate question of wages, it fell on the side of the Mining Association. The TUC favoured a settlement, but A. J. Cook, general secretary of the MFGB, was in no mood to compromise: not a penny off the pay, not a minute on the day. On 1 May 1926 the lock-out began.

The previous day D. R. had returned home from London and then travelled to Aberdare where he addressed May Day meetings before going back to Swansea where large crowds braved the high winds to hear him and other speakers in the town's Victoria Park.[6] He took his listeners through the details of the various proposals and counter-proposals, and denounced the Mining Association's 'scandalous and contemptuous' attempts to reduce wages to a position where 'a married man was to receive 6s. 8d. a day – the price of a lawyer's letter'. There was, he said, 'no word in the English language fit to describe' what was on offer, 'a strike would find stubborn support all round'.[7] At a subsequent meeting that evening he warned that the owners' terms would set the miners back at least ten years as far as their purchasing power was concerned, and he warned that there would never be a return to the seven-hour day if the eight-hour day was conceded.[8]

As one of the miners' MPs, D. R. was present throughout the meetings held between the MFGB Executive and the PLP immediately before the General Strike was called, and privately became increasingly concerned about the behaviour of the MFGB leadership.[9]

He took heart from the reaction of Britain's rank-and-file trade unionists, as more than 1.6 million people stood united in support of the miners for nine days. In his own constituency,

David Morris, secretary of the Gorseinon Trades and Labour Council, could take pride in reporting that trade unionists throughout the Swansea RDC area had been absolutely solid in their response. In Swansea itself, where Andrew Murray rallied the troops for 'the most historical moment known in the history of the working-class movement', work at the docks, in the road haulage industries, on the trams and the buses, stopped at midnight on the Monday night. The steel and tinplate works all stopped at the end of the afternoon shift.[10]

Even so, D. R. could see quite clearly the extent to which the government was ready for a battle with organised labour, having armed itself with an arsenal of legislative and organisational powers which it had acquired since the tactical retreat on Red Friday. On 6 May the government invoked measures under the Emergency Powers Act 1920, which the PLP challenged with an amendment moved on grounds of civil liberty and freedom of expression. Seconding that amendment in the parliamentary debate, D. R. condemned the powers that would be given to the authorities to disperse gatherings of people.

> Very little regard is given to the interests of the working people who must in the next few weeks resort to hundreds of thousands of meetings. Every single meeting will be subject to the possibility of disaffection brought about, not by the people themselves but by magistrates and police officials who, like the Government have lost their heads. If the Government cannot keep their heads, how can they expect a magistrate or police officer to do so?[11]

He warned:

> You can adopt these Regulations, but you will not stop the British working people, and the British people generally, from exercising the rights won for them all along the centuries. The working people will insist upon holding their meetings and upon having their processions, and if the Government

gives this kind of cue to the magistrates and induces the magistrates to forget the liberties of the British people, the Government will rue the day.[12]

D. R. began a tour of English towns to garner support for the Labour movement in its struggle, beginning with a meeting at Handfield on 7 May before proceeding to Tunbridge Wells, and then to Haywards Heath and parts of Surrey and Sussex.[13] He recalled later, 'The people in the villages were wonderful and I was satisfied that we could go on for a time despite the *British Gazette* and all the government effort to break up our movement.'[14] The workers' response had surpassed his wildest expectations and gave him 'more satisfaction than anything that I have known in politics or industrial action'.

As he took part in the discussions between the MFGB and the PLP for the nine crucial days, he felt increasing despair at the tactics adopted by the MFGB Executive, describing to Mansel how its President, Herbert Smith, had made the inexplicable decision to allow someone as distrusted by the miners as the railwaymen's leader, J. H. (Jimmy) Thomas, a free rein in the parliamentary debate on 3 May.

Before the General Strike was declared we had a meeting of the Parliamentary Party at which the TUC negotiating committee was to prepare for a debate in the House after 8.15 that evening, and I was astonished to hear Herbert Smith making a statement in almost those words, 'Mr Chairman, we have come here this evening to tell you what we think of the discussion to-night and to arrange with you about having the miners' case put. We have decided to ask you to let [J. H.] Thomas put the general case for the miners. A great many things have been said about Thomas. I may have said things myself but, with all that, I think there is some good in Thomas yet... We think he will make a good case for the miners; some will want to know why we have not chosen a miner to put our case. I do not speak with any disrespect, but when one of our chaps gets up, he is so full of the conditions of his industry, he knows all about his own industry and he may forget to put the general case which we want out here to-night.' Herbert Smith then met the miners' group in a private meeting immediately afterwards. 'I have called you together because I want to tell you that, although Thomas is in this affair, I do not trust him, and he may yet twist. If he does and your case is not properly put, I want one of you to get up and put out a case as it should be put.'[15]

D. R. went on: 'I can assure you that I came to the conclusion that... our people were quite incapable and utterly unworthy of the great responsibility imposed upon them by the members all over the country.'

D. R. was also critical of private discussions between Samuel and Herbert Smith, which had produced what he described as, 'very valuable proposals [that] gave us all the safeguards we required with a firm prospect of effective re-organisation without which the industry must continue to decline... a victory which only required prompt acceptance by the MFGB to conclude highly satisfactory terms for the miners and a complete political triumph over a badly divided Tory party torn with dissention and rent by personal rancour.' But the terms had not been considered by the MFGB Executive. 'I am pained to think that the greatest industrial victory of our history, after being won by the splendid solidarity of all classes of workmen, has been thrown away by the incompetent leaders of the miners themselves... it is extremely unfair to the Labour movement to allow the TUC to bear the blame for the "fiasco" which has resulted from the disloyalty of the miners to the TUC resolution and their incompetence in meeting the strategic advantage which was offered as a gift from the blue on 13 May.' He went on, 'The movement is doomed to sterility and failure unless we rid ourselves of the sham class philosophy which looks for traitors by either hand, and reeking of suspicion and treachery makes it impossible for clean straightforward loyal and mutual effort to be maintained.'[16]

Wherever the blame lay, it was clear to D. R. that rank-and-file trade unionists were not prepared to give up the fight when the TUC declared the strike was at an end on 13 May. Nowhere was this more evident than in south-west Wales where delegates at a meeting at the Dockers' Hall in Swansea on the Thursday morning were incredulous at the TUC's actions, and a large number of those present determined to defy TUC instructions. In the rail industry, the Associated Society of Locomotive Engineers and Firemen (ASLEF) and NUR branches in Swansea and Llanelli refused to accept the terms demanded by the railway companies and continued with the strike.[17] The following day, an even more resolute gathering met at the Brighton Hall in Gorseinon, addressed by D. R. and other local trade unionists representing steel, tinplate and other workers, as well as the miners, and called for a resumption of the General Strike. There was a major disturbance at Weaver's Mill where most of the workers ignored their leaders' instructions to return to work.[18] Men at the Cwmbwrla Tinworks remained on strike, and were still idle a month later.[19] In Gorseinon and Pontarddulais there were protests from across the different unions against the victimisation of men not re-instated.

With the MFGB blaming TUC leadership for the capitulation, a special conference was held to consider government proposals that included a ten per cent wage cut, abolition of the national minimum, an end of the seven-hour day and compulsory arbitration to replace collective bargaining, but even those terms were not accepted by the Mining Association which demanded more draconian measures.[20] For D. R., any decision to return to work on the coal owners' terms would be calamitous. He told the *South Wales Daily Post* that forcing the miners back to work would only build further resentment and lead to more trouble within a year.[21] No solution that allowed the owners to profit from any national subsidy should be accepted, and instead international agreements were required to facilitate the free distribution of coal and to address the issue of the loss of foreign markets.

In parliament he was at the forefront of Labour's opposition to the Coal Mines Bill, which the government sought to rush through the House in order to suspend the seven-hour working day for five years. He denounced those Tory MPs who wanted to offer the miners a choice between reduced wages or longer hours, reminding the House of the reality of the so-called 'eight-hour day'. He castigated the Bill for extending the working week, supposedly in the name of 'freedom':

> The Minister of Labour said this was only giving freedom to a man to work longer hours, and an Hon. Member on the other side tonight said that this freedom to work any number of hours a man chose was quite in accordance with his view. 'Freedom' is a much-abused word. There will be no freedom to work anything less than eight hours if this Bill goes through. There will be no freedom to deviate from the maximum hours of the Bill. Some years ago, the late President Wilson gave a series of addresses on the new freedom. I should like some of the Members of this Government to read those addresses and see whether they can find in them any justification for the application of the new 'freedom' to what is their policy at the present time. There was a war for freedom some time ago, all the people in this country were invited to join in, and the war was won. Was freedom won? Is this the first instalment of the freedom? Is this the interpretation of the new Tory democracy?[22]

The Bill, he maintained, would not secure its objective of peace in the coal mining districts but only serve to accentuate agitation for reform.

Throughout the summer he continued to tour south Wales and the west of England, addressing support meetings and fund-raising events.[23] In his own constituency concerts and carnivals were held, supported by local choirs such as Côr Glandulais and the Llangennech Male Voice. Religious leaders were prominent in support of their communities, as men like the Rev. T. F. Jones, the Rev. Ben Davies, and the Vicar of Pontarddulais, the Rev. W. G. Morgan, led work to support miners' wives and children. Soup kitchens were organised in chapel vestries, money was raised, and clothing and shoes donated.[24]

At the beginning of September he was again present at the MFGB conference where he listened as the SWMF unsuccessfully opposed the decision to re-open negotiations with the Mining Association. South Wales was, however, vindicated within a matter of days when the employers flatly refused to take part in any national negotiations.[25] Instead, the MFGB was confronted by revised proposals from the government that reneged on the previous commitments by requiring miners to resume work on terms negotiated on a district-by-district basis.[26] D. R. was clear that the miners could not return to work on such terms. Their case was as strong as ever, it was a fight which they had not chosen but which they had been forced into. The owners were profiteering at a time of general poverty and wage cuts. 'There are many who would like to see Mussolini in this country,' he declared, 'but there will be thousands of dead men in this country before Mussolini gets here. We are fighting for our standard of life and the standard of all of the workers in the country.'[27]

The miners' MPs, meanwhile, continued to use the platform of the House of Commons to highlight the government's complicity in curtailing civil liberties in an effort to break the strikers' morale. Following an incident in Cannock Chase in October 1926, when A. J. Cook was prevented from speaking, D. R. gathered a dossier of such cases: Herbert Smith and another speaker, W. P. Richardson, had been debarred from addressing meetings in Staffordshire; in Derbyshire, a local preacher had been prevented from addressing miners on

Biblical teachings ('Scripture banned by the order of the Home Secretary,' was how D. R. put it); in Tredegar, Superintendent Edwards had intimidated the local lodge officials, threatening baton charges; police had been busy taking notes at D. R.'s own meetings in the Gower constituency, and miners' officials were being prevented from addressing their members. He contrasted the temperate language used by the miners' leaders with the flowery extremist and unconstitutional tones habitually used by the Home Secretary, whom he accused of 'violating the decencies of social relationships in this country' by misusing his powers to defeat the miners.[28]

By then he recognised that the overwhelming combination of State and employer power could not be resisted indefinitely, however much heroism was displayed. If the men found themselves unable to resist any longer, there was nothing that could be done other than to attempt to secure the best terms possible.[29] He saw the desperation that prompted the SWMF to increase the stakes, proposing to withdraw the safety men. Their proposal was approved by the MFGB special conference and ratified by a subsequent ballot.[30] However, the MFGB was faced with the stark reality that mining communities were being forced into submission by the strength of employers supported wholeheartedly by the government. At a conference held at the start of November, delegates heard vivid descriptions of the suffering and also the loyalty to the cause being displayed across the British coalfields. For Arthur Horner from the Rhondda, a member of the SWMF executive, the struggle had to continue, a view shared by S. O. Davies who denounced the alternative as accepting 'terms of abject surrender'. Others were convinced that the men could not be expected to continue the sacrifice indefinitely, a position articulated powerfully at the conference by Bob Smilie and Aneurin Bevan. D. R. concurred, telling delegates that it was impossible to ask rank-and-file miners to carry on the battle without an end in sight. Men were going back to work, any hope of a national settlement had disappeared, and they had to obtain the best settlement they could in each district.[31] In the longer term, legislation, not negotiation with the employers, offered the best way to regulate working hours and achieve a national minimum wage.[32]

Throughout the remaining years of the Baldwin government, D. R. continued to build his factual evidence on the mining industry.[33] He accumulated a wide range of contacts among doctors specialising in lung conditions and medical research, along with a masterful knowledge of the body of evidence on these issues. He also augmented his own extensive understanding of mining engineering through personal study of the impact of mechanisation and deep mining on miners' health. Detailed questioning of government minsters, and long hours spent in the House of Commons library and other research institutes, provided him with a level of knowledge that made D. R. one of the foremost experts on these issues in parliament.[34] When a departmental committee appointed to examine the issue of silicosis in the mining industry reported in September 1928, D. R. was not satisfied, insisting that an opportunity had been lost.[35] In particular, he believed that the committee should have looked in more detail at the link between new methods of drilling and the increase in the incidence of the disease invariably affecting men who had worked more than three years with those machines.[36]

I am afraid that the Mines Department, even after the partial investigations and reports made by their inspectors, have not yet realised the great danger from this kind of disease and the great industrial loss that is occasioned by the deaths of the finest men in the industry. Men are not put on to operating these machines until they have been specially selected. It is the strongest men, the fittest men who are chosen for this kind of job. It is a heavy job, an arduous job in every way, and it is the cream of the coal-mining industry who are put to operate these machines. The men die at an extraordinary rapid rate following this kind of employment.[37]

While he welcomed the outcomes of work at the Fuel Research Station and the Colliery Owners' Research Society, he insisted that much more needed to be done, contrasting the position in Britain to that in Germany, France and the USA where scientific knowledge was being used to create safe and modern working practices.[38]

He also kept a close eye on the unemployment statistics, including those not working on a whole-time basis.[39] He rejected arguments that the crisis of over-supply was caused by the loss of overseas markets. He attributed the blame squarely on over-production in the UK, where productive capacity had increased beyond what could be consumed. Only a total reorganisation would solve the industry's problems. 'We must view it as a problem of transforming the coal industry of this country, having regard to the future uses of coal and the demands that will be made on the industry for the production of liquid fuel and the utilisation of all the valuable by-products of coal. The country which is most ready to effect this transformation is the country which will come through its coal difficulties best of all.'[40]

The evidence, he insisted, proved the case for a different form of management, rooted not in capitalist ownership but in a scientific understanding of the industry. He did not doubt that some directors of colliery undertakings were capable men, well-versed in the mechanics of the industry. Further, the amount of capital that would be required was more than private companies could bear, and this would create an intolerable burden that would cripple the industry at a time when what was needed was strategic reorganisation.

We shall see collieries getting closer and closer to the Bankruptcy Court. I can see them. I know them. In my own district I know their financial position. I know which colliery is going first to bankruptcy and I know which is going to follow. I can tell you, one by one, how many will have gone in the next 12 months unless something turns up which no one can see in sight to-day. A great deal of capital is going to be scrapped, a great many collieries are going to become derelict. Those collieries ought to be judiciously chosen. They ought not to be allowed to go under because of the exigencies of the industry. With a proper organisation we could reduce the number of productive units.[41]

Change, he argued, should be underpinned by a sense of social responsibility and include a retirement plan for all men over the age of 60, supported by proper pension arrangements and a plan to recruit and train younger men in their place.[42] He returned to the theme continuously. For example, in June 1928, he described the depths of the depression affecting the industry and the disastrous impact of such vicious competition on combines. Pointing to the impact individual colliery closures were having, he described the case of a colliery that had been closed. Because water was no longer being pumped from there, flooding had been caused in neighbouring pits, rendering more than 800 men unemployed.[43]

*

Alongside his work focusing on the issues facing the mining industry, D. R. was deployed by the PLP to oppose an array of measures brought in by the government on a very wide range of policy areas.[44] He devoted much of the winter of 1927–28 to proposals amending unemployment insurance in light of the recommendations of the Blanesburgh Report (which had examined contributions and payments under the Unemployment Insurance Scheme). The Unemployed Insurance Bill produced in response to its recommendations reduced the amounts payable to insured workers, and established more stringent criteria against which claims would be assessed. For D. R., the Bill represented 'retrogressive legislation', which would drive people in the areas of highest unemployment 'deeper into despondency and despair'.[45] The government was intent on legislation that would remove up to 200,000 people from the insurance scheme.[46] He criticised the proposals to reduce the amount payable to men – from 18 shillings per week to 17 shillings – describing the impact it would have on married men, and those unmarried and living in lodgings alike. Prolonged unemployment, he said, had eroded any savings the men were likely to have had. He demanded a weekly minimum of 20 shillings, even if it meant changing the actual limits and the contributions payable under the National Insurance Act, and he deployed the fruits of detailed statistical analysis based on the amounts paid in and out of the fund.[47]

He also took a close interest in the inquiry undertaken by the PLP in 1928 into the conditions affecting industrial communities across Britain where whole towns and villages were reduced to relying on private charity. In south Wales the Friends Home Service Committee, the Personal Service League, the York Trust, the Werner Trust, Oxbridge colleges, and the Jubilee Friend's Fund, to name but a few, were active in different ways.[48] The Bishop of Llandaff, the Rev. Joshua Pritchard Hughes, proposed that each deanery should 'adopt' a distressed area, prompting the town of Worthing to adopt Brynmawr; the Christians of the Students' Christian Movement (SCM) worked in the Rhymney valley, and St-Martin-in-the-Fields Church in London sent assistance to Merthyr Tydfil.[49] D. R. himself was involved in the work and persuaded the town of Margate to help mining villages in the Swansea area.[50] While he did not doubt the good intentions behind the myriad of charitable work being done, this was simply not enough, and an economic solution was needed to those areas' problems.

The government clearly regarded the issue simply as a matter of supply and demand that would be resolved if families upped sticks and moved where work was available. South Wales had 'surplus labour' that should move, sooner rather than later, for the sake of the nation's moral strength. The view was shared for a short time, and only to some degree, by the PLP, whose own inquiry into the plight of the 'necessitous areas' concluded that, 'Steps must be taken to effect the transference of population from areas which are hopelessly derelict to other places. This may very well commence with the single able-bodied men and juveniles, but must ultimately (unless there is some unexpected development of industry) extend to the whole population. We suggest that various forms of administrative action be taken immediately to give encouragement to such emigration.'[51]

D. R. was scathing of such approaches, and rejected the notion of abandoning whole areas like south Wales. He told the Commons, 'I do not understand anybody fooling himself with the belief that by finding jobs for some 400 men from the mining districts as hall-porters and valets and cinema attendants in residential parts you are finding a way out of the difficulties existing in our industrial districts... We have had no constructive policy placed before us [and]... believe the Government are changing their outlook on this question... between them they have not a single constructive idea for dealing with this matter next year.'[52] The government's reliance on transference, he insisted, was itself endangering recovery by driving young people about the country in a search for work in areas where they faced degradation and demoralisation.[53] He demanded purposeful relief work, re-afforestation programmes close to the mining villages, and the development of oil distillation and coal by-products.[54]

He was equally scornful of the Tory government's plans to promote emigration as a way of helping to solve unemployment. He drew on his own experience in Canada, insisting that conditions were totally different to those he had encountered as a young miner a quarter of a century earlier. How could the government suggest migration to Canada, Australia or New Zealand when those countries were already languishing in economic depression?[55] British migrants were arriving to be told there was no work for them, and the policy was merely raising false hopes, ignoring the root of the issue.[56]

*

The daily battles of the British Labour Party and trade union movement on both the industrial and parliamentary fronts, and the demands of being an active constituency MP for an area which remained politically marginal in the 1920s dominated D. R.'s time during his first years in parliament. Throughout this period he also continued his involvement on the international front, working alongside Dick Wallhead in particular. He was a prominent member of the Anglo-Russian Parliamentary Committee where he promoted the case for diplomatic and trade relations with Russia.[57] He also joined Dick Wallhead and others in highlighting the alarming evidence of the growth of fascism across Europe. As 1925 progressed, both he and Dick Wallhead received eye-witness accounts of the events in Bulgaria where the proto-fascist Tsankov regime had unleashed a regime of terror against Socialists, Communists and trade unionists. In response, the two MPs were among those who established a committee to relieve victims of Bulgarian repression in the autumn of that year.[58] Matters did not improve following Tsankov's removal from office as the Lyapchev government pursued a similarly autocratic policy. By the spring of 1927, more than 500 prisoners were on hunger strike in Bulgaria, while tens of thousands suffered as fascist organisations terrorised their opponents with succour from the government.[59] Alarmed by what was occurring, D. R. accompanied Dick Wallhead on a tour of the Balkans in April 1927, where they met with the Bulgarian Socialist leader, Pastouhov, before departing for the Bulgarian countryside.[60] There they encountered the evidence of fascist gangs, operating under the slogan 'violence is sacred', who were terrorising the peasant population with tacit compliance from government officials. Bulgaria, they concluded, was drifting towards fascism while the country's economy was collapsing under the burden of wartime reparations.[61] He supported Wallhead who accused the British government of being wholly complicit in what was happening, declaring, 'The Fascists in Bulgaria say openly that they have nothing to fear from Great Britain, which has proved herself the friend of every reactionary Government in Europe.'[62]

At the same time, D. R.'s membership of the Labour group of the India League meant he received regular briefings about the situation there, and he often highlighted issues of concern to them on the floor of the Commons, ranging from opium cultivation, tax receipts from tea production, and the use of commercial vehicles by the army.[63] Along with George Hall, MP for Aberdare, he investigated complaints in Madras where the provincial administration had not followed the lead given by the government of India in repealing the Workmen's Breach of Contract Act, therefore perpetuating penal enforcement of labour legislation in the province.[64] D. R. also pursued specific events, such as those at the Massey and Co. Ironworks, where 600 men had suffered repercussions after taking strike action against the dismissal of 30 of their workmates.

He continued to pursue these themes on the eve of the 1929 General Election in Britain, when he joined Shapurji Saklatvala, Communist MP for Battersea North, and Wilfred Wellock, Labour MP for Stourbridge and a prominent supporter of the movement for Indian freedom, in haranguing Lord Winterton, Under-Secretary of State for India, over a wave of arrests that saw prominent left-wing leaders accused of charges, including the catch-all accusation of 'conspiracy to deprive the king of the sovereignty of British India'.[65] D. R. focused on issues such as the arrests at the Burman Publishing Company and at the Vidyodda Press, Calcutta, part of broader measures to curtail civil liberties and the press when opinion in India was already inflamed by the lack of any Indian representation on the Simon Commission.[66] Despite their tenacity, however, the MPs' questioning was stonewalled continually by Lord Winterton until the dissolution of parliament. Nothing would change while the Tories enjoyed such overwhelming dominance in the House of Commons.

*

After nearly five years in office, Baldwin was bound to call an election at some point in 1929, and eventually he set the date for 30 May. The great Socialist thinker R. H. Tawney, charged with drafting the party programme for the election, sought to combine the gradualism of the Fabians and the moral purpose of the ILP in *Labour's Appeal to the Nation*.[67] In it, the Tories were castigated for the breakdown of industrial relations in the coal industry, for the failure of government in the General Strike, and for their misuse of workers' insurance funds.

Labour promised to act through public works, in particular housing and slum clearance, land drainage and reclamation, electrification, reorganisation of rail and other forms of transport, including the construction of new roads and bridges, afforestation, and promotion of small holdings. A Labour government, it declared, would restore the prosperity of the depressed areas, stimulating economic recovery by increasing the purchasing power of the working class and look to extend Britain's export markets overseas. Export credits and trade facilities guarantees would be used to boost demand for iron, steel and other manufactured goods. There would be more generous unemployment benefits and increased pensions for the aged. The school leaving age would be increased to introduce secondary education for all. The coal industry would be nationalised. In international relations, Labour stood for the League of Nations, arbitration and disarmament. It pledged to support the International Labour Office, raising the protection enjoyed by workers' rights and reducing working hours. Taxes on food would be replaced by a more graduated income tax and taxation of land values. Legislative assemblies were promised for Wales, Scotland and England. A special appeal was made to women voters. It was a fine blueprint for a Labour government and one which D. R., for one, had no difficulty in endorsing.

The election was fought on the new franchise whereby women from the age of 21 were entitled to vote as well as men. This added an estimated five million voters to the electoral roll across the UK, including around 12,000 in the Gower constituency. The Labour leadership hoped for a united, essentially moderate campaign, in tune with the new mood of 'realism' emanating from the TUC since 1926, and typified by the line taken by the *Daily Herald*. D. R. faced Alan Lennox-Boyd, a 24-year-old Oxford graduate, described in Tory propaganda as a young democrat and 'brilliant orator' as well as an expert in de-rating.[68] Like Ernest Nethercote in 1924, he sought to garner the anti-Labour vote, highlighting the failure of the Liberals to unseat the Socialists in the constituency and emphasising the importance of 'safeguarding' industry, and the importance of foreign investment in Britain. The Liberals were, however, not prepared to relinquish their challenge to Labour in the constituency, having found new vigour as a result of detailed policy development work funded by the secretive Lloyd George Fund, and published in *We Can Conquer Unemployment*, which promised public works, deficit funding, and harnessing unused capital for industrial investment. It was doubtful whether all Liberal candidates grasped, let alone endorsed, such ideas and this was almost certainly the case in Gower where Fred Davies was again selected as their standard-bearer and proclaimed more traditional Liberal beliefs on the role of the State.

D. R. undertook a typically active campaign, addressing meetings in every part of the constituency, supported by prominent speakers from the Labour movement in Swansea and the surrounding area, in particular Dr Elvet Thomas, Dr Neville George, the Rev. Ingli Jones, and Ithel Davies.[69] The election was not without its incidents. In Pontarddulais, Labour supporters drowned out Fred Davies by singing the 'Red Flag' after taking offence at his remarks, and attempts to counter them by singing 'God Save the King' served only to inflame matters.[70] Meanwhile, growing prominence in the Labour movement meant D. R. was drafted to support candidates elsewhere – in Aberavon, Neath, Llanelli and Rhondda West, and in west Wales where he addressed meetings in support of Daniel Hopkin in the Carmarthen division, and in Pembrokeshire where he spoke on behalf of William Jenkins.[71]

Throughout the campaign he emphasised the crucial need for a change of government if the issue of unemployment was to be addressed. The Labour programme, he told his listeners, 'touched life from birth to the grave', offering hope and a better future for young people through reform of education, and 'a decent and honourable pension for the men with white hair and a bent back'.[72]

When the votes were counted, the Tories had added a million to their total in 1924, but Labour soared to poll more than eight million, while the Liberals polled 2.2 million more than their previous tally. In Gower, D. R., with 20,664 votes, won a majority of 9,609 over Fred Davies, with Alan Lennox-Boyd a distant third. His victory was a reflection of a broader trend in Wales where Labour polled over half a million votes (45 per cent of the total) and won 25 of the 36 seats. They formed a strong contingent among the 287 Labour MPs elected that year who faced 260 Tories and 59 Liberals. The composition of the government was announced on 5 June. Philip Snowden again held the position of Chancellor of the Exchequer, with Arthur Henderson appointed Foreign Secretary, J. R. Clynes Home Secretary, and J. H. Thomas Lord Privy Seal with responsibility for combating unemployment. Other notable appointments included Margaret Bondfield as Minister of Labour, Arthur Greenwood as Minister of Health, and George Lansbury as First Commissioner of Works. From Wales, Charles Edwards held the office of Chief Whip, and there were junior ministerial appointments for George Hall at the Admiralty, and Morgan Jones at Education. Again, there was no position for D. R., although on this occasion Morgan Jones asked for his services as a Parliamentary Private Secretary.

Charles Edwards found him something else to occupy his time. He secured his appointment as a member of the Forestry Commission, one of two such appointments from either side of the House, a body responsible for overseeing a radical plan of afforestation designed to replenish the country's supply of timber. The crisis in British forestry had been evident before the Great War, as successive clearances meant that the supply of woodland had declined to dangerous levels. Shortly before the outbreak of war, the acreage of land covered by woodland was a mere four per cent of the total land mass, compared with 18 per cent in Belgium and France, and 26 per cent in Germany. The issue was thrown into sharp focus when demand for timber during the war exposed the country's reliance on foreign supplies. A Timber Supply Committee (TSC) was set up in 1915, and recommended increasing the acreage given over to woodland to 1,700,000 acres, through a programme of planting, buying arable land and using the opportunity to settle discharged soldiers to the land. In addition, the TSC advocated the establishment of a forestry authority, which was eventually established through the Forestry Act 1919. It faced the task of addressing the issues, identified before 1914, which had been compounded as additional areas of woodland were cut down hurriedly and without a plan due to the urgent needs of war. The Forestry Commission received its funding from the Treasury but was independent of government. It was empowered to purchase or lease land and buildings and erect the necessary buildings on that land to enable it to carry out its functions. It was able to plant trees on its own account and to make grants – paid to individuals and local authorities – to do so. The Commisson could also undertake the management and supervision of woods and forests belonging to other persons and establish or aid woodland industries. D. R. remained a member until his appointment as Secretary for Mines in 1940, and during that time he addressed his duties in light of the work of policy specialists, particularly those associated with the Fabian Society. In doing so he managed to graft their thinking around timber supplies, rural regeneration and the revitalisation of mining districts to the Forestry Commission's functions, issues which are discussed in greater detail below.

*

Throughout its two years in office, the second Labour government was thwarted by its lack of parliamentary majority – being reliant on the Liberals' goodwill – and inability to countenance the radical economic policies to which the party was committed. The government was not without ambition and had some achievements to its credit.[73] It reached an agreement at a conference in The Hague that removed much of the remaining restrictions on Germany, enabling Allied troops to withdraw from the Rhineland. Ministers also pursued a policy to limit armaments. It restored diplomatic relations with the Soviet Union, and removed Lord Lloyd, High Commissioner of Egypt, as a necessary prelude to negotiations for self-determination. In terms of domestic policy, Arthur Greenwood's Housing Act of 1930 maintained subsidies for local authority building and empowered them to deal with the issue of slum clearance with renewed vigour. The Education Bill increased the school leaving age to 15 and provided maintenance allowances for pupils over the age of 14 years. But passing legislation was not enough. The implementation of the Housing Act was delayed and its provisions regarding slum clearance did not come into force until 1934 (and not after the national government had reduced the housing budget). Meanwhile, the Education Bill did not reach the statute book because of delaying tactics causing a backlog in the House of Lords.

D. R. could also applaud the government's decision to commission detailed research into the issue of silicosis and other pulmonary diseases. Regulations had been issued by the Home Office in February 1929 acknowledging the liability of employers to pay compensation for the disease.[74] These regulations served to highlight the geographical concentration of the problem, given that no fewer than 386 of the 424 registered cases came from south Wales. D. R. joined Daniel Hopkin, William Jenkins and Dr J. H. Williams, among others, to pressurise Home Secretary J. R. Clynes to establish an expert committee of the Medical Research Council (MRC) to examine the whole range of pulmonary diseases, from silica and other dusts. The committee would be expected to work closely with researchers at the Beck Laboratory in Swansea who were already examining fibrosis in the lungs among miners in the Anthracite Area coalfield.[75] But the revised Silicosis Order eventually produced fell far short of what D. R. and his colleagues had envisaged, and the Workmen's Compensation (Silicosis and Asbestos) Act provided insufficient redress. Before compensation could be paid it was necessary to demonstrate the presence of silica / fibrosis of the lung, leading to partial or total disablement. It was clear to D. R. that the Silicosis Order, as worded, was far too limited in terms of its scope and the compensation which it afforded its victims, and it meant that men clearly suffering the effects of working in the mining industry had no hope of compensation after being forced to cease work. Almost immediately it led to renewed efforts in support of more comprehensive provision, and D. R. spoke for many in believing that an opportunity had been lost.

More broadly, the government pursued a cautious approach

in relation to the future of the coal industry, encapsulated when Ramsay MacDonald appointed Ben Turner – the man who had represented the TUC in discussions with Alfred Mond in an effort to secure more consensual industrial relations – as Secretary for Mines in his second administration. The Coal Mines Bill, introduced late in 1929, represented a change in policy given that it explicitly established the interests of the State in the coal mining industry and recognised the destructive impact of the free market on the way it operated. The Bill created a mechanism to regulate output based on a standard production quota for each colliery for domestic and export purposes. This was the only way by which the unsustainable competition for the home market could be prevented from bankrupting the entire industry. The President of the Board of Trade, William Graham, was clear, 'Whatever may be our party faiths, whatever divides us in economic policy as between an individualist and a Socialist policy, does not really apply. We are not dealing with an industry which responds to the ordinary economic tests. The demand is not elastic. Even if there was an improvement in industrial conditions, it is by no means clear that there would be any appreciable increase in the total quantity of coal consumed.'[76] Alongside these production quotas, the Bill proposed a marketing scheme and established a Coal Mines Reorganisation Commission that was to be given responsibility for developing schemes to reorganise collieries into more efficient and sustainable units.

The miners group of MPs pressed for legislation to repeal the Eight Hours Act and replace it with a seven-hour working day 'bank to bank', and saw an opportunity because the Eight Hours Act, passed by the Baldwin government in 1926, was limited to a period of five years and would expire in 1931.[77] They had a strong case – the notion of a seven-hour day had been agreed in 1919 and the change would have brought the British coalfields closer to the policy of the International Labour Office (ILO) which recommended a seven-hour working day, inclusive of winding time, in all collieries. The government offered a compromise – a working day of seven and a half hours, which was accepted with reluctance by the MFGB despite opposition from several areas. A series of amendments, proposed by the MFGB Executive, were placed before the PLP but were rejected by MacDonald, as were demands for the creation of a National Coal Mining Board to determine matters of policy in areas such as hours of work, wages, production and working conditions, and a national wages agreement to replace negotiations in individual districts.

Even so, the compromise of a seven-and-a-half-hour working day proved a step too far for the House of Lords, who amended the legislation to give employers flexibility to spread the maximum permitted hours over a fortnight. This prompted MacDonald to intervene personally in an attempt to persuade the MFGB to accept the Lords' amendment, but the SWMF members on its executive remained resolute that this was one compromise too far.[78] Matters came to a head the following winter when the employers gave notice to the effect that the 90 hours' maximum would be worked over a fortnight.[79] This prompted unofficial action across the south Wales coalfield and demands for the resignation of Enoch Morrell and Tom Richards as SWMF officials.[80] MacDonald again resorted to personal appeal, pleading with the SWMF Executive to accede to the 90 hours spread over until part one of the Act was enacted, a proposal subsequently accepted by a special conference held on 13 December.[81] Even this compromise, however, was not sufficient for the south Wales mine owners who demanded that the question of wages be opened for discussion. In any case, the attitude of the men had hardened by Christmas 1930. A special conference on 30 December rejected the owners' terms and resolved that all collieries in south Wales would stop work on New Year's Day. What began as an unofficial action was now endorsed by the whole of the SWMF, resulting in a week of stoppages until the SWMF Executive agreed to the terms of negotiations proposed by the Board of Trade, forming the basis of a compromise that was accepted by a special conference.[82]

The compromise did not remove the deep-seated grievances both in south Wales and further afield, in particular over the length of the working day. The MFGB's pamphlet, *The Claim for Legal Minimum Wages for Mineworkers*, showed clearly the extent to which wages had declined in real terms, especially in south Wales, Scotland and the north-east of England. Ministers who met the MFGB at Downing Street in March were left in no doubt that the miners were in no mood to allow this state of affairs to continue.[83] The strength of feeling within the SWMF in particular was evident at two special conferences convened by the MFGB in June and July 1931. It was clear that Ramsay MacDonald had exhausted any remaining goodwill as far as the south Wales miners were concerned.[84]

*

It had been Labour's fate to have taken office in the circumstances of the Wall Street Crash. Britain's economy was already suffering from the impact of a prolonged slump that was then compounded by the events in the United States. D. R. had never held J. H. (Jimmy) Thomas in high esteem, especially after the role he played in the General Strike, and watched with embarrassment for two years as the man charged with finding a solution to unemployment showed time and again that he was out of his depth. What was more, he saw Sir Oswald Mosley's erratic proposals for planned foreign trade, State direction in industry, and the use of credit to finance expansion, as too outlandish for serious consideration. Tom Johnston, appointed Lord Privy Seal at the end of March 1931, offered a more considered strategy and a pragmatic set of proposals that included a massive expansion of public works schemes. But his ideas rested on changes to public finances totally at odds with the Treasury orthodoxy to which Philip Snowden was committed.[85] A combination of an alarmist report by the MacMillan Commission appointed to examine the United Kingdom's trading position (which exaggerated the balance of payments problem), combined with proposals for drastic reductions in public expenditure recommended by the May Committee, appointed to consider ways of economising, set the background for the political crisis which engulfed the Labour government in the second half of 1931. While economists and financial experts questioned many of the basic assumptions under consideration (in particular over repayments to the 'sinking fund' and the solvency of the Unemployment Insurance scheme), the May Committee's recommendations became the 'orthodox' position for government officials, and was accepted by ministers. The government would need to reduce its expenditure by almost £100 million each year, including a significant cut to the rate of unemployment relief. A run on the pound in August undermined confidence even further, while a financial and diplomatic crisis in continental Europe added to the panic. Concurrently, the City of London began to dictate the terms by which a crisis it had created would be solved.

The Labour government did not offer an alternative solution. Instead, it sought agreement on where the axe should fall. As a member of the PLP's Consultative Committee, responsible for liaison with ministers, D. R. watched as the Cabinet split, eleven of its members accepting reductions in expenditure with nine against. He endorsed the course taken by George Lansbury and Tom Johnston as they battled against the proposed cuts with varying degrees of support from Arthur Greenwood, J. H. Clynes, and another five cabinet members. At no point did MacDonald consult with the PLP nor the wider Labour movement, isolating himself from his own party and any alternative proposals which they might put forward.[86] As the events unfolded, D. R. told the *South Wales Daily Post*, 'I had hoped it would have been possible to preserve a solid Labour Party, and, unpalatable though the most moderate of the economy measures that were considered would necessarily have been, that the party would have recognised that the situation required wide and national consideration rather than a merely narrow, partisan one.' But, within hours, MacDonald had formed a new government that included himself, Philip Snowden, J. H. Thomas and Lord Sankey, together with a small number of junior ministers, and supported by a few Labour backbenchers, alongside Tories and Liberals. An emergency budget on 8 September left those least able to pay to bear the greatest burden. Police pay fell by five per cent, those of public officials by a tenth, teachers by 15 per cent. A second run on the pound caused further drain on foreign credits prompting the Exchequer to suspend the Gold Standard.[87] A departure from Treasury orthodoxy was taking place, but at the cost of the second Labour government.

CHAPTER 6

The Statesmen are the Criminals Themselves

THE ELECTION CAMPAIGN – fought on the single issue of the 'doctor's mandate' to give Ramsay MacDonald and his allies the authority to do as they saw fit in response to the financial situation – placed the only man to serve as Labour Prime Minister of Great Britain in the position of leading a vitriolic campaign against the movement to which he had given his life, with the support of those who had been his most bitter enemies. For his old party, he was guilty of the 'shameless pretence of being the instrument of national unity', the puppet of the Tories, there to do the bidding of bankers whose irresponsibility had caused the crisis in the first place and whose remedies would plunge working people into destitution. Labour hurriedly prepared its own prescription: nationalisation of the banks, a National Investment Board to drive recovery, economic planning, price control, international agreement on monetary policy, and rejection of tariffs. But despite its cogency in the circumstances of 1931 – with the overwhelming strength of the Establishment, the press, and the business world against it – this was a message that was always doomed to fall on deaf ears.

In common with all of the other Labour MPs in south-west Wales, D. R. was uncompromising in denouncing his former leader, considering his actions a betrayal of principle that could never be forgiven. In Gower, the combined forces of the Conservative and Liberal parties were this time represented by Sir Edgar Jones, a former MP for Merthyr Tydfil and at one time a close ally of Lloyd George. Throughout the campaign, Jones enjoyed the wholehearted support of the local mass-circulation newspapers, especially the *South Wales Daily Post* which was plastered with appreciative articles and editorial comment in his favour throughout the weeks leading to polling day.[1] Its pages told the readership of 'Packed halls for Sir Edgar Jones' as the leaders of Swansea's business, industrial and landowning community united in his support. Aeron Thomas, President of the Swansea Liberals, joined Lady Blythswood, Miss Dillwyn, T. J. Thomas, Lillian Folland, and Fred Davies to urge support for a 'first-class businessman, parliamentarian, and philanthropist'.[2] He was, they insisted, the man who had brought new prosperity to the country's fruit and vegetable growers through his work at the national canning authority, and he would do the same for Britain's economy as a whole. Edgar Jones, for his own part, basked in the prospect of national unity, declaring, 'I feel an element of pride and a greater buoyancy of spirit than I used to feel in the old days carrying the party flag. I carried the party flag to victory many times. I shall be terribly disappointed if I have not carried to victory the National flag.'[3] The alternative would be devaluation and a repeat in Britain of what had befallen Germany.[4]

Faced with such a powerful challenge, D. R. focused all of his attentions on the task of defending his own constituency, often addressing around half a dozen meetings each evening as well as campaigning in daytime.[5] Old friends and comrades rallied to the cause: Caradoc Jones, Syd Cadogan, William Evans, Ithel Davies and E. A. Martin prominent among them.[6] For D. R. there was no doubt: the country's problems stemmed from Ramsay MacDonald's failure to stand firm the previous August and tell the financiers, 'It is you who have made a mess of things,' and they should pay the price for recovery, not the working population. He refuted the need to reduce unemployment pay, 'a dastardly act, in a country which was still the richest in the world'.[7] A national government, he warned, would be 'a puppet government, worked from behind either from New York or London by high finance'.[8] The mechanism of finance had failed while the over-valued pound undermined efforts to export. 'The world was now in the position of a business that was over mortgaged, and nothing could benefit this country if they err to force the people into misery and despair.'[9] A fortnight before polling day a mass rally was held in Swansea where D. R. shared a platform with Sir Stafford Cripps, who provided a detailed critique of the national financial crisis and its causes. Free capitalist competition had failed, Cripps insisted, and what was needed was government control of the banks to drive a process of industrial reorganisation for the benefit of the community as a whole.[10] The banks had to become the handmaidens if industry was to recover and enable Britain to export once more. Radical measures were needed to balance the budget and these should include a surtax on the rich. Why should the captains of capitalist industry be allowed to swill champagne in the bars of the Ritz while the unemployed were facing cut after cut to their allowances?[11] D. R. was no less eloquent, denouncing the 'dictatorship from America' by which the power of wealth had been used to the detriment of mankind.[12] He derided Ramsay MacDonald's call for a doctor's mandate saying, 'He has performed a very serious surgical operation upon the unemployed already, and that has not been a cure.' Had Ramsay MacDonald stood firm with the financiers, the world would have rallied round, but he had capitulated, and that was no commendation in the crisis facing the country.[13]

In the event, there was no escaping the electoral carnage that befell the Labour Party which polled 6.3 million votes, two million fewer than in 1929. There was a slightly different picture in Wales where the Labour vote held at nearly 480,000, and a similar percentage to that obtained in 1929. D. R. won with 21,963 votes, a majority of 2,806 over Edgar Jones, a highly creditable result under the circumstances. Elsewhere, even in Wales, Labour suffered heavy defeats. Two seats were lost in Cardiff as well as Llandaff and Barry, Newport fell, Daniel Hopkin was defeated in Carmarthen, Walter Samuel lost Swansea West, and Robert Richards was beaten in Wrexham.[14] Despite winning over six million votes, Labour were left with a mere 52 seats in a House of Commons that was dominated by 470 Tories, sitting alongside the National Liberals and Labour defectors. D. R. was in no doubt that Labour should take defeat on the chin and prepare for the next time. It was inevitable that the 'National' government would eventually fall prey to its own internal divisions and open the way for Labour to return from the wilderness.[15] Such confidence was desperately needed as Labour's remaining parliamentarians faced the overwhelming strength of the 'National' government which had free rein to do as it wished throughout the 1931–35 parliament. There was to be no escape from public expenditure cuts, public works schemes were delayed, local government exchequer grants were reduced, and the school building programme was curtailed. Throughout, three and a half million men were unemployed.

The PLP elected George Lansbury as leader with Clement Attlee as his deputy. Ever since his election in 1922, D. R. had worked closely with Lansbury as one of a 'ginger group' that had called on Ramsay MacDonald to provide more robust opposition to the Tories, and move away from what Lansbury derided as 'being respectable courteous party men'.[16] An interesting question, raised by the historian Ben Pimlott in *Labour and the Left in the 1930s*, published in 1977, is why none of the miners' MPs was nominated for the position of deputy leader, and specifically why D. R. did not seek the position. In Pimlott's estimation, D. R. was well-suited for the role and it is certain that he could have commanded the necessary support from the miners' MPs and others from south Wales which would have been more than enough for him to muster the numbers he needed.[17] However, there is no evidence that D. R. sought or coveted the position. Instead he was elected to the PLP Executive and given the job of shadowing successive ministers from the opposition front bench.[18] He was also appointed as one of the PLP's delegates to the National Council of Labour (NCL), where he served alongside George Lansbury, Clement Attlee, Herbert Morrison of the London Labour Party, and trades union leaders Ernest Bevin and George Gibson, for the rest of the decade.[19]

His first incursion against the government came on 12 November 1931 when he made his maiden speech from the dispatch box in a debate on the King's Speech which outlined the government's programme. After Sir Stafford Cripps, the prominent KC who had been elected for Bristol East at the election, had provided a detailed critique of the government's response to the economic crisis, it fell to D. R. to outline Labour's alternative for a worldwide approach to tackling the depression. This consisted of a deliberate policy of relief from war debts and a removal of the crippling international gold liability.[20] Labour, he promised, would fight any proposals that threatened exports or would increase the cost of food.[21]

Within weeks, he was again on the offensive, moving an amendment to the protectionist Abnormal Importations Bill which he insisted would be 'entirely ineffective in redressing the balance of trade, will only accentuate the prevailing dislocation of world trade, will destroy the re-export trade in the articles affected, and will still further hinder the full exchange of goods and commodities between the peoples of the world upon which a rising standard of life depends'.[22] Britain relied on exports, and any policy of tit-for-tat tariffs would have disastrous consequences, especially in areas like south Wales which depended heavily on the overseas market.[23]

He pursued similar themes, deploying bread-and-butter

arguments in the new year in response to the government's Import Duty Bill that proposed a general tariff of ten per cent on all goods, albeit with certain exemptions, and its proposed duties on horticultural products.[24] The impact on the cost of living, D. R. warned, would be felt across the country as people paid the price for 'this artificial method of stimulating production of vegetables and flowers [which] can lead only to inefficiency at a cost to the consumer, for the consumer will certainly have to pay in all these cases. The man who buys a bunch of flowers, the woman who buys vegetables for the family, will have to pay an additional price.'[25]

As the government sought to broaden the policy at the Imperial Conference in Ottawa, held the following summer, D. R. watched as the first signs of dissention within the government emerged, when ten Liberal ministers resigned from the government.[26] When the tariffs that formed the cornerstone of the Ottawa agreement came before the House, he again led for the opposition, predicting that it would do nothing to conquer unemployment and would merely subsidise prosperity in the dominions at the expense of working people in Great Britain.[27] The agreement represented a British 'imperial customs union', excluding other countries, who in turn would erect their own trade barriers. Any additional imperial trade would never compensate for other lost markets, and it was only the government's political obduracy that prevented it from potentially far more profitable trade with Russia and also with the Irish Free State.[28]

He was equally scathing in his criticism of the government's proposals to stimulate British farming through the Agricultural Marketing Bill, introduced in March 1933. Existing legislation in the form of the Agricultural Marketing Act 1931, piloted by Christopher Addison, Minister of Agriculture, in the last year of the second Labour government had reached the statute book and was designed as a means of promoting the interests of British farmers through price regulation and more efficient marketing techniques based on agreed schemes for different types of agricultural produce.[29] For D. R., the national government's alternative represented a dilution of the provisions and relied solely on voluntary agreements. Once again, government proposals would lead to an increase in the cost of living when what was needed to save British agriculture was a proper marketing system accompanied by the application of science and better management to increase production for the benefit of the industry and its consumers.[30]

He was given an opportunity to take a broader overview of the government's economic approach during the second day of the debate on the King's Speech held on 23 November 1933. Here, he drew on his own expert knowledge of the coal industry and the dismal state of the manufacturing sector. Exports of coal were down by over three million tons, exports of glass and glassware had declined by eleven per cent in two years, exports of pig iron were down by 50 per cent, and machinery by 20 per cent. There was, he maintained, no justification in the government's assertions of 'confidence' in economic recovery when domestic trade had collapsed and exports were blighted by tariffs.[31] The government had accumulated more powers over the economy than any other peacetime administration, but these were not being deployed for the common good. The rich were getting richer, and the poor getting poorer every year. While national wealth was accumulating, wages were falling as working people paid the price of deflation. The King's Speech failed to mention how the government would tackle unemployment, but proposed to regulate the relief paid to those who were out of work. 'I say to the Government that if they permit masses of people to remain idle and show no desire to remove them from than condition, the statesmen are the criminals themselves.'[32]

Throughout these years, D. R. harried the government day after day, in debate after debate, gathering information on a vast range of issues in the hope of exposing a weakness, embarrassing a minister, or cornering his opponents into making some unguarded comment that could be used against them in the future. He challenged ministers over the repayment of the loan made to the USA to keep Britain on the Gold Standard, on interest on government stock, and why duties intended for luxury items were affecting the whole of Britain's vegetable and fruit production.[33] He drew attention to slum housing and malnutrition, the inadequate arrangements to combat tuberculosis. He criticised increases in the naval estimates, and deplored the unreasonable cost of officer training.[34] He ridiculed Sir Robert Horne (Hillhead) and berated the Duchess of Atholl (over Russia in particular).[35] But it was J. H. Thomas who was his favourite target, as D. R. enjoyed watching his prey stumble over his words, being left speechless, in a state of fury, in debate after debate in response to a riling by D. R.[36]

*

Alongside the range of new duties that fell to D. R. to fulfil in the aftermath of the 1931 election, he continued to be vigilant about matters affecting the mining industry, as Britain's collieries languished due to low prices and, especially in the case of south Wales, the loss of overseas markets. He spearheaded the work of a cross-party group of MPs from south Wales who met from the second half of 1932 to examine how to revitalise the industry. This subsequently led to wide-ranging proposals to improve research and marketing activities and more effective working practices.[37] He was prominent in work to bring about closer collaboration between the miners' MPs and the MFGB as a means of forging closer cooperation between the political and industrial sides of the movement, and continued his work on health and safety in the mines.[38]

He was also keenly aware of the impact of the Coal Mines Act 1930 on the Western District, and his own constituency in particular, which had suffered unintended consequences because the calculations of output undertaken under the Act (which established the quota for every colliery) had been made during a period of abnormally low production.[39] This effectively prevented any prospect that quotas could be increased or that any mines could be re-opened. The issue was placed in sharp focus when an improvement in the steel and tinplate trade in south-west Wales generated an increased demand for coal, which could not be supplied by local collieries under the quotas agreed under the Act, and which meant that collieries like Killan, Copper Pit, Mynydd Newydd, Birchgrove, Glynea, Acorn, Samlet, New Pool, Pentre and Moody were being prevented from re-opening.[40] He denounced the situation in regular communications with government ministers. He wrote of how the Berthlwyd Colliery, which worked the Penclawdd and Penlan seams, had developed a new opening to overcome geological abnormalities, but production had been curtailed in 1930 following a fatal explosion. The company proposed to use electrical machinery to be able to work the Glylid seam (at much greater depth), but the standard tonnage of 22,000 tons was inadequate if the three seams (Glylid, Penlan and Penclawdd) were to be worked profitably. At the Garngoch No. 3 colliery, a stone drift had been developed to allow for the working of the Five Foot seam left by the premature closure of the Tirdonkin colliery – 'a most hopeful enterprise [which], given a chance, will produce steam coal of good quality at reasonably low cost' – if the standard tonnage was revised. Likewise, the future of the Beili Glas Colliery in Loughor could be assured if its quota was changed. Isaac Foot, as Secretary for Mines, was not unsympathetic to the evidence of the special factors affecting south Wales specifically, but he was among the Liberals who resigned from the government in 1932, and his successors did not show the same consideration. As a result much of the Western District remained practically derelict, with only 13 of a total of 43 collieries left open by 1939, and a loss of 7,000 jobs.

More broadly, Britain's miners were once again in battle when Walter Runciman, the President of the Board of Trade, introduced measures to extend the provisions of the 1930 Act, including its stipulations about the seven-and-a-half-hour working day, until 1935, thus postponing the question of whether to introduce the ILO recommendation of seven hours. The government's underlying view of the world was revealed clearly when it invited the Mining Association to discuss the issue, but failed to extend the same courtesy to the MFGB. Moreover, Runciman's proposals did not address the question of a minimum wage, the principle of national agreements were rejected, and all that was offered to the men was a commitment not to reduce wages for a period of one year. Not for the first time, the MFGB found itself presented with the terms of an agreement without an opportunity for negotiation. At the MFGB conference at the end of May 1932, the SWMF was at the forefront of demands for a militant policy, articulated forcefully by W. H. Mainwaring and Jim Griffiths.[41] Meanwhile, the weakness of MFGB Executive's position, that the PLP should seek to amend the legislation, was exposed within days as the massed ranks of Tory MPs marched through the lobbies to defeat the miners' demands.

D. R.'s response was to use private members' legislation to introduce the Coal Miners (Minimum Wage) Act (1912) Amendment Bill which would establish a minimum wage in the mining industry for both underground and surface workers.[42] The minimum wage would be based on the 1914 list, adjusted to take account of the cost of living. The system would be regulated but a court proposed under the Industrial Court Act of 1919, and a National Wages Board, would be created to establish uniform agreements throughout the separate coalfields as a first step towards addressing anomalies, and begin the process of addressing the loss of earning power. Introducing the Bill, D.

R. described how his amendment would allow for an increase to account for the cost of living and would extend the coverage of the Act to include some who had not been covered in 1912. It would strengthen the agreement by preventing employers from making certain deductions (for example, to cover the cost of explosives used in the mining process), and introduce penalties against employers who broke the agreement. It also introduced a higher minimum wage and a lower subsistence, and extended the Act's coverage to surface workmen.[43] Once again, his efforts were to no avail. The Tory members 'talked out' the Bill at its Second Reading and Britain's miners were left at the mercy of a wage agreement determined by coal owners.

*

At no point in the 1931–35 parliament did the number of unemployed in Britain fall below three million and, for the government, reducing the cost of relief rather than dealing with the substantive issue was the main priority. The payment of transitional benefits to those workers who would not otherwise qualify under the Unemployment Insurance Act had been used by different governments in the 1920s to provide relief in an unprecedented period of prolonged mass unemployment. The caretaker government formed in September 1931 decreed that insurance benefits should be limited to 26 weeks in any year, and that any transitional payments should be subject to a 'needs test' (i.e. a Means Test) that would be administered by the local authority public assistance committees. On 26 November 1931, the PLP moved that these regulations (the Unemployment Insurance (Transitional Payments) Regulations) be annulled.[44] First to speak for Labour was Jack Lawson, MP for Chester-le-Street, County Durham, who pointed out that the regulations, which affected over 900,000 people, among them 'some of the finest craftsmen and skilled people in the world... robbed of the opportunity of exercising their skill and their craft', had never been debated by parliament, but had the effect of withdrawing benefits from the disabled, those receiving compensation for injuries sustained during the war, or in pursuit of their livelihood, and those who owned their own homes. As the debate proceeded, D. R. turned to the position in south-west Wales, with its high rate of home ownership, and in doing so captured the essence of the society from which he hailed and the difficulties it faced:

> I represent, perhaps, the most thrifty and independent section of working people in this country. They are people in west Wales, of whom a large proportion have endeavoured for generations to retain that independence which the possession of a house gives, and I believe I am right in saying that in that portion of west Wales there is a larger proportion of work-people owning their own houses than in any other part of the country. There has been wide unemployment for the last eight or nine years in the district that I represent. More than half the pits have been closed down in the last ten years, and the number of miners in employment has gone down from 10,000 to 4,000. A large proportion of those people have toiled for years, patiently and doggedly, working and striving and stinting in order to own their own houses. A large number of them have been successful in preserving their own roof over their families, and have gained self-respect and dignity because they were not subject to the whim and caprice of an unscrupulous landlord, and liable to be thrown out of their homes at any time.[45]

The circular issued by the government, with its questions on property, income and financial arrangements, was completely abhorrent:

> I should like to express my utter abhorrence of the circular that has been issued. One of the questions put is: 'Have you

135

pawned any of your belongings?' I represent a district where there is not much pawning; where the people have been able to live above that standard, but in the large cities and in many other parts of the country there are people who have to resort to the pawnshop every week of their lives. They have to produce their pawn tickets to show that the meagre personal assets sheltered in their homes are their personal possessions. It is a scandalous thing. These are questions affecting the morality of the family and they are to be put by the public assistance committees. I would appeal to Hon. Members in all parts of the House, to men who call themselves Liberals, to men who call themselves Conservatives and, most of all, to those who are members of the National party. Are not these people part of the nation? Are not the work-people who are unfortunate enough to be unemployed, part of the nation? Have they not the right to protection at the hands of those who call themselves a National party?[46]

A succession of Labour members followed but, as Aneurin Bevan, already recognised as one of the most effective voices on the Labour benches, pointed out, no more than ten MPs had been present on the government benches at any point during the debate as the mother of parliaments discussed 'the desolate condition of hundreds of thousands of people'. They deserved no respect from working people. The parliamentary arithmetic spoke volumes: 41 for the Labour motion, 248 against.[47]

In the following months D. R. sought out the details by interrogating ministers about details – the number of insured unemployed and the position of the registered friendly societies, the impact of the government's failure to control rents, how many ex-servicemen were affected, what was the effect in specific groups of workers – and went on the attack again when ministers proposed to extend the system of means testing.[48] He drew attention to 200,000 insured workers who had exhausted their payments and who would have to resort to the indignity of the poor law.[49] The minister had no sympathy, D. R. insisted. 'His only admonition is in respect of those areas where sympathy has been shown, where a Means Test has been applied with an element of sympathy and understanding.'[50] Once again, the government was attacking those who had strived to buy their houses, the thrifty, the backbone of industrial society who now felt as though the whole machinery of government was being turned against them:

> Over two million people have passed before the public assistance committees. Their circumstances have been enquired into and their family incomes have been subject to examination. All kinds of intimate questions have been put to them, and all kinds of enquiries have been made about them. There is not an unemployed man in the country who does not resent the whole scheme of things which the Minister now so tardily and scantily proposes to amend.[51]

His feelings were clear:

> Resentment was recently expressed by the hunger marchers who came to this city. Resentment against the Means Test has been shown in at least half-a-dozen large cities in the country within the last two or three months, and the public resentment has only been quelled – as it affects a large number of people – by the ostentatious and brutal use of force by men who are themselves well-fed and free from the distress of unemployment.[52]

He pointed to the strength of opposition among members of the Public Assitance Committee (PAC), churches and chapels of all denominations, ex-servicemen's organisations, to name but a few. The Bill 'does discriminate, and it discriminates not against the worst, not against the unthrifty, not against the idler, not against the waster, but against the industrious person, against the thrifty person. It makes thrift and industry an offence and a crime for which people have to pay a very heavy penalty.'[53]

On the ground, responsibility for public assistance rested with the County Councils' PACs, and Labour leaders in local government sought to operate the system as humanely as possible by adopting the most generous scales of relief permitted. This was evident in the statistics which showed Glamorgan making 'full determination' in more than 94 per cent of cases while, at the same time, refusing to introduce the detested Means Test. Government officials like James Evans, the Ministry of Labour's chief officer in Wales, were outraged by such tactics and demanded that Whitehall should force its will on the councils.[54] An early shot was fired in February 1932 when the Ministry of Health issued a warning to the south Wales authorities, alleging that the PACs were ignoring 'substantial' household incomes when determining applications for relief, that the earnings of family members were not being counted, and that rent from houses owned, income from investments or payments by lodgers, were also not being declared.[55] Furthermore, it was claimed, 'It is apparently the rule of certain sub-committees to ignore automatically, and as a matter of principle, all payments received by way of disability pensions, service pensions or accident compensation.'[56] Faced with repeated threats from the Ministry of Health, local authorities were faced with a stark alternative: comply or lose responsibility for public assistance and hand the task to government-appointed commissioners, as had happened in the case of the Bedwellty Board of Guardians a few years earlier.[57] Glamorgan revised its regulations in April 1932 to comply with the stipulations, but Swansea PAC remained defiant and refused to adhere to the new regulations, prompting the Ministry of Health to appoint a commissioner in their place.[58] It fell to D. R. to seek a compromise which was worked out when he and the Rhondda East MP, Dai Watts-Morgan, along with Lewis Jones, MP for Swansea West, met C. W. G. Eady at the Ministry of Labour and succeeded in obtaining a three-month period of grace, during which responsibility would be restored to the Swansea PAC.[59] The reality was clear: unless Labour councillors capitulated to Whitehall, they would be stripped of their powers and with them any ability to defend the communities they were elected to serve.

*

While his work during the 1931–35 parliament was primarily concerned with domestic issues, D. R. was also deployed to cover matters affecting India, working closely with Clement Attlee who led for the PLP on the issue.[60] While Attlee focused on strategic issues arising from government policy, D. R. concentrated on the details of the situation on the ground across the Indian subcontinent. He pursued the Secretary for India, Samuel Hoare, over the beheading of Burmese rebels by government forces, the events at Berhampore (when pickets were dispersed by lathi-charges before a crowd of protesters were shot by police), the number of arrests made for erecting the Congress flag on government buildings, disturbances in Kashmir, the alleged flogging of prisoners, the arrest of pearl fishers dissatisfied with their pay, the details of the Meerut conspiracy trial, political arrests, the failure of Lord Lothian's Indian franchise committee to include a representative of Indian labour among its members, forest development, the growth of the Indian co-operative movement, and issues concerning the census.[61]

Throughout, D. R. insisted on the need for constitutional reform that would empower ordinary Indians to achieve a better standard of life by addressing social and economic issues alongside matters of government. Speaking in the Commons during an adjournment debate prior to Easter 1932, he declared that there needed to be a fundamentally different approach to that being pursued by the government:

> The Indian people must be told that we do not wish India
> to remain for ever under this oppression and tyranny, for
> tyranny it is, in its application to the everyday life of the
> Indian people, those millions of people labouring under
> disabilities of all kinds, especially the great disability of
> poverty. We here know something about unemployment and
> economic depression, but the British workman can still spend
> in shillings where the Indian workman spends in pennies. He
> has at least twelve times the purchasing power of the Indian
> worker.[62]

When Samuel Hoare moved to appoint a joint select
committee of the Lords and the Commons to consider the
future government of India and to examine and report upon
the proposals in March 1933, D. R. and his fellow Labour
MP from Yorkshire, Tom Williams, were deployed to support
Clement Attlee in a detailed critique of the proposals. Attlee
affirmed Labour's commitment to the right of the Indian
peoples to full self-government and self-determination based
on the consent of all sections of the population. India should
become an equal partner within the British Commonwealth,
and her government based on a new constitution in
accordance with the Gandhi-Irwin Pact. He condemned the
way the second round-table conference, representative of
a wide range of opinions in India, had been dismissed and
replaced by hand-picked, unrepresentative delegates whose
presence had been largely advisory, while the government
took the real decisions. Labour could not accept a White Paper
that did not specify when the power of the Governor-General
would be relaxed, when the role of the Secretary for India
would end, or when the Indian Amy would be reformed. The
proposals created a diarchy in which ministers, responsible
to an Assembly, would exercise their powers alongside the
Governor-General responsible to the Secretary for India,
with supervisory powers in all areas of responsibility. The
proposed Council of State was unrepresentative and the

limitations which would be placed on the franchise for the Assembly were undemocratic.[63]

The following day, 28 March 1933, D. R. concentrated on the details of the latter points. He denounced the proposition to limit the franchise, accusing the Tories of negating democracy by denying the vote to millions of people across the Indian subcontinent. He derided the proposals for an All-India Federation, by which the 'Indian States' would remain subject to the autocracy of the native princes (under the proposals there was no intention to assimilate government and administrative operations across both the native states and the provinces). In his opinion, such an approach completely failed to provide what was really needed, which was a recognition of the desires of Indians to self-government and of them as a people and a sovereign state, coupled with a policy of economic regeneration:

> No one knows the capacity of the Indian for self-government and for economic improvement until he has been allowed a chance. India is reaching out for the cup of freedom. Do not let us remove it from her grasp. Rather, let us bring it nearer so that she may drink deeply from the cup of freedom and liberty, and then we shall all share in the benefit of the greater freedom which we extend to her.[64]

He poured scorn over the British government's insistence that it should retain control over the police in India, noting that 'the question of law and order for India always suggests a measure of suppression, the keeping down of the Indian people'.

Once again, however, the outcome of three days' worth of detailed debates was that the PLP could muster a grand total of 42 votes against the government's proposals in two divisions in which more than 400 MPs voted with the government.

A survey of *Hansard* in the 1933–34 parliament demonstrated the extent to which Labour was totally reliant on the efforts of a small group of MPs. Aneurin Bevan filled 252 columns, followed by D. R. with 248 columns, with George Buchanan and Sir Stafford Cripps closely behind.[65] Whatever the strength of their arguments, the effective turn of phrase, the oratorical excellence with which Labour pressed their case – what Gideon Clark of the *Daily Herald* described as a PLP that was 'outnumbered but not overwhelmed' – the truth was described by Ellen Wilkinson MP. 'This isn't a parliament, it's a joke,' she declared, adding:[66]

> This need of opposition is shown in so many ways. Opposition isn't just a question of making speeches telling the Government of the day that you think it is the worst ever, as people who have never been MPs seem to think. A powerful and inquisitive opposition is necessary to keep the civil service, as well as the Government, up to the mark. I know from experience what a stir behind the scenes may be caused by a well-directed question. But it is mainly a queer impression of lop-sidedness that this House gives, as though the coach had three big wheels on one side and one on the other.[67]

Side by side with parliamentary work, therefore, Labour had to be rebuilt across the whole of Great Britain through a programme of campaigns and political education and by strengthening the party's organisational efficiency. D. R. spared no effort on top of his onerous parliamentary duties, addressing campaign meetings in halls in towns and villages throughout England and Wales, nurturing enthusiasm and cultivating the green shoots of Labour revival.[68] He was particularly involved in work to try to garner support for Labour in the rural areas, drawing on his work in agriculture and food policy on the front bench and his continued membership of the Forestry Commission.[69] As the months progressed, he took some comfort from the by-election results. In March 1932 Tom Johnson came close to regaining a seat in Dunbartonshire.[70]

The following month, Arthur Greenwood was returned at a by-election in Wakefield, and later Labour gained Wednesbury. Not long afterwards, D. R. was joined in the Commons by two men with whom he had worked in the SWMF, W. H. Mainwaring, elected for Rhondda East, and S. O. Davies, for Merthyr Tydfil.

During the summer and early autumn of 1932, D. R. spent several weeks in Cardiganshire assisting in the by-election caused by the resignation of Rhys Hopkin Morris, the county's sitting Liberal MP, addressing meetings in Aberystwyth, touring the north of the county and spending much time in the lead mining districts further inland. The outcome was disappointing, though little else was to be expected in light of the almost total blackout in the local press of any reference to the Labour campaign – but the by-election proved essential in galvanising the nascent Labour movement in the county.[71]

Meanwhile, Labour in Wales took the bold step of launching the *South Wales Tribune* to provide a platform that could not be obtained through local papers unsympathetic to Labour. The newspaper's content, which included articles in both English and Welsh, naturally focused on Labour councils' efforts to protect communities from the excesses of government policies, the effect of trade policies on Welsh industry, and the social consequences of the depression. These were intermingled with international issues, ranging from events in continental Europe, articles on India, and discussions of Russian politics.[72] D. R. was one of the paper's most frequent contributors, discussing the broad picture of the political situation, mostly in articles written in Welsh.[73] He defined his task in terms of 'dinoethi' (unmasking) the government's record, and set about doing so in forthright terms. 'Nid oes dim tosturi at y tlawd' [There is no mercy for the poor] was his summary of the tax on food, and he discussed the economic impact of the government's intransigence towards the Irish Free State.[74]

He and his wife Beatrice also played a full part in Labour's determined fightback in south-west Wales, where efforts focused on winning back the Swansea West constituency. The Swansea Labour Association, based at its impressive headquarters at the Labour Hall in High Street, embarked on a programme of political education and social activity, especially during the winter months, that culminated in the annual May Day celebrations. The association's secretary, Joe Davies, built a formidable ward-by-ward organisation underpinned by the involvement of affiliated trade unions.[75]

The establishment of the Llwchwr Urban District Council, with its headquarters in Gorseinon, provided a new dynamic to local politics in the area which had remained under the jurisdiction of the Swansea RDC since 1918. The locality had also benefited from the construction of Gorseinon Hospital, a gift from the tinplate manufacturer W. Rufus Lewis who provided the building free of charge at a personal cost of £100,000 and funded several further extensions. Rufus Lewis had remained in Gorseinon and consolidated his role as the generous benefactor of local causes after selling his interests in the steel and tinplate industry to the Grovesend Steel and Tinplate Co. in 1919. The extent of his philanthropy had included the church hall at St Catherine's, the pavilion at Parc y Werin, Argyll Park, the vicarage, and several other ventures.[76] Although patients from Gorseinon and Pontarddulais enjoyed access to the Swansea General and Eye Hospital (where the quality of service was recognised to be high), its capacity was insufficient for an area that took in the county borough and the Swansea Valley, the Llwchwr area and the Gower peninsula. Moreover, the high prevalence of heat cataract cases among tinplate workers added to the pressure on the hospital. At the same time, there were continual disagreements about the level of contributions expected from the workmen and employers in Gorseinon, Pontarddulais, Loughor and Gowerton towards the maintenance of the Swansea hospital. Rufus Lewis' offer to endow beds solely for use of patients from the Gorseinon area had been refused. He therefore funded Gorseinon Hospital as a separate institution. The hospital was managed by a governing body which included the trustees, local authority representatives, medical staff, ministers of religion, employers, trade unionists, and representatives elected by the main workplaces in Gorseinon, Loughor, Grovesend, Gowerton and Pontarddulais.

After an appeal, the workers of the district raised sufficient funds to pay for a bronze bust of Rufus Lewis to be commissioned, which D. R. unveiled. He declared that he was there 'to unveil a portrait of a man whose benefactions had been of great benefit to mankind... future generations would see the life-like image of Mr Lewis and realise that the Gorseinon Hospital was in being because of him.'[77] Later, when opening one of the extensions which Rufus Lewis had funded, D. R. referred to 'his great kindness to his fellow men in erecting such an up-to-date and beautiful hospital in their midst. It was,' he added, 'a great source of comfort to a neighbourhood, for the people to know that near at hand was a place where the finest medical skill and the finest appliances of science were at their disposal.'[78]

More broadly, D. R. recognised the importance of Labour in local government as a way of enabling the party to reverse years of decline and mismanagement of municipal life both in Llwchwr and in Swansea itself. The city, not the State, would be the basis of the organisation of social wellbeing. A typical declaration came on the eve of the Swansea CBC election in 1933, when he predicted, 'We will capture that council chamber and will put our domestic policy into operation... I believe this will be a landmark in the history of the town's politics and will enable us to remove the disgusting and disgraceful features in our borough life as we find it to-day.'[79] Thereafter, he watched as the Labour majority on the CBC was used to accelerate the housing programme, deploy relief work, and establish a municipal milk centre to stop private profiteering and the cost-cutting that resulted in adulteration of supplies.[80] Likewise, in Llwchwr, D. R. watched as the council, led by his older brother, W. J., proceeded with its own ambitious public health and housing schemes, extended district nursing, midwifery and maternity services in the years before the Second World War. They also found work for some of the more prominent trade unionists in the area, blacklisted by previous employers. Throughout these years, D. R. denounced the government for cutting its grants to the local authorities, accusing ministers of washing their hands while people were living in unfit houses and starving to pay the rent.[81] He was particularly critical of proposals to restrict new housing to the prosperous areas, and Whitehall's implied message (made explicit by individuals such as James Evans, at the Ministry of Labour) that while slum clearance could be justified, the solution to overcrowding lay in industrial transference and the mass migration of families from south Wales.[82]

In addition, D. R. continued to serve as a member of the Forestry Commission, which by 1933 was responsible for 180 forests on more than 330,000 acres in England and Wales, and 79 forests on more than 375,000 acres in Scotland. D. R. took a close interest in its work in Wales and took his fellow commissioners on a tour of some forest land in north Wales during the summer of 1933.[83] But D. R. was aware of the impact made by budget cuts following the May Committee's report in 1931 and the impact this had both on supplies of timber and on the area of land that it was able to take for afforestation. He elaborated on his ideas for the future in a detailed paper submitted to the New Fabian Research Bureau in January 1934, in which he argued the case for national investment in forestation, demonstrating how the potential returns over a period of 40 or 50 years would more than justify the capital outlay. He emphasised two key issues.

Firstly, the desirability of employing men on a part-time basis –around 150 days a year – to enable them to continue farming land adjacent to the forest, a proposal which could have helped to make some smallholdings financially viable, especially in upland areas. Secondly, he highlighted the opportunities which existed to make use of land acquired by municipal corporations for water supplies and other purposes for use as forest land.[84] D. R.'s memorandum reflected the Forestry Commission's own view that its role could be an integral part of rural development and help to regenerate those parts of Britain that were suffering the most as a result of the Depression, now designated 'Special Areas', in response to reports on the affected areas commissioned by the government in 1934. One suggestion made in this respect was that the Forestry Commission should purchase 200,000 acres of land in the areas worst affected by the depression, but this policy met with significant obstacles, not least in acquiring land and developing the necessary training. Although the Commission set itself a target of developing 600,000 acres (349,000 acres of which were to be in south Wales), the total acreage that was ever acquired was 30,800, almost all of which was in south Wales.[85]

CHAPTER 7

Labour Calls for Power

ON 29 SEPTEMBER 1934, the whole of Britain was shocked to the core by news of the devastating disaster at the Gresford Colliery, close to Wrexham. A total of 266 men lost their lives, most of whom were killed outright in an explosion at the Denis shaft, an area half a mile into the mine, lying at a depth of over 2,200 feet from the surface. The ferocity of the fire and the fact that several explosions occurred in quick succession thwarted rescue attempts.[1] D. R., familiar as he was with mining tragedies, immediately recognised the scale of what had happened in north Wales. He hurried to Wrexham where he met with Ted Jones of the north Wales miners, along with their solicitor Cyril O. Jones, and made his way to the colliery where desperate efforts were still being made to rescue the men. Within a fortnight, a Commission of Inquiry was appointed by the Minister for Mines, chaired by Sir Henry Walker, Chief Inspector of Mines, who sat alongside John Brass, nominated by the Mining Association, and Joseph Jones, President of the MFGB.[2] Past experience had shown that many of these inquires had been little more than a formality and, as a result, Cyril O. Jones advised the North Wales Mineworkers' Union (NWMU) to engage Sir Stafford Cripps, who brought with him two supporting barristers, Geoffrey Wilson and Arthur Henderson Jr. D. R. also joined the team as its special advisor on mining issues, providing expert technical knowledge which none of the legal team possessed.[3] He was soon given the additional task of acting as simultaneous translator for those who addressed the inquiry in Welsh, and was able to convey the implications of nuances in the use of language which might otherwise have been lost.

In preparation for the inquiry, D. R. produced a detailed introductory report based on documentation provided by the Commissioners which showed the layout of the mine and the way it was worked. In it, D. R. identified deficiencies in the airways in the area where the disaster had occurred, and the woeful inadequacies of the means of entrance and egress. This provided the basis for Sir Stafford Cripps' opening statement which set the tone for the uncompromising way in which he cross-examined witnesses throughout the 28 days of the inquiry. He would, he declared, expose a situation of 'wholesale neglect of all safety precautions [and] innumerable breaches of the law laid down by Parliament to protect the miners', in circumstances in which 'the behaviour of the Inspectorate [of the Ministry of Mines], so far as this pit and occurrences connected with it are concerned, to say the least, were utterly deplorable.'[4] He went on, 'It may not be possible to point to any single incident which with certainty caused the explosion, but it is, I shall submit, quite easy to deduce from the evidence that the conditions in certain parts of the pit were such that any untoward incident might have caused an explosion, since all the most dangerous, inducing conditions were constantly present due to the criminal – and I use the word advisedly and with a full sense of responsibility – conduct of those responsible for the management and running of the pit.'[5]

For the next four weeks Sir Stafford Cripps cross-examined witness after witness to reveal the deficiencies in the way the mine was managed. The company had tried to reduce administrative costs by making an accountant responsible for work that should have been done by a qualified engineer. The plans of the Denis section were out of date; the managers had not driven an intake and return airway to the shaft, thus reducing the amount of air that circulated. Ventilation was therefore inadequate, and the air that flowed was of poor quality. Air measurements had not been recorded. Was it true, he asked, that shot-firing had taken place in an area where gas was present in an effort to produce coal more quickly? Was it the case that men's lives had been endangered on successive occasions because they had not been given time to withdraw from the area when shot-firing had taken place? Men were working shifts that exceeded the maximum time allowed by law, and were not being required to take an eight-hour break between shifts, he alleged. Subjected to a combination of Sir Stafford Cripps' cold logic and D. R.'s technical knowledge, the company's representatives, in particular William Bonsall, the colliery manager, were powerless to prevent a damning exposé of the totally inadequate practices by which the colliery was run.

Throughout the first stage of the inquiry, the colliery company refused repeated demands by the miners' representatives for an investigation of the area where the explosion had occurred and, in consequence, proceedings were adjourned in December 1934 without producing an interim report. Six months later, in April 1935, it resumed, by which time T. S. Charlton, the son of W. J. Charlton, District Inspector of the Mines Department, had been appointed colliery manager.[6] This immediately aroused suspicion in the locality that they were witnessing a conspiracy to avoid accountability. This was articulated by Cyril Jones: 'There certainly ought to be a regulation precluding a District Inspector or his Assistant from inspecting a mine managed by his own son... I know that the Mines Department has already whitewashed the occurrence in Gresford Colliery but I can assure you that the miners in this district are very disgusted with what has occurred and feel very dissatisfied to think that, after the holding of the Inquiry, the Inspector's son should be in charge of the colliery. It makes them feel suspicious and believe that no real attempt is being made to prevent what they regard, and rightly so, as corruption in high places.' To make matters worse, the colliery company continued to resist an inspection of the affected area by repeatedly rearranging the agreed dates.

By the summer of 1935, the MFGB had lost its patience and D. R., accompanied by Herbert Smith, Joseph Hall, and Edward Jones, arrived at the pithead in their work clothes ready to go underground, only to be refused admittance.[7] The demonstration had the effect, however, of forcing the company into a corner. They then announced that that part of the mine would be abandoned altogether.[8] Ben Francis, describing the mood in the village in the *Daily Worker*, wrote:

> The decision to abandon the mine struck a chill into the hearts of the widows at the pithead and they returned home with desolation and grief marked on their faces. But in their breasts, there was also bitter indignation and resentment. For months their menfolk had returned from work to relate terrible stories of the conditions in the pit. I recall even now after 12 months the burning anger of one widow, when she related how her husband had told her that, despite the fact that he worked in only boots and short knickers, he had to take his boots off to empty out the sweat. It was common talk throughout the villages that the pit was heavily laden with gas, and frequently one had said: 'The pit will blow up some day.'

Having presented detailed information about the low wages paid by the companies – and the money they made selling the coal – Ben Francis went on to describe the anger felt locally at the failure to bring those responsible for the safe operation of the mine to justice.[9]

Without doubt, D. R. shared this sense of disgust. Men had lost their lives, leaving behind wives, families and a neighbourhood that deserved answers. In September he told the TUC conference that the facts, once revealed, would bring horror to every trade unionist in the country.[10] It was a view shared across the Labour movement, and D. R. determined to make sure that the Gresford disaster and issues it revealed remained at the forefront of the public conscience in the following years.

*

D. R. continued to shoulder heavy parliamentary responsibilities, in particular as a member of the front bench leading the opposition to the government's Unemployment Bill, which proposed to transfer responsibility for determining the amount of transitional payments (paid to the long-term unemployed who had exhausted their contributions under National Insurance) from the local authorities to the Unemployment Assistance Board (UAB). Furthermore, the amount of relief which would be payable was to be 'proportionate to need', assessed according to a prescribed Means Test that took account of household income, savings and other funds to which an individual could have recourse. Such proposals were anathema to D. R., his fellow Labour MPs, and above all to the thousands of affected families in the communities they represented, what D. R. memorably denounced as 'a measure that ignored the tradition of frugality, and provided an incentive for home wrecking, by which individuals would be deprived of the fruits of their lifetime's work by dent of a set of economic circumstances over which they had no influence or control'.[11] Throughout, D. R. worked closely with the SWMF leadership which was pivotal in forming the national campaign of resistance to the new regulations.[12] He presented a lengthy report to the SWMF special conference in August 1934 in which he outlined the social implications in considerable detail.[13]

As author Neil Evans has demonstrated in his study of the protests against the UAB's proposals, over the succeeding months a coalition of political, trade union, religious, and ex-servicemen's organisations, those representing the disabled, clubs and social organisations, came together to denounce the proposals and demand their reversal.[14] Notwithstanding the bitter internecine battles that dominated the coalfield's politics, a joint council of action was formed that convened a conference which drew together more than 1,600 delegates from across south Wales to demand the withdrawal of the regulations.[15]

D. R. was in no doubt about the indignation that was felt throughout south Wales about the UAB and its Means Test.[16] On 18 January he told a mass meeting in Gorseinon that, while 'backward areas of the kingdom' would benefit from standardisation, it would be inimical to areas like south Wales where the local authorities had implemented the regulations as generously as possible.[17] Later that month, mass meetings were held across south Wales in some of the largest ever demonstrations seen in the area.[18] At a meeting at the Globe Theatre in Clydach, D. R. described the effect of the loss of purchasing power endured by coalfield communities since the war, and the impact of prolonged unemployment on family circumstances. Government ministers were trying to reduce the standard of living of the most vulnerable and the new regulations were part of that plan.[19] The following weekend, further mass protest meetings were held, including a large gathering organised by the Swansea Labour Association at the Plaza Cinema, where D. R. warned the government that the situation would not be resolved until the regulations and the Means Test were removed.[20] The same afternoon he addressed a crowd of over 3,000 men, women and children who had marched from Morriston, Bethel, Halfway, Heol Las, Birchgrove, Llansamlet, Bonymaen, Glais, Lonlas and Skewen – and led by the Llansamlet Silver Band – to another mass meeting at Primrose Park in Peniel Green, Llansamlet.[21]

Political leaders were joined by a range of social and religious groups. The Gorseinon Chamber of Trade passed a resolution of protest, decrying the regulations as 'ridiculous and unreasonable' at a time when public authorities were talking of reversing the economic cuts of 1931.[22] The West Glamorgan Congregationalists, meeting at Clydach, passed a resolution moved by the Rev. Gwynedd Jones, Pontardawe, and seconded by Gwilym Bedw, condemning the government's actions. But despite outward signs of consensus, the relationship between some of the protesting organisations was far from easy. This was clearly evident in Gorseinon where the United Front Committee, chaired by Thomas Williams of Grovesend, an independent councillor on Llwchwr UDC, sought to fuse the local Chamber of Trade, voluntary organisations and the Communist Party; however the Llwchwr Labour Party refused to participate in its work. Indeed, D. R.'s attitude towards the 'United Front' was scathing, as is revealed in his letter to the Gorseinon United Front Committee in March 1935 in which he stated, 'the people you represent are all in their power to return the national government... [I] do not intend to regard you as a representative, as I know the malice of your policy towards us.' Tom Williams, for his part, was unbowed, accusing his local MP of placing the needs of party before those of the unemployed, and stoutly defending the role played by the Chamber of Trade in leading the campaign. Tradesmen, he insisted, had gone bankrupt trying to help the community and the MP had no business in causing disunity.

The national government sought to defuse the situation by abandoning the most contentious parts of the legislation which gave counties like Glamorgan at least some opportunity to use local discretion to save families from its worst excesses. The Means Test left deep scars. It was repugnant to families who derived their livelihoods from some of the hardest and most dangerous occupations imaginable, who took pride in the haven of home, and were robbed of what little they had in the face of the sickening evidence of blatant spendthrift consumption in the fleshpots of London.[23]

*

Fair treatment for the unemployed victims of capitalism was essential but only industrial recovery through a revival of traditional industries and the development of new employment opportunities would provide the genuine release from destitution that Britain's working-class communities demanded. Throughout these years, D. R. accompanied his fellow MPs from south Wales to meeting after meeting with the Board of Trade and the Ministry of Labour, to argue for government direction of industry to the distressed areas and the establishment of a body to finance new development. Ministers' reactions only varied according to the degree of pity they displayed, while their substantive response was always the same: salvation would only come through a general revival of trade; government was powerless; firms could only be expected to locate where it made commercial sense; people had to move to where the work was, and neighbourhoods that became derelict were merely episodes in the history of capitalism. The challenges preventing recovery in south Wales in particular were stark. At the start of 1932 it was estimated that around 200 firms were looking for new premises but none were prepared to locate in Glamorgan, Monmouthshire or Carmarthenshire, allegedly because of the region's reputation for industrial militancy and historic labour troubles. Meanwhile, capital for investment in south Wales was almost impossible to obtain.[24]

In response to accusations that it was ignoring the problem, the government commissioned reports to examine four 'necessitous areas' (West Cumberland and Haltwhistle, Durham and Tyneside, south Wales and Monmouth, and Scotland).[25] Cabinet ministers took direct responsibility for the reports on the two English regions, but the task of preparing the study of south Wales was given to Major Wyndham Portal, chairman of the paper manufacturing firm that produced England's banknotes. D. R. used the opportunity to prepare a memorandum outlining the case for relocating new industries in south Wales but, although Wyndham Portal's report provided a good descriptive account of the situation (of use to historians of the period if nothing else), it had few remedies to recommend. It categorised Blaina, Brynmawr, Rhymney, Merthyr Tydfil, Dowlais, Ebbw Vale, Senghenydd, and other mining communities as 'derelict'. Employment in the basic industries had disappeared, and the potential of existing concerns to provide any additional employment was limited. The coal, iron, steel and tinplate industries would not be capable of providing for more than 164,000 workers even if demand could be created for their produce.[26] The outlook for Welsh steam coal was particularly poor due to the loss of export markets and Admiralty contracts, and there was no imminent prospect of stimulating demand through gasification or oil extraction.[27] There was little hope for the development of new industries and the thrust of public policy should continue to be directed towards transference, taking 'the cream of the population... from the depressed districts, leaving the older and less adaptable people to bear the burden of existing social services.'[28]

In response, Neville Chamberlain, on behalf of the government, announced that Commissioners for the Special Areas would be appointed with a budget of £2 million. However, there would be no change to the government's main policy of transference, and work to move juveniles and unmarried men to other areas would be increased. Economic free markets would determine where people would live, and those left behind were a 'residual problem' to be helped through land settlement, occupational centres, welfare work, public works, drainage and afforestation and minor housing schemes. The subsequent legislation to establish the role of Commissioner for the Special Areas confirmed the government's ability to create administrative machinery of government, but the approach lacked any concrete proposals. In Neville Chamberlain's own words:

> What we want here, as it seems to us, is something more rapid, more direct, less orthodox if you like, than the ordinary plan, and if we agree to do what seems to me even more important than the improvement of the physical condition, if we are to effect the spiritual regeneration of these areas, and if we are to inspire their people with a new interest in life and a new hope for the future, we have to convince them that these reports are not going to gather dust in some remote pigeon hole but that they will be the subject of continuous executive action.[29]

The task of making sense of the government's intentions fell to Malcolm Stewart, Chairman of the London Brick Company, seen by many as a progressive employer, who was appointed as Commissioner for the Special Areas, while Geoffrey Crawshay, a descendent of the Merthyr Tydfil ironmasters, Liberal activist, one-time rugby player, and prominent member of the South Wales and Monmouthshire Council of Social Service, was appointed as District Commissioner with responsibility for south Wales.[30] Malcolm Stewart's first annual report was itself an indictment of the government's failure to deal with the problem: the 'more rapid, more direct, less orthodox' approach had seen investment in training opportunities but little else.[31] Government regulations made the commissioners' task virtually impossible: they were prevented from offering financial assistance for the construction of roads and bridges, and no concessions were made to the demand for intervention in the location of industry. Businesses which had been prepared to exploit the former industrial areas showed no sense of responsibility. The Federation of British Industry was resistant to any suggestion to support work in south Wales especially, blaming the region's inaccessibility to markets and high rates, even if they did not openly admit their members' political motivations.[32]

Malcolm Stewart's report had the positive effect of providing ammunition to the Labour members' arguments for a policy of directing work to the distressed areas and financial support to local authorities in the form of loan cancellations. D. R. joined W. H. Mainwaring, S. O. Davies and George Daggar in a blistering attack on the government, in which they highlighted the lack of progress and castigated its lukewarm response to Stewart's recommendations.[33] At the same time, D. R. worked closely with Hilary Marquand at University College Cardiff to develop alternative proposals, by obtaining detailed factual evidence through parliamentary sources to supplement publicly available material, and information from a network of Labour councillors which local officials had refused to release.[34] This provided essential subject matter for *South Wales Needs a Plan*, in which Marquand argued forcefully that the policy of transference was fundamentally flawed, and was not merely 'callous as regards the lives of the individuals and the communities concerned, but also... misconceived even if such considerations are laid on one side'.[35] His arguments were taken further by the young economist Brinley Thomas, who showed convincingly how the south Wales economy had been deprived of investment as the proceeds of dividends, royalties and other income generated by coal and steel had been spent elsewhere.[36] In the absence of such investment, Thomas insisted, the State had a responsibility to communities suffering as a consequence of a depression brought about by the government's own policies.

D. R. saw at first hand what the consequences were, as communities lost thousands of people through migration, as well as the bitter experiences suffered by many of those who had moved as they sought work in the Midlands, London and the Home Counties. Each week he met individual victims of government policy, who spoke of anti-Welsh attitudes in England as they existed on low wages in unstable occupations. Meanwhile, the local authorities across the distressed areas were having to provide services to an increasingly dependent population on diminishing resources, and social capital was wasted. None of the perpetually repeated arguments against locating industry in south Wales could withstand scrutiny: the cost of high rates could be offset by low land prices; the area was not inaccessible – it had good rail links and the road network could be transformed by a small number of strategic projects, in particular a bridge over the Severn; 'labour troubles' were no more prevalent in south Wales than elsewhere, and in any case, those that existed in the coal industry stemmed from its specific context.

D. R.'s own detailed research focused on the impact of trade policy and how it could contribute to economic and industrial recovery. He collected a battery of statistics on the purchase of commodities and the impact of tariffs and protectionism. Central to his thinking was the need for a process of industrial reorganisation through economic planning, combined with a policy of cheap money and a plan to stimulate employment through public works schemes that included afforestation, land settlement, drainage schemes, construction of new roads and bridges, recreational facilities, trading estates, hydro-electric power generation and iron ore mining. This would be accompanied by a policy to control the location of industry that diverted employment to the areas of highest unemployment.[37]

For D. R., 'The failure of our industrial system to provide for the distribution of its products has led to violent and brutal social changes over a large part of Europe. The alternative to violence is a reasoned plan for ensuring a higher standard of life for all, in which production and consumption can be maintained in balance at a steadily increasing height of equilibrium. Towards that goal of plenty, Labour must walk straightly armed with knowledge and justified by its faith in the justice and wisdom of its cause.'[38]

He was able to pursue these themes in detail in *Labour's Way To Plan Prosperity*, which he published in 1935 as one of eight volumes of the *Labour Shows the Way* series edited by Clement Attlee that also included works by Walter Citrine, Arthur Henderson, and George Lansbury and other members of Labour's front bench team, Arthur Greenwood, Tom Williams, and John Wilmott.[39] In its 118 pages, D. R. traced the decline of world trade and its effect on production and employment. Primary producers were setting prices so low as to be ruinous, and this called for a reappraisal of economic thinking, both on the part of individuals and governments. 'Changes are taking place rapidly and old ideas have to give way to the more appropriate to the times. The economics of the last century are now proved unsuitable to the world's need. Individualism has been carried far beyond its proper sphere. It is now in conflict with the interests of the people of all lands.'

He went on, 'The question now is, how can industry be put on a sound foundation so as to bring security and ordered progress instead of the uncertainty and distress arising from the present system... Has the time arrived for State planning of industry, and what are the principles upon which the State is to extend its function in regulating her production and distribution of communities and to supersede private enterprise in the service?'

Modern industry, he argued, was inseparably associated with government. 'No important sphere in production can be removed from contact with political life. Changes in industrial methods give rise to new social conditions and call new political forces into action.' Capitalism, he believed, had always sought the State's assistance to win supremacy and security from competitors; a glance at British industrial history revealed the role the State had played in securing new markets overseas through political power.

In analysing the impact of the war on the industrialised economies, he described how, 'Capitalism has reaped a rich harvest from those four years of war. Foreign finance ran its course long after. An orgy of speculation overshadowed industry and commerce and destroyed the slender foundations upon which international trade might be rebuilt.'

A fitful boom in coal and steel soon gave way to depression, all world trade was reduced to small proportions, compared with its pre-war capacity. Clearly, expansion would have enabled production and employment to be maintained.

'The reverse course was taken on the advice of banks and financial advisers in credit, with disastrous consequences.' Put simply, 'the moneylenders took charge of European politics'. Profiteering in industry, in housing, furnishing, clothing, food, travel and entertainment, was pursued irrespective of its social consequences. Capitalism was exposed in all its anarchic inadequacies. Mass unemployment, bad housing, social unrest, revolution, and political dictatorship testified to the industrial collapse which brought all the countries to the verge of ruin and destruction. The system had failed to prevent unemployment and had not been able to lower the hours in work or give decent wages to safeguard the health of the workers. 'Capitalism makes provision for a few and deprives the million.' International trade was causing friction and was not benefiting consumers.

He pointed to Britain's rich potential in terms of coal, iron ore, and other resources, as well as the infrastructure which had been created, together with reserves of human skill, organising talent, and technical knowledge. Instead of using technology to put men out of work, Labour would ensure that economic power was used to benefit society as a whole. This would be achieved through the reorganisation of all main industries, coal, transport, iron and steel, and electricity, through a national planning council responsible for establishing the general direction for industry and for planning exports and imports.

Alongside this, individual action plans would be developed for each industry. These would include unification of electricity supply and work to extend provision to rural areas. Control of banking would be achieved. The cotton industry would be reconstructed under national ownership. The reorganisation of the coal industry would be part of a scheme for a National Fuel Board that would delegate day-to-day functions to a network of district fuel boards. Pit committees would be established, on which the miners would be represented, and would address defects in individual collieries and thereby increase efficiency and maximise production. Modernisation of iron and steel would be overseen by a corporation, who would own and control all undertakings manufacturing iron and steel products. The railways would be nationalised and coordinated with road transport to plan the system as one complete whole. A National Building Board would organise the industry, harnessing workmanship and artistic design.

Labour's plan encompassed the principle of equal pay for all workers. D. R. argued, 'Equality of work should carry equality of pay. In planning industry, no distinction should be drawn between workers, beyond those of fitness and capacity for special duties. The machine has come to lighten the physical burden on labour. Industrial operations in the future will require less strength of body but great deftness and precision… Women and men will know the duties of industry and administration without discrimination.' To accommodate the change it would be necessary to limit the working hours and working years of men and women.

*

In terms of the immediate situation facing south Wales, D. R. was involved in negotiations with the Irish Free State to enter into an agreement with Britain for a supply of approximately 1.2 million tons of coal a year (alongside an increase in the cattle trade), offering the potential to restore orders that had been lost in 1932.

D. R. claimed direct responsibility for the outcome, having acted as an intermediary between the Dominions Office and the government of the Irish Free State from March 1934. In January 1935 he told the *Daily Herald*, 'My job has been trying to get something done for the coal industry, and I think the agreement will be of benefit to south Wales as well as other British coalfields.'[40]

D. R. also had to deal with issues arising from far-reaching changes in the steel and tinplate industry that threatened the future of thousands of jobs in south-west Wales, nowhere more so than in his own constituency. He knew well enough that the future lay in the creation of a small number of works capable of mass producing steel, and that this would be mirrored in the case of tinplate manufacture. Since the start of the 1930s, he had advocated the creation of a public utility company for the iron and steel industry to oversee such a modernisation process and ensure that it was undertaken in a way that took account of social as well as economic considerations.[41] What he did not accept was the argument that future developments should be located in Lincolnshire and Northamptonshire, close to the iron ore fields, involving the transfer of huge numbers of workers and causing further unemployment in the traditional steel-producing areas. This would undoubtedly be the consequence of the decision taken by Richard Thomas & Co., who announced in July 1935 that it intended to develop an integrated strip mill at Redbourn in Lincolnshire. This meant that the main steel and tinplate manufacturer in south-west Wales was about to abandon the region, thus destroying any hope of an economic revival.[42]

Immediately, D. R. was at the forefront of Labour MPs' work to convince the government to intervene to prevent such a catastrophe. On 16 July he was one of three MPs who met Stanley Baldwin to warn of the disastrous consequences

163

that lay ahead if the company was allowed to proceed.[43] He pressed Walter Runciman, President of the Board of Trade, to say whether he was aware of the company's proposals and whether he had considered its impact on south Wales, and left him in no doubt about the sense of shock and anger at the proposals. Allowing the Redbourn proposals to proceed would create yet another derelict area, he insisted.[44]

He moved quickly to demand a parliamentary discussion of the issue, and used a parliamentary debate to draw attention to the impact the development could have in south-west Wales, where nine-tenths of the world's tinplate production was based.[45] He blamed the government's trade policy – in particular its agreement in Paris to agree to reduce Britain's quota of tinplate exports by one-third from twelve million to eight million boxes without any consultation with the workforce – for the situation which had arisen. 'They were bargaining not only in regard to tinplate boxes but with the homes and lives of the workpeople, the businesses of struggling shopkeepers. These were pawns on the table in these negotiations between those who met at Paris. I wish to restrain sentiment if I can this afternoon, but I know what is involved in this to south Wales, and what is implied in what has taken place last week.'

Turning to the need to reorganise the industry to close obsolete works, he castigated comments by Sir William Firth, chairman of Richard Thomas & Co., who called for government compensation to the owners of those firms when he had made no comment about the plight of those working in the industry whose lives would be devastated by changes. 'They want statutory powers ... to enable them to scrap their plant and machinery, but there is not one word about the homes and lives of thousands of people and the community services which are involved.' He went on, 'I represent the working people in this industry. I am their political representative in this House, and I wish to give them full and adequate representation. I do not wish them to be neglected and ignored whenever political measures are considered which affect their lives.'

What was more, Sir William Firth was seeking government money to be able to do so. A government committee of inquiry to be set up immediately, he believed, should take account of the social impact of any reorganisation plan and consider its impact on the balance of the inter-dependent industries – coal, steel and tinplate – across south Wales. 'I warn the House that a social catastrophe is ahead. If we add those unemployed to the 175,000 already unemployed, the burden and the loss of income will be the last straw to break the backs of the people in that part of the country.'

What was required was not an attempt to maintain expensive and unproductive production, but the same consideration that the government was giving to other industries by pursuing its trade policy. He concluded, 'Calamity can be averted by timely action. The responsibility devolves upon the State. Its first duty is to resist deterioration in the localities. It must bring forward a well-considered plan for comprehensive industrial reorganisation on new lines and for fully utilising the facilities and resources of this area ... Has the Government an answer to the claim of south Wales? Is it to go forth that all the experience, the energy, the civic effort and the community pride of that area is to be sacrificed in order to enable private firms to find a minimum level of cost and a maximum level of profit? Is this government a national government? If the answer is "Yes", they are under an obligation to show it in this matter.'

At the end of October D. R. led another deputation from south Wales to meet Walter Runciman, whose response suggested a slight softening of the line taken by the government the previous summer. He also insisted that there was no prejudice against the development of any industry in south Wales, no irrevocable decision had been made and the company was alive to the arguments, he insisted.[46]

This change of heart was confirmed by the announcement,

made at the start of November 1935, that Richard Thomas and Co. planned to develop at Ebbw Vale rather than Redbourn. This was a cause of relief and celebration in an area of south-east Wales that had been described by Wyndham Portal as being on the verge of dereliction, and where the very existence of entire communities was under threat. But the announcement brought little relief to south-west Wales which did not feature in the company's plans, despite the thousands of jobs that depended on steel and tinplate in the region. These concerns intensified when it became clear that Richard Thomas' plans meant that a great deal of the tinplate production would be based at Ebbw Vale, while steel production at Redbourn would be increased. Why, it was asked, did the company need any more steel capacity in Redbourn when it could be developed at Ebbw Vale, allowing more of the tinplate production to remain in the south-west.[47]

The matter was reignited the following year (after the Conservatives had boasted of their role in promoting Ebbw Vale in the 1935 election) when Richard Thomas and Co. announced proposals for a new strip mill at Irthlingborough in Northamptonshire. This was in direct contradiction to the impression the company had given at the end of 1935 that they would not be financing any new plant other than at Ebbw Vale and, that while plants in south-west Wales would be required 'for years to come', the transfer of workers elsewhere in the future could not be ruled out.[48] Again, D. R., along with neighbouring MPs, met Walter Runciman to reiterate the central message that any transfer of productive capacity from south-west Wales would have disastrous consequences for the region. He repeated the message that an industry enjoying protection through State policies should be responsive to the government when determining the location of any future developments.[49] Furthermore, any proposal to move production from south Wales to Northamptonshire flew in the face of the policy of encouraging development in the Special Areas.[50] Once again,

Walter Runciman's platitudes and the government's attitude provided little assurance for south-west Wales.[51]

In the meantime, D. R. worked closely with Captain Leighton Davies of the Baldwin Co. to develop the economic case for south-west Wales as a centre for tinplate manufacture. Whatever their political affiliation, the Davies family were influential figures in the social life of Gowerton where Leighton Davies' father, Sir John Cecil Davies, had been one of the pioneers of the industry. Leighton Davies was convinced that the combination of coal supplies, railway links, skilled labour and the variety of the products being produced meant south-west Wales was well-placed to maintain its pre-eminent position in steel and tinplate production, provided that production was concentrated in a smaller number of more modern works. It was a good location to export tinplate, and could soon benefit from any increase in home consumption. He consistently rejected Sir William Firth's insistence that any proposal to build modern works in south Wales, other than at Ebbw Vale, would be 'absurd and against the national interests'.[52]

D. R., for his own part, took strong exception at comments made by Sir William Firth at the company's annual meeting about the position of Welsh workers: 'Apparently [Firth] does not approve of the Welshman's loyalty to his country. Wales is as well endowed with the labour and resources for industrial prosperity as any part of Britain. It is due to the Welsh people that a fuller explanation of the industrial reasons which actuate Sir William Firth should be given. He does not help the issue by references to the Sunday or weekday habits of the people of Wales. He should be able to appreciate the discipline and restrained habits in the people with whom, as an employer, he has been in contact.'[53]

Firth's statements also concealed two underlying truths. Firstly, that the Richard Thomas Co. could not build any more strip mills under the terms of the licence granted to them by the American owners of the patent for producing steel strips. Secondly, they were not in a financial position to do so because of the cost of the Ebbw Vale development which eventually brought the company to its knees and required intervention by the Bank of England to save the situation.[54] Walter Runciman's complacency, in response to D. R. and other representatives of south-west Wales, testified to the national government's apathy, and only the respite provided by war and the subsequent reassessment of industrial policy enabled the region to carve a future in the post-war steel and tinplate industry.

*

D. R. was, by now, approaching his mid-50s and had never been as prominent in political life. To his onerous duties in Westminster were added the regular weekend campaigning across England and Wales, as well as ministering to the needs of his own constituency in Gower. He was ably assisted by his wife Beatrice, who served on the executive of the Swansea Labour Association and spearheaded work as a Labour candidate in the Mumbles. His daughter Eileen took responsibility for administrative and secretarial work for her father for the following decades. Both women were formidable political thinkers and strategists in their own right, even if the public face was that of D. R. His eldest brother, William John, in addition to serving as leader of the Llwchwr UDC, deployed his administrative talents as the full-time secretary of the Gorseinon Housing Co-partnership which had built the Garden Village estate on the outskirts of Gorseinon – a role which combined the work of directing the company with day-to-day work, overseeing rent collection and ensuring tenants kept their dwellings in good order. He lived with his sister, Anna Jane, who had married John Griffiths and settled at Gwynfa, Mason's Road, opposite Libanus Chapel. She was a prominent school manager (governor) and a faithful member at Libanus where she often acted as the voice of the congregation in matters of church governance. Brother Ivor remained at Penhafod and became a skilful and knowledgeable water and sewerage engineer. Brother Mansel fulfilled his promise as an adult educator, eventually being appointed west Wales organiser for the Workers' Educational Association.[55] His work included setting up tutorial classes throughout west Wales and administering grants made by the South Wales and Monmouthshire Council of Social Service to support work with the unemployed. He fulfilled a longstanding ambition by opening Fellowship House, in Mumbles, as a residential centre for adult students which provided a haven for many of those involved in adult learning, both to discuss first principles and to make plans for local activities.

The strength of D. R.'s position among fellow Labour MPs was revealed in the annual elections to the PLP Executive, held each autumn, in which he regularly topped the poll, or came second only to Sir Stafford Cripps, in each of the elections held between 1931 and 1935. Even the return of so many of Labour's prominent figures in the 1935 election did not threaten his position and he did not slip to below fifth position in any ballot held between November 1935 and his appointment as Secretary for Mines in 1940. He sat on the Miners' Welfare Scholarship Committee and served on the executive of the Empire Parliamentary Association. Meanwhile, his seniority among the Welsh Labour benches led to his election as chairman of the Welsh PLP.[56] Along with other MPs, like Rhys Davies, Gordon Macdonald, Will John, William Jenkins, S. O. Davies and Morgan Jones, D. R. fitted the mould of Labour leaders, reared as Nonconformists even if some were no longer adherents to the cause, active in Welsh circles, particularly when they visited the National Eisteddfod field every year. The *Western Mail* parliamentary columnist, 'The Junior Member for Treorchy', recalled the days when he had been seen as one of the wild men of south Wales, when William Jenkins (MP for

Neath and a former Miners' Agent) and Ivor Gwynn (who D. R. had beaten for the Labour nomination in Gower) had been aloof towards him in the most ostentatious manner.[57] 'At first sight he reminds one of John the Baptist, who loved to live in the wilderness and to seek his sustenance in wild locusts and honey,' but now he had mellowed. 'There lurks behind that rugged exterior a tenderness of heart, which endears him to those who are most intimate with him.' Confirmation of this seemed to come with the publication of the 1935 Birthday Honours list which saw D. R. awarded a CBE (Clement Attlee was made a Privy Counsellor, and Walter Citrine, Arthur Pugh and Charlie Edwards got a knighthood each).[58]

As Labour prepared for the coming election it was clear that, despite Labour's efforts to castigate the national government's domestic record, international issues and the country's response to the rise of fascism across Europe would be the decisive issues in the forthcoming contest. A commitment to peaceful solutions to Europe's problems were a testament of faith for George Lansbury and most other Labour leaders, D. R. among them, who deplored the campaign of vilification waged against the peace movement by prominent Tories, described vividly by D. R. as 'a whispering gallery of alarms and suspicions that threatened war'.[59] Britain, D. R. believed, should cultivate a higher standard of moral responsibility in world affairs, but disarmament would never be realised while Sir John Simon and his ilk were at the helm.[60]

As the decade progressed, D. R. and his colleagues on the Labour benches watched in despair as European governments danced around the issue of disarmament without securing any meaningful agreement. As early as March 1933, after Ramsay MacDonald and the Foreign Secretary Sir John Simon returned from the Disarmament Conference in Geneva, D. R. had warned that there was no indication that Europe would reach any significant measure of disarmament in the following five years.[61] This he attributed squarely to the failure of those at the Geneva conference to understand the issue as a matter of rejecting war as an instrument for settling human affairs rather than a question of maintaining the balance of power in Europe through the respective strength of the 'great powers'.[62] This resulted in a situation whereby 'everywhere, dictatorships are springing up, with the weapons of murder and destruction, with the morality of the thug and the method of the bully, oppressing and coercing people all round'. What was needed, he insisted, was a policy that would bring together the body of people, present in each country, who believed in peace at home and abroad.[63]

Furthermore, he linked the failure to secure disarmament to the economic conditions prevailing across Europe.[64] 'There is,' he said, 'immense genuine poverty all over Europe. Millions of people are driven to desperation. Despair rules over Europe, at the same time poverty is increasing day by day. Hungry and desperate men will swallow the nostrum or gospel prescribed to them, but men equally desperate occupy high office in various countries.' Britain's duty was to use its influence to promote economic cooperation as a means of eradicating international rivalry.[65]

Throughout the summer of 1935, D. R. watched as Britain forged its response to the threat to peace posed by the actions of Mussolini in relation to Abyssinia. With the government committed to sanctions short of war, Labour was put in an impossible position. Should a party appalled by Italian fascism be demanding tougher action? What would Labour do in the event that sanctions failed? The party continued to vote against the defence estimates (which D. R. denounced as a 'suicide club... for self and mutual destruction'), and advocated a policy of pan-European disarmament through the League of Nations.[66] But for Walter Citrine and other prominent figures in the trade union movement, Ernest Bevin in particular, such thinking did not recognise the reality of the international situation. They demanded action against Italy, even if it meant a risk of war. D. R. listened in pain as Ernest Bevin launched a ferocious attack on the leadership's position, and George Lansbury personally, at the party conference in Brighton in 1935 and was heartbroken on 8 October when George Lansbury resigned as Labour Party leader unable to betray his Christian Socialist principles by supporting any form of sanctions of war whether by an individual country or the League of Nations.[67] Since his election to parliament, D. R. had been closer to George Lansbury than to any other of Labour's senior figures, and considered him to be 'as near perfect in human virtues that I've seen'.[68] This view was shared by thousands in the Labour movement and more broadly, not least in communities across Wales where George Lansbury was admired widely for his integrity and the sincerity of his principles. But D. R. could see that in the circumstances of autumn 1935, with Labour confronted with an international situation that created questions about its pacifist principles that would only intensify in the following four years, it was a tragic reality that George Lansbury's vision of international understanding had been destroyed by the politics of 1930s Europe, and in which Britain's 'national' government stood complicit in all its sordid aspects.

As the PLP met to elect George Lansbury's successor, it fell to D. R. to propose that Clement Attlee, as deputy leader, should take charge for the election that Baldwin had called for 14 November.[69] This was seconded by Tom Williams and carried unanimously. Clement Attlee's position as deputy leader remained vacant. In the weeks leading up to polling day, Labour went on the attack, denouncing the 'national government' and its record over unemployment, the Means Test, and its failure to deal with the housing crisis. It had undermined the League of Nations, debased the principle of collective action, been weak in the face of Japanese aggression in the Far East and that of Mussolini in Abyssinia. A Labour government, on the other hand, would cooperate with the

League of Nations on the basis of a collective peace system, while maintaining sufficient defences pending a process of disarmament that would include the removal of national air forces and subject civil aviation to international control. This would be alongside a Socialist economic policy encompassing public ownership of banking, coal and its products, transport, electricity, iron, steel, and cotton, action to address the needs of the Special Areas, improved workers' rights, agricultural reform, reform of the education system, and vigorous changes to health services, including a specific commitment to combating maternal mortality. Once again it was a manifesto to which D. R. could ascribe without any difficulty at all.

In Gower, D. R. was opposed by Geoffrey Hutchinson, a London barrister whose campaign was full of thankful praise for the 'sane and honourable' representatives of the national government. 'Not only the country, but the whole world had confidence in the men who were at present in charge of our destinies.'[70] The government, he insisted, had kept Britain clear of a disastrous war against Italy in the Mediterranean at a time when those on the Labour benches had offered no consistent alternative policy. He implored on people to 'record their votes against Socialism', citing an industrial recovery that he attributed entirely to the national government.[71]

For D. R., cheered in Swansea as 'a man who deserves a government position', much of the election had to be spent away from the constituency, addressing meetings in Midsomer Norton, in the heart of the Somerset coalfield, before proceeding on a relentless tour that took him to Corwen in Merionethshire, Shrewsbury, Rhyl and King's Norton. As polling day approached he spent time closer to home, in Brecon, speaking for Leslie Haden Guest, and then to Merthyr Tydfil in support of S. O. Davies, an old acquaintance from the days of the ILP in Gorseinon. He made repeated visits to support Percy Morris in Swansea West, where the sitting Liberal-National member, Lewis Jones, had resorted to blistering personal attacks on his Labour opponent in an attempt to save his seat. One of his favourite accusations was that Labour's commitments on old age pensions represented a form of political bribery. This drew a forthright response from D. R. who declared, 'if that were true, then he [D. R.] stood before them as the greatest sinner of all.[72] He fought his last election with that promise in his election address. And he would fight every election as hard as he could until that was accomplished. If the member for Swansea West, and those who helped him in that kind of controversy, felt assured that that was corrupt, then for goodness sake let them close down politics. All politics was corrupt if every effort to sweeten the lives of the aged and infirm was corrupt.'[73]

The 'national' government he said, had won the biggest majority of any in living memory on the false pretences of dealing with unemployment, but it had failed to do anything for the distressed areas. He highlighted Labour's demand for public works schemes as a means of helping to deal with the crisis of unemployment, and demanded a radical and drastic policy to deal with international industrial and economy difficulties. This, he insisted, should include measures to increase the purchasing power of the country to stimulate consumption and demand.[74]

At the same time, he derided the national government's attempts to secure a mandate for 'Peace and Security' as nothing short of 'a fraud and deception on their part'.[75] D. R. insisted that the results of the Peace Ballot, and the response to the public meetings called as part of that campaign, demonstrated clearly that the government was out of step with public opinion. He maintained the need for loyalty to the League of Nations and a repudiation of any policy of 'unilateral rearmament'. Peace would only be secured by establishing peaceful coexistence with people in other countries and not by committing the country's resources to a wasteful arms race. The Labour Party, he told his audience, 'are all out for peace, but not a peace by the spending of large sums of money on armament, or by asking for a blank cheque to go on increasing armaments, but by the pooling of goodwill and by the co-operation among all people and all nations of the world. International action was needed to solve unemployment and it was Labour that would get the job done.'[76]

In the event, across Britain, Labour polled eight million votes, an increase of 1.6 million on 1931, but still well behind the Tories' 11.8 million. The number of Labour MPs increased to 154, while the Liberals returned 20. The Conservatives and their allies, with 432 MPs, still dominated the House of Commons. D. R. himself could take satisfaction in his own result in which he polled two-thirds of the vote to secure a majority of 13,393 over his 'national' opponent. Elsewhere in Wales, Labour, with a total of 396,000 votes, polled a similar percentage to 1931, but this disguised the party's real achievement because of the large number of Labour MPs who were returned unopposed in 1935. The election saw Daniel Hopkin return in Carmarthen and Robert Richards in Wrexham. In Britain as a whole, the party's vote increased by a fifth, even if the number of seats gained was disappointing. Labour was, however, much better placed to launch a challenge in a dozen or so other seats in Wales. This progress rested on the efforts of those who led the rump of Labour MPs re-elected in 1931, 'bearing the heat and burden of the days during the years of opposition'.[77] D. R. Grenfell could take pride in the part which he had played in that work, both inside and outside parliament, in one of his party's darkest periods.

CHAPTER 8

A Remarkable
and Gifted Man

A FORTNIGHT AFTER polling day, the PLP met to elect its leader for the new parliamentary session.[1] Once again, D. R. proposed Clement Attlee for the post and canvassed the support of the miners' group of MPs for his chosen man. This proved vital in ensuring that Attlee led in the first round with 58 votes, fourteen more than Herbert Morrison. Arthur Greenwood, who mustered 33 votes, was eliminated and most of his supporters switched to Attlee in the second round. Arthur Greenwood was then elected deputy leader. D. R., meanwhile, successfully sought re-election to the PLP Executive, securing fifth place among the dozen elected – only J. H. Clynes, Hugh Dalton, Tom Johnson and Herbert Morrison could garner more support among Labour MPs.[2]

Within days, D. R. faced a different type of challenge, when he was asked by the NCL to visit Vienna, along with John Parker, secretary of the New Fabian Research Bureau and MP for Romford, and the future Labour cabinet minister Elwyn Jones, who had previously spent six months based in Austria.[3] For years D. R. had taken a close interest in the development of the democratic states that emerged from the Austrian-Hungarian Empire. He had been deeply impressed by the achievements of the Social Democratic Party in Vienna where a fifth of the electorate were paid-up party members, and where the Left had presided over an impressive municipal programme and sustained vibrant social and cultural organisations that dominated the city's leisure and recreational life. The Wiener Höfe, replete with its parks and recreational facilities, health, childcare, and educational facilities, presaged a brave new Socialist world.[4]

But Red Vienna was not the whole of Austria. Even though Otto Bauer's Social Democrats polled more than two-fifths of the votes across the country in both 1927 and 1930, they remained a minority in parliament, out-voted by the representatives of rural, conservative, Catholic Austria in the Christian Social Party and other smaller parties of the Right. Moreover, by the end of 1933 Austria was surrounded by authoritarian right-wing regimes: Fascist Italy, the Gyula Gömbös regime in Hungary, and Nazi Germany. Political tensions within Austria, already evident in the rise of support for the Far Right following the economic crisis of 1931, intensified from January 1933 when railway workers intercepted Italian arms which they were convinced were destined to support fascist insurrection in Vienna. Two months later, in response to a national railway strike, Chancellor Engelbert Dollfuss declared a state of emergency and proceeded to establish rule by decree, and prevented the Austrian parliament from assembling. In the autumn, miners in the Upper Styria coalfield took strike action which was defeated with immense brutality. Faced with this situation, the Left abandoned Bauer's cautious approach and prepared for a general strike supported, if necessary, by armed insurrection. Sixteen days of civil war in February 1934 resulted in defeat for the Left's fighting forces. The Socialist leadership was exiled, mainly in Prague, and Dollfuss was able to enact a corporatist constitution modelled on Mussolini's Italy.

D. R. had visited Vienna immediately after the uprising and he met some of the leaders of the International Labour Defence organisation who were operating a clandestine network of support for those facing persecution from both the government and right-wing paramilitary groups. He had reported on his experiences in an interview with the *Daily Herald* in which he called for support for the Austrian Workers' Fund (which raised almost £12,000 within a matter of weeks, money that helped over 8,000 families whose breadwinners were in prison).[5] Shortly afterwards, he had again returned to Vienna in an unsuccessful attempt to resolve the controversy over the way the Society of Friends (which was permitted by the regime to operate openly) was distributing the money. Since then he had maintained close contact with Elwyn Jones and John Parker, and through them he developed a large circle of friends among the Austrian dissidents who had sought refuge in London. The three men also met Hugh Gaitskell and Naomi Mitchison, both of whom had spent long periods in Vienna, who warned them of what they could expect there on arrival: Socialists were subject to police surveillance, meetings were prohibited, and organised gangs were terrorising left-wing activists with the enthusiastic collusion of the police and government officials.[6]

They flew to Vienna after D. R. had abandoned his plans to watch Wales play the All Blacks, and were met by Sir Walford Selby, the British Ambassador, who advised them to abandon their mission. As John Parker recalled, 'He received us very formally and told us very firmly over drinks that we had wasted our time coming to Vienna, and the Chancellor would certainly not see us. David Grenfell nearly floored him by telling him we had an appointment next morning at 11am.'

Parker goes on to describe their arrival at the centre of Austrian government. 'It was a cold, sunny day when we went to the Chancellor's headquarters which was massively guarded – as we walked to the stairs machine guns were trained on us. We were then placed in a little ante-room where the previous Chancellor Dollfuss had been murdered by the Nazis... After receiving us, he [von Schuschnigg] asked David Grenfell to present our case. He listened nervously tossing his leg up and down in his shiny black boots while Schmidt (later I believe one of Hitler's interpreters) translated. When Schmidt cut out anything, Grenfell interrupted in German to insist on its inclusion.'

D. R. and his colleagues remained in Austria for a further three days during which they met many of the country's Socialist leaders, always under the watchful eye of plain clothes police. Discussions were arranged in cafés frequented by the Left, where the British delegation would be sent to reserved corner tables surrounded by members of the Social Democratic Party, out of earshot of the police or anyone else who might be eaves-dropping. These bodyguards included Dr W. Gifford, a prominent figure in the Socialist Medical Association in Vienna who had played a leading role organising medical aid to those injured in February 1934. A few years later, Parker and D. R. were instrumental in helping him to escape after the Anschluss to Britain where he established a practice in St Helens that pioneered mass radiography for workers at the Pilkington Glass factory.

The immediate outcome of the visit was a symbolic victory – von Schuschnigg agreed that all prisoners other that the men who had been armed at the time of their arrest, around 200 in total, would be released in time for Christmas 1935. But this was an empty gesture. Those deemed to be armed, whose number included many whose only 'crime' was to promote Socialist propaganda, remained in prison. Austria was but one example of what was happening across Europe and, for D. R., it was time that the British Left alerted public opinion to the reality already facing millions of oppressed people throughout the continent. He told the *Daily Herald* that a political tyranny ruled in Austria, where the police enjoyed unprecedented power, but that the workers were determined to continue their fight for political and trade union rights.[7]

In Skewen he warned his audience that Europe could be heading for war unless action was taken, warning that small states were being forced along a programme of attempting to achieve economic self-sufficiency though burdened with external obligations, and were therefore easy prey to neighbouring oppressors.[8] He coupled his message with a consistent refrain of the idiocy of the mad race to rearm.[9] D. R. was scornful of the British government's approach and reserved special contempt for the Foreign Secretary, Samuel Hoare, who he believed was doing nothing but giving succour to dictatorships across the continent.[10] The government, he insisted offered, 'no indication of any effective policy for the restoration and maintenance of peace, the reduction of armaments by international agreement, or the removal of the economic causes of war'.[11]

It was a sentence that encapsulated D. R.'s standpoint on foreign affairs. The British government was a mere bystander on the European stage, watching as fascist regimes across the continent were flouting international agreements and ignoring what machinery existed to enforce them. He remained firmly opposed to any military solution – that represented the failure of politics and diplomacy at huge human cost – but called for robust international political action to prevent fascist regimes from interfering in other states, coupled with support for the political movements that challenged them in their own countries. This was not a matter of appeasement nor a matter of rearmament, and it was a political argument to which D. R. adhered even though it was severely tested by the events of the following three years.

*

Upon his return from Vienna, D. R. threw himself into the campaign launched by the MFGB in support of a national agreement on wages and working conditions.[12] At the time of the 1935 general election, Britain's miners voted overwhelmingly in favour of strike action in a national ballot, with 93 per cent across all coalfields and a 95 per cent vote in south Wales. Shrewdly, this threat of industrial action coincided with an effort to appeal to society's conscience through a campaign of public education designed to alert civil society to the amount of money being taken by retailers and middlemen, as well as profiteering by industrial consumers of coal.

Throughout that autumn D. R. had used his platform both inside and outside parliament in support of the miners. The collier's value not being acknowledged was one of D. R.'s constant themes, and the problems confronting the industry stemmed from the way it was organised under private ownership.[13] He dwelt on how vast profits were being made by major customers, such as the electricity and gas producers, at a time when the coalfields were crippled by unemployment and the miners barely subsisting.[14] Faced with the refusal of the Mining Association to concede a national agreement, the MFGB resolved to issue notices from mid-January. D. R. was convinced that, on this occasion, the miners enjoyed public sympathy. He told the University Labour Federation in Cardiff that, 'the men working in this industry, given better conditions, can run this industry very much better than it has been run in the past. I have known no industry in which there is more technical inefficiency and where there has been so much waste, and I am perfectly convinced that it would be of infinite advantage to the industry if a large measure of workers' control were adopted.'[15] The threat of strike action was enough to instigate negotiations between the larger colliery companies and some of their main consumers – including most of the large steel and tinplate manufacturers, the gas industry and other bulk purchasers, such as ICI, who relented to an increase in the price of coal in order to allow for a wage increase.

However, the agreement varied by district and had minimal impact in areas, like south Wales, which were most dependent on the export market. A proposal made by Jim Griffiths, president of the SWMF, to continue the fight until a national agreement was reached was rejected by the MFGB leadership. D. R. shared the SWMF's frustration, but bitter experience of history had taught him that industrial action under such circumstances as existed in south Wales in 1935–36 would be futile. Instead, he joined those who sought to make use of the propaganda weapon, using his column in *Labour* magazine to highlight the agreement's deficiencies, in particular the disparities that existed across the different coalfields, and demanding international arrangements to share world markets.[16]

*

By the start of 1936 he had also accepted an appointment to the Royal Commission on Safety in the Mines, set up in response to the Gresford disaster, which for D. R. offered an opportunity to grapple with some of the most serious issues confronting the British coal mining industry. The Commission's terms of reference required it to examine 'whether the safety and health of mine workers can be better ensured by extending or modifying the principles or general provisions of the Coal Mines Act, 1911, or the arrangements for its administration, having regard to the changes that have taken place in organization, methods of work, and equipment since it became law, and the experience gained.'[17] D. R. sat alongside ten other members – Lord Rockley, a former Tory MP descended from Lord Salisbury, Sir Malcolm Delevingne, a retired Home Office civil servant who had specialised in workplace safety; Sir Henry Walker, Judge George Allesbrook, a mining engineer who held various positions within the industry; Edward Brown and W. H. Tefler, both directors of colliery companies; John Walker, a colliery manager; Ebby Edwards, secretary of the MFGB; W. T. Miller, president of the Firemen, Enginemen and Deputies' Association; and John Walker. Over a 14-month period they gathered evidence from a total of 53 witnesses, together with a significant body of written evidence, including legislation from other countries, official reports and an array of research evidence.[18]

During its sittings, D. R. questioned witness after witness on a whole range of issues which he knew needed to be addressed if the Commission's work was to make any difference to the lives of those working in the British coal mining industry. In doing so, he focused on the details: the basis on which calculations of accidents were undertaken should be changed so that it was done on the total number rather than the number per ton produced to take account of increases in output per man shift; the rate of accidents in mines where conveyors were used instead of loading by hand; the dangers caused by the use of electricity underground; the possible use of compressed air as an alternative; the link between low wages paid to electricians in the industry and the rate of accidents; instances where existing safety proposals had not been implemented; and the magnitude of the situation whereby one in five miners suffered an accident requiring them to be away from work for three days or more every year.[19] He rounded on those who sought to attribute safety problems to 'human error' on the part of the miners, and pressed witnesses about the right of workmen to prosecute mine-owners in the same way that managers were allowed to prosecute workmen for safety breaches.[20]

He gave full vent to the deep frustrations felt in British mining communities. When Dr S. W. Fisher, the Medical Inspector of Mines, gave evidence, D. R. was totally dissatisfied with his efforts to skirt around the cause of lung diseases. 'While the experts fail to agree on the general causes of silicosis, there are men dying of this dreadful disease,' was his retort to the doctor.[21] In April 1936 he was involved in heated exchanges with Thomas Ashley, Divisional Inspector of Mines for the Swansea Division. 'Have you had many complaints from the men that they have to work in gas in the pits in your division?' D. R. asked. 'No, we have had very few,' Thomas Ashley replied. D. R. continued, 'When you find that ventilation is bad and that the presence of gas is suspected, do you consult the men at all?' Thomas Ashley replied, 'No'. D. R. then asked, 'Are the men allowed to work in ignorance?' Thomas Ashley, 'If it necessary to withdraw the men they are withdrawn.'[22] D. R. then asked Thomas Ashley whether he paid any attention to complaints sent in by workmen regarding the presence of gas. When Ashley denied that any such reports had been received, D. R. raised the specific example of the North Navigation collieries in his area, but Thomas Ashley refused to be drawn.[23]

Thomas Ashley's underlying social attitudes were captured by Ben Francis who covered the exchanges in detail on behalf of the *Daily Worker*. On 8 April 1936 he reported:

> There were several heated arguments at the Royal Commission on Safety in Mines when it resumed yesterday morning at the Caxton Hall, Westminster, between Mr D. R. Grenfell MP and Mr T. Ashley, Divisional Inspector of Mines for the Swansea Division, who continued his evidence before the Commissioners. Mr Ashley's attitude of antagonism to Mr Grenfell and Ebby Edwards, the two members representing the miners out of 11 members on the Commission, is in striking contrast to his unctuous 'My Lord' when replying to the Commissioner. Time and time again, Mr Ashley replied to even the most elementary questions put to him by Mr Grenfell and Ebby Edwards by saying 'I didn't know' or 'I have no information', or he had not considered the question. This is the most unsatisfactory witness yet to appear before the Commission, and it was a waste of time to question him.[24]

Later that month, D. R. again clashed with Thomas Ashley over the question of measures to prevent silicosis, which he insisted had only been introduced when mine-owners realised the extent of their liabilities for workmen's compensation.

True to Ben Francis' description, Ashley refused to be drawn other than to admit there was a problem.[25]

As the inquiry progressed, D. R. pursued issues around the right of miners to carry out their own safety inspections by electing men to examine conditions and identify potential dangers. When Sir Alfred Faulkner, Permanent Under-Secretary for Mines, appeared to deny allegations that colliery companies were refusing to facilitate such inspections, D. R. leapt to the attack.[26] He clashed with E. H. Frazer, Divisional Inspector for Scotland, who had alleged that workmen's inspections were being manipulated for political reasons, and he criticised the lack of attention to injured miners, drawing on his own experience in evidence.[27] Some of the bitterest exchanges occurred when George Spencer, of the Nottinghamshire Miners' Industrial Union, appeared before the Commissioners. The leader of the 1926 breakaway union believed that the right of the men to undertake inspections should be removed and replaced by a system of teams consisting of workmen, owners' representatives and government appointees. These teams, he insisted, should be selected and not elected. Spencer's claim, that men were obtaining the role of workmen's inspectors through popularity rather than by ability to carry out the job, infuriated D. R. as a libel on the body of mineworkers and, if George Spencer's suggestions were implemented, 'You might as well have a board of burglars and housebreakers to elect the policeman.'[28]

Likewise, when W. J. Charlton, Inspector of Mines for the area that included Wrexham, appeared before the Commission, D. R. ignored the chairman's ruling not to focus on the specifics of the Gresford disaster and raised the question of the fire damp at the colliery before the explosion, insisting that an accumulation of gas should not have been allowed to happen. W. J. Charlton replied, 'That I don't know'.[29] D. R. understood fully that W. J. Charlton was attempting to use his appearance before the Royal Commission – before Henry

Walker summed up the evidence in the Gresford inquiry – to pre-empt its conclusions. The Royal Commission was receiving the evidence of the father of the man who was responsible for bringing the colliery into profitable production, on behalf of the company that sought to minimise its liability towards the families of nearly 300 miners who had lost their lives in the disaster, and D. R. was not about to be hoodwinked by such an obvious ploy. Furthermore, W. J. Charlton's subterfuge reinforced what D. R. already knew about the relationship between the Mines Inspectorate and the colliery owners, and provided proof, if any were needed, of the need for radical changes in the way safety and working practices in British collieries were overseen.

An attempt was made to visit the scene of the disaster on 6 February when D. R., along with other representatives of NWMA and the Mines Inspectorate, spent over three hours in the Gresford colliery trying to access the affected area in advance of the inquiry re-opening, but they were unable to gain access into the Dennis shaft.[30] This could have added essential testimony but, in any event, Sir Stafford Cripps as their counsel was able to present a damning indictment on the owners and managers of the colliery in his summing-up statement which extended to over 150,000 words. Sir Stafford Cripps' case centred on the issue of ventilation and the fact that an additional intake was required but had not been provided. As a result, coal dust had been carried up the ventilation current and had built up. He was personally scathing of the manager who 'rarely visited the face in the Dennis District. He appeared indifferent to the evidence of deterioration in the airways and the falling off in the volume of ventilation.' Later, when Hartley Shawcross (himself a Labour MP in due course and prosecutor at Nuremburg) summed up on behalf of the company and sought to undermine the credibility of much of the miners' testimony, D. R., sitting alongside Sir Stafford Cripps, did not conceal his anger. In his notes, D. R. scorned the young barrister's entire case and dismissed as nonsense his contention that there was adequate attention to safety at the pit.[31]

*

In between sessions of the Royal Commission, D. R. played a full part on the opposition front bench shouldering much of the work on unemployment and the industrial situation. No matter how much the government sought to boast of economic recovery, the reality in south Wales, as in so many other parts of industrial Britain, was of prolonged mass unemployment and destitution, while the government responded by telling those young, fit and able enough to do so to move to wherever there was work. Amid escalating criticism of the UAB, the PLP used an Easter adjournment debate to denounce the government's treatment of the unemployed and the specific practices used by officers responsible for implementing the UAB regulations.[32] Opening the debate, D. R. did not spare the rod, castigating the UAB as an unelected and unaccountable organisation whose guiding principle was, above all, to save money and cut the cost of relief. The UAB was practically immune from any political accountability. More than four and a half million people were being forced to exist below the recognised minimum required to put food on the table. Families were being tormented by enquiries from officials taken 'almost to the point of indecency' while 'the good appearance of a house is a disability to the applicant' and 'neatness and evidence of family pride constitute a save-ability, and the applicant receives less on that account. The person who has striven and struggled and made sacrifices to avoid incurring debts is under a disability.'[33] Meanwhile, the Exchequer was collecting more than ever in death duties – a clear sign that the rich were getting richer amid the poverty suffered by others.[34]

The following month he joined more than 20 Labour MPs who signed a letter to the Minister of Labour demanding the abolition of the Means Test.[35] Their protest made no impression on the government which introduced new regulations to the Commons at the beginning of July. Immediately D. R., along with George Hall and George Daggar, attended a meeting of the SWMF Executive to report on their implications, declaring that the proposals would have a particularly inimical effect in south Wales given the high concentration of unemployed, and warning that family break-up would undoubtedly ensue.[36] Later, the Joint Unemployment Council for South Wales met the NCL to agree a plan for another united campaign that was to start with an 'all-in' conference at the end of August to include representatives of the Labour Party, trade union organisations, the Communist Party, the ILP, co-operative societies, the British Legion, unemployed organisations and chambers of trade, among others. They gathered at the Cory Hall in Cardiff where Jim Griffiths, speaking from the chair, reported on the discussions with the NCL. He was followed by D. R. who, reviewing the parliamentary discussions, warned that the government's actions represented a subtle form of British fascism. [37]

As was the case nearly 18 months earlier during the first weeks of 1935, large meetings were held in protest at the new regulations. D. R. addressed a crowded meeting in Swansea where he denounced the unfairness of the new scales.[38] Some weeks later, the Joint Unemployment Council organised a march to London and vociferous protests were made to the Ministry of Labour. D. R. supported their arguments on the floor of the Commons, where he denounced the government's total failure to tackle the question of unemployment.[39] Its legislative programme was, he said, designed to do nothing for the unemployed or those on low wages, but instead protect the interests of the rich and comfortable owning classes. Paying tribute to an earlier speech by Ellen Wilkinson, he highlighted the 'spectre of decay' in Jarrow and the 'complete collapse of industry and of industrial existence' there and in the other Special Areas. Labour would not allow the government to disregard the disgraceful state to which Jarrow and Merthyr Tydfil had been allowed to deteriorate. The government's policy towards the Special Areas was totally inadequate. A government elected by the richest and most comfortable in Britain, committed to safeguarding the interests of the owning classes, could not possibly offer a solution to the problems of those areas suffering from the collapse of industry.[40] Across whole swathes of the country 'there is evidence... of the undermining of the physical constitution of the people who live there. The government had created a situation whereby one half of the people were unable to buy 9s. worth of food in a week, leaving millions under-fed, and undermining the physical constitution of those who lived there.'[41] The Means Test had taken more money out of south Wales than the Special Areas Commissioner had ever been given to pour in as investment.

> We have made them poorer and poorer, and poorer. We are receiving no assistance at all from the government in our period of trial and difficulty. The people are waiting in pathetic and tragic anticipation for alternative employment of some kind. What shall the answer be? What is the answer that we shall have in this debate? What will the Right Hon. gentlemen say next week when he goes to south Wales, to be received as courteously as he would be in any part of the country? Those people have not forgotten their good manners in these days of distress but let him not mistake that courtesy for effusive affection. They distrust him, and whoever accompanies him will share their disfavour.[42]

*

Throughout this period D. R. kept up his close involvement in the Labour Party's international work through his membership of the NCL and several working groups within the PLP, and it fell to him to become chairman of the Labour group of the India League as the implications of the India Act, passed by the national government in 1935, were becoming apparent.[43] As the British Raj resorted to its own brand of authoritarian repression, D. R. used parliamentary privilege to highlight cases of oppression referred by the India League, in particular the case of M. R. Masani, joint secretary of the All-India Socialist Movement, whose movements within the Commonwealth were restricted by order of the India Office.[44] D. R. insisted that it was Masani who spoke for the millions of Indian Socialists, whose strength had been demonstrated in the 1936 legislative elections. He endorsed Masani's central message that political independence alone was not sufficient, and that private ownership, even by Indian nationals, would lead to continued exploitation. For D. R., M. R. Masani offered a more realistic analysis of India's need than that voiced by Gandhi who appeared to offer little more than a policy of returning to the villages as an answer to India's problems. M. R. Masani, on the other hand, demanded action to meet the problems of the large crowded cities, maintaining that, 'If India follows Mahatma Gandhi's economic prescription, it will remain internationally weak and militarily defenceless... Rather than level down the plane of existence to that of the rustic, let us prevent the growth of inequality by harnessing the genii of machine to the chariot of State control and planned economy. That is the Socialist alternative to the Romanticist solution of Mahatma Gandhi.'[45]

It was natural that D. R. played a prominent role when Jawaharlat Nehru, newly released from prison, visited Britain in February 1936. He joined Sir Stafford Cripps, Aldous Huxley, John Jagger, Harold Laski, Tom Williams, Ellen Wilkinson, and Sehri Saklatvala at a large meeting in the Caxton Hall to welcome the Congress leader. Nehru's uncompromising message was that what was happening in the sub-continent, at the behest of the British, mirrored the behaviour of the fascist regimes in Europe.[46] Politics in India, he declared, was not a profession but an irresistible urge. The India Act, he insisted, would not bring peace. What was needed was a programme of social and economic reform.[47] It was a message that D. R. had no problem in endorsing and he accompanied Nehru a few days later when he repeated his stance of outright opposition to the India Act at a subsequent meeting at the House of Commons.[48]

That spring D. R., along with three other parliamentary colleagues, took the opportunity to visit Soviet Russia. After a stormy voyage across the North Sea, then the Kiel Canal and the Gulf of Finland, the delegation toured the Russian mainland for a week where they enjoyed the hospitality of the Soviet authorities – receptions at the Kremlin and the British Embassy followed by visits to art galleries and the state theatre. Their hosts proved less enthusiastic when D. R. insisted on visiting churches in Moscow where he witnessed packed congregations. His stubbornness may have been one of the reasons why he was the only one of the MPs not to receive a ticket for the annual May Day celebrations in Red Square. Undaunted, he again strained Russian hospitality by insisting on visiting a collective farm. This required a journey to Kharkov (nowadays Kharkiv, Ukraine) where the delegates could see for themselves the working of a model of agricultural organisation. But no amount of Soviet propaganda could conceal what he saw en route – the main reason why he had wanted to travel there – which convinced him that all was not well in the workers' paradise. There was no hiding the poverty of the countryside or the primitive conditions that afflicted the rural areas.

The men returned home via Warsaw and Berlin where the crescendo of persecution and hatred to which the Jews were being subjected was already evident. For D. R. it was incomprehensible that a minority community, representing a mere one per cent of the German population of the Austria and Germany, could become the focus of such intense and irrational hatred. He recalled, 'I have asked myself time and time again why should the 99 show such malevolence against the one? Why should not the 99 so order their lives that it is possible for the one to live in peace among them? I have never been able to understand why that could not be done. The Jews have done much to enrich that country, and not merely by money. Money is not all to the Jews. The Jew is sometimes charged with being a very acquisitive person, but nobody gives more readily of the fruits of his labours than the Jew does when he gets the opportunity. He has given much to Germany and has given much to the world in the arts, in literature and in science.'[49]

He redoubled his efforts on behalf of the victims of Nazi tyranny and maintained a regular correspondence with leading Social Democrats in both Austria and Germany. He joined a cross-party campaign to secure the release, or trial, of Ernst Thälmann, the German Communist leader who had been imprisoned by the Nazis, and late the same year joined those demanding action against the German government following the execution of Edgar André.[50] The extent to which the German authorities had been concerned about his activities on behalf of dissidents in the country was revealed by a bizarre event in Hamburg in June 1936, when a prominent British Communist, Major Grenfell (late of the Royal Army Medical Corps), arrived to witness the trial of Edgar André but was arrested by the Gestapo before he could attend the court. He was then subjected to a seven-hour interrogation before being ordered to leave the country, during which they produced a vast dossier which turned out to contain information not about the Major but about his namesake, David Rhys Grenfell.[51]

Against this background, the Labour Party remained steadfast that international cooperation was the only solution to the situation engulfing continental Europe and that there should be no resorting to force. When the National Peace Congress convened in Leeds, its platform included trade union and cooperative organisations who viewed the League of Nations as the guarantor of peace and were totally opposed to rearmament. D. R. subscribed to this policy fully and unconditionally, scarred as he was by the experience of the Great War. He was Mansel's brother, and also close to those in Gorseinon, Loughor and Pontarddulais who had opposed the war on political or religious grounds, for whom military action was never a solution to international conflict. Economically and industrially, the Great War had been a cataclysm for the British working class and the cause of the misery to which industrial Britain had been subjected ever since. D. R. was among those who addressed the Labour Party's demonstration for peace in Hyde Park on Sunday, 28 June 1936 (a separate gathering but coinciding with the National Peace Congress), where he condemned the government's betrayal of the League of Nations and its decision to abandon sanctions, and called for the hand of friendship to be extended to the German people.[52]

But the reality of the European situation in the summer of 1936 forced the Labour Party to face the question of whether it could adhere to the principle of total rejection of military means of resolving international situations. The Left in Britain had reason to celebrate the election of the Popular Front government in Spain in February 1936 as a glimmer of hope, when country after country was falling victim to fascist dictatorship. They therefore watched with foreboding when rebel Spanish generals marched on Madrid while an elected government had to resort to arming its own supporters to repel the insurrectionists. As someone who had been part of the SWMF's efforts to provide support for the miners in the Asturias coalfield in north-west Spain in 1934, D. R. was aware of the brutality of Spain's reactionary forces and the carnage that was now being unleashed on the whole country.

The British government's policy of 'non-intervention', with its operation entrusted to an international committee, was merely evading the question.[53]

As General Franco's forces captured a large swathe of western Spain with the open support of Europe's fascist regimes, non-intervention was clearly a byword for a refusal to intervene in support of the elected government.[54] No other response could be expected from the men Britain had returned to power in November 1935, but Labour too found it increasingly difficult to justify its position. D. R. sensed the dissatisfaction in the months leading up to the Labour Party's annual conference in Edinburgh in October, where the depth of feeling among the rank and file could not be concealed.[55] Why, delegates demanded, should an elected government not be supported against an illegal armed insurrection by rebel generals? It fell to D. R. to second the NEC resolution that reiterated Labour's commitment to the decisions of the Socialist International in Paris the previous month. The party's position, he reminded delegates, had been adopted in response to requests by the Popular Front government in France that any escalation of the conflict would result in war with Germany. Britain had been at fault for not supporting the Spanish government earlier, when its intervention could have tipped the balance against the fascists, but this did not happen and that reality, caused by its failure, had to be faced. Crucially, any alternative course to the one being pursued by the party leadership risked escalation to world war.[56] As the debate continued, he was supported by Arthur Greenwood and Ernest Bevin, and Arthur Deakin on behalf of the Transport and General Workers Union (TGWU), but denounced by the MFGB, including delegates from the SWMF who insisted that Gower's MP did not speak for them. Under such circumstances, it was little consolation that the leadership position was carried by 1.8 million to 519,000 votes.[57]

Publicly, at least, D. R. adhered to the official Labour view, reiterating the line agreed collectively by the Labour leadership. As Darren Leeworthy has highlighted however, his own view was that a pacifist response, while genuinely reflective of Labour's abhorrence of war, was no answer to the situation engulfing Spain.[58] This was clear from the views he expressed in the confines of the NCL Executive meetings, where he argued that the government should raise the arms embargo to enable the Spanish people to obtain the necessary material and arms (a position close to that of the MFGB which had mandated their group of MPs to advance those arguments).[59] However, in parliament and open meetings he remained more guarded, verging on the facile, warning of a drift to war because of the government's failure to promote a collective peace system to defy Europe's dictators, insisting on the need for unity against fascism (but short of working with other parties in Britain) and insisting that, if Spain fell, France and Belgium could soon follow suit.[60] He was walking a tightrope, compelled to adhere to the leadership position (unlike Aneurin Bevan or Jim Griffiths who were both free to speak from the back benches), knowing full well that any resignation from the PLP Executive over the issue would be a futile gesture that would only provoke a crisis for the government to exploit. Given all that he had done to rebuild the PLP over the previous five years, such a course of action was unthinkable.

In the meantime, volunteers from across Britain, but particularly from south Wales, joined the International Brigades on the battlefields. There they witnessed at first hand that the notion of non-intervention was a clear fallacy. The fascist forces could count on a steady supply of Italian and German armaments and military personnel, while the elected government was starved of resources. For D. R., it was time for British parliamentarians to see that reality for themselves. He instigated a parliamentary delegation to visit Spain, which left for Paris at the end of November despite efforts by Tory whips to prevent any government MPs from going.[61] Their aim was ostensibly to investigate the condition of the civilian population, prisoners, the sick and the wounded, and were granted safe passage by the Spanish government. To D. R. it offered an opportunity to try to uncover a much broader range of issues.[62] From Paris the MPs travelled to Toulouse (where they were stranded for two days due to difficult flying conditions), and then landed in Barcelona where D. R. took part in a mass demonstration in honour of the Popular Front leader, José Buenaventura Durrutti, who had been killed the previous day. They then drove by escorted cavalcade to Valencia where they met political leaders including Julio Álvarez de Vayo, the Foreign Minister, Indalecio Prieto, the Minister of Air, Manuel de Irujo, the Basque leader and José Giral, the former Prime Minister.

They had an eventful time in Madrid where they experienced at first hand the effect of the Fascist bombardment both from the air and through continuous artillery which D. R. heard each evening from his hotel. A shell fell yards away as they were leaving the building.[63] They were lucky to escape with their lives that time but then four of the contingent – D. R. among them – narrowly escaped death a second time when another shell landed on the spot where the ambulance in which they were travelling had been standing a moment before during an inspection of the devastated areas.[64]

Upon his return, D. R. described the reality of life in Madrid where the civilian population was terrified by the atrocities inflicted upon them, and drew particular attention to the use of foreign aeroplanes there:

We noted that the people of Madrid were enduring the daily and nightly attacks with great calmness and courage, although strongly resenting the destruction of large areas of dwellings, which were the target of the insurgent aircraft. We saw evidence of damage to large blocks of dwellings in the heart of the city. Each day and in various ways we came into contact with the people; we visited hospitals, prisons, and shelters for homeless people, and we grew to admire the courage and self-control maintained by the population in their trying circumstances... There was fierce resentment against the use of foreign aeroplanes and guns in the attack on Madrid.

A quarter of the city's houses had been destroyed, and the western fringes had to be evacuated due to the bombing. Basements and underground stations were packed with sleepers and there was an urgent need for gas masks and international relief due to the shortage of food and fuel. The city's public health infrastructure had been decimated, communication virtually impossible, and evacuation hindered by the fact that there was simply no place for people to go.

On their return the group sought to produce a report that would reflect some form of consensus among MPs with widely different views about the conflict. In it they concentrated on the lack of emergency accommodation, the scarcity of air raid shelters, and the state of the hospitals which they found to be close to breaking point. Houses were being destroyed by 'Caproni and Junker bombing planes'. They explicitly referred to the clear evidence of German and Italian involvement, describing how, 'We talked with one prisoner of war, an Italian, who stated that he was a serving soldier in a Rome artillery regiment, and that others were sent with him[65]... The bombardment seems to have had exactly the opposite effect to that intended, and every bomb dropped by German and Italian planes increases, if possible, the hatred that characterises the struggle.'[66] At the same time they refuted allegations that prisoners were being mistreated at the hands of the Spanish government. 'We firmly believe that all those in authority under the Government are sincerely determined to do their best to stamp out unjustifiable detention and illegal executions.'[67] They called on 'all democrats' to support the civilian evacuation of Madrid and called on Britain to make provisions to follow the example of France and agree to accommodate 50,000 Spanish children. Such measures, they wrote, should be accompanied by the provision of gas masks, food and fuel.[68]

In addition to compiling their report, the MPs convened a meeting attended by more than 20 organisations already working in Spain. It met at the House of Commons shortly before Christmas 1936 to determine a way of increasing their efforts.[69] D. R. warned those present that thousands risked dying of starvation if Madrid continued to be sieged because of the 'wanton destruction of human life by the air raids' whereby 'old men, women and children have been killed and more than one-third of the working-class houses in Madrid are already levelled by bombing and by fire'.[70] There was, he said, a real threat of starvation and epidemics. What was required was a large-scale plan for the evacuation of Madrid to remove half of the 1.4 million people who were now living there as a result of the arrival of refugees from elsewhere in Spain.[71] Those discussions subsequently led to the establishment of the National Joint Committee for Spanish Relief as a means of coordinating the work of various humanitarian, Christian, and medical groups whose primary aim was the relief of suffering. D. R. became one of its three honorary secretaries, along with Captain John MacNamara and Wilfred Roberts, with the Duchess of Athol becoming Chairman and a staff of organising secretaries appointed to take responsibility for its day-to-day activities. Its work included supporting emergency evacuation, coordinating food parcels, medical work, convalescent homes, distributing mail and other humanitarian activities. It worked alongside others, such as the Foreign Service Council, the Save the Children Fund, Spanish Medical Aid Committee, the Youth Friendship Committee, and local organisations. Its work, and that of its associated bodies, became the focus of much of D. R.'s activities for the next 18 months.

CHAPTER 9

A Man of Real Ability

IN A PUBLISHED diary entry for June 1937, Thomas Jones, the former Deputy Secretary to the Cabinet, referred to a conversation with David Lloyd George during a weekend at the latter's home at Churt, during which the former Prime Minister had offered his observations on the leading political figures of the day. Jones recalled Lloyd George as saying that, 'No-one living today [was] built on the scale of Gladstone and with his courage. Attlee made a miserable surrender over the Government's Profits Tax. Herbert Morrison showed great parliamentary skill in the Charing Cross Bridge debate… David Grenfell had real ability and was straight. Nothing generous to say about Aneurin Bevan. Arthur Greenwood was always complaining.'[1]

The comment on D. R. reflected his profile both in the House of Commons and in the country at large over the previous year. During that period, the situation in Spain and its wider implications for peace in Europe had occupied an increasing amount of his time. Shortly before Christmas 1936, D. R. again crossed to the Continent to attend a conference convened in Paris to consider the situation in Spain and the response of the British and French governments. Immediately afterwards he embarked on an arduous schedule of public meetings held by disparate organisations which, in some way or another, were seeking to provide support for the Spanish people. He went to Birmingham to raise money on behalf of Spanish children at an event where Eduard Sõrmus, the violinist who D. R. remembered from the ILP days in Gorseinon, played Spanish items with the support of the Birmingham Cooperative Orchestra.[2] Within days of the new year, D. R. was in Cardiff where he gave a vivid description of the scene in Spain, depicting how hordes of German 'tourists' were leaving their homeland in plus fours to arrive in Spain in khaki uniforms.[3] He was a natural choice to address the mass demonstration called by the London Trades Council in support of the Spanish people on 11 January 1937, before appearing at a meeting organised by Hackney Citizens' Council, in support of the Spanish Medical Aid funds, at the Mile End Baths three days later.[4] The following month he joined International Brigadier Ken White at a meeting in Battersea Town Hall, and watched as three buses arranged by the National Joint Committee left Westminster filled with milk, food and clothing for refugees still in Spain.[5]

By January 1937, D. R. made no pretence that the notion of non-intervention was anything but a fallacy. Writing in *Labour*, he warned, 'If non-intervention does not safeguard the rights of the Spanish people, then the pact should be honourably set aside so that democracies in Europe might combine to give the Spanish people and the Government the means of preserving their rights against the usurpers at home and their Fascist allies.'[6] When the House of Commons discussed the issue on 19 January 1937, Clement Attlee provided a forensic analysis of the government's duplicity, challenging Foreign Secretary Anthony Eden over the government's use of the Foreign Enlistment Act to prevent men from volunteering on the Republican side, while at the same time ignoring those who were heading to Franco's aid. He also mocked ministers' insistence that German and Italian troops in Spain were 'volunteers' and did not constitute any significant German involvement in the country. D. R. was in combative mood when he rose later in the debate, reminding MPs that a legitimate government enjoying an overwhelming parliamentary majority had been subverted by an illegitimate force bereft of any legal status.[7] Tory claims that General Franco enjoyed the support of the Spanish people were not borne out by the facts – where were Franco's triumphs, if that was the case? Why had he been stopped at the gates of Madrid? In the lands controlled by the Falangists, Catholics were displaying a level of intolerance, violence and cruelty not seen since the days of the inquisition. Allegations that shiploads of arms were being transported by rail by the Popular Front government in France did not bear scrutiny – as a glance at the map would prove. The reality was that shiploads of arms were being taken directly to Spanish ports from Germany and Italy.[8] It was not a class war, but a battle for freedom and constitutional liberty, not a civil war but an international war fought on Spanish soil.[9]

Two months later D. R. returned to the theme, arguing that a policy of non-intervention had to be respected on both sides if it was to work, but that was not the reality in Spain. The Non-Intervention Committee, established by the Western European powers to monitor the situation the previous summer, was totally ineffective and relied on the word of governments that could not be believed:

> I believed in July and August that non-intervention was a sound policy... we have relied on the good word of various governments; we have kept to the pretence of the Non-Intervention Committee and of trusting one another, but it is all a farce. It was a great offence to this House to have it believe that there was a bona fide attempt by 27 nations to carry out the pledge not to intervene in Spain. I do not believe a single nation has carried out the pledge quite properly, although I believe this country has been closest to perfection in this respect. Non-intervention has never been a fact, and there has been intervention by almost every one of the signatories.[10]

Only a genuine withdrawal of all foreign influences from Spain, allowing the Spanish people the freedom to resolve their own internal matters, could be taken as genuine non-intervention.

Practical help was also required through humanitarian efforts to relieve the suffering. This is what D. R. had in mind in an article in *Labour* in March 1937 in which he described the pitiful sight of sick and enfeebled refugees fleeing to the cities, the perpetual epidemics and breakdown of health and medical facilities. 'Our task and duty is to relieve suffering and distress in that ravaged country. Many thousands have made the supreme sacrifice in Spain – not all of them on the actual battlefield.' He asked for donations of a shilling from every Labour Party member, calling on everyone who recognised the struggle against a cynical and brutal military force to rally to the cause.[11]

This suffering was the intended consequence of General Franco's naval blockade of the Bay of Biscay, designed as a means of cutting supplies to the republicans in the north. D. R. had used the publicity surrounding the case of the Cardiff skipper David John Jones – 'Potato Jones' – as further evidence of the government's duplicity in relation to non-intervention.[12] Potato Jones operated the *Marie Llewellyn* from Cardiff docks, and had established trade with the Basque region by exporting coal and importing iron ore. In common with other ships headed for the ports of Bilbao, Gijón and Santander, the *Marie Llewellyn* had been detained at Saint-Jean-de-Luz despite having charters and commercial contracts with the other ports. The British government refused to take any action, merely warning vessels not to enter the ports in case they were mined. As Hywel Francis has noted, Potato Jones was not one to be thwarted by a Spanish blockade. When Samuel Hoare, as First Lord of the Admiralty, made a lame attempt to defend the government's position in parliament, D. R. seized the opportunity to launch a tirade against the government front bench. He had not been satisfied by a single utterance by any minister in the House for the previous four or five days, he told MPs. While government ministers insisted on freedom for shipping to enter ports in southern Spain controlled by Franco, they had no intention of breaking the blockade in the waters around northern Spain.[13] This was a direct result of the influence of Franco's supporters in the British parliament.

He demanded that the government instruct the Royal Navy to give protection to ensure free access to all waters, insisting that failure to do so would constitute a humanitarian crime against the Basque people. 'If the Basque people are brought to surrender weeks and months from now by the privations of their people, with the food ships standing here, food ships for which money has been paid… the responsibility will fall upon the government and upon this House.'[14]

On 26 April, Fascist cruelty reached new heights when civilians were subjected to a brutal attack by land and air in Guernica. Within days, D. R. raised the atrocity on the floor of the Commons and demanded an international investigation into the events that would establish the nationality of the pilots.[15] Why was it, he asked, that Italian troops were being transferred from Liguria to Spain while Mussolini's government protested its innocence under the non-intervention pact?[16] No treaty he could remember had been evaded so palpably as this one. Spanish Fascists were removing an elected government and replacing its constitution with the open support of foreign powers.

Throughout the summer, D. R. worked tirelessly to help refugees fleeing Spain through the National Joint Committee for Spanish Relief and by addressing Labour and cooperative gatherings in England.[17] He demanded that the British government should grant protection to the vessels sent to rescue refugees from northern Spain. He also highlighted the humanitarian crisis that had engulfed the port of Bilbao, which was at breaking point in the months leading up to the fall of the city in June 1937 as people waited for vessels to carry them to safety. Matters intensified further in August as refugees tried to escape from the Basque country, prompting a group of eminent public figures in Britain, D. R. among them, to issue a public warning of the potential catastrophe if Basque refugees were not allowed to travel to Catalonia.[18]

This crisis prompted the establishment of the Basque Children's Committee, set up to help maintain 4,000 children who had been evacuated to Britain.[19] The Basque Children's Committee worked in parallel with the National Joint Committee. Day-to-day organisation was undertaken by Dr Betty Morgan, a former Liberal parliamentary candidate, and someone close to the Lloyd George family.[20] The committee enlisted D. R.'s assistance to establish camps in Wales, at Sketty Park in Swansea, Brechfa in Carmarthenshire, Old Colwyn in Denbighshire and Caerleon in Monmouthshire, with support from the Aid Spain movement.

As groups of children began arriving at the camps, D. R. led fundraising efforts and collected clothing in Swansea and elsewhere.[21] But matters did not always pass smoothly. Within a month of the arrival of the children at Brechfa, the *Catholic Times* delighted in publishing sensationalist accounts of a disturbance in the village involving 15 of the boys, who were alleged to have rampaged through the locality, breaking windows and damaging property. D. R. took personal charge of the matter, travelling to Brechfa where he found what he himself described as 'undoubted evidence of disorder', although discipline had by then been restored.

While Franco's sympathisers gleefully denounced the children and the camp organisers, D. R. pleaded for compassion. All of the boys had lived in conditions of 'incredible nervous tensions and that it would take time and careful supervision to enable them to regain a normal sense of balance'. He pointed out that some of them had been working on the construction of trenches around Bilbao, and their minds had been affected by the experiences of the previous 12 months. They could not be expected to settle down to the monotony of life in the camp without help.[22] Later, addressing a meeting of the Pontardawe and District Committee of the Basque Children's Fund at Soar chapel, he declared, 'Window-breaking is a crime not unknown in Pontardawe and I have seen a few windows smashed in my time, but it must be remembered that these children are a very long way from home, and are used to living in circumstances quite inconceivable to the average minds of persons in this country. Most of us have no idea of what they have experienced. They are severed from their family circles and driven in confusion from their homes to any sort of shelter, shaken and with no sense of direction or without guidance.'[23]

Meanwhile, the NCL looked to the League of Nations for 'immediate action... to end acts of aggression against the Spanish government [and]... restoration without delay of the right of the Spanish government to buy arms', but fell short of endorsing rank-and-file demands to denounce the principle of non-intervention.[24] But by the time of the party conference in October, attitudes had hardened, which led the Executive to accept a resolution demanding an end to the policy of non-intervention and insisting on the right of the Spanish government to obtain arms.[25] Speaking during the debate, D. R. blamed the British government who had never conceived the League of Nations as a means of resolving international issues, and had continuously lent on the side of the aggressor in every international disagreement, whether it was when Japan attacked China, when Italy invaded Abyssinia, or anywhere else. Government policy meant peace at any price, 'the peace of the cemetery, the peace of death, that lies behind General Franco'.[26] The launch of the Labour Party's Spain campaign gave him an opportunity to go further in his criticism of non-intervention and to demand the right of the Spanish government to obtain arms.[27] He addressed mass meetings at Manchester, Edinburgh, Birmingham, Bristol and Swansea, followed by an even larger rally at the London Olympia, in which he demanded an end to Fascist intervention alongside practical support.[28]

By now it was clear to anyone with a modicum of understanding that the notion of non-intervention in Spain was nonsense. In February 1938 D. R. demanded action on the 'wanton attacks' waged by countries who were signatories to the Non-Intervention Agreement which had never been implemented fairly and had favoured the Fascist insurrection.[29] He pursued Duff Cooper (who had replaced Samuel Hoare at the Admiralty) over the sinking of the *Endymion* by a Falangist submarine 16 miles south of Cape Tiŷoso.[30] Italy's role in the war was clear for all to see, he insisted, as was evident from the pages of *Il Popolo d'Italia* and *La Domenica del Corriere* where Mussolini boasted about 'his' victory in Spain, brought about 'in spite of the Pact of Non-Intervention, by flagrant and open violation, by piracy, by wanton destruction of lives on land and sea, by terrorism, by blackmail, and by political propaganda'.[31] The legitimate Spanish government was being robbed of its legal and constitutional rights.[32] Mussolini, he asserted, was bent on setting up a fascist state in Spain, and that with the wholehearted assistance of the British Prime Minister. Spain represented merely a stepping stone in the fascist take-over of Europe.[33]

*

By 1937 issues concerning the weakness of Labour's ability to respond to the rise of fascism in Europe, and its failure to unseat the 'national' government fuelled the demands for a Popular Front in Britain. A unity campaign, launched by Sir Stafford Cripps and Harry Pollitt, General Secretary of the Communist Party of Great Britain, and supported by others including George Strauss, William Mellor and Harold Laski, attracted minority support, including in south Wales where meetings began to be held in the early summer.[34] D. R. had attended the TUC conference in September 1935 which had decisively rejected the notion of a United Front between Labour and any other political force.[35] He had himself been so incensed by remarks made by Communist speakers, at a conference conveyed to discuss unemployment at Swansea in July 1936, that he had launched a blistering attack on the role of Communists in both Britain and France. D. R. had accused the French Communists of abdicating their responsibility by 'playing fast and loose' with the government led by the Socialist Léon Blum.[36] He took particular offence at remarks made by the Neath Communist, Frank Roper, for suggesting Willie Gallacher, Communist MP for West Fife, was the only one to be trusted to defend the unemployed. A few days later, the *Daily Worker* seized on the opportunity to denounce D. R.'s attitude, along with that of the Labour leadership as a whole.[37] It commented:

> There is need to combat D. R. Grenfell's attack on unity, and particularly his senseless remarks about the French Communists 'evading responsibility', when he knows full well the Communists made their position quite clear before the election. Like Herbert Morrison, D. R. Grenfell waits until after the elections to trot out this bogey. It is rather strange that Mr Grenfell MP is opposed to Communist affiliation in this country, but in France even wants the Communists to take part in the Government.[38]

D. R. opposed any notion of a United Front as a member of the NCL and in response to the unity campaign's meetings. His view prevailed overwhelmingly at a conference of the Gower divisional Labour Party in December 1936, which resolved to call on all working-class organisations to unite behind the Labour Party at the next election and reject any other route. D. R. also made his views clear at the SWMF conference in April 1937 when, together with Arthur Jenkins and Jim Griffiths (both now Labour MPs), he sought to defeat a resolution that would open the way for Communist influence in the Labour Party. Technically, the change that was proposed would give a right to all those paying the political levy to be permitted to represent their union as delegates to the Labour Party (both at local level and as delegates to national conferences).[39] For D. R. and his two colleagues, the resolution reflected a Communist plot, and manoeuvres to undermine the Labour leadership.[40]

Further evidence of D. R.'s hostility is provided by Ithel Davies who, in 1937, was a member of the Labour Party in Swansea. His vivid recollections of the episode are presented in full:

> Ni chofiaf yn awr beth yn fanwl oedd fy neges ond yn
> ystod ein trafodaeth aeth D. R. ati i ymosod ar y Cynghrair
> Sosialaidd am ddadlau dros y Ffrynt Unedig. Ceisiais innau
> egluro iddo y rheswm am hynny, a hynny oedd y dylai'r
> mudiadau Sosialaidd dynnu at ei gilydd a'i bod yn well
> fod y Blaid Gomiwnyddol yn fodlon ymuno â'r Blaid Lafur
> ar yr un tir â chymdeithasau eraill a berthynai i'r Blaid
> Lafur, oherwydd felly byddai rhyw fesur o wastrodaeth ar
> y Comiwnyddion fel ar y mudiadau eraill. Gwylltiodd D. R.
> wrthyf yn ffyrnig. Cododd o'i gadair a'm gorchymyn i adael
> y tŷ. 'Ewch allan o'r tŷ yma,' meddai â'i lygaid yn tanio. Ni
> symudais o'r lle'r eisteddwn. Erfyniais arno dawelu a thrafod
> y mater yn dawel. Edrychai fel petai'n mynd i ymosod arnaf
> neu geisio fy nhaflu'n gorfforol o'r tŷ. Llwyddais i'w dawelu
> a chyn i mi ymadael ysgydwasom ddwylo a pharhaodd ein
> cyfeillgarwch.[41]

> [I can't remember now what my message was in detail, but
> during our discussion D. R. attacked the Socialist Alliance
> for advocating the United Front. I also tried to explain
> to him the reason for that, which was that the Socialist
> movements should pull together and that it was better that
> the Communist Party was willing to join the Labour Party

on the same basis as other societies that belonged to the Labour Party, and that, in consequence of that, there would be some measure of amelioration on the Communists as on the other organizations. D. R. became furious with me. He got up from his chair and ordered me to leave the house. 'Get out of this house,' he said with his eyes flashing. I didn't move from where I sat. I begged him to calm down and discuss the matter quietly. It looked as if he was going to attack me or was going to try to physically throw me out of the house. I managed to calm him down and, before I left, we shook hands and our friendship continued.]

The accuracy of this account can be questioned if only on grounds of chronology, but Ithel Davies captures D. R.'s mood and his views on the substantive point. The Labour Party would fight on its own and would not benefit from any infusion of support from other political forces. This was the view not just of its leadership but of the bulk of its members as well, and the positioning of the Communist Party previously and in succeeding years would confirm that view certainly as far as D. R. was concerned.

*

While D. R. was busily concerned with international issues, he continued to play a full part as a member of the Royal Commission on Safety in the Mines as it finished gathering information. This now included Sir Henry Walker's report into the Gresford disaster, published at the start of 1937. Walker concluded that the whole of the Denis area of the mine was unworkable, and that the second means of egress – a mile-long airway that had been left standing and unmaintained for years – was totally inadequate for the purpose. The area suffered from poor ventilation, and Walker accepted the recollections of the men who had claimed that the presence of gas in the wind road had been known for some weeks, concluding that those responsible for inspecting the area had neglected their duties. However, Walker's report failed to provide firm and definite reasons for the cause of the explosion. While the report alluded to the possibility that the explosion had been caused by shot-firing near the airway (as alleged by Cripps), the three Commissioners could not agree that this was the case, and separate conclusions were drawn by each of them on this vital topic.

These outcomes were dismissed as a whitewash by the miners themselves, D. R. concurred, insisting that the way the Gresford mine was managed, the attitude of the owners, and the climate of fear which existed there had been totally ignored.[42] None of the three essential conditions for the protection of miners during their work existed at the shaft where the disaster occurred. The conditions at the colliery were a scandal, in which violations and evasions of the Act were practised by the management on a daily basis.[43] 'Here is not a "mistake" which inevitably led to disaster, but a deliberate and sustained piece of managerial policy,' he insisted. He was adamant that the report could not be taken as the final word on the disaster and neither was it enough to prosecute the individuals deemed responsible – essential though that was. What was required was a comprehensive inquiry into the way the Mines Inspectorate worked, and a new system whereby pit deputies were employed by the State rather than colliery companies.[44]

Parliament, he reminded MPs, had a responsibility exercised on behalf of the country as a whole to prevent such disasters by ensuring that mining was undertaken under conditions of maximum safety. The conditions that had been allowed to exist at Gresford had led to one of the most appalling occurrences of the post-war period, and the only surprise was that an explosion had not happened much sooner. He gave a vivid description of conditions at the mine and the carelessness with which it had been managed:

There is no language in which one can describe the inferno…
There were men working almost stark-naked, clogs with
holes bored through the bottom to let the sweat run out, 100
shots a day fired on a face less than 200 yards wide, the air
thick with fumes and dust from blasting, the banjack hissing
to waft the gas out of the face into the unpacked waste, a
space 200 yards long and 100 yards wide above the wind road
full of inflammable gas and impenetrable for that reason…
The scandal has been clearly exposed by workers who were
unwilling accessories to the violations and evasions practised
every day in Gresford. The management had failed because
no one in authority tried to stem the daily decadence which
ended so tragically.[45]

For D. R., the report raised fundamental questions about
the machinery that parliament had set up to monitor safety
in the mines. The Mines Inspectorate did not come out with
any credit; the divisional inspector had never even entered the
colliery, while both the senior and junior inspectors had failed
to find anything wrong in the way it was being worked. The
result was that 264 men had died as a result of conditions that
should not have existed in any mine. He reserved particular
scorn for W. J. Charlton and his allegation that the explosion
had been caused by a spark from a telephone. Such a view
typified the man who:

… rejects or ignores all the evidence as it seems most
convenient to him. He is even now unwilling to believe that
gas was present on all the lower parts of the Denis main area.
He rejects the evidence of workmen and officials who admit
the entire story of neglect and carelessness. He is impervious
to the evidence. One might almost say he is gas-proof. He had
produced a theory and falls back on futile and mischievous
speculations regarding the cause and place of ignition. There
is not a scrap of justification, not a sign or an indication
to confirm his belated exception. The telephone has been

located in the area where the gas pressure was the least and the handset was still in its box, unaffected by the explosion it was alleged to have caused.[46]

For the remainder of the debate the Secretary for Mines, Captain Harry Crookshank, showed himself out of his depth, stumbling through his speech as Aneurin Bevan, Arthur Jenkins, Robert Richards, and MPs from other mining areas followed D. R. in highlighting the inadequacies of existing regulations. Cripps paid his own tribute to the man who had advised him throughout the inquiry. 'I should like to take this opportunity of saying – and I say it without any fear of contradiction – that he is more responsible for the effectiveness of this inquiry than any other man in England. It was due to his very large and extensive technical knowledge, acting behind the representatives for the north Wales miners in the course of the inquiry, that the facts as regards the tragic neglect at Gresford were able to be brought out and made public.'[47] But there were many ambiguities in the report, and this proved crucial when the colliery company was prosecuted before the local magistrates for offences under the 1911 Coal Mines Act. Paltry fines were imposed for poor record keeping, but there was no justice for the hundreds of men killed in the disaster. It caused outrage in Gresford and the surrounding areas, belittling the lives of those killed, and was something that D. R. and his colleagues on the Labour benches were not prepared to forget.

Within days, D. R. was back at work at the Royal Commission where he faced the incarnation of colliery owners in the form of Sir Evan Williams of Fforest, Pontarddulais, President of the Mining Association, whose company, Thomas Williams and Co., Llangennech, owned collieries in Grovesend and Pontarddulais as well as on the Carmarthenshire side of the Llwchwr. D. R. was well-acquainted with Sir Evan, one of the most determined opponents of the MFGB's demands for a national wage agreement throughout the 1920s and one of the coal owners' chief strategists in the 1921, 1925 and 1926 disputes. Sir Evan's softly-spoken attempts to charm the Commission spoke volumes. 'The human element is so very difficult to deal with that accidents will remain unavoidable, largely through want of foresight or through error of judgement.' Safety legislation and the associated regulations were merely codified practices that had been evolved by the industry in response to its experiences. 'There were questions… on which those acquainted with the industry should lay down the law rather than that the House of Commons should formulate it. The Mines Department should set regulations rather than having them enshrined in legislation, and the less interference with the industry, the better for all concerned.'[48]

D. R. gave vent to his own feelings after Sir Evan refused to agree that workmen should have the right to prosecute the management. 'There are three-quarters of a million men working in the mines of this country, as good as those who own them. It is very offensive to these men to be told they have not got the same rights as others.'[49]

As the evidence gathering stages of the Royal Commission's inquiry came to an end, D. R. was chosen as one of four members, alongside Sir Malcolm Delevingne, Sir Henry Walker, and E. O. Forster Brown, charged with analysing the evidence and drafting the recommendations. This work was undertaken during the course of 41 meetings held between April 1937 and May 1938, which included discussions with divisional Inspectors of Mines, officials of the Mines Department, as well as visits to the Mines Department testing stations and the research stations of the Safety in Mines Research Board. The sub-committee also visited 19 mines selected after consultation with the MFGB and the Mining Association, including Cefn Coed Colliery in Crynant and collieries at Bargoed, Groesfaen, and Penrhiwceiber.[50]

In advance of the report's publication D. R., along with

Jim Griffiths and others, used every available opportunity to demand that the government should take administrative action to improve mine safety as an interim measure.[51] He was keenly aware of the reality of the daily accidents underground, many of them resulting in loss of life, which served as testimony to the fact that those working in the industry could not wait for detailed consideration of the merits of legislation, even less for bureaucratic niceties. Action was needed, and as a matter of urgency.[52]

The Royal Commission's report was eventually published at the end of 1938.[53] It consisted of 12 chapters, beginning with a historical overview that traced the development of safety legislation and the creation of the mines and quarries inspectorate. The second chapter explored developments in the industry from 1911, including organisation (ownership, management, output etc), the number employed, introduction of equipment, and accident rates. Chapter three focused on the administration of the law, and the role of the Mines Department and Inspectorate. The report then outlined the statutory responsibilities of different groups and the qualifications they needed to hold (owners, agents, managers, under-managers, overmen, electrical and mechanical staff, surveyors, firemen, examiners and deputies). This was followed by sections on issues relating to the working of mines – ventilation, support of workings, haulage and travelling, before moving on to examine the evidence about explosions, fire and accidents. Conditions of work on the surface, safety organisation and training, health and the prevention of occupational diseases were outlined in the final chapters.

The report acknowledged the dangerous nature of the industry and the duty of all those involved to reduce the unacceptable number of accidents and injuries. They rejected totally the argument that the industry was over-regulated and, while acknowledging that there were a very large number of regulations that had to be observed, they insisted that no streamlining should be allowed on grounds of cost. The industry collectively – owners, officials and workmen – had to adhere to the highest standards. Much of the report focused on new regulations required for mines to be worked safely using modern methods. There were a total of 179 recommendations, which included a call for higher standards of formal training with associated qualifications, stricter measures to control gas, more efficient ventilation, and revision of the standards for roof support. Dust control would have to be made more efficient, and the use of naked lights should be phased out, other than in a limited number of specific instances. Other measures recommended dealt with the use of explosives and shot-firing. To facilitate these changes, they recommended separating the health and safety responsibilities from other functions of the Mines Department, and increasing the status and pay grade of the Chief Inspector and other senior staff. These recommendations, the Commissioners insisted, needed to be implemented in their totality if they were to have the necessary impact: 'the problem of safety in mines, if substantial improvement is to be secured, must be attacked simultaneously from all sides by adequate strengthening of the administration, the setting of a higher standard of enforcement and observance, an improvement in the material conditions under which the work is carried on, and the co-operation of all parties.'

Early in 1939 the government accepted the report's recommendations 'in its general sense and purport' and promised to take steps to implement its provisions, but insisted that it needed time to consider what legislation would be required. Such prevarication infuriated D. R. and his colleagues on the Labour benches, who demanded immediate legislation to enact the Commission's recommendations and those of the separate investigation into industrial pulmonary diseases.[54] Even so, no parliamentary time could be found in 1939 and implementing the recommendations on safety was not a priority among the successive coal crises of the war years or as the Attlee government took the mines into public ownership. Indeed, almost 15 years elapsed before the Commission's recommendations were put into force, setting the framework within which the nationalised mining industry was to operate.[55]

The government produced a series of proposals affecting the mining industry that included State control of mining royalties and the replacement of the Coal Mines Reorganisation Commission (set up by the Labour government in 1931 to rationalise colliery undertakings into optimum-sized units) by a Coal Commission which would hold the royalties.[56] This represented a recognition by Tory ministers of the grievance caused by private ownership of minerals and a consensus, voiced by mine-owners and mineworkers alike, that 'scattered ownership' was 'wrong from the point of view of economical working'. This represented a belated recognition of recommendations made by both the Sankey and Samuel Commissions in the 1920s, and by subsequent investigations which highlighted fragmented ownership of the minerals as one of the main causes of inefficiency and legal disputes in the industry.[57]

D. R. regarded the government's proposals as a totally inadequate response to the industry's needs.[58] The proposals would not nationalise the mining royalties, merely provide existing owners with an unprecedented level of State largesse. He questioned the basis on which the assessment of royalties (15 years) had been made, and insisted that the amount of compensation to be paid was little short of shameful, and would burden the Commission with the task of finding over £3 million annually in interest payments, equivalent to the production of 250 million tons of coal at an average rate of 5d. per ton. Such a burden would be unsustainable in a time of slump. The industry would be bound by 'the permanent endowment of royalty owners', producing a settled income that would go on for ever. 'The State is not going to pay. It is the men who dig the coal who will pay. I stand here in the strongest spirit of revolt and protest against the idea, as a man who worked for 23 years, man and boy, in the coal pits. In the whole of the time I was paid less than £2,000 for 23 of the best years in my life spent in the mines of this country. I have given 2½ years of hard labour and servitude to a royalty owner.' The amount drawn from the miner to cover royalties was sufficient to provide every miner's family with a house with a freehold value of £500, and that should be the priority.[59]

Later, during the committee stage of the Bill, D. R. dealt with the role of the proposed Coal Commission in promoting efficiency within the industry, in particular over the question of amalgamations. The new body, it was proposed, would examine production figures and recommend any colliery groupings that would increase efficiency. In D. R.'s opinion, this vested an unacceptable amount of power in the hands of Commissioners, especially as the legislation did not provide clear criteria against which to judge the efficiency which would be made. Its only outcome would be to create a complex and bureaucratic structure when what was needed was a new technique in the management of the coal industry with stronger planning based on an understanding of the industry.[60] The Coal Bill did not address any of the key issues confronting the industry, he insisted.[61] The number of mines had declined by a third in 18 years and there had been few new shafts and little new development. More than half a million men had left the industry, new machinery had been introduced with the sole aim of increasing production rather than to promote the welfare of the men employed. Electrification had been introduced without adequate safety measures, and more lives were lost through explosions in Britain than in almost every other part of the world.[62] He concluded:

The record of explosions, with heavy loss of life, is a reproach to all of us. There is a greater strain on the nerves and bodies of the men. Dust plays havoc on the men exposed to deep mining. I trust that to-day's debate will quicken the interest and the practical sympathy, so that our responsibilities can be discharged and the utmost amelioration in mining conditions can be achieved.[63]

H. R. S. Philpott, writing in the *Daily Herald*, was clearly impressed:

Mr Grenfell's speech was one of the best he has ever delivered. Economic penetration, mining experience and a deep regard for human life that can be saved were all part of it... Out of his great experience he declared that it was not necessary for explosions to occur in this country if proper precautions are taken. That was the main theme that ran through the subsequent debate – the dreadful and avoidable peril of men being blown to pieces down in the darkness and tunnel-ways. A handful of Tory and Liberal backbenchers joined with Labour in cheering Mr Grenfell when he ended his speech, with a plea for the gravest vigilance and the most far-seeing precautionary measures.[64]

*

Malcolm Stewart's resignation as Commissioner for Special Areas in November 1936, on the grounds that public policy had failed the people of the Special Areas, highlighted the inadequacy of the government's response to the areas worst affected by the depression. He castigated business and ministers for their lack of vision and refusal to countenance the promised unorthodox measures to revive those areas.[65] The government had rejected argument in favour of State-provided inducements, such as relief from tax on profits, relief from local rates or long-term loans, or an increase in the number of government factories located in Special Areas, and it had refused to give preference to contracts for companies in the Special Areas.[66] His words summarised his sense of frustration and disillusionment at the feeble efforts made by the government:

> It has been conceded that matters which concern the welfare of many thousands of our fellow-citizens are properly to be considered in relation to their social and broad economic consequences, as well as in relation to the profit and loss account of the individual concern. If this principle had been recognised 15 years earlier, much suffering might have been avoided and the Special Areas might not have presented so acute a problem as that which they provided in 1931.

In an attempt to be seen to be taking action, the government appointed a Royal Commission on the Distribution of the Industrial Population, and introduced the Special Areas (Amendment) Bill which prolonged the duration of existing Special Areas legislation and extended the powers of the Commissioner to attract industries to those regions (a responsibility which had previously been denied to them).[67] This enabled the Commissioners to do what Malcolm Stewart accused them of failing to achieve, building factories for let in the Special Areas and providing rent, tax and rate inducements, and offering loans for companies choosing to locate in 'areas certified by the Ministry of Labour as suffering from long-time severe unemployment, where the local economy was dependent on one of the depressed industries and where there was no prospect of recovery without assistance'.[68] Later, under separate legislation, the government established the National Industrial Development Council for Wales and Monmouthshire to overcome the problems of raising capital for new ventures in south Wales, and created the South Wales and Monmouthshire Trading

Estates Company. They also introduced measures to clear derelict sites.[69]

As the Bill reached its Third Reading, D. R. (who had been prevented from taking an active part in previous discussions due to other duties), summed up for the opposition, deriding the Bill as 'a puny measure' that failed to respond to community needs, did not provide the local authorities with the support they required, and made inadequate provisions to retrain the unemployed for work in other industries.[70] The Special Areas Reconstruction Association (SARA) was 'niggardly' in its attitudes, comprised of elaborate machinery but producing very few results.[71] Youth unemployment, in particular, alarmed him, and the failure to offer any meaningful schemes in the Special Areas was particularly galling, creating the prospect of an unskilled generation destined to be nothing more than an inferior class in the labour market.[72] He demanded to know why former munition sites in Special Areas were not being used for aircraft factories, and called for training centres in the Special Areas to equip men with the skills they would need in new industries.[73]

He decried the government's policy of 'pump priming' as wholly inadequate. Demand was falling, unemployment was rising. More than a quarter of the industrial population of Carmarthenshire, Glamorgan and Monmouthshire were unemployed; there had been a 22 per cent increase in unemployment in Tumble, 52 per cent in Mountain Ash, and 85 per cent in Ogmore Vale, all due to the government's failure to maintain overseas markets, and its failure to protect the interests of anthracite producers in discussions with the Canadian government. The steel and tinplate industry in south Wales was going through a period of unprecedented change due to the construction of the integrated strip mill at Ebbw Vale, with the result that communities further west were in trepidation. Miners at the Wernbwll Colliery, near Penclawdd, had been given a choice between relocating to Irthlingborough, close to Richard Thomas & Co.'s new works, or the dole queue. Meanwhile, iron ore production was being jeopardised due to uncertainty about the future. He demanded a radical new approach including the development of an industrial research capacity in south Wales, greater financial inducements for firms to locate in the areas, expansion of the trading estates model, the direction of government contracts to those areas, immediate progress with the Severn Bridge, as well as measures to deal with the burden of rates.

Elsewhere in Wales, rural communities were suffering due to neglect of basic public health. When the Minister of Health published a report boasting of the impressive array of social services that were being built up in the United Kingdom, D. R. seized on the opportunity to draw attention to the reality facing communities across Wales.[74] He pressed the case for more to be done to develop rural water supplies, maintaining that a national effort was needed to create a national system to use water resources more efficiently.[75] Housing conditions in the quarrying areas of north Wales were often deplorable. Tuberculosis was rampant because of working conditions.[76] Furthermore, any efforts to promote good health were futile unless accompanied by new measures to deal effectively with the problem of poverty: health essentially bore down to questions of housing, rents, subsidies and age. Turning to the specific issue of tuberculosis, D. R. asserted, 'There is no escape from tuberculosis unless we make a determined effort to remove the causes of the disease. I am sure also that rheumatism would give way to suitable measures.'[77]

One immediate step, Welsh MPs believed, should be the creation of the post of Secretary of State for Wales. This was an idea which D. R. supported, and two years earlier he had insisted that this should be seen merely as a first step, 'the demands of the Principality should not end there'.[78]

In 1938 Welsh MPs, through the Welsh Parliamentary Party (WPP), prepared a case that argued for the appointment of a minister with the task of representing the nation's interests at Cabinet level and of co-ordinating the government's work, including the myriad of government departments – among them the Welsh Board of Education, the Welsh Board of Health, and other aspects of the devolved structure responsible for administering public policy in Wales.[79] Clement Davies led the charge for the WPP, along with Morgan Jones who emphasised both the principle and the practical case. Wales' position as a nation had already been recognised in successive legal enactments and the extent of the issues facing the distressed areas and rural Wales called for a cabinet minister with detailed knowledge of the issues at stake.[80] Their case gained substantial cross-party support, and from a wide range of civil organisations that included the Council of the National Eisteddfod, the Cymmrodorion, the University of Wales Guild of Graduates and several educational organisation. D. R. was among those making the case for the proposition, and he was appalled by Prime Minister Neville Chamberlain's rejection of the idea after a deputation, led by Morgan Jones, had put the case eloquently in a meeting in July 1938.[81] The Prime Minister's announcement revealed a dismissive attitude towards any claims Wales had on grounds of national status, and the government's complacency amid the crisis it faced in the inter-war period:

> Under the present system, wholly Welsh affairs are dealt with in the appropriate Government office in London, and arrangements have been made – where it is possible – for their concentration in a separate division and there are, of course, offices in Wales itself which handle individual questions of a nature to be dealt with locally... I am satisfied of the efficiency of these arrangements and I do not consider that Wales would receive any practical advantages from co-ordination of the various activities in a single department.

Having referred to the question of cost, he drew comparisons with Scotland, concluding: 'Wales… since Henry VIII's Act of 1535 has been closely incorporated with England, and there has not been, and is not now, any distinct law or administrative system calling for the attention of a separate Minister.'

To add salt to the wound, the government announced there would be no grant for a Severn Bridge, nor would a carbide factory be located in Wales. Welsh MPs were appalled, D. R. among them, as he declared, 'I see no reason why the Prime Minister should not have made a graceful concession to Wales on the lines of the concession which Scotland secured by bargaining… The present generation of Welsh people do not regard it as a matter for bargaining. Our demand constitutes an essential means for the progressive development of local government.'[82]

Scotland had asked for a great deal more and had settled for a Secretaryship of State and that was the very least Wales could expect. It was a question to which the WPP, and D. R. especially, would return to continuously over the next 20 years.

CHAPTER 10

Freiheit![1]

EVEN THOUGH THE situation in Spain took up much of D. R.'s attention during 1937, his longstanding contacts among the Socialists of central Europe left him in no doubt that they, too, would soon be appealing for the support of the international Labour movement in the struggle against Nazi oppression. Socialist friends in Germany, in Czechoslovakia, and in Austria gave him first-hand accounts of the persecution they faced.[2] In the Sudetenland, Hitler's propaganda and funding fanned support for Konrad Henlein. Of special concern was the safety of the substantial refugee community of Socialists, trade unionists and other opponents of the Nazis, who had sought refuge there since the Austrian civil war in 1934, and the thousands of others who had joined them after the Anschluss. These were the people of whom D. R.'s friend, Wenzel Jaksch, the Sudeten Social Democrat leader, had spoken about in meetings with Labour leaders in London, all of whom were marked out by the Nazis as political opponents and whose lives would be in peril if Hitler was allowed to march into Czechoslovakia.[3]

In February 1938, D. R. wrote in the Czechoslovak paper *Lidové noviny*, 'The British Labour Party is ready and prepared to come to the help of Czechoslovakia whenever her independence is threatened by military or other aggression from the side of the Fascist powers.'[4] Whatever assistance the party was 'ready and prepared' to provide still fell short of a commitment that would lead to war. In March 1938, Labour launched its peace and security campaign, in which D. R. took full part, during which over a thousand meetings were held across Britain and two million leaflets were distributed in an effort to convince the public that war could be averted and the arms race stopped if the League of Nations was re-invigorated.[5] Within months, the situation had intensified as relentless Nazi propaganda, coupled with violent persecution of Social Democrats in the Sudetenland, enabled Henlein to achieve a resounding mandate in local elections held in May 1938. D. R. watched as Jaksch's worst fears were realised, while the British government could think of nothing better than to send Lord Runciman to Prague in July 1938 to seek concessions from the Czech government that would grant the right of self-determination to the Sudeten Germans. The Sudeten Socialists clearly did not figure in Walter Runciman's investigations of the situation on the ground – he failed to visit any of the Left's strongholds during his visit to the Sudetenland – and his reports to the British government contained barely any reference to the existence of opposition to the Nazis among the Sudeten Germans. The government's mindset was confirmed on 15 September when Prime Minister Neville Chamberlain agreed to proposals to separate the Sudetenland from the rest of Czechoslovakia, forcing the country to accept a new arrangement without even being party to the discussions: Germany would occupy the Sudetenland, concessions would be granted to Hungarian and Polish minorities, and Britain and France would only intervene to support a much truncated Czechoslovakia.

Meanwhile, faced with the threat of violence by Nazi thugs trained and armed with weapons by the German government, Sudeten Socialists organised themselves in a Republican Guard to defend themselves and the organisations of the Sudeten Left against the violence of Nazi mobs determined to impose their own discipline throughout the Sudeten area.

225

In Eger, they took up arms to defend the workingmen's club against a gang of crazed Nazis. Five hundred Socialist metal workers fought to defend their comrades at the Plauert factory in Wernersdorf on 22 September, while individual acts of bravery by party officials, trade union leaders, and others demonstrated their determination to resist Nazi tyranny to the last. More than 100,000 refugees, primarily Jews and known opponents of the Nazi regime, fled to seek sanctuary in what remained of Czechoslovakia, mainly in Prague where they joined the thousands of others who had already escaped from Austria. The German government demanded their return, while Czechoslovak ministers became fearful that the presence of such a large number of migrants was likely to aggravate the unemployment problem and cause a backlash within the Czech community.[6]

The Labour Party in Britain summoned a special conference that called on the British government to join with France and the USSR to resist any attack on Czechoslovakia, and appointed a delegation consisting of D. R., Clement Attlee, Arthur Greenwood, and Herbert Morrison to a joint meeting of the Presidium of the LSI and the International Federation of Trade Unions (IFTU) to discuss the situation.[7] The British government, for its part, instigated a crisis of its own by distributing gas masks to regional centres and sounding sirens in preparation for air raids, clearly implying people had a choice between peace with Hitler or war over Czechoslovakia.

As Prime Minister Neville Chamberlain outlined his plans to make a further plea to Hitler, Clement Attlee's response, welcoming any opportunity to avoid war, came with a caveat. 'I am sure that every Member of this House is desirous of neglecting no chance of preserving peace without sacrificing principles.'[8] This sentiment was repeated by the *Daily Herald*, which while welcoming the way war had been avoided, declared, 'It appears that Czechoslovakia is to be presented with proposals demanding from her sacrifices still greater than those heavy and bitter ones she has already been called upon to accept under the "irresistible pressure" of Britain and France... If that should be the case, then when the first dominating feeling of relief from the anxiety of war has passed, the public opinion of Britain will, we believe, be profoundly shocked that such relief has been purchased at the expense of a further abandonment of a small, brave and democratic nation.'[9]

On 3 October, D. R. was at his seat at the NCL as Wenzel Jaksch reported that the battle over the Sudetenland had been lost and that the urgent need now was for the evacuation of people who had been actively opposed to the Nazi regime: trade unionists, political and social leaders, among them lawyers, teachers, authors, journalists, and artists who had used their professional or political positions to oppose Nazism and all it stood for. For D. R., the time for political delegations had passed and what was now required was practical support. He therefore welcomed the pledge by the NCL to provide financial support and guarantee that they would help maintain Socialists and trade unionists fleeing Czechoslovakia who required temporary asylum in Britain. This response mirrored that of the SWMF, who denounced Chamberlain as the 'accomplice to the murder of the smaller democracies' and demanded facilities for the trade unionists in the disputed areas of Czechoslovakia as well as protection for the Jews.[10] The Labour Party's National Executive Committee (NEC), for its part, denounced the French and British proposals for the dismemberment of Czechoslovakia as a shameful betrayal of peaceful and democratic people, and demanded the re-establishment of the rule of law in international relations, but again reiterated its faith in collective security through the League of Nations.[11]

During the debate on the Munich Agreement, D. R. listened as Clement Attlee denounced Neville Chamberlain for having given Hitler mastery of central Europe without a shot being fired.

D. R. then embarked on his own condemnation of Munich and all it represented. Chamberlain and his ministers had betrayed the principle of national self-determination and, in doing so, had unmasked Hitler's true intentions which were to seize land from neighbouring countries by force without compromise or respect for any form of democracy. Czechoslovakia, he insisted, was merely the latest instalment in a bill that democratic governments would have to pay perpetually in order to satisfy Hitler's ambitions.[12] He highlighted the plight of Hitler's German opponents. 'Germans, as German as Herr Hitler himself, Germans of pure race and of pure speech, who do not agree with Herr Hitler in politics, were being robbed of all democratic rights.' The same applied to the Czechs. '"Gwell angau na chywilydd" [Better death than dishonour] was the phrase that came to mind but for Hitler's victims there was no such choice and Britain was complicit in allowing such a state of affairs.'[13]

The fate of the 700,000 Sudeten refugees who had sought refuge in Prague quickly roused the troubled social conscience of the British public. The Lord Mayor of London, the *News Chronicle*, and the *Manchester Guardian* launched an appeal for the relief of the destitute and homeless, while the *Daily Herald* demanded that Britain recognised its responsibility for the women and children forced to flee their homes. The *News Chronicle* also demanded a plan to evacuate the refugees which echoed D. R.'s message to the NCL: warm words would not be enough, there was a need for a scheme of practical relief. Faced with such pressure, the British government committed £10 million to assist the citizens of Czechoslovakia.[14]

The NCL played a full part in these efforts and gave D. R. the responsibility and freedom of action to do what was required in response to the crisis. Following a meeting with Lord Halifax at the Foreign Office, he travelled to Czechoslovakia on 10 October 1938, accompanied by William Gillies and George Hicks, on behalf of the Labour Party, along with two representatives of Labour and Socialist International (LSI), Léon Jouhaux and Walter Scherenes.[15] Once there, D. R. and William Gillies spent the evening in discussion with Jaksch who conveyed the message that Siegfried Taub, Secretary of the German trade union movement, had received a secret warning from General Karel Husárek that the German government would be demanding the return of all Socialists who had escaped into Czechoslovakia and that, furthermore, Konrad Henlein had issued a proclamation that there would be no mercy for them when they arrived. The following day, D. R. met with Sir Walter Layton, who led the *News Chronicle*'s work on behalf of the Prague refugees, and then the British Ambassador, Sir Basil Newton, whose pro-German sympathies were no secret, who calmly reported to the Foreign Office that what D. R. had found put 'new light on the matter' and that 'if these people are not to be exposed to suffering and even death, it is felt that something must be done so as to enable them to leave the country'.[16]

D. R. and Gillies, for their part, credited the situation with a greater sense of urgency, sending a telegram to James Middleton, General Secretary of the Labour Party, via the Foreign Office, on 12 October 1938 that read, 'Extremely urgent. Communicate with General Sir Neill Malcolm and Sir Walter Layton with view to obtaining information regarding tragic outlook of German-speaking refugees here. Suggest deputation should approach Prime Minister or Foreign Secretary tonight. Our representations and suggestions already made here and communicated to Foreign Office.'[17] In the meantime, the British government requested the Czechoslovakians to allow the refugees to remain inside their border and maintain them as a temporary measure.[18]

The situation in Prague was indeed reaching a crisis, as was subsequently described by Wenzel Jaksch and Walter Kolarx in *England and the Last Free Germans*, published in 1941:

In Prague the situation by the middle of October had become
tragic. The nationalist press worked to an agitation against
the Sudeten refugees. Suddenly they were regarded as
the detested Germans who ought to go back to Germany.
The Agrarian paper *Vecer* accused the Sudeten refugees of
having made demonstrations in Czech villages immediately
after their arrival. Ridiculous as the accusation was, it had
its effect, even the Czech Left Wing was affected by the
argument that the presence of a new national minority meant
a danger, and that no Germans and no Jews were needed
in the republic. Forced transports back to Germany and
expulsion orders were in full swing. The Sudeten Germans
effectively had no hope of remaining in Prague or of escaping
elsewhere, meaning that their fate was clear – they would be
expelled to Germany.[19]

Recognising the urgency, D. R. then returned to London
where he held a succession of meetings with Labour and
Liberal leaders, and presented a report to the NCL which
described the appalling scenes in Prague and called for further
financial assistance to be given to those fleeing persecution.[20]
The NCL also formed a plan of action which D. R. would
implement in the name of the Labour Party – what Wenzel
Jaksch and Walter Kolarx later described as '18th October.
David R. Grenfell takes Action'.[21]

In doing so, D. R. enlisted the support of the Polish
government and the Polish-British Shipping Co. to arrange
places on the SS *Baltrook* at Gdynia. The following day, 19
October 1938, D. R. left for Prague to take charge of operations.
Betty Morgan, his colleague from the Basque Refugee Fund,
then travelled to Poland where she coordinated work at that end
in support of the efforts in Prague. Throughout this time, D. R.
shared intelligence with several others from Britain who had
travelled to Prague to assist with the situation, especially David
Wilks of the *News Chronicle* and Doreen Warriner, the Prague
representative of the British Committee for Refugees from

Czechoslovakia.[22] The Foreign Office alerted its representatives in Bucharest, Warsaw, Budapest and Belgrade to what was going on and instructed them 'to afford Mr Grenfell such assistance as may be possible', although it did not stipulate how and to what extent they should do so.[23] In any event, D. R. had no time to discuss his plans with anyone. On 20 October he led a group of refugees on an arduous journey from Prague to Gdynia, which took more than 60 hours to complete mainly due to late-running trains and missed connections. En route, he intervened to overcome the problems caused by trigger-happy guards at the Slovak frontier and resorted to bribing the engine driver with drinks to entice him to take the train to the Polish frontier station.[24] The desperate situation was described by Wenzel Jaksch and Walter Kolarz:

> Even the rail journey over Poland was highly problematical.
> All main line connections were cut for weeks after the
> Sudeten occupation. D. R. Grenfell, who led the first
> transport of Sudeten refugees over the Slovak frontier, had
> to pay for coal for the engine and for drinks for the driver,
> before the little train could be roused to run over to the Polish
> frontier station.[25]

The Polish authorities proved more amenable than the Slovaks, at least judging by the tone of a telegram sent by the British Embassy to the Foreign Office. 'Polish legation here have been most helpful and valuable in granting facilities for refugees to pass through Poland. As far as is known, no hitches have occurred. Mr Grenfell MP telephoned on 24 October to passport control officer from Kraków and the only difficulty that he mentioned was that trains were frequently late, and connections therefore being missed.'[26]

D. R. stayed in Kraków until Monday, 24 October, and then travelled to Warsaw where he spent Wednesday night at the station restaurant overseeing the arrival and departure of refugees. By now the situation in Poland was also becoming desperate as Jewish refugees found themselves stranded, as was evident from a second telegram sent from the British Embassy:

> Passport Control officer learns from sources, which he considers reliable, that situation of Jewish refugees who are marooned in no-man's-land is desperate and that immediate relief is required. The number involved is about 82 and includes women and children. No further reply has been received from the Czechoslovak authorities to our informal suggestion that they should be admitted into this country on humanitarian grounds, nor do I anticipate a favourable answer unless their emigration is provisionally guaranteed. My French colleague, who has also received appeals from a refugee family at Biro, is of the same opinion. He has brought the matter to the notice of his government but hitherto received no instructions. The case of these people is more urgent than that of refugees which the departure passport control office is authorised to facilitate, but, of course, without some undertaking from the German government. One result of our assisting might be to encourage the German authorities to push further numbers across the frontier.[27]

Four days later, D. R. was back in Prague where he again met Jaksch to discuss the situation in Poland. While there, he helped a second group of refugees whom he accompanied to Kraków, and then to Gdynia where they embarked on the SS *Warszawa* and, crammed into its 200 berths, sailed to England on 2 November. Recalling the events later, D. R. paid tribute to the work of both the officials and volunteers who contributed to the relief operation, but deplored the terrible human cost.[28] He was able to secure government support for the PLP's motion that guaranteed that all Jewish children from Germany, who were sponsored by an organisation or private individual, would be welcomed to Britain, and elicited a pledge from Home Secretary Samuel Hoare that the government would take measures to counteract the wave of anti-Semitism that was engulfing the country following alarmist propaganda about the number of refugees reaching British shores.[29]

But private charity and sympathetic gestures were not enough in the face of such a crisis.[30]As British opinion realised the gravity of what had been done to Czechoslovakia, D. R. joined in the chorus of outrage at the government's capitulation to Hitler's demands.[31] 'We cannot divest ourselves of the responsibility... I can see how easy it is to liquidate a state and deprive people of that pride in their nationality which belongs to every people and every nation. That will have serious consequences yet for all the people of Europe.'[32]

By March 1939, Czechoslovakia was, to all intents and purposes, under the control of German forces when Germany over-ran its remaining territories. Wenzel Jaksch recalled the impact on those of the Left who had been unable to escape:

Immediately after the occupation of the Sudetenland, more than 20,000 of our comrades were dragged into German concentration camps, still in the uniform of our militant organisation, 'Republican Guard'. They were treated with excessive cruelty... Those who dared to resist Nazism under the shadow of Hitler's war machine did so under the threat of extermination. Actually, most of the male population of Socialist strongholds were marched off to concentration camps immediately after the occupation.[33]

On 15 March 1939, D. R. held the Commons spellbound as he admonished government ministers and their actions.[34] The Prime Minister had given 'the briefest and most curt report of events of worldwide importance as if they were simply a matter of routine, an official comment which fell upon him to perform. I am quite sure that the Prime Minister is about the only person in diplomatic circles in Europe who can afford that splendid sense of isolation and detachment that he presented today. It is quite certain that no one in Czechoslovakia, either

233

those who have held responsibility on the very difficult six months through which the country had passed, or the great mass of the Czech people who have witnessed the invasion of their country, the violation of their liberties, the liquidation of the sovereignty of their country, the destruction of their independence, not one of those people could afford to preserve the calm mien which the Prime Minister has been able to preserve today.'[35]

He derided the way Neville Chamberlain had ignored the historical context of central Europe in seeking to defend his position, making no reference to the way Europe was disintegrating into violence while the British government stood aside.

For Chamberlain to claim that he had acted in good faith in Munich in 1938 was simply incredible. 'The Prime Minister talked about moral responsibilities. I think he used the words "moral wants". This country has a reputation for regard of moral principles... [but] there is nothing that rebounds to our credit in the history of the events which came so much nearer a culmination yesterday, 14th March.'[36]

British policy had been pursued with a sense of detachment as if it were a 'a kind of theoretical and academic observation' rather than dealing with the plight of real men and women subjugated to a foreign power.[37] The policy of appeasement, he insisted, was hastening the disintegration of Europe.[38] Austria had been overwhelmed. Czechoslovakia, which had stood so bravely in May 1938, had been deserted by those who promised to defend her. Pointing to his own pacifist background and beliefs, he declared that the way to a peaceful solution in Europe had been barred by the unchallenged use of force by aggressor countries.

We see armed men being led into the highways to bar the road to peace. Those armed men are becoming more numerous and their mandate is becoming more explicit.

234

They are there to invade and to overwhelm nations here and nations there. There is no security in Europe to-day. The smaller the nation, the more innocent the nation, the more is its apprehension and the greater its fear, but the large nations are not free from it either.[39]

Those who heard him were clearly moved. Sir Archibald Sinclair, on behalf of the Liberals, opened his remarks by stating clearly 'that the feelings which have been aroused in me by these events received far better expression – and I would like to say most eloquent expression… in the speech of the Hon. Member for Gower… than in the speech of the Prime Minister.' Only obscure Tory backbenchers like Patrick Donner and Archibald Southey attempted to defend Chamberlain from D. R.'s attack. 'However lamentable the German occupation of Prague is and may be, we should remember, I think, that the present occupation has been undertaken in conditions of peace and not in conditions of war,' was all Donner could muster.[40]

The following day, 'Grenfell warns hushed House of Commons' said the *Daily Herald* which reported that, 'Mr Grenfell… has recently paid several visits to Czechoslovakia and probably knows more at first hand about the position there than any other man in Parliament.' Its editorial column declared regretfully that Britain had to face the consequences of Chamberlain's agreement with Hitler –'the postscript to Munich' – and advocated collaboration with Russia, France and the United States to uphold principles of international justice.[41] *The Scotsman*'s parliamentary sketch referred to the 'uncompromising vigour' and 'sincerity and earnestness' conveyed by D. R., while William Barkley in the *Daily Express* paid a rare tribute to a Socialist:

Nothing more extraordinary could be imagined than that this Welsh miner, marked with the signs of his trade, little bits of blue blood where an explosion below put coal dust for ever in scars in his face, should make a speech cheered by Mr

Winston Churchill. Such a situation aroused controversy as to whether Mr Dai Grenfell and Mr Winston Churchill with Mr Eden, would fail to be together in the proposed new national government. The blue blood of the aristocrats and the blue wounds of the miners. Mr Grenfell made a fine speech. It was emotional, but at the same time he based his party's case on the argument that Herr Hitler has violated peaceful methods. If there were a general election, my personal vote as a Tory would be to support Mr Grenfell as a much better unpaid Socialist leader than Mr Attlee. I am very sorry that on this occasion the Prime Minister has dismissed the whole problem of Czechoslovakia with such few words and with such a scant amount of feeling.[42]

'Angry shouts arose at once of "No" from the Government side, with cries of "Yes" from the Opposition side... Amid many bursts of applause from dissident Tories like Mr Churchill and his little band, Mr Grenfell powerfully protested against the process of violence over-running democratic institutions in Europe.'[43]

That summer, Czech refugees commissioned Ernest Neuschul, a former professor of art at Berlin University, to paint a portrait of D. R. in recognition of his work on their behalf.[44] Neuschul had previously painted portraits of former President of Czechoslovakia Tomáš Masaryk and Edvard Beneš, the former Prime Minister of Czechoslovakia. Neuschul himself was a refugee from Nazi Germany, having been persecuted since the mid-1930s after two of his pictures had displeased the Nazi minister of propaganda. One was a picture of a father, mother and child that the artist intended to depict as family life. This was deemed not to be in the interests of the nation as it depicted a family with only one child. Another was a picture of workers trying to overcome the difficulties of their toil. This did not show the subjects with smiling faces.[45] During the spring of 1939 Neuschul spent considerable time with D. R. discussing his background and political activities in order to get to know his character and what drove him. Two portraits were eventually produced after D. R. insisted that the mining scars which covered his face – which were omitted from the original version – should be included. They were presented to D. R. by Wenzel Jaksch at a Labour gathering in Swansea in June 1939. One of the portraits was subsequently exhibited at the Deutscher Kulturbund (the German refugee arts organisation) in London.

In the House of Commons, D. R. recognised that war was merely a matter of weeks away, an outcome which he had spent the previous decade seeking to avoid as he pleaded with successive governments to take the required action to combat the menace of fascism in Europe. But while he was wholly convinced of the inevitability, indeed the need for a military intervention to defeat fascism, he was determined that this should not be at the expense of civil liberties in Britain. His bitter memories of the First World War and Mansel's treatment as a political objector was, no doubt, a factor in his declarations during discussions about the Military Training Bill, as he vigorously opposed the use of conscripts to bolster the numbers in the armed forces. Such a strategy, he believed, was a product of the fertile imagination of militarist 'amateur strategists' sitting in the comfort of London clubs, who believed that as long as men were compelled to join the Forces all would be good, when what was needed was a radical reconsideration of Britain's military strategy to avoid the need for mass mobilisation. The British working class would not be found lacking if war came, but it would have to be a war fought on the basis of working-class solidarity and not a requirement imposed by militarists.[46]

Haunted by memories of the treatment of those who had objected to military service over 20 years earlier, D. R. successfully moved two amendments, accepted by the government, to strengthen the position of conscientious objectors appearing before a tribunal.[47] He dwelt at length

with the second of his proposals, which enshrined the right of
a conscientious objector to be represented by a trade union.
His reasoning was deeply personal, as was revealed in his
contribution on the floor of the Commons in May 1939:

> Some of us are old enough to remember the operation of
> conscientious objectors' tribunals during the Great War,
> and I have very vivid recollections indeed of some of the
> circumstances of the hearings which I attended and in which
> I sometimes took part. I remember how sensitive, very
> intelligent and deeply conscious people found themselves
> almost unable to state their case because of the atmosphere
> and the environment of the court itself. I remember the way
> in which military representatives pressed their claims for the
> bodies and souls of the young men who appeared before these
> tribunals. I remember how very domineering, and indeed
> sometimes objectionable, was the behaviour of some of these
> military representatives. Unless a person has a very strong
> personality, he cannot do himself justice.[48]

Britain would never succeed unless the right of conscience
was recognised and enshrined in law, and that meant respecting
rather than ridiculing those who rejected war as the solution to
Europe's problems.[49]

As the government introduced the Control of Employment
Bill within hours of the declaration of war, he insisted that
the conflict would put freely organised states in a battle with
totalitarianism. The proposals would empower the Minister
of Labour to direct workers not otherwise employed 'to the
employment most useful to the nation in this struggle,' and
D. R. insisted that the freedom of the worker should be
paramount in any such schemes and that it was incumbent
on a free country to show it could defeat totalitarianism by
superior organisation, not by curtailing freedoms. Above all,
the workers had to be better treated than they had been during
the Great War.[50] He demanded assurances that parliament

would be able to scrutinise any orders, and that the unions would be recognised formally in the machinery by which the measure would be implemented. He warned that, 'There must be no Hitlerism in the factories.'[51] Only the workers, he added, could bring the country through the war, as their work producing munitions and machines was the backbone of the struggle.[52] The defeat of Nazism had to be total, and he rounded on those, including Lloyd George in October 1939, who might give the impression, however unintended, that this might not be the only satisfactory outcome.[53]

At the end of October he was one of three Labour MPs who ventured to the Maginot Line as guests of Léon Blum and declared his admiration for the spirit of the French people.[54] Throughout, he called for the war to be pursued with a clear promise of a very different future for working people, both in Britain and throughout the Empire. This, he insisted, meant changing the practices of institutions like the UAB whose treatment of working people over the previous six years had fostered a sense of alienation. This was something the country had to overcome if it was to succeed and fulfil the united determination of the British people for the defeat of Hitlerism and the creation of an Europe based on 'moral principles' and free from the tyranny of any mighty neighbour.[55] He used a speech to the Cardiff Press Club to insist on the need to focus on the prize ahead in the darkness of the situation facing Britain and the rest of Europe:

> I know we shall suffer very much… but I believe that ultimately we shall win through to a more secure state of human existence as a result of our trials in the war. In the world of the future, Germany should have equal rights with Britain, but Czechoslovakia should have nothing to fear from Germany, nor Finland from Russia… Planning for peace should commence at once; a peace that would secure free conditions for the mind, the body and soul of man… If ever a war was justified, this one was, and most of the

neutrals of the world prayed for the success of Britain and France.[56]

He continued on the same themes throughout the year. 'Freedom was in jeopardy; there was plotting against the freedom of the individual all over the world.' Free institutions were imperilled and democracy assailed. 'We must heed lest dictators succeed in stifling all our liberties... the workers of this country must now stand together to fight for freedom. Britain was the bulwark, and the workers must strengthen the nation to sustain democratic rule for themselves and for the downtrodden nations of Europe.'[57] In Aberystwyth he combined a similar message with an appeal to Welsh national pride, and gave a detailed analysis of the contradictions and dilemmas of natural pacifists confronted with the reality of what had unfolded in Europe.

Wales believed in the justice of the cause, and also believed that after the struggle there would be better things to share than ever before. He believed in the rights of human personality, and those rights were only guaranteed by a system of democracy. He believed that we had a right to be ourselves in the society of the world, a world of glorious variety. Democracy enabled every person to be as near to himself as possible. Today's struggle was against totalitarianism, which was nothing but the old despotism dressed in a new guise.

He referred to what he had observed in Spain during the civil war and believed those events should have stirred the conscience of Europe. But, instead, 'We allowed the days and the years to pass until the dictators had gathered sufficient arms to dictate to others, and there were no more attempts at conciliation.'[58]

By the end of 1939, D. R.'s friends and family were increasingly concerned about the toll on his health – by now a man in his late 50s – caused by his strenuous activities over the years, not least his involvement overseas in helping the

D. R. in the 1920s.

KEEP GRENFELL

FOR GOWER

Published by the Candidate, D. R. Grenfell, and Printed by Swansea Printers Ltd.

Election poster.

At MFGB conference. Group includes D. R., William Brace, Robert Smilie, and Herbert Smith.

At the TUC conference. Group includes Ben Tillett (far right).

D. R. at his desk in the 1920s.

The young support D. R.

Ramsay MacDonald arrives in Swansea.

Rival parties meet after handing in nomination papers, November 1923. Gwilym Bedw is standing behind D. R. To the right of the photo are W. H. Davies and H. W. Davies.

D. R. visiting the USSR, 1925.

On a visit as a member of the Forestry Commission in the 1930s.

Discussion after a meeting for women voters in Mumbles, October 1931.

The Parliamentary Labour Party after the 1931 election.

Viewing the portrait of D. R. by Ernest Neuschul. W. Grant Murray (curator of the Glynn Vivian) D. R., Ernest Neuschul, Wenzel Jaksch.

Preparing to go underground as a member of the Royal Commission on Safety in the Mines, 1939.

Colliery visit in the 1940s.

Preparing to go underground as Secretary for Mines.

D. R. at the Sea of Galilee.

D. R. with J. D. Parry, clerk to Glamorgan County Council, at the Mettoy stall at the Welsh Industrial Exhibition, Olympia, London, August 1947.

Directing operations as Chairman of the Welsh Tourist Board in the 1940s.

In Honour of

David Rhys Grenfell

M.E., C.B.E., M.P., J.P.

on the occasion of the
25th Anniversary of his
election to Parliament
(July the 20th, 1922)

❈

We have the greatest pleasure in
presenting this modest Brochure as a
Souvenir to be treasured by his many
friends and admirers, and as a mark of
the warm appreciation which he has
earned by loyal and kindly service.

D 207/11/4

Brochure for a dinner organised by Gower CLP to mark his 25 years as an MP.

Labour Party conference, Margate, 1950, with Ivor and Mattie Davies and a delegate from West Gloucestershire.

D. R. at his desk in the 1950s.

D. R. with Jim Griffiths MP and officers of NUM (South Wales Area).

Le Directeur de l'Institut de Science Economique Appliquée
et
le Directeur de l'Institut Français du Royaume-Uni

vous prient

de vouloir bien honorer de votre présence
la réception qui sera donnée en l'honneur de

Monsieur Pierre MENDES-FRANCE
Ancien Ministre

le Jeudi 27 Novembre 1952 à 5 h.
dans les salons de l'Institut Français, Queensberry Place, S.W.7.

Cette réception précèdera une conférence de
Monsieur Mendès-France
sur
"L'épargne et la politique économique française depuis
la libération".

Sous la présidence de Mr. Nicholas Kaldor, M.A.,
Fellow of King's College, Cambridge.

Invitation to an event with Pierre Mendes France, later Prime Minister of France.

COUNTY BOROUGH OF SWANSEA

Presentation of
The Freedom of the Borough

TO

The Rt. Hon. DAVID RHYS GRENFELL,
C.B.E., J.P., M.P.

Alderman DANIEL EVANS, J.P.

Councillor GEORGE WILLIAM PEACOCK.

IN THE BRANGWYN HALL,
SWANSEA,
THURSDAY, 16th APRIL, 1953,
at 3-0 p.m.

Councillor W. T. Mainwaring Hughes, D.L., J.P. Mayor.
T. B. Bowen, C.B.E., M.A.............Town Clerk.

D 207|11|1

Brochure from the Freedom of the Borough of Swansea ceremony.

Father of the House of Commons, 1950s.

The Father of the House of Commons is congratulated by PC Jones, originally from Aberystwyth.

D. R. receiving the
Freedom of the
Borough of Swansea.

D. R. heads for Canada
in the 1950s.

Opening of Parc y Werin, Gorseinon, 1951.

D. R. and civic dignitaries with Pontarddulais Choral Society, 1953.

D. R. and Beatrice, 1955.

D. R. and Beatrice with Ifor Davies, *c.*1955.

victims of Fascist oppression. Many believed that a period of rest was called for. The opportunity arose when the Empire Parliamentary Association selected him as the British representative to New Zealand's centenary celebrations.[59] The visit itself, and the stops en route in Australia, would result in a busy schedule, but the long sea voyage offered a chance for at least some relaxation and recuperation. During that time he kept a diary in Welsh of his experiences and observations of the sights he saw in the ports where the ship docked along the way, and he made detailed records of the Welsh travellers and expatriates whom he met.

D. R. was under no illusion that the visit to the Antipodes had to be used as an opportunity to promote the war effort and to explain Britain's reasons for going to war. He discussed what needed to be done with officials at the Dominions Office and, in a long interview with Sir Anthony Eden, both agreed the political imperatives for the visit which included the state legislatures of Southern Australia, Western Australia, Victoria and Tasmania, as well as the national parliaments in Canberra and Wellington.

D. R. was in combative mood when he arrived in Adelaide and denounced the Communists' attitude towards the war in front of an audience which included many who were clearly out of sympathy with the British position.[60] He declared his disbelief at the course that Russia was following in entering an alliance with Nazi Germany, a course of action which he, as someone who had sympathised with the Soviet Union for two decades, found incomprehensible. 'Russia had gone mad; Great Britain was not waging an imperialist war... as Hitlerism was the complete antithesis of all for which the Labour movement of the Empire stood for and British workers were prepared to serve and suffer to end Hitler's advance.'[61] He went further and committed the Labour Party to stand by a British declaration of war against Soviet Russia, if it ever came to that.

He pursued a similar theme after arriving in New Zealand,

telling his listeners in Wellington that Britain and France alone of the European powers were not afraid of Germany. He repeated the same message a few days later when he attended the annual conference of the New Zealand Labour Party, stating that he and his fellow Socialists in Britain were determined to support the war effort to its conclusion.[62]

CHAPTER 11

Let Your Work Proclaim Your Worth

D. R. WAS under no illusion about the danger which faced Britain when he returned in the spring of 1940, weeks before the British humiliation at Dunkirk. He had been kept informed of developments within the PLP and returned to London as the Labour Party conference on 13 May 1940 endorsed the leadership's decision to join the coalition government. It was not a decision that could be taken lightly: D. R. had spent the best part of nine years in daily battle with those whom he would now be required to support: the ministers who had presided over the establishment of the UAB and the misery inflicted on industrial Britain, the allies of the coal owners, the appeasers, the guilty men of Munich. He understood fully the strong objection within the Labour movement, the SWMF in particular, to any notion of collaboration with the Tories, especially any arrangement with such a class enemy as the new Prime Minister Winston Churchill. But, such were the circumstances in which Britain found herself.[1] Attlee, Arthur Greenwood and Herbert Morrison were obvious choices to represent Labour in the new government. The trade unions were represented by Ernest Bevin, who was given unprecedented authority over manpower issues as Minister of Labour and National Service.[2] The success of his recent visit to the Antipodes led to speculation that D. R. would be appointed

243

Dominions Secretary, but he was a more natural choice as Secretary for Mines, technically a Parliamentary Secretary at the Board of Trade, but responsible for all aspects of the coal industry.[3]

His appointment was widely seen as one that would help to galvanise the mining industry behind the war effort, with a crucial role in achieving an annual output of 270 million tons, an increase of around 40 million on what had been achieved in 1938–39. From south Wales, the *Western Mail* predicted, 'Mr Grenfell's wide knowledge of mining industry problems should prove of considerable practical benefit at a time when, as Lord Portal declared in his broadcast speech to-night, the task of increasing coal output had become a question of supreme importance. One might almost say of Mr Grenfell that he has "lived" in the industry with which he became associated at the early age of 12.'[4] For *The Scotsman*, 'He is the best type of Socialist and has no enemies in the Commons,' while the *Liverpool Echo* declared, 'He enjoys the confidence of the miners for no Member of Parliament knows more about the mining industry.'[5] Will Lawther of the MFGB committed the miners to supporting 'a practical miner' who was one of their own as Secretary for Mines, promising that they would not hesitate to do their all in the national effort.[6] The SWMF Executive, for its part, also gave a warm endorsement of D. R.'s appointment, reiterated a few weeks later at its annual conference where Arthur Horner made great play of the historic significance of the fact that, for the first time, a man who had worked as a miner now filled the office of Secretary for Mines.[7] The significance of the occasion was not lost on D. R., who used his address to describe the seriousness of the situation facing the country and the vital need to maximise coal production. He promised to resist any proposals to increase the length of the working day, at least until all other avenues had been exhausted, and to ensure that the sacrifices made by Britain's miners in such a time of crisis would not be forgotten.[8]

The address to the SWMF was one of a series of pronouncements made by D. R. in the weeks after accepting office. Within hours of his appointment, he had taken part in a broadcast talk in Welsh for the BBC, immediately followed by an English version on the same theme, in which he dwelt on the need for an increase in coal production and recruitment of more miners in order to reach the targets set.[9] He accompanied Ernest Bevin to Swansea where they used the coal trimmers' annual conference to make a rallying cry to both sides of the industry to increase output and put aside differences over wages, conditions, and working practices for the duration of the war. D. R., responding to Ernest Bevin's impassioned speech, declared that those present:

> … had listened to an inspiring speech by a brave man, who had taken up a task which no one would undertake who was not a brave man. Mr Bevin knew the serious obligations he had assumed, and that success in his new office could not be achieved unless he continued to receive the confidence and support of trade unionists. The working people of this country could make a success of his job… The masses of people of this country would be called upon to expend every ounce of energy to win the war.[10]

The *Western Mail* captured the spirit of the meeting, during which:

> Both Ministers showed a profound sense of the onerous responsibility attached to their new positions, and an equally profound appreciation of the opportunity which it afforded them of rendering conspicuous and even memorable national service. They are in key positions as regards the output and production of all the most urgently needed sinews of war, and being themselves life-long trade unionists and ardent promoters of the interests of all classes of workers, their appeals should carry powerful conviction throughout the

country… The same appeal must be addressed to employers. They, too, must face the risks of concessions which may seem at the time to jeopardise their private interests. They must employ more labour and take bolder steps to eliminate unemployment. There must be a much larger degree of co-operation with employees if the needs of the nation are to be met. Up to the present, some of our greatest industries have failed to pull their weight. They have not reached their maximum production. Obstacles, which in existing circumstances are quite intolerable, have been allowed to retard the national drive. All this must be amended at once.[11]

The MFGB insisted that maximising production could only be achieved through the creation of effective structures through which both sides of industry could work together, coupled with an immediate wage increase of at least 1s. per shift in response to the rising cost of living.[12] The owners, having failed to convince the government to meet the cost of any such increase, offered 6d. per man shift. Weeks of negotiation led to a compromise agreed by the MFGB, despite objections from the SWMF, Yorkshire and Scotland, whereby the miners would be given an advance of 8d. per man shift for adults and 4d. for juveniles. Nevertheless, the sense of dissatisfaction at the settlement remained, and was felt especially strongly within the SWMF, and intensified when the MFGB agreed to another compromise on its longstanding demand for a new wages formula that took account of the rise in the cost of living over the previous 25 years.[13] More hopefully, the MFGB spent the winter of 1939–40 surveying the position in each of its districts, compiling a list of closed collieries which it believed could be re-opened, and gathering details about the potential for more efficient shift working to increase output. This, it argued, would require around 124,000 unemployed miners and ex-miners working in other industries to return to the industry. On one thing they were in no doubt: the required output of coal would not be achieved by making the existing workforce work longer hours or by importing foreign labour into Britain's coalfields.[14]

In the meantime, the MFGB, along with the Mining Association, agreed to a proposal from the Mines Department to set output targets for each district, and, within those, each individual colliery. This agreement was supervised by the Coal Production Council (CPC), chaired by Lord Portal, which included representatives of the management and employees, and at a local level by district and colliery production committees, responsible for addressing all questions regarding production and manpower.[15] The CPC's work was to be supported by coal production advisers who were to act as the conduits between the new body and the situation on the ground. For Portal, the system recognised that each colliery had its own distinct characteristics and unique set of problems that could not be resolved by a national agreement, a view that was shared by D. R.

Both D. R. and Portal also understood that production was being hampered by the fact that so many miners, especially the younger men, had joined the Forces or transferred to other industries since the start of the war, thus drastically reducing manpower. D. R. insisted that a workforce of 800,000 men was required to reach the target of 270 million tons, and one of his first declarations as Secretary for Mines was to call for former coal miners working in other industries, and a comb-out of miners from the Forces, to return. Fifty thousand more miners would be required if output targets were to be met.[16] He also endorsed the MFGB's argument that mines which had been lying idle could be brought into production.[17]

Even so, despite the presence of a Secretary of Mines who was clearly closer to MFGB policy than any of his predecessors, the discontent that festered within the coalfields was evident, and the Labour leadership's willingness to cooperate with the Tory enemy riled many in the rank and file. This had been discussed at the SWMF Executive in February 1940,

247

which referred the matter to a special conference but with no recommendation. That conference had endorsed the notion of a war against fascism, but had welcomed Labour's refusal to join the government. After Labour reversed its decision, Arthur Horner, President of the SWMF since 1936, moved a resolution on behalf of the SWMF at the MFGB annual conference, insisting that only a government cleansed of 'all those who, led by Chamberlain, pursued the policy which has created this situation' would be capable of providing the kind of leadership that was required by the country. The Coalition should be replaced by 'a Government more representative of the people of this country'.[18] He warned that Winston Churchill's ministers would have no compulsion in betraying the Welsh MPs now expected to support it: Tories remained 'rotten with treachery' whatever they professed.[19] President Will Lawther, however, warned that, were the MFGB to follow Horner and demand a purge of the men of Munich, D. R., along with Tom Williams, George Hall, Wilfred Paling and William Whitely, would have to forsake participation and return to the backbenches, given that there was no realistic chance of it ever happening in the circumstances in which they found themselves.

To the relief of those MPs and the Labour leadership more broadly, conference rejected the SWMF motion, and supported an alternative resolution from Durham that affirmed Attlee's war aims, as outlined in his declarations of November 1939 and February 1940. The conference recognised that Labour ministers would not be able to implement a Socialist policy in the areas for which they were responsible. This would include no immediate nationalisation of the mining industry, nor reform of the Workmen's Compensation Act, nor an increase in the number of workers' representatives on the Coal Production Advisory Committee, all of which would have to wait until after the war was won.[20] D. R. had committed his life to realising such aims but he was enough of a realist to know that a government led by Winston Churchill in a parliament still dominated by the Tories would never implement any such measures. Above all, he understood that Britain's miners, while unconditional in their commitment to the battle against Nazi-Fascism, did not trust Winston Churchill or the Conservative Party, and ministers in the government needed to understand that underlying reality.

While the MFGB was articulating its plans for coal production, Ernest Bevin was already embarking on his own programme to mobilise Britain's entire workforce in support of the war effort and to reach the target, calculated by Sir William Beveridge, that half a million men were required for the armed forces.[21] Ernest Bevin brought with him an unrivalled knowledge of key aspects of British industry. Even before his appointment he had been involved in developing the detailed planning for docks and road haulage, where the pooling and transfer of labour was an accepted solution to those sectors' problems. He had also been privy to discussions which convinced large manufacturers to concentrate production in a small number of centres. The Military Service Act and Control of Employment Regulations gave the government – and the Ministry of Labour and National Service specifically – the power to direct labour and prevent the drift of workers from key industries, which Ernest Bevin was determined to use to the full.

A manpower review of the coal industry, undertaken between April and June 1940, identified that between 28,000 and 38,000 men attached to the industry were unemployed, the majority of whom had been out of work for over twelve months, of whom around 6,000 were deemed not suitable for re-employment underground, mainly on health grounds.[22] While there was broad consensus that coal mining had to be scheduled as a reserved occupation, there was no agreement over how this would work out in practice. In particular, the Ministry of Labour was under intense pressure from the departments responsible for the Services not to agree to a blanket application of reserved occupation status, and each regulation was subject to scrutiny by Lord Cherwell and the statistical section, whose aim was to maximise the number of personnel available for military service and minimise any exemptions. Consequently, while reserved occupation status was granted to underground workers aged 18, 21, 23 and 25, it was not extended to other colliery workers. Building maintenance men, engineers, transport workers, clerical staff and other employees were subject to the same regulations as those that applied to similar employment categories outside the mines. The fall of France provided further ammunition to those who sought to deny there was any manpower crisis in the coal industry, as the number of unemployed miners increased to 60,000.[23] Furthermore, decades of decay, poor management and labour troubles meant it was badly prepared for the task it was required to undertake in support of the war effort. The situation in the summer was outlined in graphic terms by Ness Edwards, speaking on behalf of the SWMF at the MFGB annual conference, who referred to the 'anarchy in the coal industry' that created a situation in which some districts were working on short time while others were working seven days a week.[24] J. Swann of Durham warned of the danger of a repeat of the 'coal famine' experienced during the opening months of 1940 unless there was a change of government policy, while Arthur Horner demanded equitable distribution of coal orders across the whole country.[25]

D. R. was given the opportunity to respond at the conference and resorted to the bare facts.[26] Britain was cut off from the coal markets of Europe, meaning all export coal had become surplus. Supplies already on ships at sea when the capitulation of France took place had been brought back to Britain and unloaded at appropriate places. This meant the plans for increased production, both for internal consumption and for export trade, had to be abandoned. He pledged that government policy would support collieries to work for four days a week as an alternative to closure, and all production in all areas needed to be maintained. On the question of stockpiling, he was able to announce that the government intended to increase stocks during the summer before the shorter days and the blackout began, and that electricity and gas producers, railway companies, and private consumers would be expected to build up their stocks.[27]

Even so, he was also aware that the Undertakings (Restriction of Engagement) Order, which came into force in June 1940 and forbade the employment of miners or men with recent experience of the industry in other jobs other than under specified circumstances, had unintended consequences.[28] As unemployment continued in the coalfields, especially Durham and south Wales, men were being kept idle when they could be working elsewhere.[29] Ever since he had been appointed Secretary for Mines, D. R. had argued forcefully that unemployed miners should be allowed to take work in other industries as a temporary measure until they were needed in the mines, and that the operation of the Restriction of Engagement Order should be suspended to enable them to do so. He also called for a programme to train new recruits through an apprenticeship scheme that included the introduction of graded wages based on an annual increment.[30]

Ernest Bevin was guarded in response to these proposals, insisting that the Restriction of Engagement Order should remain in force as a means of ensuring men did not leave for higher wages elsewhere when work was available in the mining industry.[31] However, he agreed to take 'administrative action' that enabled local officers of the Ministry of Labour to permit unemployed miners to enter other occupations, subject to the proviso that they would be empowered to transfer men to coalfields where work was to be found. In consequence, nearly 36,000 men from Durham and south Wales were either relocated to other coalfields or, more commonly, found work outside the mining industry (mostly building factories, working in the chemical industry, ironstone mining, and shipbuilding) between summer 1940 and spring 1941. The figures included an estimated 5,500 men from south Wales who went to work in non-mining industries in other parts of Britain, mainly in South and West Yorkshire.[32] The requirement to move to other districts, however, immediately created resentment, revealed clearly by the Joint Secretaries of the South Wales Production Committee when asked to cooperate in the arrangements, who made it clear they would not do so and insisted that the Ministry of Labour had no business imposing such a requirement.[33] In any event, the measures failed to prevent growing unemployment in the coalfields: in September 1940 more than 31,000 miners were completely out of work and an even greater number, 42,000, were temporarily laid off.[34]

The dissatisfaction within the coalfields in relation to the government's whole approach to the coal industry was reflected in the tone of a parliamentary debate held on 5 September 1940. From the Labour benches, Jack Lawson referred to the level of unemployment in Durham and south Wales, complaining that the plight of 40,000 miners who were out of work was being ignored as ministers focused on dealing with labour shortages elsewhere. He was scathing about the Ministry of Labour refusing to give the required 'Green Cards' to enable miners to obtain work outside the industry.[35] S. O. Davies concurred, and called for a 'complete reorganisation of coal production and distribution' through the creation of a central body 'with real authority' to direct and coordinate work across all coalfields.[36] David Adams maintained that if men were prevented from obtaining other work then they should receive their wages while not working, and he insisted that the situation could be eased by more effective distribution of orders.[37] From the opposite side of the House, Sir Cuthbert Headlam alleged gross mismanagement of the situation the previous winter (before D. R. became Secretary for Mines), and suggested looking for export markets in countries unaffected by war.[38]

D. R. was keen to emphasise positive aspects as well as recognising the difficulties. More coal was being produced per shift than had been the case for a long time. Men were being trained, but this could not be done overnight. Turning to the manpower issue, he referred to his discussions with Ernest Bevin throughout the summer, which had begun in very different circumstances for the mining industry. Thousands of men had left the industry – 73,000 since September 1939 – which meant that around 40,000, if not 50,000 more men were required to enable the output targets to be achieved. The fall of France had changed the situation completely and the government had sought to take steps to stem the rising unemployment in the exporting districts, but they had encountered practical problems in doing so. This meant that it was necessary to allow men to be released from mining until other work could be found, but only on the understanding they could be called back to the mines when work was available. However, many men wanted to join the army, creating a danger that 'we shall lose the cream of our manhood in the industry because of men going into the army unless we can find regular work for them.'[39]

Jim Griffiths, in response, endorsed D. R.'s approach, adding that it would be more effective to pay miners laid off for a short period of time than to transfer them elsewhere, because of the longer-term benefits that this would bring. It was vital, he believed, that the industry was not allowed to contract. This would be best achieved through the creation of a central body under government control to prevent coal owners from using their traditional tactic of closing a colliery when there was no demand. But any such reorganisation was outside the scope of the Secretary for Mines working under the constraints of a wartime coalition government.[40]

Shortly afterwards, D. R. and Ernest Bevin met again to

discuss how many men were required for the mines, how many could be transferred, and how many brought in from other industries.[41] During those meetings Sir Alfred Hurst from the Mines Department advised that production could be boosted by concentrating on working the most efficient mines in each district and transferring the men there. As a gesture of goodwill, he proposed a special levy to subsidise the re-opening of collieries closed in consequence of this policy after the war. Even so, Hurst believed that a workforce of 750,000 men would be required to reach the output targets. Ernest Bevin, on the other hand, demanded that at least some of the 1.3 million men required for the army should be recruited from those working in the coal industry. He was prepared to consider any scheme to increase production that was agreed by the industry, provided that it secured the required number of men to meet both its own needs and freed for the Forces. He therefore proposed to remove the exemption granted to all men aged 18 to 23, but would delay implementing it until November to allow stock-piling to take place. This, Hurst countered, would take miners away from areas already short of workers, something that could not be addressed by the transfer of men, as they would be required to move to different districts (rather than collieries within the same district). He warned that, 'It had been found by experience that transfer was always difficult, and if made compulsory led to inefficient work by the miners concerned.'[42]

The Ministry of Labour's view prevailed and, on 21 September 1940, D. R. met the MFGB Executive where he had to tell them that, despite his efforts to retain manpower, the fact that unemployed miners had not been 'absorbed' in the industry meant that the departments responsible for the Services' demands were being given precedence and that, consequently, the younger men would be subject to being called for military service. As if to rub salt into the wounds, by coincidence D. R. was obliged to outline to the same meeting the details of the government's generous scheme to compensate coal owners whose property had been affected by enemy action.[43] It was not a meeting that D. R. would want to repeat.[44] The MFGB Executive, for its part, indicated a willingness to compromise, but not to capitulate. It agreed that miners who were 'wholly unemployed' could be directed to other industries but insisted that, 'The only men who can be spared from the coal mining industry without serious interference with supply of essential requirements are those registered by the Ministry of Labour as wholly unemployed. Such men, being no longer employed in the industry, should cease to be reserved from military service for that reason, and if above the age required for such service, should be available for other industries.'[45]

The following month, D. R. again met with the MFGB Executive, Ernest Bevin, and the Mining Association to discuss coal production and the manpower issues. D. R. repeated his argument in favour of retaining an adequate labour force within the coal industry, notwithstanding the heavy demand from the Services and the munitions factories.[46] Again, Ernest Bevin agreed that men who were genuinely required in the mines could not be directed to undertake military service, and he also committed to change the reserved occupation regulations and to establish a tribunals system to determine how many men could be spared from the collieries in each district. However, he insisted that men under 30 released by the tribunals and any man who had been unemployed for more than six weeks could be called up. In his view, the tribunals should identify younger men who could be called up which would then create opportunities for unemployed older men to return to the mines.[47]

In the midst of the discussions, D. R. still found time to lead a campaign to boost production in public meetings and conferences across the country. He used a series of broadcasts to make a direct appeal to those working in the industry, declaring that under the conditions of war there were no two sides in the industry 'on this occasion, and for this purpose there is only one side', and that was the country, united in its opposition to Hitler. He went on:

> We can win this war by work. Steady, regular, hard work, its determination to win to prove we have strength as well as right on our side... My mining comrades, I know that you are loyal and brave to a man. In this time of trial, let your work proclaim your worth and your output of coal be the measure of the part you are prepared to pay for liberty.[48]

Despite such appeals, and the valiant efforts made across Britain's coalfields in the autumn of 1940, coal supplies fell drastically, especially in London and south-east England where a combination of air attacks and transport difficulties reduced the weekly supply available from 250,000 tons to 165,000 tons. Alarmist comments that the capital and its hinterland would freeze to death the following winter may have been some way off the mark (as D. R. pointed out, around 60 per cent of supplies were reaching their destination), but they had some currency given the experience the previous year.[49] Some emergency measures were implemented. Unemployed Welsh miners, mainly from the Anthracite Area, who had been sent to London to help with rescue work during the air raids, were among 3,000 men who were given temporary work in the Kent and Somerset coalfields. This followed a personal intervention by D. R., who pleaded with the SWMF Executive to persuade the men to agree to the arrangement, even though it meant they were required to work in extremely poor conditions, especially in Somerset.[50]

However, the main focus of the government's efforts was directed towards building up stocks of coal in London during the summer and early autumn. Shortly after his appointment, D. R. had announced a target that 20 million tons of domestic coal would be stockpiled in the capital or its immediate vicinity. When his officials reported difficulties in finding additional storage sites, D. R. insisted on overseeing much of the work himself, becoming heavily involved with the detailed task of identifying every conceivable place where coal could be kept, and personally monitoring the level of stocks at gas works, generating stations and those held by individual merchants.[51] He became convinced that the problem was being exacerbated by the railway organisation's refusal to prioritise the movement of coal supplies, which meant that the only option was to commandeer road haulage for the task.[52] Therefore, although a creditable supply of 30 million tons was stored in the capital by the beginning of November, D. R. realised that this was barely sufficient for the winter.

As the situation worsened during the last months of 1940, D. R. ordered that coal that could not be taken to its intended destinations should be stored in government facilities until it could be moved.[53] This decision, in turn, revealed another problem, a shortage of wagons, caused by the fact that so many of them were lying idle, loaded with coal intended for export in various docks and across Britain. The press had a simple story to tell: railway wagons filled with coal were standing idle throughout the railway system while Britain shivered.[54] The tone was set when the *Daily Express* declared:

> It is said that on Mr Grenfell's orders there are 70,000 trucks all standing full and idle in the sidings of Britain. Get them moving, they are full of steam coal for export which cannot be burned in the domestic grate. They are idle because the customers that ordered them now take orders from Hitler. Tip out those trucks, Mr Grenfell. Tip them on to dumps or tip them in the sea. No matter, so long as you get the trucks moving to the towns and the coal carts moving through the streets, it doesn't matter who is blamed or is inconvenienced. It doesn't matter which department does it. It doesn't matter how it is done. So long as Mrs Smith, Mrs Brown and Mrs Jones get coal to burn in their stoves and grates this winter.[55]

On the key question of manpower, the paper was equally unequivocal. 'Minister David Grenfell says he has knocked at Ernest Bevin's door with 20,000 coal carters. That is good. Right now, the Army can spare these men and we at home cannot.'[56]

This was the issue above all which occupied D. R.'s mind either side of Christmas 1940. He met Ernest Bevin on 4 December to discuss once again the position of unemployed miners in south Wales and Durham who needed to secure other work, and questions related to unemployment in those areas. The subsequent correspondence between them highlighted a fundamental difference over what had been agreed, both at that meeting and in relation to the substantive issue of the extent to which men working in the coal industry would be exempt from a requirement for other work or military service. This was to prove crucial in the ensuing dispute between the two men, and is outlined in detail below.

Ernest Bevin had produced a note of the meeting in which he insisted that miners 'stood off' should be regarded as available for transfer to other mining employment, or other work of national importance, in the same way as wholly unemployed coal miners. Coal miners aged 30 or over in employment, in south Wales and Durham, should be regarded as available for transfer to coal-mining employment in other districts, or to other work of urgent national importance either locally or in other districts. Miners aged between 25 and 30 in employment in south Wales or Durham should only be regarded as available for transfer to coal-mining employment in other districts, but not to any other kind of employment.

D. R. immediately responded by saying that he accepted the first point but not the remainder of the note, insisting they had not even been discussed at the meeting. He believed that Bevin had *assumed* his agreement on the key question of whether men who were in employment should be transferred elsewhere at the discretion of the Ministry of Labour, and that such transfers should be regarded as 'administrative matters'. Furthermore, he believed that such matters could not proceed while tribunals, which the Ministry of Labour itself had set up, were still considering how many men could be released for the Forces. This was particularly the case in south Wales and Durham where any analysis would be bound to be complicated by the fact that the number of men temporarily required to man the industry was lower than what was normally required, causing a false situation to be built into manpower calculations. He added that the course suggested by the Ministry of Labour would establish a dual process which would create uncertainty within the industry and cause unnecessary disruption:

> I am quite sure that the industry would object to the proposal for the reasons I have mentioned, and I do urge that we should give the tribunals a chance before taking the risk of further disturbances to the organisation of the industry by introducing another separate process for removing men from it which would be running side by side with the tribunal machinery.

Ernest Bevin responded by insisting that the points had been discussed and, while the details needed to be confirmed, he believed that D. R. had accepted the principle of transferring men who were in employment, specifically in areas where there was a surplus of labour. He went on to refute each of D. R.'s arguments, arguing that the tribunals would look first at those mining areas with the highest unemployment and then review whether men from other coalfields would be required to be made available outside the industry.

On 20 December D. R. replied, insisting that Ernest Bevin had repeated the 'inaccurate statement' contained in his previous letter which he again denied, adding that Pryor, an official at the Mines Department, concurred with his (D. R.'s) version of events. Furthermore, D. R. had looked at the Manpower and Production Committee papers which showed clearly that the mining industry had lost 18 per cent of its workforce through the voluntary transference of men to other industries. Since the previous summer, unemployed miners had been released from the industry for other work on condition that they could be required to return to the mines should circumstances allow. He demanded information about the methods that would be used to assess men in the mining industry in view of the withdrawal of reservation of men under 30 and the proposed transfer of men over 30. How could sufficient numbers of men be retained in the industry under such arrangements, he demanded to know.

Ten days later, Ernest Bevin agreed 'for the time being' not to allow miners in employment to leave the industry, other than those under 30 who might be allocated by the tribunals to be made available for the army. The same principle could be applied to miners who were briefly out of employment or working short time, 'owing to temporary transport difficulties or want of wagons'. However, 'miners who are on more or less sustained short time, owing to want of trade., should be regarded as available for transfer outside the industry'. No obstacle would be put before unemployed miners leaving to do work of national importance. He also conceded on the specific point of the Anthracite Area miners who were out of work because of loss of trade with Canada but who would be required in the mines in the spring who, he agreed, should be found some other work for the interim period. Bevin added, 'I am hopeful that they will feel no difficulty about agreeing to these suggestions which I have made in an endeavour to meet your views.'

D. R. insisted that the central proposals made by the Ministry of Labour, that men selected for release from the industry would be available for call-up, would 'produce a violent dislocation of working conditions' that would severely handicap the coal industry from making its own contribution to the war effort. Serious damage would be done to the structure of British mining and discrimination between different districts was a possibility. He was not querying the number to be released, but any such process should be implemented on the basis of particular occupational grades and colliery by colliery.

Ernest Bevin, on 8 January, interpreted that D. R.'s proposals meant that a separate and special quota from each pit would not be acceptable to the industry and would not help ensure that the right men were called up. He suggested an alternative, already being trialled in Durham, based on employment exchange areas. At least, initially, the pits in such sub-divisions would be within travelling distance of each other, thus eliminating the need for miners to relocate.

However D. R. was not convinced by that proposal either (which in any case limited the guarantee that relocation would not be necessary to an initial period only). He referred to the need to consider the implications of any requirement on miners to travel to collieries other than those where they already worked. What was needed, he insisted, was a workforce of between 700,000 and 720,000 men and a system that took account of the fact that miners were most productive when they worked in areas where they were familiar with the conditions and working practices. 'Methods of working, transport conditions to and from work, and so on, vary so much from one district to another that the individual man is seldom a fully efficient unit outside his own area, or if his own occupation inside the industry is changed.' Far from increasing production, he believed, the change proposed by Ernest Bevin could lead to a shortage of coal.

This exchange was the first in a series of disagreements between the two men, but the possibility of shortages led to an agreement on four immediate steps: first, that men would be prevented from leaving the industry; second, ex-miners suitable for employment in the industry would be transferred back; third, an examination would be undertaken to understand how existing manpower could be used more effectively; and fourth, unemployed workers from other industries would be transferred into mining.[57]

Believing that he had established these principles, D. R. began to sound a cautious note of optimism about the prospect for coal supplies. In a series of pronouncements at the start of 1941, he noted that Britain had witnessed two winters when coal stocks had been depleted because of lack of manpower and transport difficulties. Increased output and better transport arrangements meant that the country was in a better position to face its next cold period. Furthermore, some of the collieries that had stopped working in 1939–40 had resumed production, not least in the Anthracite Area in south Wales.[58]

D. R. continued with his work, battling the elements to continue his punishing schedule of speaking engagements across Britain's coalfields throughout the winter, persuading his audiences of the need for increased production and hearing for himself what was happening in the mining communities and intervening personally to resolve local disputes. He spent time in Lancashire negotiating a solution to a strike over the way a wages agreement was being implemented in the area around Manchester.[59] He travelled to Scotland to personally oversee negotiations over union membership and a 'no strike' agreement for the duration of the war.[60] He dealt with safety issues (in particular the urgent need to revise the regulations in response to the findings of a report into the disaster at the Valleyfield Colliery in Fife), sought to improve coal transportation both for industrial and domestic customers, attempted to create a more efficient distribution of orders to enable collieries facing short-term working to survive, and tried to re-open some of those pits that had closed.[61] Throughout these months, he repeated his insistence that the rate of absenteeism (which averaged between ten and twelve per cent during his time as a Minister) could not be attributed to any shortcomings on the part of the miners themselves; mining was a difficult and dangerous job undertaken in poor conditions in situations which changed with every shift, and any failure to reach the output targets should not be blamed on the colliers themselves.[62]

Given the demands on an industry working in the conditions of war, it was inevitable that his work and the contribution of coal mining to the national effort would face intense scrutiny from all quarters.[63] He faced another fractious debate in the House of Commons in February 1941, during the course of which he sought to defend the Mines Department and its work from Labour MPs who, while loyal to D. R., were nevertheless determined to attack his officials. Gordon Macdonald, the Welsh-born MP for Ince, urged him to use his powers to control orders and ensure transport was available to maximise production in all areas. The Labour MP Tom Smith asked why there was such a high casualty rate in 1940, the highest figure for ten years, before turning his attention to the problems of management and demanding that an over-riding authority be established to deal with pits threatened with closure. On several occasions the phrase 'coal famine' was used to describe the situation facing the country. D. R., responding to the debate and outlining the situation, appealed for forbearance in the circumstances. Stock-piling was taking place, the Mines Department was actively involved in developing schemes to improve distribution, using their powers to deal severely with profiteering, and a range of measures were being taken to improve safety. It was a valiant effort and, under the circumstances, it was difficult to conceive of anyone better placed than D. R. to save the government from the MPs' wrath, but the essential problems remained and had to be addressed to prevent a fuel crisis later in the year.[64]

D. R. was convinced that each criticism that had been made of the coal situation could, in some way or another, be attributed to the underlying problem of manpower. Everything stemmed from the fact that there were not enough miners in Britain to produce the coal it required. Men were working when they were not fit to do so and absenteeism arose, more often than not from total exhaustion. His own battle with the Ministry of Labour had been conducted against a backdrop of unrest in the industry and open criticism of the government's manpower scheme. The MFGB Executive declared its opposition to the Ministry of Labour's proposals, especially the transference arrangements which discriminated against certain areas, south Wales in particular.[65] The *Daily Express* described the situation in terms of personalities. 'Burly Will Lawther, President of the Mineworkers' Federation, confronting Mr David Grenfell, Minister for Mines, in London yesterday, received a promise that he will deal quickly with the manpower available in the coalfields and the fact that some collieries are flooded with orders while others in the export trade are idle.'[66]

On the ground, however, little progress was being made, even after the CPC sought to bring together both sides of the industry to discuss a way forward. The MFGB and Mining Association were at loggerheads over wage standards and the involvement of the men's elected officials in decision-making processes. They could not agree to the establishment of a joint national board, nor on the question of a guaranteed weekly wage, nor compulsory union membership, all issues that had been at the heart of the tensions within the mining industry for generations.

CHAPTER 12

I Am Glad I Trusted My Own Judgement

IN MARCH 1941 D. R., faced with another alarming set of production figures, instructed his officials to write to the Ministry of Labour requesting the suspension of any further transfer of men from the mining industry. He followed this with his own memorandum in which he emphasised the gravity of the coal situation and the pressing need for more manpower.[1] The Ministry of Labour was forced to concede, but its alternative was even more unpalatable than the status quo: manpower would be regulated by an Essential Works Order (EWO) that stipulated mining as a reserved occupation, and the men could not leave their place of employment nor be dismissed, and they would face sanctions if they were absent from work at any time. A guaranteed minimum wage would also be introduced, which would be linked to, but not directly controlled by, the EWO.

The notion of an EWO had long been resisted within the industry and the proposal generated much resentment, especially within the SWMF and among the Scottish miners.[2] The EWO, its opponents insisted, was unnecessary. The issues that came under its jurisdiction could be resolved far more effectively by the joint committees working at each colliery. Linking a minimum wage to an EWO was not sufficient, and what was needed was a guaranteed minimum wage for the whole industry. George Thomas, industrial correspondent of the *Daily Herald* and himself a product of the south Wales Labour movement where he had campaigned for Keir Hardie in Aberdare 30 years earlier, understood the resentment that would be generated in mining communities by the insinuation that such regulations would be necessary to maximise production. The miners' reasonable demand for a minimum wage was being unfairly linked to regulations that would force men into idleness because they were unable to leave the industry, he insisted. The men would be required to report to the colliery, to be told there was no work for them, and would be put at risk of a fine for absenteeism in consequence.[3] It was a recipe for discontent throughout Britain's mining communities.

This resentment was voiced clearly when D. R. met the MFGB and the Mining Association at the beginning of April 1941.[4] The MFGB insisted that the question of an EWO could not be separated from consideration of their demand for the establishment of a national board and the introduction of a protected weekly wage.[5] The MFGB could not countenance any restrictions or compulsion on the miners until a satisfactory agreement was reached on the question of wages, something which the Ministry of Labour realised would involve subsidises to the coal industry.

The extent of the distrust which existed towards ministers among the MFGB was revealed by a fairly trivial incident during the course of these negotiations. D. R. had to leave the meeting to attend a parliamentary engagement and the subsequent discussions were led by Sir Alfred Hurst. However, this was interpreted by some of the MFGB as a sign that D. R. was not prepared to discuss the difficult issues that lay at the heart of the matter. Although the misunderstanding was resolved when Ebby Edwards of the MFGB met D. R. the following morning and accepted his explanation, the key issues remained unresolved as the MFGB would not, under any circumstances, accept a situation where men were tied to the mining industry when they could be obtaining higher wages elsewhere.[6] After days of negotiation, D. R.'s patience began to fail and he insisted that it was pointless for the MFGB to bring such arguments to him as he had no authority over those matters. In any event, he could not see how the status quo could be maintained when men were leaving the industry to satisfy their own convenience, with the result that those left behind in the mines were unable to do their work.

Ernest Bevin, he insisted, had offered guaranteed amounts to prevent men leaving the industry. While D. R. retained the view that there was a need for a national board to control the industry, this again was not a matter for him. He reminded the MFGB that an EWO provided a level of security and regulation of working conditions that had not been granted previously.[7] On the other hand he, as the minister, also faced the Mining Association who adhered to their longstanding opposition to the principle of a national minimum wage and, instead, offered a bonus that would be conditional on men turning up to six successive shifts.[8]

The MFGB Executive summoned a national conference which revealed clearly the extent of the miners' opposition to the EWO and broader resentment at the way the industry was being run.[9] Despite the efforts of Will Lawther to minimise discontent, delegates from the SWMF and from Scotland led the attack, insisting that, despite promises to the contrary, the men had no real say in the way the mines were being worked. The owners were ignoring the pit production committees, while their experience of the National Service officers meant they did not trust them with the increased powers they would enjoy through an EWO.[10] They demanded that the MFGB reject any change until their grievances had been resolved satisfactorily.[11] Ebby Edwards then reported on the negotiations with D. R., expressing his 'disappointment' at the lack of progress. Others were more forthright. J. Pearson, from the Scottish miners, insisted that if D. R. believed a national board was a necessity, he should resign from the government rather than continue to serve in an administration that had rejected the idea.[12] Despite such views, and the strong opposition of the SWMF to the government's proposals, the conference resolved not to pursue a demand for increased wages due to the seriousness of the war situation, conditional on the establishment of a national minimum weekly wage of £4. This formed the basis of subsequent negotiations, in which Arthur Horner, on behalf of the MFGB, played the leading role in finding a pragmatic solution. A national agreement was secured that included provisions for a bonus which incentivised full attendance, restricted miners to working in the industry, and raised a levy of 6d. on each ton of coal paid into a pool to fund a guaranteed minimum wage.[13]

When the matter came before the House of Commons on 28 May 1941, Labour MPs remained unconvinced, referring to the potential for abuse and unfairness in the way the agreement would be implemented. They demanded to know whether National Service officers would henceforth be able to usurp the role of Pit Production Committees and criticised the decision to link the guaranteed weekly wage to the EWO. Tom Smith MP listed example after example of potential difficulties: men could be given duties underground they could not do and would not be in a position to refuse; there would be nothing to prevent colliery mangers from keeping men idle and draw down the payment from the pool rather than pay the men to do essential maintenance work. Sandy Sloan MP, speaking for Scotland's coalfields, made a passionate speech denouncing the very notion of an EWO in the mining industry.[14]

As the attacks on the government intensified however, members from both sides began to express personal support for D. R. Gordon Macdonald deplored the way D. R. had been treated by the press. 'I did not like the references which were made to the Secretary for Mines during the week-end. Some sections of the Press for some reason have set out to belittle him,' he declared. The Ulster Unionist MP Sir William Allen, Deputy Grand Master of the Orange Order, also referred to the minister's expertise, stating that, 'In this House we have a Secretary for Mines who ought to know all about the subject... I am quite satisfied, as an outsider who does not understand the first thing about coal, that he has the interests of the miners just as much at heart as the interests of the coal owner, if not more.'[15]

Meanwhile, the Mines Department warned of the prospect of a national crisis the following winter unless coal production was increased substantially. It presented the evidence in stark terms to representatives of the MFGB and Mining Association, based on calculations that indicated that 112.6 million tons would need to be produced by September 1941, equivalent to a production rate of 4.5 million tons each week.[16] The reality was, however, that output had fallen from 61,974,100 tons in June 1940 to 51,064,600 in June 1941. As the miners' historian R. Page Arnot concluded 20 years later, the failure of the government to heed D. R.'s warnings was a major cause of the crisis. 'Amid the winter Blitz of 1940–41, the warnings of the Secretary for Mines had not come home to the Government. Week by week and month by month, man-power and output was falling. The crisis was growing, but it was not until the spring of 1941 that the Government realised the development of a coal crisis.'[17]

The assessment that the country needed more than 112 million tons to survive the winter strengthened the Mines Department's case for additional manpower, and prompted D. R. to demand that a labour force of 765,000 be maintained, representing an increase of at least 50,000 men over the existing workforce. This was at a time when the industry was losing 1,000 men every week. To achieve this, the Mines Department advocated enticing ex-miners working in other reserved occupations, through improved wages alongside other inducements, such as additional food rations and a training and apprenticeship scheme to attract juveniles.[18] Their case was, however, challenged throughout by Lord Cherwell, whose regular private memoranda sent directly to Winston Churchill continually questioned the Mines Department's figures. He argued that the winter of 1939–40 should not be accepted as the basis for estimating supply requirements as it had been unusually cold, far colder than 1940–41. Consumption needs were being exaggerated, and far from needing men, the mining industry could release several thousands for call-up to the Services.

Ernest Bevin may or may not have seen Cherwell's memoranda but their tenor was certainly conveyed to him, as is clear from the discussions he and his officials had with D. R. and the Mines Department at the end of May 1941.[19] D. R. put the case for allocating an additional 50,000 men to work in the mining industry as part of the Mines Department's argument that releasing men from the Forces would be a better option than sending men from other industries, some of whom had left coal mining as they were not suited to such work.[20] Ernest Bevin resisted, declaring that he was 'not prepared in any circumstances to support an application for the release of men required for the Forces. To do this would interfere with the training of the Army at a critical period.'[21] His view was echoed by Ministry of Labour officials who insisted that 'they could not continue to tolerate the continued unemployment of these people if there were work they could do, even if not efficiently, if their work could release men at present engaged on surface work for more strenuous work, particularly underground.'[22] The same official went further, and offered to send representatives of the Ministry of Labour to collieries to advise how men could be used more effectively.[23] With his lifetime's experience of the mining industry, D. R. knew better than anyone around the table that such a suggestion would be guaranteed to provoke outrage across the coalfields, but he still faced the difficulty of getting others to understand the situation.[24] The meeting agreed to a compromise whereby ex-miners not engaged in priority work would be encouraged to return to the industry, and authorised D. R. to make a public appeal to this effect.[25] This he did in June 1941, but he was almost instantly undermined by Ernest Bevin who threatened that young miners 'who did not pull their weight' could lose their reserved occupation status, and reiterated his opposition to the release of former miners serving in the Forces.[26]

Undaunted, D. R. continued his battle, declaring to the Commons that the government would be arresting the leakage of manpower, and charging his officials with the task of developing a scheme that would guarantee that wages would be paid to men during the period when they were temporarily laid off.[27] The Ministry of Labour, meanwhile, introduced a registration scheme to make it easier to transfer men back to the areas from which they had come voluntarily and new regulations also stipulated that men found fit for work underground would not be permitted to take other work, unless under special circumstances.[28] But the general view of what transpired was that the Ministry of Labour had succeeded at the expense of the Mines Department. As D. R. ruefully told the *Daily Herald*, 'I have made representations… but I am not responsible for the balancing of considerations. There may be other considerations that overweigh the claims I make.'[29]

It is clear that both Winston Churchill and Clement Attlee were both aware and alarmed at the tension which clearly existed between the Mines Department and the Ministry of Labour, and the increasing animosity that was evident in the skirmishes between D. R. and Ernest Bevin. The extent to which Ernest Bevin had briefed against D. R. by the summer of 1941 – if he had done so at all – is not proven but, crucially, his case echoed that being put by Lord Cherwell who certainly had the Prime Minister's ear. This induced Winston Churchill to discuss changes to ministerial appointments which he discussed with Clement Attlee in July 1941, that included a suggestion that D. R. should be removed from the government and offered the position of Governor General of New Zealand as a consolation. The correspondence between the two indicates that Clement Attlee was not enamoured by the idea on several grounds. He argued that, 'to send Grenfell to New Zealand would be considered there as providing a place for someone not wanted at home'. While he recognised that D. R. had made a good impression there and in Australia, he was very committed to his work at the Mines Department. 'I think it very unlikely that Grenfell would accept under these circumstances. He might indeed be very upset.' Furthermore, such a change would jeopardise relations with the miners and, in particular, the MFGB which were already in a delicate state. Despite these reservations, Clement Attlee did indeed broach the matter with D. R., who was adamant that he wished to continue with his work at the Mines Department. The Mines Department was the place where a man of his background and experience was best placed to serve, and he had sought to exercise his duties faithfully since his appointment. For the time being, Clement Attlee agreed, and the option of New Zealand was not discussed further. Even so, it was clear that D. R. had powerful enemies within the government, who would have been more than happy to see him removed.[30]

The gravity of the situation in the mining industry, and the weakness of Ernest Bevin's arguments, became even clearer over the summer when local officers of the Ministry of Labour established special panels consisting of their own officials and representatives of the miners and employers to examine the detailed situation in each area and concluded that, of the 2,000 men initially interviewed, only a quarter were fit to work in the mining industry.[31] Meanwhile, the Ministry of Labour faced resistance from employers who had taken on miners and were reluctant to release them to return to mining, especially if the men were deemed to be engaged on work of national importance. The actions of a public contracting company in Northamptonshire, which refused to release 40 men to return to Saron Colliery, near Ammanford, was one of many such examples, several of which were only resolved when the firms were threatened with prosecution under the DORA.[32]

Addressing the MFGB conference later that summer, D. R. insisted that he remained 'a good coalminer, willing to take it, driving through the hard ground' in his work as Secretary for Mines. Turing to the manpower and production issues, he implored the conference to look to the future that could be secured. 'I cannot give an exact outline of the world peace structure that is to be, but I will name some fundamental conditions, and that is the concession of common right to abundance, to prosperity, to contentment and security for all nations.'[33]

In the interim, his arguments concerning the manpower situation were boosted when the committee chaired by the Lord President, Sir John Anderson, recognised what D. R. had been saying since the start of the year and warned that the country faced a coal crisis in the winter unless urgent action was taken. While the position in south Wales, Durham and Scotland was deemed to be fairly satisfactory, there was a significant shortage of miners in north-west England and the Midlands.[34] The MFGB responded, blaming the EWO and insisting that no solution was possible until it was removed. Former miners would not return underground voluntarily, they declared, if they would be required to abide by such restrictions.[35] Furthermore, to rely on recruiting ex-miners was a fallacy, as revealed by the fact that, of the 104,000 men examined, nearly half were unfit or rejected as unsuitable, and most of the others were unavailable.[36] The Executive was also clear where the blame lay. 'They had great sympathy with him [D. R.] as one of our own MPs, whom they believed to be placed in a difficult position by officials of his department and by the ministers in the War Cabinet,' but they would not be prepared to compromise on questions of principle when dealing with the government.[37]

By the time the winter came, unemployment in the mining industry was below 5,000 men, but this failed to avert the predicted coal crisis. A memorandum from the Mines Department described the situation. 'The men were working a longer week than before, stocks were three million tons larger than the year before, and they thought that the position would be fairly safe for the winter, although no doubt local and temporary shortages might occur. The Secretary for Mines wished to maintain the existing numbers until the spring when a new recruitment drive might be undertaken.'[38] This issue was referred to an inter-departmental committee involving the Ministry of Labour, the Mines Department, the Mining Association and the MFGB which repeated familiar conclusions: the falling birth rate, the long-term drift in population from the mining areas, lack of security of employment, and poor working conditions were responsible for the manpower problems. What the committee failed to do was to agree on any concrete measures that could be taken forward.[39]

At the end of 1941, an attempt was made to bolster the role of the CPC to enable it to become a genuine forum that would drive efficiency in the mining industry. D. R. had less than favourable views in its effectiveness or potential in fulfilling its aims, and this was clear from the amount of attention which he devoted to it. Others, notably Arthur Horner, a CPC member from the end of 1941, were more positive and worked out in detail what the body could achieve.[40]

In the intervening period, a committee of inquiry on the post-war organisation of the British coal industry, chaired by the experienced civil servant Sir Ernest Gowers, began its work by taking evidence from both sides of the industry and relevant Whitehall departments. D. R. believed that one of the most urgent measures would be to amend the Coal Act,

1938, which intended that all interests of coal, other than the leasehold interests, should be vested in the Coal Commission from July 1942, and also to remove a range of 'legal evasion' techniques that were being used by financial estate companies to demand extortionate payments for working seams after the initial lease had expired. He declared, 'I would go so far as to describe the activities as a piece of gross "racketeering" which, unless an amending Bill is passed into law promptly, will net a rich profit for the estates.'[41] He believed that little would be gained by acquiring the minerals from private owners if they continued to own mining property and equipment.

D. R. argued, 'Most of us had hoped that the transfer of property rights in unworked coal would coincide or immediately precede a transfer of mining undertakings from private to collective ownership. It is going to be very difficult to reconcile private ownership of mines with unification of mineral property under State control.' In future, he argued, the industry should be organised in larger units, which private ownership could not provide. He warned that while company amalgamations had taken place, they had not led to benefits in terms of safety and working conditions.[42] The mining industry was not showing the same level of improvement as other industries, and lack of investment meant there was little prospect of developing modern mines working at greater depths, introducing mechanisation and more scientific working methods. He therefore rejected the suggestion that the government should confine itself to purchasing mineral rights, which he believed would only create a confusing situation whereby private ownership of mines existed alongside State ownership of the minerals.

As an alternative, he proposed unifying properties region by region or coalfield by coalfield, under the control of regional entities modelled on the London Passenger Transport Board, ideas which he had previously discussed with Arthur Greenwood. D. R. believed a unified structure, created for the whole power industry, should also include gas and electricity supply.[43]

This would then be subject to oversight by a national board that would supervise the general operations of the whole industry.

> The ownership of the mines could well be vested in the Regional Board after a form of amalgamation and valuation laid down by Acts of Parliament. The stockholders would still own shares in collieries but would not, in the capacity of shareholders, enjoy the right of managing the pit or determining the conditions of sale of the coal produced in any of the pits. I could justify the setting up of Regional or District Production Boards with the abolition of private control of mines and the guarantee of shares in joint district enterprises where planning and economic development could be carried out and made effective from every standpoint.

He added, 'I do not wish to wade into the political considerations involved in a radical reorganisation of production and distribution of coal and fuel,' but the technological case stood notwithstanding those arguments.[44]

Even so, it was the practical problems facing the industry and those who worked in it which were foremost in D. R.'s mind. He sought to resolve problems with bus and train services used to carry men to the collieries, which operatives considered unremunerative and which colliery companies believed were unsatisfactory because of the unreliability of the vehicles used. D. R. chaired an inquiry on the payment of travelling expenses to mineworkers which recommended that all fares over 3s. should be paid by the Treasury. This led to considerable procrastination on their part, who suggested that the costs should be borne by a tonnage levy, a proposal vigorously rejected by the Mines Association.[45] D. R. also faced frustration in his discussions with the Ministry of Food and other departments on the issues of clothing coupons, food, and soap rations for all men employed in the coal industry, including surface workers.[46]

While the policymakers deliberated largely away from the public eye, rank and file miners faced the daily privations of a country at war and an industry suffering from all the consequences of decades of under-investment. These were made worse by the continuing sore of the EWO which left men penalised for absenteeism, even when the circumstances were beyond their control, such as when they were unable to get to work as a result of enemy action. D. R. estimated that around 360,000 tons of coal had been lost in production due to minor industrial disputes that had occurred because of the general discontent across the British coalfields.[47] A strike at Betteshanger colliery in Kent, over the issue of back pay, lasted 19 days and threatened to spread more widely after lodges in south Wales offered to act in support of the claim. D. R., accompanied by Ebby Edwards, travelled to Deal and agreed a settlement.[48] Later, D. R. led a deputation to the Home Secretary, Herbert Morrison, which secured the release of three imprisoned miners from the colliery.[49] D. R. intervened in the dispute at Cortonwood Colliery in South Yorkshire where 1,800 men were on strike.[50] In Cumberland he was called in after the Miners' Association reported that some of their members were refusing to be associated with the production committees, as they could be responsible for bringing disciplinary action against their own members.[51] In Lancashire and Cheshire, he dealt with complaints that an arbitration award had not been implemented fully.[52] A dispute in the Scottish coalfield, that started over a question of absenteeism, escalated and was on the verge of spreading throughout the area before D. R. managed to arrange a settlement.[53] Men in four collieries in Durham went on strike demanding that two youths be released from prison.[54] The men employed at Gresford, north Wales, demanded higher wages, while their counterparts at Hafod Colliery near Ruabon also took strike action, while the haulage men at Llay Main Colliery complained about their wages.[55] Closer to home, D. R. sought to deal with issues in the Anthracite Area when juveniles risked prosecution under the DORA by taking action (against the advice of the Federation) which spread to 18 other collieries.[56]

All of these disputes compounded the immense difficulties already affecting the mining industry in Britain. An analysis of the production figures for the first week of April 1941 showed an output per man of 6.01 tons, against a target of 6.392. By the corresponding period in 1942, that had fallen to 4.969. The following week, output stood at 4.554 (71 per cent of the target for the week) and by the week ending 18 April it was 5.821.[57] At the same time, D. R. was concerned by reports that coal was being produced by reducing safety levels in mines, as suggested by accident statistics which revealed that, during the first quarter of 1942, 321 accidents had occurred underground compared with 28 in the corresponding period the previous year.[58] He returned to the question of manpower, warning the War Cabinet that coal supplies would become insufficient to cope with the impact of air raids and loss of shipping unless at least 720,000 men were allocated to the industry.[59]

He won a partial victory: the Cabinet agreed that former miners should be released from the Forces, providing an additional 23,000 men, though this was far short of the 82,000 men previously employed in the mining industry who had joined the armed forces in the first months of the year.[60] A few weeks later it was decided that a further 11,000 men would be released from both the Forces and other industries to return to the mines as part of the effort to revitalise the industry, with priority being given to the most productive seams and collieries. These decisions were taken despite strong objections from Lord Cherwell, among others, who continued to subject the Mines Department and its statistics to a sustained barrage of criticism. He accused Sir Andrew Duncan of being 'alarmist' in his descriptions of the coal situation, alleging that the deficit had been greatly exaggerated and advocated moving men to the more productive pits, challenging the medical exemptions that were being issued, and enforcing rigorous measures to increase output per head.[61]

Amid this tension, four separate but related developments occurred that were to impact significantly on government policy, but which also hastened D. R.'s removal from its ranks. Firstly, Hugh Dalton was appointed President of the Board of Trade and he, in turn, commissioned Sir William Beveridge to develop a scheme to ration coal supplies. Beveridge concluded that any rationing scheme should be applied to all fuel supplies – gas, electricity, paraffin, as well as coal – and warned of the danger of price inflation unless some form of regulation was introduced. This, he recommended, should be based on a points system, administered through coupons, applied on the basis of households rather than individuals, and calculated on current need not prior consumption. Each household would be required to register with a supplier and this would form the basis of the distribution arrangements. In order to conserve supplies, the amount of coal available for domestic customers would be cut by 12.5 per cent, equivalent to a reduction of one ton in eight. When Hugh Dalton outlined the basis of the plan to parliament, it was clear that there would be opposition, especially from Conservative MPs worried about the impact on large domestic consumers, and from many on the Labour benches convinced that such a scheme failed to grapple with the real issues, in particular the manpower problem. This was the view of the *Daily Herald*, which quoted earlier statements made by D. R. about the need to increase coal production, and described the scheme as, 'A poor substitute for a bold and constructive fuel policy... In the summer of 1941 both sides of the coal industry were agitating for the release of young and vigorous miners from the Services in order that industrial and domestic needs could be met.'[62] The government had resisted until it had to relent, but it was yet to be seen if sufficient numbers would be released from the armed forces. The Labour paper could not have put a better case for what D. R. had been telling his fellow ministers for almost two years.

Secondly, the appointment of a separate committee, chaired by Sir John Forster, prompted yet another examination of manpower problems, this time focusing specifically on the question of juvenile labour, which a previous investigation had failed to resolve the year before.[63] The Forster Committee echoed the longstanding arguments of the MFGB that a history of insecurity and low wages were the main factors why young men were reluctant to return. Despite Ernest Bevin's insistence that enough manpower would be found if ex-miners working in other industries were transferred back into the industry, the Forster Committee recognised that this would not be sufficient and that a younger workforce, prepared through a proper training scheme, was required if Britain was to produce the coal it required.[64]

Thirdly, changes to the structure of Whitehall departments created a new Ministry of Fuel and Power with responsibility for the oil, petrol, electricity and gas sectors, as well as coal.

Fourthly, the government produced its White Paper on the coal industry which declared its intention to take control, but not ownership, of the coal mining industry. The system was to be overseen by regional controllers, who would work alongside a National Coal Board with responsibility over production matters. A separate body (appointed under the chairmanship of Lord Green) would oversee wage issues. The pit production committees would continue to address matters relating to productivity, but would not be responsible for dealing with absenteeism. These proposals fell far short of the MFGB and Labour Party positions, both of which insisted that full nationalisation was the only answer. The MFGB's 'Coal Plan' formed the basis of a memorandum prepared by Morgan Phillips which linked the issue of nationalisation to the war effort, arguing that it would lead to increased production of coal by addressing longstanding problems in the industry. Its logic spoke for itself: the State was already setting the price of coal, it was responsible for supplies to industry, it collected levies to maintain uneconomic mines when their production was necessary, and it met the expenses of men transferred from other industries. In short, 'the State accepts the burden of all deficiencies but leaves all of the benefits of the profitable mines to the owners'.[65]

It is clear that from the very start of March 1942, Hugh Dalton was plotting to remove D. R. According to Ben Pimlott, 'Dalton regarded Grenfell as stupid and incompetent, and wanted him sacked,' and the only question in his mind was how this could be achieved.[66]

Hugh Dalton's diaries certainly reinforce this judgement. For example, the entry for 2 March gives a clear picture of Hugh Dalton's intentions, Clement Attlee's position, and also the views of Lord Hyndley (Chairman of Powell Dyffryn Colliery Co. and a longstanding advisor at the Mines Department): 'Grenfell, he [Hyndley] says, is frightfully conceited and really does not understand what it is all about. He has been very difficult to handle by my predecessors and there have been scenes in public.'[67]

Clement Attlee was said to have 'put his foot down against the PM's wish to shut Grenfell,' as he could not stand a second row about firing a Labour minister after Arthur Greenwood. Hugh Dalton went on to demean D. R., claiming that he would have to humour him and carry out his duties. He then turned his guns on the rest of the mining group of Labour MPs:

I said that… Grenfell was no use. If he stayed it would mean that I should have to spend infinite time humouring him, and then do most of the job myself. I would much have preferred, if it had to be a miner, Jim Griffiths. Clement Attlee said he did not think any other miner would be willing to take Grenfell's place. They would all stick together and say he has been victimised. He begged me to do my best to work with him, and, if I found it was impossible, we could consider it again after an interval.[68]

Sir Stafford Cripps was reported to share his views but wanted Hugh Dalton to take responsibility for the decision. He developed a ruse whereby D. R. would be made Postmaster General, which had been rejected by Clement Attlee who knew that he (D. R.) would see through such subterfuge.[69]

Hugh Dalton had clearly conceived his ideas early in his tenure at the Board of Trade, and this is reflected in his diary entries throughout March 1942. 'I have to carry Grenfell with me all the way with compliments and encouragements. He is my Calvary.'[70] He was irritated by the repeated and detailed discussions involving D. R. and Ernest Bevin.

Hugh Dalton was again disparaging on 19 March when be warned D. R. to stay silent and let him do the talking at a meeting with the Mining Association, in order for him (Hugh Dalton) to declare how he looked forward to discussing how the coal industry could contribute more fully to the war effort through a national authority to which both the men and the owners would be represented. This prompted a lengthy response from Evan Williams, 'as hotly as his advanced age and temperament allow,' who 'had blamed all of the industry's problems on political interference': the owners would like to increase wages, but the money was not there to do so; a national authority was politically motivated and would do no good at all; there were no problems in the industry when there was no political interference; the owners would consider, on merit, any proposals to improve the efficiency of the industry.[71] This encapsulated what a lifetime had taught D. R. about the Mining Association and its leaders but did not change Hugh Dalton's views of his colleague. 'I am succeeding in keeping Grenfell quiet' summed up his attitude.[72]

On 20 March, Hugh Dalton recounts in his diary that the War Office had miscalculated their figures, prompting the

Lord President's committee to charge him with undertaking a broad review of the manpower question. 'This is a perfect remit, given to me and not to Grenfell who makes a very poor impression, bumbling on about how difficult everything is. Ernest Bevin says to him at one point, "Of course I know you will always defend everything in the industry. You are the biggest conservative I have ever met."'[73]

On 25 March, Hugh Dalton attempted to meet the officers of the Mining Association without D. R.'s knowledge (D. R., however, immediately found out about the subterfuge when he saw those who had met Hugh Dalton waiting for the lift outside his office).[74] D. R. was, however, under no illusion that Hugh Dalton was attempting to sideline him by giving him mundane tasks to perform, and he made no secret of his resentment.[75]

When Ernest Bevin agreed to release 7,000 ex-miners from the Forces, there was an immediate clash between D. R. and Hugh Dalton about the impact this would have on coal production. Hugh Dalton assumed that it would result in additional production of more than 5.5 million tons, whereas D. R. estimated it would be less than half that figure. For D. R., it could not be assumed, given the age and condition of the workforce in the mining industry, that the additional men would all be deployed at the coalface in addition to the existing face workers, an argument which Hugh Dalton refused to accept.[76] Even this was too much for Lord Cherwell, who continued to press the case that the men were required in the Forces.

By the start of May 1942, D. R. was at the point of resignation. He told Clement Attlee that he had 'never been treated as a proper minister', had not been included in key discussions and that his warnings about what would happen if miners left the pits for the Forces had been ignored. He summed up his grievance saying he had been 'led about like a dog on a string'. Clement Attlee responded by saying that it was the wrong time for any resignations, but Hugh Dalton was unrepentant, countering that he had included D. R. in meetings with the miners and the owners and that, 'He has wasted my time abominably'. Hugh Dalton recalls in his diary that Clement Attlee tried to have D. R. included in the government, possibly as the deputy to Lord Hyndley in the new Ministry of Fuel and Power, something which Hugh Dalton opposed, as it would leave D. R. dealing with all issues relating to the department in the House of Commons. Another of Clement Attlee's suggestions was that D. R. be moved to the Department for Overseas Trade or to be a Parliamentary Secretary at the Foreign Office.[77] In any case, Clement Attlee's good intentions came to nothing. For months, rumours circulated that D. R. was among the junior ministers who would be removed and Winston Churchill was determined to act.[78]

Nina Fishman, in her biography of Arthur Horner, considers that D. R.'s removal was inevitable. 'Grenfell had made no attempt to persuade the MAGB and MFGB to agree on changes in working practices and conditions. Consequently, unlike their counterparts in charge of shipbuilding, aircraft and engineering, civil servants in the Department of Mines were unable to promote practical measures to increase labour productivity, working hours and management efficiency.'[79]

She refers to the failure of D. R. and Oliver Lyttleton, President of the Board of Trade until June 1941, to deal with D. R.'s 'evident weakness'.[80] She also argues that:

> Veteran observers, such as Ernest Gowers and Lord Hyndley, were well aware that it would not be possible to expand coal production sufficiently to meet the growing demand from industry while continuing to supply coal for domestic consumption at its peacetime levels. But in March 1941 they occupied positions on the periphery of the Department of Mines. Their political masters, Grenfell and Lyttleton, were apparently unwilling to face this grim reality.[81]

284

She maintains that D. R. showed little interest in the CPC, and concludes that, 'The Government had now acknowledged that the solution of the coal problem depended on resolving the Grenfell problem.'[82]

Hugh Dalton's perfidious conduct towards D. R. and the thoughts he committed to his diary need to be taken in the light of his unvarying disparagement of his colleagues and the fact that he was hardly a model minister himself, be it as Parliamentary Secretary at the Foreign Office under Arthur Henderson, as the man in charge of economic warfare, in his running of the Special Operations Executove (SOE), or memorably after the war as Chancellor of the Exchequer.[83]

To understand the significance – and limitations – of Hugh Dalton's views, it is important to look in detail at his observations from the period in which he entered government with other Labour members in the summer of 1940, and his acerbic comments on his own colleagues within the Labour movement: Ernest Bevin talked too much in meetings and trampled any opposition in the mud; south Wales members were 'hysterical' on the question of local defence arrangements; Jim Griffiths combined slyness with innocence.[84] He may have been more impressed by Arthur Horner, 'lucid in discussion', but Horner blotted his copybook by consuming too much whisky during discussions, so much so that he had to be helped into a taxi, ironically enough by D. R.[85]

Dalton was an abrasive and offensive man with a habit of undermining colleagues in his own party and whose relationship with officials left much to be desired.[86] D. R. evidently had other detractors, as Fishman in particular has highlighted.[87] But much of the negativity about D. R. as Secretary for Mines came from the observations of officials and colleagues who found themselves on the opposite side to D. R. at important periods during the war. D. R. brought with him a lifetime's experience of the mining industry and his cautious approach – the conservatism which Ernest Bevin derided – owed much to his close understanding of the delicate relationships within the industry, the importance of recognising local agreements and practices, and his determination to minimise unnecessary industrial action. Ernest Bevin may have berated his conservatism, but he ignored the fact that the coal industry had never seen the kind of Mond-Turnerist reforms which his TGWU had secured across swathes of British industry in the inter-war years. D. R.'s lack of engagement with the CPC should be placed in context by Hugh Dalton's revealing comment, 'I have let him take the chair of the CPC partly because it is a mere talking shop and a waste of my time, and partly to appease Grenfell.'

D. R. had good reason to be wary of some of the senior officials both at the Mines Department and elsewhere in government, based on his previous dealings with them as a backbench MP involved in the miners' struggles on wages and conditions. He may have underestimated the determination of MFGB leaders, Arthur Horner specifically, to work with the government but, again, Horner's analytical and coherent approach to policy in the mining industry did not mean he did not have his own battles to fight within the MFGB and its constituent parts. The fact that the miners' group of MPs were, with few exceptions, wholeheartedly loyal to D. R. throughout his period in office, speaks volumes, as does the fact that Jim Griffiths would not countenance taking his colleague's ministerial post. The same loyalty was shown by the most informed industrial correspondents of the day, and this was by no means confined to Fleet Street's Welsh contingent.

It remained that, when, on 4 June 1942, it was announced that Gwilym Lloyd George would become Minister of Fuel and Power, there was no room for D. R. in the government. In the context of wartime censorship it was perhaps understandable that no mention was made of the reasons for the change. What was less understandable was the fact, clearly demonstrated by subsequent correspondence, that Clement Attlee did not give

D. R. any personal explanation for the change at the time, and was extremely coy about the issue subsequently.[88] Others were more gracious. D. R. enjoyed the sympathy of his old comrades in the PLP, especially the Welsh Labour MPs, and immediately threw himself into the work of the WPP. The MFGB was also loyal, thanking him for his support throughout his time as Secretary for Mines, and declaring, 'No miner has ever gone to a place with the bottom in, the sides coming in, the roof down, and the weight pulled down to such an extent as he did when sent to your Mines Department. There is no single Minister did more than Dai Grenfell', was how Will Lawther put it.[89]

More broadly, Trevor Evans of the *Daily Express* had correctly interpreted the tensions in the government and went as far as censorship would allow in blaming Ernest Bevin, and exonerating D. R. for the problems that had bedevilled the government's fuel policy.

> Don't let it be said now that no one was to know in the summer of 1940 that we were to be in the plight of today. There was one minister, an under-minister, who forecast what would happen. He was David Rees Grenfell, the Secretary of Mines. He went to the Manpower Board in September 1940, and declared solemnly that if the mining population was permitted to fall below 750,000, there would be a desperate coal shortage within two years. He said, 'If you must, let the miners go into other jobs, then keep their places open. You'll need them.' He was right. 'Ernest Bevin's second mistake,' he declared, was not to restore ex-miners to the pits.

As far as the coupon scheme was concerned, Trevor Evans noted, 'I have already mentioned that their minister, David Grenfell, was alone in forecasting disaster. He and his experts were not consulted in formulating the coupons scheme which has been so unceremoniously postponed.'[90]

Publicly, D. R. remained silent over these issues, but when rumours subsequently began to circulate that he had opposed

the government's decision to take over the mines, he wrote
to Clement Attlee to demand an explanation, adding, 'I have
been very anxious in the interests of the party to keep my self-
imposed pledge not to raise the question of my treatment and
dismissal from office last June.' Clement Attlee's response, four
days later, sought to reassure D. R. that he had done his utmost
to press his case, but did not elaborate on what had entailed.[91]
D. R. summed up his own feelings, declaring:

> I have been severely criticised. Much advice has been offered
> to me. Much dangerous advice. I am glad I trusted my own
> judgement. I now have the satisfaction of knowing the coal
> industry is intact. My personal position does not matter to me
> much. It is enough that I kept faith with my party and with
> the men in the industry to which I belong.[92]

CHAPTER 13

The Labour Movement Stands for Liberty

D. R. LEFT the government in the summer of 1942 and returned to the opposition benches. Never again in his remaining 17 years as an MP was he to hold any ministerial office in government. He was able to resume his work as a member of the PLP Administration Committee and with it the NCL Executive, and played a leading role in the WPP for the rest of the decade. He continued to do his utmost to support the war effort as a national figure within the Labour Party, addressing public meetings across Britain and enjoying success as a radio broadcaster in both Welsh and English for the BBC.[1] Increasingly, however, he found himself at odds with government policy especially in relation to manpower issues, and challenged its decisions over matters that affected civil liberties and over foreign policy. Inevitably, this marked him as an implacable opponent of Tory ministers, but he also found himself at odds with the Labour ministers in the wartime coalition, and continued to clash repeatedly with Ernest Bevin and Herbert Morrison as he took part in several of the most famous backbench rebellions of 1942–45.

An immediate issue arose during the second half of 1942 when the Ministry of Supply announced that tinplate works, including several in Pontarddulais and Llanelli, would be requisitioned for storage purposes as part of the government's 'concentration of industry' scheme that would also require thousands of people to move to the English Midlands where production would henceforth be based. A conference of local authority leaders, trade unionists, employers and local MPs, held at Swansea's Guildhall the following spring, was unanimous in its condemnation.[2] For D. R. the result would be a 'creeping paralysis' which would affect the community were it to lose skilled workers and young people. He insisted that there should be no return to the experiences of the Depression once the war was over. He also took the opportunity to call on the Ministry of Fuel to reopen collieries like the Berthlwyd, Whitewalls, and Gelli Hir, and demanded a subsidy to enable others, like the Wernfawr Colliery in Treboeth and the Broadoak in Loughor, to continue production. [3]

Looking to the future, D. R. produced a detailed memorandum on post-war reconstruction which stressed the need to address longstanding structural economic issues if a lasting solution was to be found to the problems faced by south Wales.[4] He traced the historic context whereby industry became dominated by large trusts, managed by men with little interest in the business, whose only aim was to extract profits, often doing so irresponsibly and with no regard for the future. This, along with the glut caused by German war reparations in the 1920s and the behaviour of socially-irresponsible owners, created a situation whereby, 'In 14 years of depressed prices and unemployment, this prosperous area has fallen back 40 years in living standards. Men at work in the coal industry are producing coal for less real wages than at any time in the period.' This, together with 'rationalisation' of the steel and tinplate industry, threatened to create a state of 'permanent dereliction' with the result that, 'In such areas the houses, streets, reservoirs, schools, hospitals and public works, upon which the public debt is secured, are threatened with depreciation to the point of complete breakdown in values.' Rates would be raised against the falling rateable value to the point of community breakdown.[5] Such a situation was not inevitable if the political will was there to avoid it. 'That calamity can be avoided by timely action. The responsibility for that action devolves upon the State. It should lend its authority and its resources to the work.'[6]

As the months passed, D. R. watched as the changes introduced as he was leaving the government in the spring of 1942 failed to resolve the coal industry's inherent problems. Production difficulties continued and threatened Britain's supply of fuel for industrial and consumer needs. Issues around the role of pit committees and the welfare and training of juvenile miners remained unresolved, and while miners' wages increased following the Green Award in July 1942, they were below those of other workers. Matters were inflamed further in September 1942 by the introduction of the Essential Works (Coal Mining Industry) (Amendment) Order which brought in new regulations relating to absenteeism and persistent lateness that were enforceable under the DORA.[7] These matters were at the forefront of D. R.'s mind in October 1942 when he made his first major contribution to a parliamentary debate since leaving the government. D. R. recalled how, when he joined the government, Whitehall had been under the misapprehension that manpower and supplies in the coal industry were plentiful. They had ignored the realities of an ageing workforce and the problems caused because not enough men were working at the coalface.[8] A few days later Aneurin Bevan articulated the critics' case, dwelling at length on the issues of authority within the government and the way in which Ernest Bevin and his officials were able to ride roughshod over other departments.[9] They were the first salvos in what was to become a full-frontal attack on the Minister of Labour the following year.

Before that, D. R. and his parliamentary colleagues from south Wales – Jim Griffiths, Ted Williams, and S. O. Davies in particular – had another target in the form of the government's Workmen's Compensation Bill, which failed to provide benefits for victims of pneumoconiosis and did not give adequate support to miners' widows.[10] This question went to the heart of issues which had been at the core of D. R.'s work throughout his time as a parliamentarian and as a minister. Men rendered unfit for work in the mining industry were being denied compensation because of the strictly limited criteria under which such payments could be made. It was blighting lives across the coalfield, but in particular in the western areas, and the coalition government's refusal to take the steps D. R., his colleagues and the SWMF deemed necessary said all about its political priorities and social attitudes.

More broadly D. R., along with other Labour MPs, welcomed the vision of a future based on the principles of social security and full employment, as outlined in Sir William Beveridge's report in November 1942. However, his suspicions were aroused when the matter came before the Commons in February 1943, when the most that could be elicited from ministers were vague promises.[11] More to the point, it was clear to him and others in the PLP that the Tories were determined to use consideration of the Beveridge Report as an excuse to delay any reform of the insurance system in the intervening period. Despite a threat by Ernest Bevin to resign from the government if Labour MPs put forward a critical resolution, backbenchers, led by Jim Griffiths, placed a motion before the House expressing dissatisfaction at government policy and demanding early implementation of the Beveridge plan.[12] Although D. R. spoke only briefly during the debate to make technical points, he joined a total of 97 Labour MPs in the lobbies against the government.[13]

Three months later, in May 1943, the Pensions and Determination of Needs Bill came before the Commons, which proposed that the amount of capital a person could hold before qualifying for supplementary pensions be increased, enabling women under 60 who were receiving widows' pensions to qualify as well. The Bill also stipulated that household income would no longer be considered when determining applications for out-door poor relief (a provision already made in relation to supplementary pensions and unemployment assistance). Aneurin Bevan used the opportunity to raise the objection that the proposals failed to increase the level of the main pension and did not address the recommendations contained in the Beveridge Report.[14] During the debate ministers were accused of tinkering with the issue while pensioners were living in poverty. If an increase in the basic rate of pension was not possible, they argued, then the supplementary allowance should be raised. On this occasion, D. R. was among 59 Labour MPs, led by Aneurin Bevan, defying the government whips in the lobbies.[15]

*

Throughout this time, D. R. continued his work on behalf of those facing Nazi persecution across Europe in his roles as Vice-Chairman of the Parliamentary Committee on Refugees, a member of the National Committee for Rescue from Nazi Terror, and as a trustee of the Czech Refugee Fund. He was also contacted regularly by Jewish refugees and others who had managed to escape from central Europe, and personally interviewed many of those who had witnessed atrocities.[16] When the outcomes of the Anglo-American conference in Bermuda in April 1943 were discussed in the Commons, D. R. drew on the evidence he had gathered from those refugees. He also gave an account of his own first-hand experiences in central Europe, describing the frenzy of hatred towards the Jews generated because, 'Germany is suffering and has been suffering for years from a kind of mania movement based on anti-Semitism, which is anti-Christian, and anti-everything which is not Nazi, looking for culprits in every corner of German society, and getting the Germans to hate the Jews.'[17] This, he insisted, was indicative of a much wider 'pernicious moral element at work in Europe' that was directed against the political opponents of Nazism as well as the ethnic groups it despised, which was a matter of revulsion for all decent-minded people.[18]

He spoke of his absolute conviction that the situation being described by the refugees was truly desperate as thousands of Jews, including women and children, were being killed on a daily basis. Britain, he insisted, had an international obligation to secure the safety and welfare of the Nazis' victims, and no argument of cost or practical difficulties would absolve the country of its obligations. Talk was of no use when faced with such deadly danger, the government should act immediately.[19]

As already noted, he himself was also much involved with the work of the Czech Refugee Fund, established to oversee the use of the money voted by parliament to assist the work of the British Committee for Refugees from Czechoslovakia, the 'Victims of Munich', who included both Czechs and Sudeten Germans under threat of persecution.[20] Prior to his appointment as one of the trustees, D. R. had been made aware of the crisis within the Czech refugee community and, in particular, the accusations that the Communists were seeking to gain control of the refugee organisation for their own ends. One of his associates from the work for Spain and in Prague, Dr Betty Morgan, had sought to mediate between the various political groups while working for the Czech Refugee Fund in 1940 and 1941. Her efforts had not been able to overcome the deep-seated enmity which had grown among different elements of the Czech community, and she left the organisation in April 1941. Meanwhile, allegations of Communist control proliferated, and detailed complaints about aggressive behaviour and misuse of funds were reported to the Home Office and security services by, among others, William Gillies, of the Labour Party's international department, Janet Chance of the PEN Club, Mary Ormerod, formerly Deputy Chairman of the British Committee, and Doreen Warriner, who had been alongside D. R. in Prague.[21] The allegations were investigated in minute detail by officers reporting to Roger Hollis, at the time the head of the MI5 F Division, who collected voluminous evidence from informants, the police, and their own agents on both the refugees and officers of the trust throughout 1940 and 1941. However, many of the issues could be attributed to a combination of personal animosity and poor management, and were not solely related to political tensions, and the overall outcome was that many of the trust's employees lost their jobs in a subsequent reorganisation.

Thereafter, it fell to D. R., alongside two other trustees, Sir Lionel Heald and Sir Alexander Maxwell, to restore a semblance of normality to the trust's work for the remaining years of the war. Despite continuing political tensions within the Czech refugee community housed in its hostels, they provided the equivalent of £935,000 in assistance to more than 8,000 people, most of whom were helped to emigrate overseas, although a small number were provided with financial support to study in British universities. This latter group included a least ten doctors (one a consultant at Carmarthen psychiatric hospital), a dentist, academics, architects and industrial designers. D. R. was to remain associated with this work for the rest of his life, only retiring shortly before his death, by which time the focus had changed to that of looking after the welfare of the new wave of refugees who arrived in Britain in the late 1940s.

*

Throughout 1942–43, the problem of manpower was still evident in the coalmining industry, indicated by the gravity of the situation during the winter and the failure to produce enough coal in the following spring and summer to guarantee the required supplies for the following year. Privately, several officials and some minsters began to acknowledge the case made by D. R. about the difficulties facing the industry, in particular the way production was being held back by the older age profile of the workforce, and the fact that 'natural wastage' meant the industry lost around 38,000 men per year, many of whom were not being replaced. A review, chaired by Arthur Greenwood, led to the appointment of the Labour MP Ellis Smith to make a detailed study of how to boost production, and to consider alternatives to the use of the EWO as a means of dealing with absenteeism. The evidence he collected vindicated D. R.'s arguments both in relation to manpower and the broader need to reorganise the mines into large units which, in turn, would be arranged into more rational production units. Management, it was argued, should be undertaken by regional fuel controllers and for as long as the war lasted control of production should be the given to a mining engineer. These changes should be accompanied by a more effective use of manpower to maximise output achieved by giving miners appropriate transport and pay for accommodation if they needed to be away from home. Exact hours of production and shifts would be organised to suit individual collieries.

In the meantime, D. R. used every available opportunity both inside the House of Commons and elsewhere to call for State control and to harangue ministers for the difficulties affecting the industry. He reiterated his argument that the capacity of idle mines should have been kept, and that the services of any miners who found themselves unemployed at any time during the war should be retained until they were needed in the industry.[22] An adjournment debate on 12 October 1943 provided him with the opportunity, at last, to raise the issues that had been festering in his own mind ever since he left office. At the outset, Gwilym Lloyd George realised the tense atmosphere that was developing in the chamber, and asked for a calm discussion of the issues as he provided an overview of the government's position on production, manpower issues and working conditions. D. R. then questioned the figures which Gwilym Lloyd George had quoted from 1942. He was followed by Aneurin Bevan, who demanded that a more senior minister than Gwilym Lloyd George should respond on behalf of the government. Others, including Jack Lawson, Seymour Cocks, and Ness Edwards, followed suit.[23]

The following day, Aneurin Bevan's request was heeded when Winston Churchill addressed the House and sought to gloss over many of the difficulties.[24] He was followed immediately by D. R., who attacked the Prime Minister's complacent attitude when confronted with such a dangerous situation. Production was down by 400,000 tons from the level of 1941, not because of any restriction in output by the miners (as Winston Churchill had implied), but due to loss of manpower and the age of the workforce. He fiercely denounced the Prime Minister's allegation that many of the problems were caused by miners preparing the ground for a future conflict with the owners.[25] His distrust of Winston Churchill and his whole attitude towards the miners, in south Wales in particular, was obvious. D. R. pointed to the sense of public responsibility that was to be found among the coal miners and the efforts which they made to maintain production whatever physical or human obstacles they faced. It was an insult to accuse them of keeping output low in order to settle scores with Winston Churchill's government or to prepare the ground for a future conflict. The answer lay in more effective management and better recognition to the men engaged in the task of producing the fuel upon which the nation depended.[26]

Pointing to the heavy labour involved in the work, he challenged Gwilym Lloyd George's figures presented the previous day and what they implied about the men working in the collieries. Production, D. R. insisted, had been highest when he was Secretary for Mines, and what was needed above anything else was better management. Turning to the manpower problem, it was clear from the outset that D. R. would not be taking prisoners and the drama of the debate reflected both a sense of his own anger and the way in which

Ernest Bevin's conduct inflamed the situation. The exchange between the two men, discussed in Chapter 11, reflects the importance he put on the matters at issue, as does the fact that the letters are preserved in his papers at the West Glamorgan Archives. He outlined the way he had pressed the case for an allocation of 720,000 men – a number required to address the weakened state of the coal industry at the start of the war – and how the figures had been continually challenged by the Ministry of Labour and National Service.[27] His warnings had not been heeded and requests to allow flexibility for unemployed miners to find alternative work on a temporary basis had fallen on deaf ears. Instead, he had faced a constant refrain from Bevin that the mining industry was holding on to too many men and needed to make a greater contribution to the war effort in terms of making manpower available. Had the government pursued its intended course with regard to miners in Durham and south Wales, then coal production would have been reduced by 20 million tons and the war effort would have broken down because of a lack of fuel.[28]

D. R. then quoted from letters he had received from ex-miners pleading to be sent back to the collieries instead of marking time sweeping floors or peeling potatoes when there was an urgent need for coal. Turning on Ernest Bevin, he declared: 'The Minister of Labour is responsible. He will intercept other young men from going into the Army to bring them into the mines, from which he wrongly took the men away.'

Ernest Bevin retorted that, with 77,000 men out of work, they had to be put to do other work, but D. R. would have none of it. Referring to letters from Welsh MPs, he accused Ernest Bevin of failing to discuss any of the details with him during the crisis weeks in the winter of 1940–41. He cited, in particular, a letter from his fellow Labour MP, Arthur Jenkins, in which Ernest Bevin said he would be discussing the issue with D. R., but no such meeting ever took place. Instead, Bevin had been busy trying to convince other MPs that the problem lay with Grenfell. D. R. accused Bevin in the strongest terms:

> He was colluding with those people, getting them to write letters to me instead of meeting me as a colleague. There is no question of it, and if the Right Hon. gentleman disputes, I will have every word that I have written examined impartially. I will make this case: I make the assertion now that if the proposals of the Right Hon. gentleman had been accepted by me, the industry would have been ruined, and Durham and south Wales would never have recovered for the duration of the war. That is a fact.[29]

The debate laid bare the sore that had been at the heart of the government's problems over coal production and the manpower the industry required throughout D. R.'s tenure as Secretary for Mines. Matters were clearly not helped by Bevin's attitude – comments like, 'I don't care what you do' – during the debate. Once again, D. R. could rely on the support of members from mining backgrounds, especially from south Wales, against the brick wall of government ministers who were clearly unimpressed by the arguments that coal mining was a distinct entity and that this meant that policies implemented in other industries were wholly inappropriate when applied to it. Whatever else, D. R. had highlighted that the mining industry's problems did not stem from absenteeism or a lack of commitment to the war effort on the part of the miners, a point which he reiterated continually for the remainder of the war.

Later that month, D. R. again found himself criticising another senior Labour member of the coalition government when he joined Ness Edwards, Aneurin Bevan and others in criticism of the Workers Compensation (Temporary Increases) Bill, for which Herbert Morrison was responsible. The measure, designed to simplify compensation arrangements and to revise the maximum payments to be made, reached its committee stage in October 1943. The government had sought the unions' views through a joint committee consisting of employers' representatives and nominees of the TUC. But the proposals did not satisfy Labour's rank and file and, despite an instruction to Labour MPs not to move any amendments, Ness Edwards defied the whips and denounced the provisions as totally inadequate. As it stood, it provided the minimum possible to injured workmen and excluded married women and children, with the consequence that 90 per cent of those who might benefit were excluded. He was supported by Labour MPs from the north of England, in particular those sponsored by the MFGB, alongside William Beveridge and rebel Tories.[30]

But the most trenchant criticism came from south Wales – it was the occasion of Aneurin Bevan's famous 'third-rate Tammany Hall boss' description of Morrison ('squalid back-stairs Tammany Hall politician' was another version) – and even if D. R. lacked Aneurin Bevan's colourful language, his critique was equally devastating.[31] He highlighted the decline in the value of compensation payments ever since the first Compensation Act was passed in 1898, and insisted that any amount should be set at no less than two-thirds of earnings. He derided the government for their failure to present any meaningful arguments in support of their proposals, other than the fact that they were considering the Beveridge proposals 'something quite extraneous for the moment' that 'leave people 11s. 6d. short' of what had been done 45 years previously. Once again, he joined the rebels in the lobbies in defiance of the whips and continued to press issues around equality of the sexes in compensation issues, highlighting anomalies within the existing legislation in subsequent discussions.[32]

D. R. clashed with Morrison for a second time when he challenged the decision to release Oswald Mosley from prison on grounds of supposed ill-health. D. R. had tabled an amendment to the address, along with George Strauss and John Parker, placed before the Commons in early December 1943. D. R. provoked a furious response from the Tory benches, Quentin Hogg in particular, by contrasting the treatment handed to Mosley with that of miners struggling to work under pain of the EWO, declaring:

> These men, who are in a much worse medical condition than Oswald Mosley, are told that, in addition to travelling long distances to their work, to performing heavy and arduous duties for long hours in the mine and to a long journey back, they must turn out for Home Guard parade and go on a march of 10 or 12 miles. They are sent to prison because they cannot stand the strain and they say so.[33]

An exchange between D. R. and Commander R. T. Bower, Conservative MP for Cleveland, spoke volumes. D. R. described the comfort enjoyed by Mosley during his incarceration at Holloway, 'the acme of luxury and comfort and that despite the fact that he was a proved enemy of this State'.

'Not proved,' Commander Bower interjected.

'He was a proved enemy of the State. Does anybody dare to say he was not?' responded D. R.

'Yes, I do,' stated Commander Bower.

It was clearly more than D. R. could stand and he launched a tirade against Mosley and his behaviour – organising gangs of bullies to attack defenceless people before the war. The government's actions would embolden his sympathisers. British fifth columnists were no different to those who had wreaked havoc in Norway, Belgium and Holland, who were looking to the future with Mosley:

> Sir Oswald Mosley must be glorying in a triumph. He is free from Holloway. He is allowed a country house to live in, allowed the attendance of servants and we have had the most frivolous explanation of his medical treatment that I have

heard for some time. We have been told that he is suffering from phlebitis with a kind of superimposed or incipient thrombosis and must be given a chance to take vigorous exercise. I would give him some. Let him work in a coal mine. Other men equally good are required to work there every day and do their job for the benefit of this country.

Labour MPs whose constituents had witnessed Mosley and his supporters at first hand before the war rallied to D. R.'s support, and few were convinced by Morrison's emphatic denial that any accommodation had been reached with Oswald Mosley. In the event, D. R. was joined by 62 of his colleagues in opposing the government, but again to no avail.[34] More broadly, his actions were criticised bitterly by Labour ministers in the coalition who regarded the amendment to the address as a vote of censure on Herbert Morrison and set out to persuade the PLP to take action on those who had supported the amendment.

A further incident, in April 1944, risked even more serious repercussions for D. R. when he joined backbenchers within the PLP, led by Aneurin Bevan, to challenge the government, and Ernest Bevin directly, over the issue of regulations making incitement to strike illegal, with the threat of custodial sentences for anyone leading such action. The order, Regulation 1a(a) of the Emergency Powers (Defence) Acts, 1939 and 1940, had been denounced by the SWMF in particular, because of the associated publicity which had been given to recent mining disputes in south Wales, alongside others in the Yorkshire coalfield, as well as strikes on the London buses.[35] Aneurin Bevan denounced the regulations, both on principle and ground of practicality: any minor dispute between employers and employees which led to strike action could result in prosecutions. For Aneurin Bevan, a sense of proportion was needed. 'Small strikes, small disputes are the vent valves of society. They do not hold up the war. These minor adjustments in industrial relations are the means by which the whole apparatus is kept smoothly functioning. To make those minor disturbances major offences under the law is lunacy.'[36]

On this occasion D. R. found himself among the 25 members who supported Aneurin Bevan in the division lobby (mainly the Clydesiders and other ILP members and left-wing by-election victors such as Tom Driberg and Hugh Lawson). Immediately, Aneurin Bevan was threatened with disciplinary action and there was also the question of what punishment would be meted out to D. R. and the other Labour rebels.[37]

Their cause was championed both by *Tribune* and the *Reynolds News* whose Welsh editor, David Raymond (David Thomas Raymond Jenkins), a native of Llangennech and close confidante to both D. R. and Jim Griffiths, was a perceptive and well-informed commentator on Welsh Labour politics. He warned the Labour leadership not to ignore the strength of feeling on the ground in mining communities throughout Britain, most especially in south Wales:

> From everything I hear, south Wales is particularly incensed by the anti-strike regulation, 1a(a), and will not allow its Members of Parliament to be gagged by any attempt to set a party caucus… The miners especially have always insisted that their representatives, whether in Parliament or in the Trade Unions, must be answerable for what they do, and this is a democratic instinct that cannot be eradicated. The Labour Movement will ignore it at its own peril.[38]

He went on to point to the fact that in south Wales, 'a deep-rooted democracy and independence are reinforced by bitter memories of 20 years of Governmental neglect', and quoted D. R. as saying, 'The Labour movement… stands for liberty. It would be fatal if we were to assist in losing that liberty. That is the great danger now. I shall go on fighting it with all my remaining years.'

Those views were echoed by David Raymond who told his readers, 'No Welsh MP who surrendered himself body and soul to a caucus forbidding him to speak for the Welsh people would survive another election.'

D. R. himself escaped any serious retaliation by the PLP and, in discussions on the NCL, was determined to prevent action being taken against Aneurin Bevan, who enjoyed the support of the SWMF and other unions, in particular the National Union of Distributive and Allied Workers (NUDAW). At the PLP meeting which followed the vote, he supported the resolution against withdrawing the whip and insisted that if action was to be taken, then all of the rebels – himself included – should face the PLP's censure. When all else failed, he joined fellow Labour MPs Emanuel Shinwell, Jim Griffiths, George Daggar, Ellis Smith and Alfred Barnes and others in voting against the PLP's 'ultimatum' to Aneurin Bevan to give an assurance that he would abide by its Standing Orders.[39]

As 1944 drew to a close, D. R. began to turn his attention to the day when Labour would once again be fighting an election free from the shackles of the coalition.[40] He was enthused by the Labour Party conference held in London in December 1944 at which he spoke in the debate on coal nationalisation in support of the resolution, moved by the Durham miners' leader Sam Watson and seconded by Jim Griffiths, that demanded there would be no further delay in implementing the policy. D. R. used the opportunity to reiterate his longstanding view that this was the only way of resolving the problems of under-investment and poor industrial relations that had held the industry back for generations.[41] The only remedy for the problems affecting the coal industry lay in mechanisation and the effective planning that could be achieved through nationalisation linked to a UK-wide scheme that covered production, distribution and coal consumption.[42]

He also took the opportunity to repeat the argument when the Coalition brought forward legislation to enable the Ministry of Fuel and Power to continue their function in peacetime (in the face of opposition from Tory MPs), insisting that the ministry's powers were not sufficient in a situation when the country was heading for a fuel crisis.[43] However, even the minor administrative reform that the government proposed proved too much for ministers after Robert Foot, Chairman of the Mining Association, proposed an alternative that would allow for reorganisation but which rejected any requirement for State control.[44] When Sir Charles Reid's committee on the technical reorganisation of the industry recommended radical reorganisation and re-equipment, D. R. seized on the opportunity to demonstrate that such measures were only possible under public ownership. He declared, 'The industry is going down and down, and not a word the Minister said today will stop it.'[45] He went on, 'When the Minister was discussing the industry it was not clear whether he was turning over a patient on the way to hospital or a corpse on the way to the grave' and, in such a situation, 'you get quacks telling us how to deal with the problem... The quack is Mr Foot, a man who earns his salary under false pretences.'[46]

D. R. concluded with a rallying cry for a new beginning for the mining industry in Britain:

This industry, of which I form a part, to which I belong, which has drawn from me the best of my physical and mental powers, this industry in which I am still intensely interested, which is the foundation of our national life and our political activity, and upon which the whole superstructure of Britain's life, commercial and industrial, has been built for the last 150 years, this industry which has given strength and prestige to Britain as nothing else has, is now subjected to neglect and selfish exploitation and to a lack of patriotic interest. Public ownership was the only means by which the necessary investment could be made to give Britain a modern, safe coal-mining industry in which men would be enabled to work in modern conditions.

Dissatisfaction with the continued presence of Labour ministers in the government intensified as the Tories pursued their own reactionary agenda on the world stage. Anglo-American support for right-wing elements in Europe – the Pietro Badoglio government in Italy and the royalists in Greece among them – were an abhorrence when Labour could look to the Socialist hope of a European future shaped by left-wing resistance movements. When Winston Churchill proffered the hand of friendship to the Spanish government in June 1944, it was more than Labour MPs could stomach. D. R. joined Harold Laski and other prominent Labour figures in a blistering attack on the Prime Minister, issuing a joint statement that declared:

> Franco has used his victory to make of Spain a vast prison house in which there are denied to ordinary men and women all the freedoms for which the United Nations are fighting. Franco has sent troops to assist Hitler against the Soviet Union. He has made Spain a centre of supplies and espionage on behalf of our enemies. He has executed thousands of citizens who were loyal to the form of government they had chosen constitutionally, and he has forced into prison many hundreds of thousands. Before Quisling himself, Franco was the first quisling. The Spanish people wish ardently for a victory of the United Nations, convinced that, when those nations have overpowered fascism everywhere, they will no longer support it in Spain. Then, think the Spaniards, at last their chance will come to drive out the usurper. [They warned] fascism, entrenched in Spain and Portugal, would be in a position to extend its influence and power over large portions of South America, the Mediterranean basin and Catholic Europe, and to prepare the third world war.[47]

Shortly afterwards, he was one of several Labour MPs who criticised Winston Churchill over his policy in Greece, in particular his denunciation of all leftist forces as Communist, and the way he consorted with suspected Fascists and dubious pro-monarchists.[48]

Any change in policy would never be achieved by a coalition government dominated by Tories complicit in the shame of the Depression and the policy of appeasement. It was time for Labour to put its case to the country. On 20 May 1945, all Labour ministers resigned from the government, a caretaker government took over, and the election date was set: polling would take place on Thursday, 5 July, the votes would be counted three weeks later.

Throughout the election campaign, Clement Attlee, Sir Stafford Cripps, Herbert Morrison, Hugh Dalton and their colleagues on the Labour front bench set the tone of the campaign that promised State intervention, the defeat of poverty, full employment and a welfare state, alongside an internationalist world view. Their opponents could offer little more than Winston Churchill's record of wartime leadership, a vote for 'nation' above party, and a diet of negativity about what was possible for Britain in the situation in which it found itself in in the summer of 1945.[49] As the weeks went on, the desperation in the Tory and Liberal camps became clear. A Labour victory could lead to defeat in Japan, it would threaten personal freedom, nationalisation would mean the end of private property, and a Socialist Gestapo would be established, modelled presumably on the one claimed by the Tories to be preventing their canvassers from campaigning in the valleys of south Wales.[50]

On this occasion, Labour's front line did not feature D. R. Grenfell.[51] Despite his long experience haranguing ministers over both domestic and international issues throughout the dark days since 1931, and his experience as a government minister, he was not called upon to take part in the radio broadcasts, nor was he deployed to cover public meetings in the marginal constituencies. Instead, he concentrated his efforts in Gower, supplemented by occasional forays to other areas, in particular to support Tudor Watkins in Brecon and Radnor, and Iwan Morgan in Cardiganshire.[52] His own result in Gower was decisive; he polled 30,676 votes (nearly 70 per cent of the total), giving him a majority of 16,561 over Aeron Thomas.

CHAPTER 14

You, As Our Leader

IN JULY 1945, the voters of Britain provided the Labour Party with the clearest of mandates, a resounding and emphatic victory delivered by an electorate full of hope about what the future could hold for them, their families and their communities. Labour's tally of 393 seats and 48 per cent of the vote was unprecedented, and nowhere was the victory more absolute than in Wales where the party polled more than three-quarters of a million votes, 60 per cent of all those cast. Labour's triumph constituted a rejection of the economic policy that left vast swathes of industrial Britain languishing in depression. It was an end to the belief that people unable to find work in those areas should simply move elsewhere, and combined with a repudiation of a foreign policy that was reconciled to fascism and accepting of Munich.[1] Labour showed that a better future was possible, both materially and in the essence of the society that was to be built, as presented in the immediate blueprint of *Let us face the future* and, more profoundly, in the fruits of more than half a century of Socialist thought and propaganda.

D. R. voiced his jubilation in a radio broadcast, *Wales at Westminster*, declaring, 'Wales has never figured so prominently before and Welsh talent has never been as fully recognised as it has been in the formation of this Government.' He went on, 'We have come back to the House of Commons pledged to do better for the maimed, the aged and the afflicted members of society.'[2]

The Welsh talent that was recognised did not include D. R. himself. He had reason to expect a call to serve as a minister on at least four separate grounds, long service to the Labour Party as an MP since 1922, stalwart of the opposition front bench in the 1930s, loyalty to Clement Attlee and the part he had played in enabling him to become leader in 1935, and as one of few Labour MPs with previous ministerial experience. This was not to be, and the way in which Clement Attlee conveyed the news reflected no credit on Labour's greatest Prime Minister. In a somewhat curt letter, dated 4 August 1945, Clement Attlee told D. R. that he regretted that he had been unable to find him a position in the government, but did not elaborate on his decision. When the news became known, most Westminster commentators expressed surprise having expected great things for Gower's MP.[3]

For a long time afterwards D. R. wondered why he had been denied any role in Britain's first majority Socialist government. He had never been given a full explanation of the reasons for his removal from the government in 1942, and neither did Clement Attlee see fit to elaborate on his decision to exclude him from his own ministry, as revealed in a letter from D. R. to Clement Attlee in March 1947 in which D. R. requested a meeting to discuss the events so that he could be clear in his own mind about the circumstances. 'I do not know what has been said against me,' he wrote. 'That is my complaint. All I know is that I carried out the duties allocated to me with loyalty and efficiency. I have the greatest pride in the service I have given to the mining industry and to my country. If you prefer not to speak about it I shall always regret your silence... When I feel I can do so without doing harm to anyone, I shall speak on my own behalf and will claim what ordinary justice appears to me as a right.'[4] There is no evidence that such a meeting ever took place and D. R., presumably, was never given satisfaction over the issue.

He had some consolation when he was elected to the

chairmanship of the WPP where he soon became something of a father figure to some of the newly-elected Labour MPs, Goronwy Roberts of Caernarfon in particular, and he watched two of those for whom he had campaigned take their seats – Percy Morris for Swansea West, and Tudor Watkins for Brecon and Radnor. He was also recognised with other positions open to a backbench MP: Chairman of the newly-formed PLP Fuel and Power Group, a member of the BBC Welsh Advisory Committee, and a leading participant in the Franco-British Parliamentary Group.[5]

He was also closely involved in making the needs of disabled ex-miners a matter of government policy during the first months of the Clement Attlee administration. The issues had been placed in sharp focus by a deputation which met representatives of the Ministry of Labour and Board of Trade in September 1945, which heard Evan Phillips, Chairman of the Amalgamated Anthracite Combine Committee, describe the effects of prolonged unemployment on those prevented from working by disability.

Within weeks, he accepted chairmanship of a cross-departmental working party committee appointed by the government and sat alongside D. J. Williams (an old friend of D. R.'s who had been elected MP for Neath at the start of 1945), Evan Phillips, David Davies, the Secretary of the Amalgamated Anthracite Combine Committee, three local leaders, County Councillor Frank Davies of Ammanford, councillors William Lawrence of Aberdare, and H. Griffiths of Port Talbot BC, as well as G. Tracey Phillips, Clerk to the Ammanford and Cwmamman UDCs.[6] They were joined by Col. R. W. Broadhead, the Board of Trade's Factory Controller; C. G. Hillier, Wales Regional Officer of the Ministry of Labour; L. W. Hooper, Research Officer for the Wales Regional Office of the Board of Trade; Harold Finch of the National Union of Mineworkers (NUM) and Dr A. Harper, a radiologist based at Ammanford.

D. R. had been determined to address the needs of disabled ex-miners who were unable to continue working underground but were capable of working in a clean environment. This matter came increasingly to the fore after medical screening in the industry meant increasing numbers of men were suspended from work, which included more than 3,500 men examined during the war years. While the need was evident throughout the industry, it was particularly acute in south Wales, especially in the westernmost portion where a concentration was identified in the Ammanford, Tumble, Ystalyfera and Garnant areas.

The committee focused on men who were fit to work but not underground. They challenged the misconception that those men were no longer employable, citing evidence of the successful re-employment of ex-miners at the Treforest aircraft factory in support of their argument. What was needed was, firstly, the introduction of light industry, where men could work in conditions that were free from dirt or dust under normal industrial conditions. Secondly, sheltered employment under special conditions, requiring some form of State subsidy. The recommendations concentrated on the first group. Rent rebates could be provided for firms who committed to employing at least half their workforce from those certified as being unable to work underground. On the question of terms and conditions, the report was clear: 'We consider it to be of the utmost importance to avoid the sense of inferiority and dependence which would be inseparable from the segregation of this class of workers from their fellows.' This would only reinforce the danger of the 'adverse psychological effect and feeling of being outcast and unwanted,' what one witness had described as the state of 'waiting for the undertaker' which affected so many ex-miners in this position. The committee therefore believed that alternative work should be provided to enable men to give up mining while their health was relatively unimpaired. Those employed would be relatively fit, able to do a full day's work without the special arrangements and handicaps which might be involved in the employment of a high percentage of seriously disabled workers.[7]

Importantly, they specifically rejected the notion of offering work on the surface to this group of miners (an issue which was later revisited by the Pneumoconiosis Board). Government-owned factories could be provided across the whole of south Wales, they believed, but with a special emphasis on the westernmost part due to the reluctance of firms to locate in that region.

The committee's recommendations were accepted by the government which agreed to build an initial ten factories to be let. But progress in implementing them proved painfully slow and the anticipated jobs did not materialise as hoped. In Ammanford, the Harden Valve Co. had difficulty in recruiting the nucleus of skilled workers which would enable it to reach the requirement of 50 per cent ex-miners in significant numbers. Charles McCloskey Ltd, in Tumble, experienced delays in importing the required specialist machinery. Philip Owen Screen Printing in Ponthenri went into receivership after a short while. Cyc Arc at Garnant was bedevilled by poor industrial relations. Further east, factories at Aberbargoed and Llwynypia, which produced for the car industry, enjoyed greater success, while the Grenfell factory (this kind of factory was called a 'Grenfell factory' after D. R.) in Aberdare, linked to Hoover in Merthyr Tydfil, was allowed significant flexibility which enabled it to absorb its quota of ex-miners across various plants. However, as author Steven Thompson has clearly shown, the implementation of the scheme, coupled with duplication from the Remploy scheme (to provide employment for a broader category of disabled workers), meant that the Grenfell factories did not meet initial expectations.[8]

It was not long, however, before D. R. began to show signs that he would not be an unquestioning supporter of the government, and once again his old adversary, Ernest Bevin, was the focus of his discontent. The event itself was innocuous enough – a Commons motion tabled in D. R.'s name and signed by 120 members from all sides of the House that urged the government to take all measures necessary to prevent disaster in Europe. The key messages were in the detail. The motion called for the policy of expelling Germans from Eastern Europe to be postponed until the winter was over. If it were to take place it should be done in an orderly way, along with intensified efforts to maximise coal production in the Ruhr, to increase supplies of food and other necessities, and the establishment of a Supreme Economic Authority to coordinate efforts at reconstruction.[9] D. R. had been lobbied by his contacts among the Sudeten Germans, among them Wenzel Jaksch, over this issue and the implications for them of the Potsdam Agreement.[10] But, more broadly, the subsequent debate provided an opportunity for members to offer a critique of the Potsdam Agreement with noted contributions from several MPs, Michael Foot in particular. However, it was clear that Ernest Bevin had no intention to have policy determined by Labour backbenchers, let alone the Labour rank and file, clearly suggesting the approach he was to take for the subsequent five years.[11]

A few weeks later D. R. was again in critical mode as the most senior Labour member involved in a backbench rebellion demanding an immediate increase in the old age pension. Jim Griffiths, speaking as the Minister for National Insurance, sought conciliation by recognising the backbenchers' case, but insisted that no such commitment could be made while the government was engaged in a much broader reform of national insurance that required comprehensive new legislation. This reassurance did not satisfy D. R., who joined fellow MPs Sydney Silverman, Jennie Lee, Barbara Castle and others to reiterate the demand for an immediate increase during a subsequent meeting with ministers.[12] Not for the first or last time in his life, Jim Griffiths was put in the position of defending the official government position, whatever his own views may have been, but the revolt strengthened his position in subsequent discussions both with government ministers and his own officials, and resulted in changes to the National Insurance Bill as it proceeded through the Commons the following May.

In the meantime, D. R. became embroiled in another conflict with ministers over the terms of the American loan to Britain, negotiated by Maynard Keynes as an interim arrangement following the abrupt end of the lend-lease arrangements.[13] D. R. understood the need for some form of temporary assistance as British industry readjusted to peacetime conditions. He knew from long and bitter experiences what the consequences of not doing so had been in the 1920s, especially in areas like south Wales that had relied so much on the export market for coal and for tinplate. Keynes had undoubtedly secured as much as he could get from the Americans, but it was also clear that Britain would pay a high price indeed for what little was on offer. US support would only come if Britain committed itself to free trade, the end of imperial preference, acceptance of the Bretton Woods monetary plan, alongside a potentially crippling commitment that sterling would be convertible with the dollar within twelve months of Congress approving the loan, together with the payment of an annuity to the United States far in excess of the value of British exports to America before the war.

D. R. was appalled by such extortion and shared a deep suspicion that the real motive was to undermine the government's ability to implement a fully Socialist policy at home and on important international questions. This view was shared by others including Aneurin Bevan and Emanuel Shinwell, both of whom denounced the terms of the agreement when it came before the Cabinet. When the Commons was asked to approve the order on 13 December 1945, dissenting voices on the Labour benches revealed their deep distrust

315

both of the Americans' intentions and of the implications of accepting the Bretton Woods agreement and the institutions that would subsequently be created (the International Trade Organisation, the International Monetary Fund and the International Bank for Reconstruction and Development). Why was it, the critics demanded to know, the government had not pursued alternative proposals that would have drawn support from governments in Europe and Australia that were far more attuned to its political agenda? Once again, D. R. found himself among the rebels in the PLP, joining W. G. Cove of Aberavon and the newly-elected L. J. Callaghan of Cardiff South from among the ranks of the Welsh Labour MPs on this occasion.[14]

However, D. R.'s criticisms were insignificant when set in the context of his support for the Labour government's determination to drive through its legislative programme and implement the key tenets of the manifesto on which it had been elected. D. R. watched as the nationalisation programme saw civil aviation, Cable and Wireless, and the historic enemy of Labour governments, the Bank of England, taken into public ownership during the government's first year in office.[15] Most celebrated of all its achievements was the Coal Industry Nationalisation Bill, introduced in December 1945, which passed through its parliamentary stages the following spring, reaching its third reading on 20 May 1946. On vesting day, 1 January 1947, the Labour movement's cherished goal of a coal industry owned by the nation would become a reality.[16]

To celebrate, D. R. published a short book, *Coal*, written against the backdrop of the fuel crisis of 1946–47 in which he presented a detailed account of the issues impacting production. He began with a brief sketch of the development of the industry since the Industrial Revolution, and then described the disastrous events of the inter-war years. He outlined the geological factors affecting different coalfields and noted that the prospects for most areas were bright if production was centred in deeper mines. This would call for new ways of working which could only be financed through expensive reorganisation schemes. Mining conditions in Britain, he insisted, had never kept abreast with those overseas, as was clear from the safety figures and the extent of silicosis and pneumoconiosis. He called for international collaboration to understand medical aspects alongside safety measures. This would require an investment programme of £75 million over 15 years to improve transport, ventilation and pumping in existing collieries, and research into the use of longwall methods of mining underpinned by geological investigations and evaluations of fuel usages. Looking to the production of coal in other countries, he declared, 'the whole outlook as far as coal production is concerned is satisfactory... [but] some of the older coalfields everywhere have been recklessly and wastefully exploited, and no country can afford to neglect the planning and consumption of its reserves.'

D. R.'s analysis repeated many of the arguments he had deployed in his discussions with the Ministry of Labour during his time as Secretary for Mines. The coal industry suffered from manpower problems stemming from the way that half a million men had been lost from it in the previous 25 years. Young men would not be attracted to jobs in which the working day had been lengthened and there was no guarantee of continuity of employment. Such issues would only be solved when the conditions of employment compared favourably with those of other occupations. He called for better training and career opportunities to enable men to progress to working as engineers, managers and other professional roles. Such reform needed to be made in the context of a wholly different mindset about the way the industry was run: 'The market price of coal is determined by market conditions. But the value of coal is represented by the measure of the additional production which it brings about and the services which are made available by its use.'

He went on to outline the responsibilities which would, in future, rest on the State to manage and plan the industry in ways which capitalist coal owners had failed to do, to the detriment of Britain as a whole:

> The State must carry out the development work neglected by generations of colliery owners... The failure to plan, to take national review, to maintain sufficient labour, has brought the British coal-mining industry close to ruin. It nearly caused a breakdown which would have brought about military defeat. Many warnings had been given by authoritative advisors, but the objections to nationalisation were too strongly held. As a result, Britain had to wage total war with a weakened coal industry, in which there was no reserve of pit-room.[17]

When vesting day came on 1 January 1947, D. R. attended civic functions in Gower before proceeding to the Mayor of Swansea's New Year's Day event. Amid the euphoria of the day, D. R. recognised that nationalisation was only a first step towards a much deeper transformation that was as much about a social as an economic change, in which he had a clear view of the responsibility of the way the industry should operate. 'The National Coal Board (NCB) must be the acknowledged instrument of the national work and the symbol of loyalty and cooperation in the mining industry.' The miners had to be given the recognition and status they deserved for the vital part they played in the country's economy.

But D. R. also realised the responsibility that now fell on the government: it could no longer blame the coal owners for any crisis, it was answerable for production crises, for working conditions, and for the pitiful condition of collieries across Britain, nowhere more so than in the Western District of south Wales. Difficult decisions faced the NCB as they took responsibility for colliery closures and grappled with the work of developing the modern, deep mines that were the industry's future. Along with Jim Griffiths and D. J. Williams, D. R. had to lobby hard to prevent the NCB alienating mining communities in south-west Wales, virtually from the start of its existence. The Broadoak Colliery in Loughor, which closed within a year of nationalisation, was beyond saving but the future of the Steer and East Pits in Gwaun-Cae-Gurwen (which were threatened with closure following an unofficial strike over piecework price lists) became a matter of intense argument between the NCB and the NUM.[18] D. R. himself faced criticism in Gorseinon for defending the NCB's insistence that large tracts of land at Mynydd Lliw should not be developed until plans for future mineworking were prepared, with some doubting whether they would ever materialise. A change of ownership did not remove the daily challenges of mining in geologically complex collieries such as Graig Merthyr, the Mountain and the Garngoch collieries, as well as the remaining small mines across the Gower constituency.

At the same time, D. R. was in constant discussion with Whitehall departments as he supported work to attract alternative employment to the area. The Labour government had signalled its intention to use the powers of the Distribution of Industry Act, 1945, passed by the coalition government despite opposition from some die-hard Tory free marketeers, to influence as never before where factories were set up to ensure that work was brought to the people. It was a repudiation of the dogma of transference that had seen half a million people leave Wales in the inter-war years.[19] By October 1945, over 600 firms had sought Industrial Development Certificates indicating that they wanted to locate in south Wales, including ICI and Viscose in Swansea.[20] These included several earmarked for the Gorseinon area, such as Swears and Wells, Durex Abrasives, and Western Light Castings.[21] These were in addition to the large manufacturing units at the Ystrad Road trading estate in Fforestfach which were taken by various light manufacturing concerns.[22] D. R. actively promoted the area, approaching companies directly and facilitating meetings with ministers and officials in Whitehall and in the House of Commons.[23] He demanded investment to modernise Swansea docks, and took considerable interest in the possible development of the Fairwood Aerodrome as a fully-fledged airport providing regular scheduled services to London and Dublin.[24]

Progress was by no means smooth. Durex Abrasives withdrew from a commitment to develop a factory in Garngoch.[25] There were concerns that the western part of south Wales was not being promoted adequately by the Board of Trade, and that companies were put off by the vista of dereliction as they approached the area through the lower Swansea Valley.[26] D. R. was keenly aware of the difficulties, particularly the view of many of the local authorities that the area was being ignored. He was also aware that the problems being experienced across Wales were generating a growing dissatisfaction with the progress being made by the Labour government. More than 70,000 men were out of work in the spring of 1946 and the exodus of people, especially the young, continued unabated as the Welsh supplied the needs of industrial areas in the English Midlands and the towns of the Home Counties. He joined fellow members of the Welsh Labour group to demand urgent action, complaining that too many of the newly-built factories were lying empty.[27] A deputation of MPs, led by George Daggar, met with Clement Attlee in July 1946 to outline the problems being faced. A few weeks later they met with Sir Stafford Cripps, who insisted that government schemes would provide employment for 47,000 people and that those who had been forced to move out of Wales would be helped to return once economic conditions improved.[28]

Such assurances did not satisfy the MPs and fuelled the arguments for the creation of a Secretary of State for Wales as the head of a 'coordinating ministry' who would 'advocate on behalf of Welsh interests' across the different government departments. D. R. had, of course, supported the demand for a Welsh Secretaryship when the WPP raised the issue in 1938 and again in 1943, but to no avail. The matter remained in abeyance when Labour were elected in 1945, and Clement Attlee's words in February 1941 that, 'Wales is not just an industrial region... it is the home of a separate nation,' had been widely interpreted as a statement of intent to create a Welsh Secretaryship. Furthermore, D. R. had referred specifically to the need for such a ministerial position in his election address in 1945, as had Goronwy Roberts and his colleagues in north-west Wales who campaigned on the *Llais Llafur* manifesto that promised distinctive action to meet specific Welsh needs.[29] These views were shared by MPs such as S. O. Davies, W. H. Mainwaring, Tudor Watkins, John Evans, Robert Richards, and George Daggar, all of whom were appalled by the crisis still facing Labour's Welsh strongholds. They were convinced that only a Secretary for Wales would provide the required leadership and coordination.

These and other issues were placed before Clement Attlee and Jim Griffiths by a delegation from the WPP at the beginning of March 1946, but no decision was taken, merely a promise that the matters would be considered by the Prime Minister, an ambiguous response that elicited sharp comment from within the Welsh Labour movement.[30] David Raymond, in *Reynolds News*, reiterated his paper's longstanding support for the creation of such a post by reminding Clement Attlee of his previous commitments on the issue and declaring, 'I hope that when Mr Clement Attlee has given his promised consideration to the demands made by the Welsh MPs he will be seen not to have changed his mind now that he has the power to do something.'[31]

Likewise, John Roberts Williams, editor of *Y Cymro* which had a large circulation in north and west Wales at the time, published an open letter on 15 March 1946 which reiterated an identical statement it had made to Winston Churchill in June 1943. *Y Cymro* drew attention to the lack of progress in housing, rising unemployment and declining coal output, asserting, 'We know that in the past you have under-estimated the solid feeling that exists in Wales behind this demand. Let us assure you, that has become the battlecry of the Welsh people in their struggle for their very existence as a Nation.'

It touched a raw nerve when the newspaper declared: 'It is melancholy in the extreme to imagine that a new Government which received such a mass of progressive support in Wales and which raised seven south Wales members into office, with two members in the Cabinet, should show so little cognisance of the soul of this ancient Principality.'[32]

Unsurprisingly, both papers rounded on Harold Laski in May 1946 after he appeared to dismiss the notion of a Secretary of State as something that would produce nothing for Wales except confusion.[33] Why, asked David Raymond in *Reynolds News*, had Laski not consulted some of the Welsh Labour MPs before taking upon himself to speak on the issue?

D. R., Goronwy Roberts and W. H. Mainwaring then took responsibility for drafting the detailed case for the establishment of a Secretary of State, which dwelt on the special social and economic difficulties facing Wales. They produced a catalogue of complaints with which they were having to deal. Welsh MPs, despite their best efforts, had never been able to obtain adequate consideration from Whitehall during the inter-war years, while government policy meant people were 'voluntarily or forcibly [being] moved to England'.[34] The situation in which they now found themselves was one in which 'dread and fear of the future are widespread' due to the growth of unemployment. The war had created demand and 'served to lift the clouds of economic depression in Wales' but, unless action was taken, Wales would suffer the same plight as had been its experience in the inter-war years. They warned that people's patience was already exhausted. 'The thousands of unemployed are already restless. They grow cynical, extremely cynical, of promises.' The MPs listed specific failings. The Board of Trade had a long list of agreed or contemplated building programmes for factories, but few of them had been built. Sites were not being cleared and building was not proceeding. There were complaints about the work of the Treforest Trading Estate Co., which had been given responsibility for projects across the whole of Wales. Bureaucratic delays were causing frustration. There was no effective machinery to hold officials to account. The MPs described the Welsh Reconstruction Advisory Council as 'useless'.

The WPP's concluding statement in support of a Welsh Secretaryship brought together the national, economic and political arguments in its favour:

> In further support of this suggestion, it needs to be emphasised, while Wales is a part of the economy of Britain, it would be folly indeed to dream of the possibility of it being otherwise. Wales and the Welsh are a nation with a language and culture they desire to maintain. A condition of existence for most nations is that a livelihood is made available for the people in their own country.
>
> There is a sense of frustration spreading throughout Wales, and this is fostering the growth of resentment against whatever Government may be in power. It is only right that the anger of ignoring the manifestations already made, and of others that will follow, should be made known to you. The country is united as never before in the demand for proper recognition and effective measures to facilitate the development of its resources, the growth of industry, and administration of Welsh affairs on satisfactory lines. It is now our fervent hope that you will be able to make some statement likely to restore the confidence of the people and enable them hopefully to face the future.[35]

A Welsh Office, located both in Wales and Whitehall and headed by a minister, would be able to co-ordinate government functions in Wales and discharge parliamentary duties 'in

connection with administration in the several departments now
or to be represented regionally in Wales, dealing with Health,
Education, National Insurance, Employment, Agriculture and
Fisheries, Transport, Local Government, Works, Development'.
This would be achieved through supervision of the activities of
each department in Wales, with a duty to report on that work
to parliament. This would detect and address its shortcomings
of administration affecting Wales, and ensure plans for
development in every branch of industry on a five-year cycle.

This memorandum formed the basis of a discussion with
Herbert Morrison in February 1946 but, while he recognised
the MPs' frustration, it was clear from his reaction that neither
he nor the Prime Minister had any sympathy with the course
they proposed as a solution.[36] Writing to D. R. from Paris a
few months later, Clement Attlee noted that the regional
organisation of government departments had developed
during the war and that such structures would be retained.[37]
He promised that civil servants based in Wales, as part of the
regional structures of Whitehall departments, would enjoy
enough autonomy to address the issues facing the country, and
that the relevant government ministers would ensure that they
fulfilled those duties:

> It is our intention that ministers should pay particular
> attention to ensuring that the Welsh Sections of their
> Department are staffed in a way which secures that the
> application of general Government policy to Welsh conditions
> receives skilled and sympathetic attention, and that there
> is no unnecessary reference to Whitehall of matters which,
> by the exercise of a proper degree of responsibility, can be
> settled in Wales.

For Clement Attlee, a Welsh Secretaryship would
merely complicate administrative structures and delay the
implementation of government policy: 'The appointment of
a local minister would have complicated the Government

machine at a time when greater simplicity and directness in administration should be our general aim.'

Unlike Scotland the civil and criminal law was not different to England, which he alluded was the sole argument for maintaining a separate office for Scotland. With regard to an economic plan, he argued: 'Wales should be able to exercise her undoubted right to ventilate her special claims in the economic sphere, but on broad organisation the proper course is to ensure that Wales takes her place in the general economic plan for the whole country.'

When Clement Attlee's attitude became public knowledge later that summer, the WPP was reported to be 'indignant'. The *Western Mail* sought to maximise Labour's discomfort over the issue, sarcastically chiding the party's failure to respond to the demands of its most faithful heartland.[38] The decision was also condemned forcefully by *Reynolds News* and by John Roberts Williams in *Y Cymro*, who warned: 'Nid yw Cymru'n mynd i anghofio ar frys y gwarthrudd hwn a ddaeth oddi wrth blaid mawr Llafur a'i Llywodraeth.'[39] [Wales will not forget this impudence in a hurry, coming from the great Labour Party and its government.]

Later that month the same paper warned Aneurin Bevan against the dangers of swallowing the idea that all salvation must necessarily come from Whitehall on all occasions.[40]

D. R. was by no means prepared to let the matter rest and immediately entered into a detailed correspondence with Clement Attlee who was at the Paris Peace Conference at the time. In a letter to Clement Attlee dated 15 August 1946, D. R. repeated the views of the WPP meeting and conveyed its disappointment at the government's reply which did not address the proposals they had made, and suggested that the idea of a Secretary of State and Welsh Office had not even been subjected to serious examination. Indeed, 'The reply is the same simple negative which was given by the coalition government and by leaders of the Labour Party in the Coalition.'

Turning to the Welsh ministers in the Attlee government, D. R. went as far as to allege that, 'We cannot explain their change of opinion and find it difficult to believe that they are personally committed to the terms of your letter.' Wales was being treated as a region of England which was simply not good enough. He made a clear appeal for a different policy which he justified on the grounds of Welsh nationhood:

> The general impression is that the Labour Government
> is opposed to the slightest recognition for Wales. The
> administration is to remain regional. Wales will get as much
> as the North East, the North West, The Midland regions,
> but not as much as Scotland or either part of Ireland... The
> Welsh Parliamentary Party is authorised to make as strong a
> claim to autonomy as either of the four nations in the United
> Kingdom. The reply of the Government seems to repudiate
> entirely the claims of Wales as a nation. It will not satisfy the
> supporters of the Government nor the majority of people in
> any party in Wales. The Welsh nation has occupied a proud
> place in the line-up of democratic peoples. It will not be
> content with sentimental substitutes for the right of equality
> and self-government. The Members of Parliament for Wales
> have, in the interests of the people, made a united demand
> for better government, in Wales, for Wales, by the people of
> Wales.

The government's reply, he went on, was 'un-conciliatory' to that part of the United Kingdom which had supported it more than any other, and the letter 'makes no acknowledgement that her loyalty and the political respect due to a proud and progressively minded people seeking to make a stronger contribution to the better government of Wales and the United Kingdom.'

The kind of proposals which the government were making merely continued the arrangement that had existed throughout the inter-war years. They had failed to prevent the country deteriorating into depression and a designated Special Area.

Clement Attlee responded to the WPP in a letter, dated 5 September 1946, in which he insisted that the matter had been considered by the government with the most 'sympathetic understanding of the needs and feelings of the Welsh people than had ever been shown before'. Government policy in Wales would lead to important changes in the machinery of government which included strengthening the staffing and organisation of government departments in Wales and ensuring more effective coordination between them in relation to Welsh issues, most notably through the requirement for the heads of all Welsh regional offices to meet on a regular basis and examine policy together in the light of what was happening on the ground. The idea of an annual White Paper on Wales, which the government was pursuing, would enable ministers to be held to account for the implementation of their policy in Wales as never before, and would act as a stimulus to the government, and especially to ministers, to keep Wales at the forefront of their minds. Clement Attlee insisted there was no difference between his aims and those expressed by the WPP, merely a disagreement on how they might be achieved:

> I feel that we are in agreement about the objective – meeting
> the true needs and interests of the Welsh people – and
> differ only about the best means of achieving it. I suggest
> that the scheme which I have proposed ought in fairness
> at least be given a trial rather than pronounced inadequate
> beforehand… I do not disguise from you our belief that it
> would be a mistake to think that Wales can achieve economic
> well-being altogether apart from considerations of policy
> for Britain as a whole; nor do I accept the view that the
> appointment of a Secretary of State would solve the economic
> problem.[41]

Those supporting the notion of a Secretary of State continued to press the matter throughout October 1946, clearly refusing to accept Clement Attlee's response to be the end of the matter. Goronwy Roberts, addressing D. R. as, 'you, as our leader', declared, 'I hope a good many of us will say that we do not intend to liquidate the agitation as a result of the Government's refusal to create a Welsh Secretary. Indeed, Wales will not allow us to do so.'[42]

As a first step, D. R. and W. H. Mainwaring held another meeting with Clement Attlee and Herbert Morrison, following which it was agreed that a parliamentary debate would be held to allow MPs to air their grievances.[43] D. R. and Goronwy Roberts were determined to make the most of the opportunity they had been given, and arranged the detailed tactics to be deployed in the Commons. W. H. Mainwaring would open the debate and relate the national argument to the economic case. D. R., Goronwy Roberts, Tudor Watkins, Robert Richards, John Evans and George Daggar would all come at the issue from different angles. The conclusion would be the same: the government's machinery in Wales was inadequate and could only be put right by a dedicated Secretary of State. In advance of the debate, D. R. and W. H. Mainwaring took to the pages of *Reynolds News* to put their case, in which they made much of the specifically national claims of Wales in support of their argument:

> Scotland has a Secretary of State; Northern Ireland has a Parliament of its own; Eire is a Dominion. Wales and her people, whom no one will deny to be something distinct from England, with her own language, an ancient culture and traditions, has always looked with jealous eyes at the recognition long given to the separate nationhood of her Celtic sister nations. In the past it was on the basis of national sentiment that Welshmen again and again asked for the recognition of their own claims.

Having lost almost half a million people in population during the Depression and further dislocation in the war years, Wales needed special attention, and they insisted that the structural problems facing the Welsh economy, stemming from generations of decline and mismanagement, reinforced the case for change:

> The transition from war to peace brought with it a dislocation of industrial activity which once again lays bare the evils that had afflicted Wales in the pre-war years. The return of a Labour Government encouraged the renewal of a demand for a Minister charged with the responsibility for planning economic and social reconstruction... What gives special urgency to the demand now is that Wales at the moment has an unemployment figure of 60,000, by far the highest in the Kingdom... The unemployment is not the fault of the Labour Government. It is largely the heritage of the past: it arises from the fact that, as soon as war-time industry was wound up, Wales fell back on an ill-balanced, unplanned economy, which grew up in the years of the industrial revolution.

The need was to generate employment and this required a minister charged with directing and driving a plan for promoting a balanced industry with full employment and develop Wales' rich natural resources. Pointing to the cross-party support for the proposal, echoed by business, trade union and local government leaders, they insisted, 'Parliament is becoming overburdened with legislative and administrative discussions and some method must be devised to ease the pressure at the centre.' Clement Attlee had, they claimed, implied that he recognised the need for some form of devolution in his answer to the WPP during the summer, but this had been administrative devolution bereft of the required democratic scrutiny and political direction:

> He has proposed that the heads of Government departments in Wales should have frequent meetings to advise on questions of policy. But this proposal of his, which he

suggests as an alternative to a Welsh Minister, delegates powers to civil servants which are the proper business of Parliamentary representatives and of Ministers responsible to them... Constitutionally, it would be a dangerous precedent and is no real alternative to the considered proposals of the Welsh MPs. In these days of revolutionary changes, when the whole economic structure of the country is being recast, the objection of constitutional difficulties in creating a Welsh Ministry cannot be valid... The High Court of Parliament has full authority for making all the changes necessary to ensure Britain's complete recovery. And in this connection, who will gainsay that there can be no real recovery for Britain if the needs and claims of such a vital economic area as Wales are overlooked.[44]

David Raymond in the same issue of *Reynolds News* pointed out that, as diverse a range of commentators as the *Observer*, the *Sunday Times*, the *New Statesman* as well as his own paper, all recognised the validity of the Welsh demands.[45] He found it difficult to reconcile Clement Attlee's response that the government had gone so far to meet Welsh demands and could go no further, with the reality of the 60,000 unemployed in the country.[46] The Welsh MPs, he insisted, were merely asking for fair play. They 'are not asking for economic or any other kind of separation; they are asking for measures to make sure that Wales gets her fair share of the economic well-being of Britain as a whole, instead of having the tough end of the unemployment problem.'[47]

On 28 October, the Welsh backbenchers made their case in a debate on the government's White Paper on Wales. Sir Stafford Cripps introduced on behalf of the government, and during the course of an hour's oration sought to reassure MPs that the government was serious about tackling unemployment, and would do so by bringing Wales into the mainstream of British industrial life. He referred to the programme of factory construction, the roads being built, and the clearance of derelict sites. The problem with Welsh ports, explained the Bristol MP, was that they had been designed primarily to export coal which meant it was difficult for them to be adapted to other uses. He rejected the argument for a dedicated Minister, insisting that the matters of concern were not specifically 'Welsh' problems but ones that demanded the attention of the government as a whole. Scotland needed its own machinery of government because of constitutional and legal issues, which did not apply to Wales. Under any circumstances, a Secretary of State for Wales would only cause delay and inefficiency.

He made the ill-judged remark that, 'With an area and population to draw upon so small as that of Wales, it would be quite impossible to maintain the standard of administration, in purely Welsh services, as high as that which is possible when these services cover the entire country.' This immediately provoked an angry response from Tudor Watkins and W. H. Mainwaring, before Sir Stafford Cripps contradicted his own logic by acknowledging that, 'it is most important to have the maximum possible devolution of responsibility to departmental officials working in Wales.'[48]

D. R. had not intervened during Sir Stafford Cripps' speech but rose at 4.46pm to begin a 30-minute contribution which set the tone for the debate. He began by regretting that the Minister's opening remarks failed to provide a satisfactory answer to any of the issues raised by the Welsh MPs. What was the government's response to the situation confronting Wales?

Does not the population alarm the Government?… There are 300,000 fewer people in Wales than in 1926. The young men have gone away, the old have tarried; and the old people are not so productive or reproductive as the young people. This is a time when the economic fabric of Wales must be re-examined, but not by patchwork, by tinkering or local alleviation. There must be a plan for Wales. We are as entitled as anyone to have a plan; we are the people who have suffered most for the want of planning.

A massive £100 million per year had been lost in wages between 1920 and 1935, along with £2.5 billion in capital loss and property values. But throughout those years the government's only response was transference, and the Labour government appeared to be following the same counsel of despair:

> The Welsh unemployed are told, 'Go somewhere else. Swim in the streams of prosperity elsewhere.' That has not been the history of people who have been compelled to go elsewhere. It has been found that their standard of living has been permanently reduced when they have had to move to other parts of Britain. We are determined, so far as we can, to explore the possibilities of a scientific economic organisation in Wales for the benefit of Welsh people, for their full employment, and the return of prosperity to Wales.

He accused the government of abandoning Wales as more people would be forced to leave the country, and this at a time when Britain was governed by a party which had historically relied on the loyalty of its people. He continued, 'We stand here today and all we ask, not as a concession or a favour, but as a contribution to the better Government of Wales, that the Government shall give us this power, let us have a plan, and let the Welsh people have a voice in it.'

D. R. was followed by a succession of MPs, initially from the opposition benches, during which Gwilym Lloyd George, David Price White, Nigel Birch, Henry Morris-Jones, Megan Lloyd George, W. J. Gruffydd, Emrys Roberts and Rhys Hopkin Morris joined to support the national claims of Wales in various ways. From the Labour benches, Charles Edwards, George Daggar and D. L. Mort focused mainly on constituency issues, before Tudor Watkins put forward a practical and moral case for a radical change in the machinery of government in Wales. His contribution was followed by Goronwy Roberts who, while welcoming the government's use of Socialist planning to respond to Wales' needs, insisted that such an approach should be refined through the appointment of a dedicated Minister and a Royal Commission on the possibilities of national assemblies for Wales, Scotland and England. He was supported by John Evans who acquiesced with both the notion of some form of Minister for Wales and the demand for devolution.

This was not the only view. D. J. Williams believed that the economic problems were more intense in Wales – as was evident from the level of unemployment and continued out-migration of people – but he advocated an Economic Planning Authority rather than the appointment of a Secretary of State. Similarly, James Callaghan was opposed to the notion of a Secretary of State but supported some form of regional devolution and a federal system within Britain.

W. H. Mainwaring concluded the backbenchers' contribution to the debate, describing the practical difficulties faced by Welsh MPs who were being sent around government departments, and veered from specifics (charges against the Treforest Estate Co., in particular) to the general. 'Of what value will Welsh culture be if Wales is denuded of its population?' He reminded the House that the Labour Party had committed to a Secretary for Wales as a way of addressing the needs of the devastated areas. 'It was made at a time when they were not embarrassed by official responsibilities; made at a time when they had not the embarrassment of meeting these demands; when the men who made that report were free to devote their minds to the problems.'

He was followed by Aneurin Bevan who rose to sum up for the government. He managed to say that the government had delivered 'every syllable' of the manifesto promises, and that it had implemented 'executive devolution', the 'machinery to give executive drive to government policies', before being unceremoniously interrupted by D. R.:

333

D. R.: 'Upon whom have they [the powers] been devolved?'

Bevan: 'They have been devolved on regional officers, regional directors and civil servants, because these are the executive agents of the Government.'

D. R.: 'Irresponsible elements.'

Bevan: 'If the argument is to be that we should have elective regional authorities, there is an argument for that, but it has not been advanced tonight.'

Crucially, Aneurin Bevan did not dismiss the case for elective devolution and conceded that radical changes in Britain's constitutional arrangements could well be required as the State increased its sphere of responsibility:

> Indeed, it is obvious that as the Government more and more intervenes in economic affairs, we may have to reconsider the whole structure of local government, and consider whether any new constitutional devices are necessary in order to put into the hands of elected persons at the regional level the obligation to carry out a good deal of Government administration.

But he then got diverted, making largely irrelevant points about the extent to which the ability to speak Welsh should be a requirement for office (which had not been suggested), before resorting to the administrative argument in opposition to a Welsh Secretary.[49]

Aneurin Bevan's description of D. R. as 'querulous' during his concluding remarks may well convey the mood of the occasion, and was reflected by David Raymond in *Reynolds News*, who reported that, 'The vehemence of some of the speeches, especially those of Grenfell, Mainwaring and Daggar, surprised the Ministerial benches, from what I can gather.'[50]

*

Within months, D. R. was again to find himself opposing the Labour government's actions in Wales, this time over the issue of compulsory purchase of large tracts of land in rural areas for military training purposes. The announcement that half a million acres of land in Wales would be taken by the War Office came at what was already an awkward moment for the Labour government, as it coincided with a left-wing revolt over the direction of foreign policy. Now Welsh Labour MPs, many of whom were already disgruntled at Clement Attlee's response on the question of a Secretary of State, demanded to know why there had been no consultation with them or other interested parties in Wales. Why, they asked, was Wales expected to contribute proportionately three times as much as England and nine times as much as Scotland?[51] Within weeks the extent of public anger in Wales was clear. 'Ni bu cymaint o ddeunydd tân yng Nghymru er dyddiau'r degwm' [There has not been so much fuel for the fire in Wales since the days of the tithe wars], was John Roberts Williams' comment in *Y Cymro*.[52] Civic organisations ranging from the Women's Institute to Undeb Cymru Fydd, local authorities, voluntary organisations, and tourist bodies joined in a chorus of opposition.[53]

There were student demonstrations across Wales while the Welsh Nationalists, now led by Gwynfor Evans, quickly seized on the issue as yet another demonstration of the Labour government's failure to live up to Welsh expectations.[54] D. R. recognised that opposition did not only come from the tiny Welsh nationalist movement. For him the real issue cut deeper; it went against the grain that a Labour government was commandeering land in peacetime on an unprecedented scale to prepare men to go to war when it should be revitalising the economic and social life of the very communities that would be worst affected. Tackling rural depopulation, making small family farms in upland areas viable through subsidies and guaranteed prices, extending water and electricity supplies to villages and promoting tourism, was what a Labour government should be doing in rural Wales if it was to be true to itself and worthy of its Welsh roots.

He agreed to chair the national conference convened by Undeb Cymru Fydd in Llandrindod Wells in March 1947. Over a thousand delegates attended, including several of D. R.'s Welsh Labour colleagues – Tudor Watkins, whose Brecon and Radnor constituency was directly affected, along with Goronwy Roberts, S. O. Davies, Will John, George Daggar and Robert Richards.[55] They joined the Liberal MPs Gwilym Lloyd George, Henry Morris-Jones, and Emrys Roberts, the trade unionist Huw T. Edwards, and religious leaders such as the Welsh Baptist, the Rev. Wyre Lewis, and the Bishop of St Asaph at the conference. In an address from the chair, D. R. defended Wales' record at a time of war and insisted that what was being asked was an unreasonable burden to bear:

> We are the representatives of a small country... and we do
> not desire to hand over large areas of its land for permanent
> military purposes. Wales has borne its part in all Britain's
> struggles abroad. We have never sought exemption from
> the burdens of war, but we do object to the steps now
> proposed, for purely military reasons, to take over an entirely
> disproportionate part of our small land... We have great pride
> in our country, and we opposed this ruthless annexation
> when the schemes were first announced. The whole of the
> proposed acquisition of land totals about half-a-million acres,
> and that seems an outrage on Wales. We have yet to learn
> that consideration is to be given to the people of Wales in this
> matter.[56]

Not everyone in the Labour Party agreed with D. R. or those of his colleagues who had travelled to Llandrindod Wells. The Executive Committee of the Pontypridd Divisional Labour Party wrote supporting the government's 'fairness' in allocating the quota of land required to fulfil Britain's obligations to the United Nations Organisation (UNO), but drew a swift response from D. R. 'If the Executive Committee of the Pontypridd Divisional Labour Party wishes to give a blank cheque to the military authorities, it should be done in plain terms.'[57]

He repeated his objections during a meeting with Clement Attlee, Fred Bellenger, the Minister for War, and John Freeman in April 1947, but the outcome was again disappointing. While the Prime Minister gave a commitment to hold public inquiries in each area, he gave no undertakings on the substantive issue.[58]

Over the next six months individual areas were withdrawn until eventually it was announced that the total amount of land required in Wales would be reduced by a third.[59] Despite this concession, the opposition in Wales continued. The Welsh Committee on Training Areas met with Emanuel Shinwell at the start of 1948 amid a vociferous 'Hands Off Wales' protest, but he rejected their demand that the quota to be taken in Wales should be reduced to one half.[60] Properly-run training centres, he insisted, would have no effect on Welsh culture; farmers would be compensated and protected, and he insisted that an army had to be maintained at the size proposed.[61] Public protests continued throughout the spring which forced the War Office to make further concessions that reduced the amount of land to be taken even further.[62] This was not sufficient to placate the opposition in Wales, as was made clear to Emanuel Shinwell when he visited Aberystwyth in February. He was involved in a memorable confrontation with the future Labour politician Gwilym Prys Davies over the matter.[63] Shortly afterwards, the Ministry of Town and Country Planning appointed Sir Wynn Wheldon to undertake public inquiries in the most contentious areas, which led to some concessions to local opinion in certain areas. However, festering resentment continued in the affected areas and it was seized upon by Labour's opponents in Wales for many years to come.

The campaign coincided with parliamentary discussion

on the National Service Bill which the Attlee government introduced to counter the decline in the number of voluntary recruits for the armed forces. The government proposed continuous compulsory military service for men aged 18–26 from 1 January 1949 for periods of 18 months to two years, with safeguards for individuals who could prove that it would cause personal hardship, and conscientious objectors. The proposals drew sharp criticism both from committed pacifists on the Labour benches, in particular Rhys Davies and others who seized the opportunity to criticise Ernest Bevin's foreign policy more broadly.[64] The level of opposition had been evident earlier in the year when 50 Labour MPs signed an amendment opposing the proposals, and they were prominent in the two-day meeting held in April 1947 in which Rhys Davies insisted that a Labour government should not countenance military conscription in peacetime and deplored the influence enjoyed by unelected military chiefs on the ministers' proposals.[65]

When the matter was put to the vote, the government found itself in the unenviable position of receiving the support of Winston Churchill and the Conservative opposition, itself sufficient condemnation of any Bill according to its Labour critics. D. R. did not speak during the debate but was among the 85 Labour MPs who entered the lobby against the government.[66] Reflecting on the revolt, John Roberts Williams of *Y Cymro* expressed the disappointment felt by many, not least because the Bill had received so much support from the Tory opposition. His parting shot, 'A'r dwthwn hwnnw yr aeth Herod a Pheilat yn gyfeillion' [That day, Herod and Pilate became allies], cut to the quick for many Labour stalwarts, among them those who remembered Socialist opposition to the Great War.[67] No doubt D. R. appreciated John Roberts Williams' advice to Labour MPs that it would be better for them to 'dilyn ôl troed hen warior fel Dai Grenfell sydd â cryn dipyn o'r tân Cymreig yn llosgi ynddo o hyd' [follow in the footsteps of an old warrior like Dai Grenfell, who still has so much of the Welsh fire burning in him].[68]

Within a fortnight, D. R. spotted another opportunity to challenge the Bill during its committee stage. He seized on the fact that, despite the strong objections of Ulster Unionist MPs, compulsory military service did not apply to those living in Northern Ireland. This situation had existed ever since the outbreak of the Second World War and stemmed from the wartime coalition's fear of antagonising Irish Republicans and the government of Eire. If Northern Ireland could be excluded, then the same exemption could be claimed for Wales with its tradition of internationalism and commitment to peace.

But the amendment to this effect, moved by W. J. Gruffydd, MP for the University of Wales, secured the support of only 21 MPs, including D. R. and several of the Welsh MPs who had opposed the government's proposals the previous month, and a similar fate befell the Rev. Campbell Stephen's efforts to get Scotland excluded.[69] The revolt made little impression on Ernest Bevin who wrote to Clement Attlee saying, 'I realised it was chiefly the Welsh and I always anticipated that they and a few conscientious objectors would oppose.'[70] The reality that the Welsh, whom he dismissed, represented the part of the United Kingdom who had consistently shown most loyalty to Labour was not lost on D. R. and his fellow rebels. Compulsory military service might have been a necessary evil to defeat fascism in 1939 but it was no way for the party with the internationalist inheritance of Keir Hardie and George Lansbury to behave in these very different circumstances in 1947.

CHAPTER 15

D. R. and the New Jerusalem

By THE SUMMER of 1947 the Labour government, through the Iron and Steel Board, were in a position to begin the transformation of steel and tinplate production by means of a comprehensive restructuring and modernisation process. Already, the Board had announced that a third strip mill would be built at Margam, and its selection represented a victory for industrial and economic planning and showed the government's determination to support the regeneration of south Wales, despite fierce opposition from free marketeers within the industry who demanded that the new works should to be built close to the ore fields in the East Midlands.[1] The scale of the development was more than a single manufacturer could undertake. As a result, a conglomerate of the largest steel manufacturing firms, Richard Thomas & Co., Baldwin's, GKN, John Lysaght, and Llanelli Associated Tinplate Co. established the Steel Company of Wales to drive the process of change. The new works represented the dawn of a new industrial era in the history of the western part of south Wales. The livelihoods of more than 29,000 men and 3,500 women, approximately a fifth of the region's insured population, relied on it. As far as tinplate manufacturing was concerned, the days of the hand-mills that had been the mainstay of the industry was coming to an end, as production would henceforth be concentrated in modern cold-reduction facilities that would be supplied from Margam.[2]

D. R. knew that such momentous changes presented great opportunities for the region but that only detailed planning would prevent thousands from losing their jobs in the process. A Labour government was duty-bound to ensure all workers were either redeployed or given alternative work in order to prevent any return to the uncertainties of the inter-war years. A sign that such an approach would be taken was given by ministers serving in the wartime coalition. Hugh Dalton, as President of the Board of Trade, made a commitment that the new cold-reduction facility would be situated west of the Margam plant, in Swansea. Dalton's geography had been vague, but D. R. believed there was no doubt that 'Swansea' meant a site adjacent to Llangyfelach, at the point where Swansea County Borough met the Llwchwr Urban District, close to existing tinplate-manufacturing centres like Gorseinon, Pontarddulais, Morriston, Llansamlet, and accessible to areas like Clydach, Pontardawe, Ystalyfera and Ystradgynlais in the Swansea Valley.

On 21 May 1947, D. R. joined the other MPs representing the region in a meeting with John Wilmot, the Minister of Supply, and Sir Archibald Forbes, Chairman of the Steel Board. It was announced that Llangyfelach would be the preferred site. The decision was welcomed by those present, with the exception of Jim Griffiths whose Llanelli constituency was further from the Llangyfelach site. He declared in no uncertain terms, 'I will fight for my town inside the government', adding that Llanelli had been badly let down by the ministers responsible for the decision.[3] Notwithstanding his opposition, more than 300 men began work to prepare the site at Llangyfelach, while Llwchwr UDC entered into agreements with Swansea CBC to upgrade water supplies. Surveys were prepared, and engineering estimates commissioned.

D. R. was therefore incandescent – no other word could

describe his reaction – when John Wilmot announced the following month that the preparation work at the Llangyfelach site would be abandoned and that, instead, a new plant would be built at Trostre, on the outskirts of Llanelli, in recognition of the social impact the original decision would have on the workforce there.[4] Following heated exchanges in the House of Commons, D. R., with the support of fellow MPs D. L. Mort, Percy Morris and D. J. Williams, demanded the appointment of a select committee to look into the issue.[5] Jim Griffiths, for his part, avoided the temptation to enter into a bitter exchange with his parliamentary neighbour and sent an urgent letter to his agent, W. Douglas Hughes, warning the Llanelli Constituency Labour Party (CLP) and its affiliates not to seek to portray the matter as a victory for them over Swansea.[6] He emphasised that the choice of the Llanelli site reflected the way decisions should be taken in the new era of economic planning, in which industry would be organised to serve people. 'In deciding issues of such magnitude and importance, the Government is bound to consider the sociological as well as the economic factors involved.'[7] This was the only way of avoiding the kind of mistakes made when Stanley Baldwin was Prime Minister, which had bedevilled the local economy during the inter-war years, he believed.[8]

Such arguments cut no ice in Swansea. Local officers of both the ISTC and AEU declared their personal support for the Llangyfelach site, although their regional leaders remained silent on the matter.[9] Llwchwr UDC, which stood to lose most in rateable value by the change, was unanimous in its opposition to the change. Likewise, the neighbouring Pontardawe RDC, led by Richard Roberts who was himself a prominent trade unionist in the steel and tinplate industry, declared its total opposition to the plan, which they believed would jeopardise the whole future of their own area. They refused to countenance a more conciliatory approach suggested by Jack Maunder, the Communist councillor from Craig-cefn-parc, who believed they should instead seek a guarantee that an alternative use would be found for Llangyfelach.[10] In the meantime, the *South Wales Evening Post* took the opportunity to blame the ideology of the Labour government, stating, 'Loss of money, waste of labour, and an artificially created delay due to the interference of politicians with the advice and experience of experts, are allegations that have always been made in arguments against Government control and nationalisation.' Cabinet members, it claimed, were making decisions that should be left to trained professionals and industrialists.[11]

A conference of those opposed to the decision was held at the Brangwyn Hall in Swansea, at which D. R., clearly angry with all that had happened, declared that the decision would have ramifications for the future of the steel and tinplate industry throughout the UK. It was not a local quarrel but a matter of the future of the industry.[12] He produced a battery of statistics in support of the Llangfelach site, and returned several times to his central argument – that most of the tinplate workers rendered unemployed by the closure of old works lived in its vicinity rather than in Llanelli. 'Reversal of a decision taken on such sound ground is an act which can only be tolerated if there is some overriding case of which we know nothing at all. I dissent most strongly from the view that Llanelly is to suffer more than any other district.'[13] Any impartial inquiry, he insisted, would decide 'against taking this plant away from the site selected by the Steel Board and confirmed by the Government,' before it reversed its decision. Llangyfelach was 'perfectly without flaw as a site', suitable in terms of geography and free from any future mineworkings. He was supported by Percy Morris, who viewed the battle as one for effective economic planning. 'We want to save the government making a serious mistake. We want to help them in their planned economy, and if the Llangyfelach site is not utilised it means the very negation of planning as we understand it.' D. L. Mort warned that world markets would be lost due to the slightest increase in cost, and this would be the effect of locating the plant at Trostre.[14]

The *Evening Post* predicted difficulties for Labour in Swansea in the future and delighted in 'an open split... between incensed local Labour and its own Government, which has so far grievously disappointed it... The stability and proximity to substantially the larger number of tinplate works and employees which would ultimately be affected by the change-over at Margam and the cold-reduction plants, have all been shown clearly to constitute a case decisively strong in favour of Swansea, on every conceivable ground.'[15]

Notwithstanding the conference's decision to demand that ministers revert to the Llangyfelach option, Clement Attlee was unmoved, calmly writing to D. R. 'I can assure you that the question has been considered in the light of all the facts and the decision reached only after very careful thought.'[16] But D. R. continued his campaign, telling the *Daily Mirror*, 'Three hundred men have worked round the clock at Llangyfelach to get the site ready. A marvellous job has been done and £80,000 spent. The Government says the site will be utilised in time. But we want to see tinplate rolling away as soon as possible. A switch to Llanelli would throw production back a year or two.'[17]

He pursued Sir Stafford Cripps to demand that the evidence on which the decision had been taken should be published, specifically whether any advice had been received from within the tinplate industry and whether any recommendation had been made by the Steel Board.[18] Within days, he went further and used the committee stage of the Supplies and Services (Transitional Powers) Bill to propose that, before there was a transfer of any industry, there should be joint consultation with representatives of industry, local authorities and local MPs rather than leave the matter to civil servants. He said that he disagreed most strongly with the entire Bill. 'In every line, the Bill confers greater power for the Government bureaucracy. I have no confidence at all in that. Civil servants are ill-trained for this work. They cannot direct industry as they have no technical knowledge… They have, to my knowledge, made very grievous mistakes with permanent ill-effects on the industries of this country.'[19]

Such an argument went to the heart of the discussion about how a nationalised industry would work in principle, and gave succour to the Tories who seized on the arguments as testimony of what would happen in the event of the steel industry being nationalised. But D. R. had no qualms about giving succour to the opposition. He accused the government of abandoning his constituency to mass unemployment and challenged the 'sociological' argument in favour of Trostre, accusing the government of ignoring the advice of the Steel Board. Early in 1948, he shared his thoughts in a radio broadcast to demand that the economic case for Llangyfelach should supersede the social argument for Trostre. He believed that the matter needed to be assessed in a broader sense of the most advantageous location for the whole region.[20] He estimated that Trostre would cost an additional £125,000 per annum, a sum which would either fall on the taxpayer or increase the cost of its output, affecting its trading position. Llangyfelach was the technologically superior site and the proposed work could be built there much more quickly than at Trostre.[21]

An announcement that a second cold-reduction plant would be built at Llangyfelach failed to satisfy him, especially when building work was delayed.[22] Furthermore, the fact that many of D. R.'s own constituents, particularly in the Loughor, Gorseinon and Pontarddulais areas, found employment at the new works at Trostre was no consolation.[23]

D. R. and Jim Griffiths had a close working relationship as Labour leaders in neighbouring constituencies for over 30 years. D. R. had undertaken an annual programme of speaking engagements in the mining villages around Llanelli throughout the 1920s and 1930s, and had worked closely when

Jim had been building up the Labour organisation in advance of Dr J. H. Williams' election in 1922. Thereafter, both had worked together after Jim was elected Miners' Agent for the Anthracite Area and later as President of the SWMF. When Jim had sought a senior post with the TUC in 1931, he had enlisted D. R.'s support in canvassing prominent trade union leaders. Moreover, both men had collaborated on mine safety and disability issues in parliament, each one specialising in aspects that complemented the work of the other. There was to be no such collaboration after the controversy over Trostre. The scars remained unhealed, certainly as far as D. R. was concerned. There was no reconciliation even when Griffiths' brother David, the poet Amanwy, used his weekly column in *Y Cymro* to try to mediate.[24] Not even the warm words of an old friend could reconcile D. R. to Jim Griffiths.

*

The arguments over the location of the new cold-reduction plant coincided with the financial situation that occupied the Labour government's attention throughout the summer of 1947. Under the terms of the American loan, 'full convertibility' had to be restored by mid July but, from the start of the year, the Treasury's dollar reserves began to decline at an alarming rate due to the escalating costs of food and raw materials imported from the United States. The government halted convertibility on 8 August before reaching a temporary agreement with the Americans two days later. To no one's surprise, American assistance came at a heavy price: imports of food had to be reduced, resulting in further reductions in rations, and a substantial increase in exports – set at £31 million per month – would be required to enable the UK to meet its obligations. The government sought to mobilise public opinion through the twin efforts to maximise industrial productivity in order to boost exports, and to make funds available to ministers by means of investment in national savings. Throughout late summer and early autumn, ministers toured the country emphasising the need for the massive national effort needed to save the situation.[25] Labour leaders warned the rank and file there could be no improvement in working conditions until the current crisis was resolved.[26] Sir Stafford Cripps portrayed the export drive as an essential part of Britain's goal of economic freedom, a battle that had to be won if the country was not to be tied by economic strings to the political priorities of other countries, a clear reference to American influence in British policy.[27]

D. R. played a full part in the effort to galvanise public opinion behind the national effort, recognising its political importance as a means of freeing Britain from the shackles of its reliance on the USA. He supported the National Savings Silver Lining campaign, which in Swansea set a target of £400,000.[28] He made an explicitly political appeal, telling the Workers' Education Association (WEA) in Pontarddulais that the export drive was a vital component in enabling the Labour government to create the world machinery necessary for international economic and political security.[29] In the circumstances, he did not need to add that it needed to be a world system that was not determined by the American government or its big business interests.

*

The following December, D. R. belatedly celebrated 25 years as Gower's MP with a programme of events organised by the constituency Labour Party. A grand dinner at the Brangwyn Hall heard more than 20 tributes from across the political divide. They included D. L. Mort, who summed up his parliamentary neighbour as 'an international figure who did his greatest work on his own doorstep'; D. J. Williams talked of his Socialist idealism; Hopkin Morris referred to the breadth of his political talents; and D. H. Thomas, manager of the Mountain Colliery in Gorseinon, commended his great knowledge of the coal industry. The Mayor of Swansea, Sir William A. Jenkins, went further, reproaching the government that his services were not being used to the fullest extent.[30]

The young Goronwy Roberts, for whom D. R. had great hopes, was asked to prepare an address in Welsh for the commemorative brochure. Noting D. R.'s 25 years' service, he wrote:

Yn ystod yr amser maith hwn, rhoes wasanaeth amhrisiadwy i'w genedl ac i'r byd, a chyrhaeddodd safleoedd o anrhydedd a gallu... doniwyd ef â meddwl cryf. Dysgodd fwy iddi'i hunan nac a wnaeth Prifysgol i lawer dyn ffodusach ei amgylchiadau ond llai ei grybwyll. Meistrolodd wyddor mwynyddiaeth – er hyrwyddo achos ei gyd-lowyr; dysgodd brif ieithoedd Ewrop – er bod o wasanaeth i heddwch a gweriniaeth mewn llawer gwlad; daeth yn awdurdod ar lu o broblemau gwleidyddol ac economaidd – er perffeithio ei hunan fel Seneddwr a Gweinidog y Goron... Llafuria yn ddibaid, a gwna ddefnydd o bob munud. Fel Gweinidog y Mwynfeydd yn 1940–42, rhoes esiampl o ymroddiad, a thybia mwy nag un heddiw y dylid fod wedi 'gwrando ar Grenfell' yn y dyddiau hynny. Fel Cadeirydd Plaid Lafur Cymru yn y Senedd er 1945, bu'n batrwm o arweinydd diflino a phenderfynol... y mae Grenfell yn ŵr o gymeriad. Hynny yw sylfaen ddisygl ei bersonoliaeth fawr a'i apel arbennig i'r ieuanc. Ni ellir adnabod 'D. R.' yn hir heb sylweddoli ei fod yn ŵr gonest ac argyhoeddiadol yn anad dim arall. Y mae rhywbeth yn ei safiad cydnerth, ei drem ddiwyro, a'i lais treiddgar a enilla barch a serch pawb a ddaw i gyfathrach ag ef. A dengys ei weithredoedd fel seneddwr a person preifat nad oes twyll na rhagrith yn perthyn iddo. Yn sicr, dyna ei gryfder – a dyna ei neges i Gymry ieuainc heddiw. Wrth ei longyfarch ef a'i briod heddiw, talwn deyrnged i Gymro pur, Gwerinwr cywir, ac yn bennaf un, boneddwr gwych.[31]

[During this long time, he gave invaluable service to his
nation and to the world, and reached offices of honour and
ability... He was gifted with a strong mind. He learned more
by himself than a university did for many more fortunate in
their privileges, but with less ability. He mastered the science
of minerals – in order to advance his fellow-workers; he
learned the principal languages of Europe – in order to serve
the cause of peace and the common good internationally;
he became an authority on a host of political and economic
problems – in order to prepare himself as a parliamentarian
and minister of the Crown... He labours ceaselessly, and
makes use of every minute. As Minister of Mines in 1940–42,
he was exemplar in his hard work and dedication, and many
today believe that 'we should have listened to Grenfell' in
those days. As Chairman of the Welsh Parliamentary Party
since 1945, he has been a model of tireless and determined
leadership... Grenfell is a man of character. That is the
foundation of his unstinting great personality and appeal
to the young. It is impossible to know D. R. long without
realising that he is an honest and convincing man above all
else. There is something in his resilient stance, his relentless
principles, and his penetrating voice that earns the respect
of all who come into contact with him. His actions as a
parliamentarian and in private show that there is no fraud
or hypocrisy about him. That is certainly his strength – and
that is his message to the young Welshmen of today. In
congratulating him and his spouse today, we pay tribute to
a pure Welshman, a true servant, and most of all, a great
gentleman.]

The money donated to the Gower CLP Silver Jubilee Fund
was used to purchase an annuity of £1,000 which was used to
support the Beatrice Grenfell prize at the National Eisteddfod,
issued to the winner of a competition for a work on industrial
history or development.

Meanwhile, as his constituents across the Gower
constituency adapted to the challenges of life in post-war

Britain, D. R. joined D. L. Mort and Percy Morris in lobbying government ministers over the reconstruction of Swansea's devastated town centre, demanding compensation for those whose properties had been damaged, and measures to control future development so that they were planned and speculators thwarted.[32] A regular stream of people approached him on a weekly basis seeking help, service personnel hoping for release due to personal or family situations, miners who had been called up when they would have made a greater contribution to post-war life had they remained underground, European volunteers in the tinplate industry threatened with deportation, personnel serving in the armed forces concerned about their welfare facilities, a doctor posted abroad when his services were desperately needed in Gorseinon, and a brilliant student who would have been prevented from taking up a postgraduate scholarship because of the requirements for National Service were it not for D. R.'s intervention.[33] He was inundated with requests to assist families across the constituency who were in desperate need of housing. He took up the future of Bwlchymynydd post office, supported those opposing the building of a dog track with betting facilities in Grovesend ('atal hap-chwarae ar y rhedegfeydd cwn' [preventing gambling on the dog races] was a particular concern for those who had approached him). He demanded that the British Transport Commission (BTC) should improve local rail services and facilities at stations, called for the development of Fairwood Aerodrome for use for civil aviation, supported proposals that Mynydd Lliw should be developed as a site for factory development, similar to what was proposed for Fforestfach, pursued the need for more adequate public lighting in Gorseinon, and raised the concerns of local farmers who were faced with the rigours of post-war regulations.[34]

*

In parliament, D. R. joined his old comrade Rhys Davies MP in another challenge to ministers, this time over the Control of Engagement Order, presented to the Commons in September 1947. The Order empowered the government to direct workers to industries essential to the national interest, although individuals were free to move between different employers within a particular industry.[35] For Rhys Davies, the regulation represented the antithesis of a Socialist society in which he believed there should be more individual freedom than was ever possible under capitalism.[36] He told the House of Commons, 'I am in favour of harnessing, controlling and owning by the State or municipality of those inanimate things necessary for the life of the community, but I draw this fundamental distinction. I object to the State treating human beings as if they were things and inanimate material.'[37]

No government, he insisted, could do better than was being done to provide homes and food for the people. But this did not justify restricting the freedom of individual workers. 'The difference between a slave and a free man is that the free man has the right to strike and the right to choose his own job instead of being told by a clerk at an employment exchange what job he must accept.'[38]

D. R., in seconding Rhys Davies' motion, was equally forthright and based his argument on half a century's involvement in the Labour movement fighting for individual freedom and workers' rights. He challenged the right of anyone, least of all a government bureaucracy, to interfere with an individual's choice of occupation:

I have myself been a firm believer in personal freedom. I have watched this great movement of ours grow. I was in it before there was a beginning of social reform. I was a member of the Labour movement more than 50 years ago. I have preached these things, and I believe today that there is no advantage to be gained by trying to coerce the working classes of this country to enter or to leave occupations at the will of the officials of bureaucracy, of the Government now in power, or of any other Government.[39]

The workers, he insisted, would give more when they were free to choose their own employment. The government's Order was one of the worst pieces of labour legislation that he had seen. 'When a man is caused to change his job under compulsion, he is also caused to leave his home under compulsion, and he may be forced to part with and break associations he has maintained all his life.'[40]

While it was the Cabinet Minister George Isaacs who led for the government, it fell to another product of the south Wales coalfield, Ness Edwards, now Parliamentary Secretary at the Ministry of Labour, to try to defend it from the criticism levied by the rebel MPs. Special measures, he insisted, were needed in the circumstances in which the government found itself during the convertibility crisis. He outlined the specific targets for each industry and insisted that the Order offered the only means by which this could be achieved. In a clear appeal to the Left, he insisted that Britain could not avoid economic subservience to America without such measures.[41] Neither the American loan nor Marshall Aid were at issue in the debate, but Ness Edwards knew well enough how repulsive dependence on the USA was in the minds of the rebels from Wales.

Within months of this debate, D. R.'s name was mentioned in two separate controversies related to foreign policy in which he was said to be challenging the government's pro-American line, although on the first occasion he denied categorically that he was involved in any way. The first occurred when it was claimed that D. R., along with other Labour backbenchers including Bessie Braddock, Lester Hutchinson, John Platts-Mills, Julian Silverman, and Sidney Swingler, and Gordon Schaffer of the *Reynolds News*, had agreed to serve on the editorial board of the Democratic and General Press Agency. The company had been established in 1937 by Eric Cook, a former member of the New Zealand Communist Party, and his wife Freda, and specialised in providing news for the overseas press from a left-wing perspective. The Cooks had been subject to surveillance by the British security services, and the Labour Party had formally disassociated itself from their organisation.[42] D. R. immediately denied he was a member of the editorial board, insisting that he had no association with it and that his name had been used without his knowledge. There is no evidence to the contrary, and he was one of several MPs who found themselves in the same position.

The second controversy arose when his name appeared on a list of Labour MPs who had signed the 'Nenni Telegram' declaring support for the Italian Socialist Party in the 1948 General Election, despite the fact that they had entered into a popular front alliance with the Italian Communist Party which the Labour leadership had condemned.[43] D. R. had met Pietro Nenni, the leader of the Italian Socialist Party, on several occasions and had worked with him on international issues in the 1930s. He was aware of the difficulties facing the Left in Italy and of the continuing danger posed by fascist elements that were defeated, but by no means eradicated. Nevertheless, under pressure from the Labour NEC, he agreed to remove his name from the list before the NEC threatened disciplinary action, as did other signatories from south Wales, though both W. G. Cove and S. O. Davies did so only after being given a week to comply.[44]

It is clear from the number of times that D. R. deviated from the leadership's position during the first three years of the Labour government that he was unhappy with some of the key decisions that had been taken with regards to international policy. This is alluded to further in a letter which he sent to Clement Attlee in May 1948, in which he expressed his discontent with the way the PLP was operating, in particular its emphasis on holding individual members to account and its failure to drive government policy. He wrote:

> I have long held the view that our party meetings have not
> been used to advantage in discussing party policy and the
> new situations arising from the working out of the party's
> programme... I feel I must express my protest against
> the publicity given to personal charges made against
> ministers and ordinary party members by men who have
> little experience or knowledge of the background of our
> movement... The attack on Mr Shinwell by James Callaghan
> has already done great harm to the party: while there are
> matters in which the regular meeting of the PLP could
> deliberate with advantage, personal attacks of this kind
> cannot fail to injure the morale of the party inside and
> outside the House... I think the party should be invited to
> drop these narrow-minded methods of exorcising personal
> and doctrinal errors in the name of our party. We shall need
> more unity and forbearance. I hope the party meeting will
> be strongly urged to refrain from petty persecution of men
> who differ in views and in expression without sacrifice of
> conviction and party unity.[45]

There is no direct link between D. R.'s suggestion that
PLP meetings could be used to better effect to discuss party
policy, with his own concerns about the government's foreign
policy. But his continued dissatisfaction with its approach to
international issues came a few weeks later when, against the
backdrop of the Berlin crisis, he joined more than 40 other
Labour MPs in signing the 'Stop the Coming War' manifesto,
instigated by the Socialist European Group of the Labour
Party (SEG). They had produced a memorandum outlining
their own vision for Western European collaboration,
arguing for a policy of non-aggression towards the Soviet
Union as long as no European territory was violated, no
interference in the internal affairs of Eastern European
countries, the promotion of east-west trade, a rejection of
the military use of land in preparation for action against
the USSR, and the ending of both military cooperation and

military conversations with the USA.[46] SEG argued that the burdens of austerity 'will be borne in vain unless the result is an independence of the USA so decisive as to convince the USSR of the genuine sincerity our Socialist intentions'. The use of integrated economic policies across Europe would enable the implementation of democratic Socialist policies that would promote political security in conditions of independence from any outside (i.e. American and Soviet) influence.[47]

The Stop the Coming War manifesto attracted a much wider circle of Labour MPs than groups such as Keep Left had done on previous occasions. A broader range of MPs critical of the government's international policy came together. The signatories included W. G. Cove, Percy Morris, Robert Richards, Goronwy Roberts, George Thomas, and Tudor Watkins from among the Welsh Labour members.[48] The declaration they signed recognised the need to accept the financial assistance available through the Marshall Plan, but only if it was used to ensure the country had sufficient economic strength to pursue an independent foreign policy, free of American influence, as a precursor to the creation of a democratic Socialist block. At the same time discussions between the Big Four, namely Great Britain, USSR, France and the USA, should be restarted to negotiate a programme of disarmament, and see the use of atomic weapons repudiated. Support for a Western European Union should be conditional on whether it pursued Socialist goals.

This emphasised a theme pursued by D. R., most notably at an address in Cwmllynfell earlier that spring during which he insisted that Russia should not be condemned to isolation without first being given an opportunity to live in the world community. The economic power of the United States should not blind the world to the problems of the economic system which it upheld. 'Our Labour government must not evade any issue. The danger of war can be removed and the Socialist plan for world unity is not a shibboleth but a solution of world troubles.'[49]

*

At the start of 1948, 18 months after the Labour leadership had rejected outright the appointment of a Secretary of State for Wales, the Welsh Labour group produced a new memorandum focusing primarily on the need for administrative reform in Wales. Its immediate priority was for a Minister for Welsh Affairs, a Welsh Economic Conference or Advisory Council similar to that already existing in Scotland, and the appointment of a member of the Cabinet Secretariat with special responsibility for Wales. It also called for reform of administrative structures by which a Permanent Secretary in each department would deal with matters relating to Wales, and the regional controllers of government departments in Wales would be responsible to the Welsh Permanent Secretary. In addition, more parliamentary time should be spent discussing Welsh issues, expenditure on Wales should be made clear in all estimates presented to parliament, Wales should be treated as a distinct unit in all legislation, and a Welsh members' committee should scrutinise all relevant legislation.

The Welsh Council of Labour (WCL) remained equivocal, adhering loyally to the course taken by government ministers but forced to concede in private that the government might face a backlash unless ministers were seen to be doing more to address the issues of which the Welsh PLP complained. A memorandum produced by the WCL in the summer of 1948 warned that Labour would be wrongfooted in Wales unless it was more alive to changes in public opinion on the question of self-government:

While it is open to question that the Welsh Nationalist Party, as such, by reason of its immaturity and irresponsibility, will gain considerably in strength as the political vehicle for the expression of Welsh interests, it is certain that the Labour Party will be confronted in some from or other in the next four years with a considerable development of Welsh opinion demanding more adequate means of self-expression and more responsibility in public affairs.

Noting that Liberals could find a home in the ranks of the Nationalists, it stated, 'In this interesting and potentially valuable period of political development, the Labour Party occupies an entirely negative and unsatisfactory position.' It had rejected the notion of a Secretary for Wales, was making inadequate progress towards diversification of industry, and alienated people by permitting the claims of the military on Welsh land.[50]

In response, the WCL proposed the establishment of a consultative body comprising representatives from local government, trade unions, business and civil society, alongside some other fairly modest suggestions. This prompted some concessions from the government: it would produce an annual report on government action in Wales which would be presented for debate at the annual Welsh Day debate, and an appointed advisory body – the Council for Wales and Monmouthshire – would also be created.[51] As expected Cliff Prothero, on behalf of the WCL, described the measures as the greatest offer to Wales made by any government in 400 years.[52] Goronwy Roberts was also remarkably quiescent, welcoming the decision to recognise Wales as an entity but hoping that the Council's composition and terms of reference could be reformed at a later date. D. R. was more forthright, arguing that the details should be addressed before the body was constituted. Not surprisingly, S. O. Davies was a critical voice, denouncing the proposals as 'a petrifying, ridiculous scheme', and repeating his demand for a national representative council as a way of overcoming top-heavy, bureaucratic centralisation.[53]

Furthermore, the proposals did not allay the dissatisfaction with the way government policy was bring administered in Wales, prompting D. R. and several other members of the Welsh PLP to put their names to a memorandum drafted by S. O. Davies concerning unemployment in Wales. The document drew attention to the fact that successive meetings and deputations had met ministers but, despite their assurances, unemployment remained tragically high throughout Wales. Shortages of materials meant 'promising factories' were forced to close down or lay off workers. Government contracts were being issued without regard to where the work would be done. Recent cuts in capital investment had been disastrous as far as south Wales was concerned. Schemes on which work had already started had been abandoned, new factories had been left half-built, and prospective employers were discouraged by an atmosphere of uncertainty. As if to add salt to the wounds, the 'Grenfell' factories were not proving successful, despite the good intentions of some of the industrialists who had taken them over, because the Ministry of Labour's Disabled Persons Employment Corporation insisted on creating its own Remploy factories, few of which were operational. The memorandum reiterated previous demands for administrative changes, but fell short of reopening the question of a dedicated minister. It also advocated that the NCB should be instructed to develop facilities for manufacturing colliery requisites and equipment in south Wales to provide employment for some of those formerly engaged in the industry. Also, priority be given to the development of trunk roads, and changes to the arrangements for housing key workers. Work to remove coal tips and other industrial scars should also be undertaken as a matter of urgency.[54]

This memorandum formed the basis of discussions with Herbert Morrison, and subsequently with Clement Attlee in the spring, focusing on the need for government action and specific policy changes.[55] They pointed to the appointment of the Council for Wales and Monmouthshire but that very few specific commitments were ever elicited from ministers. Not for the first time, the Welsh Labour MPs were left looking weak and ineffective when faced with ministers' cavalier attitudes.

*

Despite the fact that he was now in his mid-sixties, D. R.'s energy remained undimmed and he continued to involve himself in the work of an extremely wide range of organisations, both in Britain and internationally, alongside his constituency work. He devoted much of his attention to three areas of particular attention: the issue of leasehold reform, his work as a member of the BBC's Welsh Advisory Committee, and his position as Chairman of the Welsh Tourist Board (WTB), each of which is discussed in more detail below.

Throughout his time as MP for Gower, issues affecting leaseholders had been a recurring theme in D. R.'s postbag. The practice of leasing land either to individuals or large-scale builders, usually for a period of 99 years in return for an initial payment and annual ground rent, was the normal arrangement in the industrial part of the Gower constituency, as elsewhere across south Wales, including both coalfield communities and the larger conurbations. In 1884 the Royal Commission on the Housing of the Working Classes examined the question of whether leaseholders should be given the right to acquire their freehold, but concluded that this would not lead to any improvement in the quality of the housing stock. In the succeeding decades, the rapid expansion of Britain's industrial areas generated a housing boom and rich pickings for the landowners concerned.[56]

D. R. had contributed frequently to the debates on the issue throughout his time as an MP and member of the Leasehold Association of Great Britain. He and other south Wales MPs had been prominent supporters of a private members' bill, brought forward by Walter Higgs, Tory MP for West

359

Birmingham in 1938, when D. R. had described the existing system as 'a conspiracy against the poor classes of people'.[57] But while he had supported that legislation wholeheartedly, D. R. considered it to be merely a starting point on a journey that would eventually lead to leasehold enfranchisement to provide a return to the leaseholder for the work done on a property.[58] Progress was made by 1946 when Leslie Hale, MP for Oldham, produced a draft private members' bill which D. R. commended to Clement Attlee as something which the government should adopt as part of its own legislative programme.[59] The Prime Minister's reply was disappointing however, stating that, 'I do not myself think that the Leasehold Enfranchisement is important enough in the programme over the many areas which are striving for a place in our home programme.'[60]

Undaunted, D. R. persisted, and continued to demand a short bill that would establish the principles of leasehold reform and making it easy for all those affected by the system to get security at a fair and reasonable price. At the 1947 conference in Margate, D. R. moved the Composite Resolution on Leasehold Property that committed Labour to approving the principle of leasehold enfranchisement, the substitution of the term of 999 years for any lower period in an existing lease, and to allow for the acquisition of freehold at any time by the lessee on a purchase price equal to 25 times the covenanted annual leasehold rental. He gave detailed descriptions of abuses, and denounced the existing system as a 'real social grievance and a social injustice to the workers of this country'. It was purely a British phenomenon that did not exist elsewhere and represented a 'tyrannical form of ownership'.

His arguments elicited a sympathetic response from Aneurin Bevan, on behalf of the NEC, who discussed the matter at length with D. R. and others shortly afterwards.[61] Despite Aneurin Bevan's commitment, leasehold reform did not feature among the government's priorities, however. It appointed a committee, chaired by Lord Uthwatt (later chaired by Lord

Jenkins), to examine whether a change in the law was necessary. Meanwhile, D. R. continued his own detailed investigations into the system based on an analysis of leases from all over Britain and published, in the form of a pamphlet produced by Gower Labour Party, *A Plea for Leasehold Reform*.[62] In it, D. R. traced the development of land tenure since the Middle Ages with specific reference to south-west Wales. He highlighted the process of industrial development in the nineteenth century and the demand it created for housing, most of which was held on the basis of leasehold tenure. This was a common pattern, affecting around half of the population of Wales, including around 50,000 families in south Wales who were facing the imminent end of their leases. In his evidence to the Uthwatt Committee, D. R. referred to the 'very serious apprehension which affects profoundly the life and peace of mind of a very large proportion of the people in the industrial area. Due to the leasehold system, his home became less and less secure with the passage of time.' The leases granted in the 1850s and 1860s were rapidly approaching their expiry date, which meant unscrupulous landowners were in a position to demand exorbitant amounts in ground rents as the redemption date drew nearer. While no one would resent paying a reasonable amount for commutation, some owners were demanding a hundred years' rental income, while others were refusing to sell at all. He drew particular attention to the behaviour of limited companies who had bought freehold interests and were responsible for some of the worst abuses. Among those he named were Western Ground Rents, who owned the Bute Estate in Cardiff, who were offering to renew ground rents at five to ten times the previous amount. In Llanelli people were being refused permission to sell and a landlord had demanded £400 in repairs. Elsewhere in Carmarthenshire, the company controlling the Dynevor Estate was demanding that a chapel pay £100 a year, whereas previously it had paid 10s., while the owners of freeholds in Pembroke Dock had increased ground rents to £18 from £1. D. R. demanded that the term of all leases be extended to 999 years, terminable by a payment of 25 years' rental in order to provide security of tenure alongside measures to deal with iniquities of dilapidation payments.

The outcome of the Uthwatt Committee was disappointing to say the least. The committee failed to agree on the central issue as the majority believed that there was no need for further legislation.[63] The minority report, signed by Leslie Hale and the Labour MP for Llandaff and Barry, Lynn Ungoed-Thomas, called for legislation for leasehold enfranchisement by which owner-occupiers should be able to purchase their freeholds at a fair and reasonable cost. Even so, the issue remained unresolved when Labour was returned to power in 1964, by which time the WCL's policy document, *Signposts for Wales*, produced in preparation for the establishment of the Welsh Office, made Leasehold Reform a central pledge. This led to the Leasehold Reform Act 1967, which addressed many but by no means all of the issues highlighted by those demanding justice.

*

In 1946, D. R. was appointed to serve on the newly-created Welsh Advisory Committee of the British Broadcasting Corporation (WAC), a body established as part of the evolving structure of the Corporation's Welsh Region established nine years earlier. D. R. had been among those Welsh MPs who had advocated the creation of a Welsh Region during the protracted discussions in the 1930s in the face of resistance from the BBC's senior managers in London. Throughout the intervening years, D. R. had been a frequent broadcaster in both Welsh and English, especially during his time as Secretary for Mines, when his regular appeals to the mining communities had been a vital part of the government's efforts to maximise coal production. He had also taken part in programmes produced in German which sought to appeal to trade unionists and other opponents of the Nazis.[64]

The Welsh Region's development had been severely curtailed by restrictions imposed during the war. D. R. was well aware of expectations among listeners for an increased output once the normal service was resumed. But those making such demands sat in two very different camps: one powerful lobby demanded a commitment that more programmes should be produced in Welsh, while another equally determined group called for more programmes in English relating to Wales. During D. R.'s time on the WAC, the BBC's Welsh Region, under the stewardship of Alun Oldfield-Davies, expanded its output thanks to the work of talented producers and directors like Mai Jones, John Griffiths, Sam Jones, Aneirin Talfan Davies, P. H. Burton, Alun Llewelyn-Williams, and John Ormond. They were responsible for a flowering of radio broadcasting in Wales after the war, as the BBC Welsh Region emerged as a patron of creative writing and culture in both languages.

D. R. made a wide-ranging contribution on the WAC. He advocated creating a BBC publication for Wales that would provide an opportunity for people to read about programmes after they had been broadcast (something that was achieved when the Corporation began publishing *Llafar*, edited by Aneirin Talfan Davies). He also insisted on trade union rights for BBC staff, urged that the orchestra should not confine itself to Welsh music, joined the prominent internationalist Gwilym Davies in demanding a radio station on the Cambrian coast, and warned against offending the French government through an over-sympathetic portrayal of the Bretons (to the annoyance of another WAC member, Gwynfor Evans). He made a stance (supported enthusiastically by Kate Roberts) against the use of mongrel Welsh on the airwaves, and he welcomed the Corporation's development of a form of standardised Welsh that sought to overcome regional variations within Wales for broadcasting purposes, and offered a more contemporary idiom than the literary, 'pulpit' Welsh that was its main alternative.

However, determining the right balance between the two languages and how much attention should be paid to different parts of Wales proved to be a much more difficult part of the work, and this issue dominated many of the WAC's meetings.[65] For Sir Wynn Wheldon (the former Permanent Secretary of the Welsh Department of the Board of Education, who was appointed to several advisory boards with a remit for broadcasting), the need for Welsh-language programmes was the primary reason for the existence of a BBC Welsh Region. Kate Roberts maintained that English speakers had plenty of other choice already, while G. H. Jones believed too many people were being excluded from positions with the BBC because they did not speak Welsh. As the discussion continued, complaints flooded into the Corporation maintaining that those who wrote in Welsh were at least twice as likely to have their material accepted as those who wrote in English.[66] Others objected to an output that included so many programmes in a language they did not speak.

As a proud Welsh speaker representing communities in which Welsh was still the language of most homes in the late-1940s, D. R. was well aware of the demand for more programmes in the language. But he also recognised that the experience of English-speaking industrial Wales had an equal claim on Welsh nationality and it was right that the culture and values that emanated from those communities found articulation on the airwaves, as in Welsh life more broadly. Nothing would be gained from the two extremes of the narrow bigotry of those Welsh speakers contemptuous of the English-speaking majority, nor from English speakers jealous of any opportunities enjoyed by those who wrote or performed in Welsh. D. R. recognised there was some justification in both viewpoints and endeavoured to defuse the situation by advocating a policy informed by evidence. Was it true, he asked, that sets were being turned off during Welsh programmes? Did the programmes reflect too much of the mindset of a generation which had passed? What kind of programmes did people want to hear? How did the BBC know what talent was available in different parts of Wales? His experiences on the WAC exposed D. R. to the extent of the deep cultural divide that bedevilled Wales throughout the second half of the twentieth century, a situation made worse by the agitation on both sides of the argument of many irreconcilable, truculent and uncompromising individuals. Under such circumstances, D. R. was not sorry when his term of office on the WAC came to an end.

*

He had an equally challenging experience trying to reconcile the different interests within the tourist and hospitality industry in Wales. D. R.'s extensive travels across Wales meant he was fully aware of its great potential as a tourist destination, both in terms of its resorts and the untapped opportunities in rural areas. However, in common with the rest of Britain, the Welsh tourist trade was in a desperate state by the end of the Second World War. The sector had seen little investment, and many establishments bore the scars of having been requisitioned for successive uses by the armed forces, temporary workers and others desperate for any form of accommodation during the war. Some hotels, particularly in the countryside, were full of permanent residents and unable to accommodate holiday travellers. Rationing restrictions created their own challenges. Addressing the situation called for a combination of government, municipal and private investment to address a list of impediments that included poor road and rail services, the lack of cleanliness in some hotels and restaurants, the inadequate quality of the food served, as well as the absence of local amenities such as parks and theatres in some places. The

Labour government was not oblivious to these issues, both as a means of attracting visitors from overseas and also to cater for middle-income and lower-income earners in Britain who had been granted holidays with pay, but had few opportunities to do so. Consequently, Harold Wilson, as President of the Board of Trade, pledged government support for the tourism industry, beginning with a grant of half a million pounds in 1948–49.[67]

A revival of the Welsh tourism industry also required better marketing and promotion through the creation of more effective structures than were provided by the multitude of organisations that operated in the field.[68] This was recognised within the industry itself and was also a recommendation of the Welsh Advisory Council on Post-war Reconstruction.[69] A conference in Aberystwyth, attended by industry representatives and several MPs in May 1946, led to the establishment of the Welsh Tourist and Holidays Board which operated as part of the National Industrial Council for Wales and Monmouthshire.[70] Their efforts secured a prominent place for the tourist industry at the Welsh Industries Exhibition held later that year, and led to the production of a holiday booklet in readiness for the following season.[71] However, progress was hampered by the rivalry between the several different organisations which continued to exist in Wales and the duplication this caused. This prompted the WPP, in conjunction with the British Holidays and Tourism Board, to begin the work of establishing a unified body to promote the industry in Wales.[72] Such was the discord within the industry that D. R., at the request of Arthur Bottomley, the Minister for Overseas Trade, agreed to chair a conference convened in Shrewsbury in February 1948 which began the work of establishing a unified tourist body.[73] Speaking after the conference, D. R. sought to promote a vision of the future rather than dwell on the problems. 'Wales must have a single, representative, efficient, and authoritative body to act and speak for her in such matters, and to co-ordinate the many interests involved,' he told the assembled delegates.[74]

Within weeks, he presented a draft memorandum and articles of association for the new Welsh Tourist Board as a company limited by guarantee 'to promote tourism information and publicity, to inspect premises, and support the improvements which would increase visitor numbers.'[75] It was to be financed by an annual grant of £3,000 from the Board of Trade, supplemented by voluntary contributions by local authorities.[76] As its first chairman, D. R. took every opportunity to promote the new body, addressing meetings across the length and breadth of Wales, meeting existing bodies such as the North Wales Resorts Association, the Cardigan Bay Resorts Association, and the Central Wales Resorts Association, and attending meetings with civic leaders in south and west Wales.[77] He quickly identified the importance of public investment and lobbied the BTC over a range of issues concerning public transport, including the need to maintain services during the winter months, run chartered tourist services to north and west Wales, and to repair dilapidated stations. Such investment, he insisted, should be part of a wider plan that should include the development of civil aviation in Wales. D. R. also insisted that the future of tourism in rural Wales was dependent on improvements to water and electricity supplies, and that such work should be expedited urgently.[78] Meanwhile, the WTB organised conferences, sent its secretaries to promotional events in Welsh costume, trialled helicopter rides in Wales, promoted events as part of the Festival of Britain, used rugby internationals to highlight Wales, and hosted visits by travel agents from Britain and Europe.[79]

Alongside this work, D. R. recognised the importance of promoting awareness of Wales both within the United Kingdom and further afield.[80] He took a close interest in the preparation of the WTB's tourist guide to Wales and provided an introduction in which he described the attractions and beauty of the scenery. 'The northern part is generally cold and often austere. Mid Wales is less visited, but there are wide highland areas from which the larger Welsh rivers start their course to reach the sea a hundred miles away. South Wales has its beauty spots lying around its busy industrial regions,' he declared. At the same time he made a direct link between the WTB's work and the government's economic crusade by placing a strong emphasis on marketing Wales to the Americans as part of the 'Come to Britain' campaign being run in the USA. It hoped to attract at least 130,000 visitors to the UK.[81] This led the WTB to hold an exhibition on the beauty of Wales in Madison Square, New York, aimed at Americans heading to the Festival of Britain. It sought to establish links with Welsh communities overseas.[82]

Even so, the WTB continued to face challenges. It proved difficult to persuade local authorities to affiliate, including the County Borough of Cardiff which chose instead to affiliate to an unofficial body set up to promote south Wales.[83] Most of the local tourist associations continued to operate, as did the tourist section of the National Industrial Development Council of Wales and Monmouthshire (NIDCW) and much of the WTB's energies were spent coordinating the work of local publicity officers.[84] Furthermore, the WTB complained that its work was hampered by the lack of a dedicated office in London, which meant that efforts to market Wales were often lost in the broader work of the British Tourist Board (unlike the situation in Scotland).[85] D. R. did not give up and remained chairman of the WTB until November 1950, when he informed the board that due to the government's small majority he was unable to commit to attending its meetings.[86] His tenure as chairman, however, had proved crucial in establishing the need for the WTB and in setting its priorities. Above all, he had demonstrated the extent of the challenge but also the huge potential of creating a world-ranking holiday, tourist and leisure sector in Wales.

CHAPTER 16

Father of the House

IN FEBRUARY 1949, D. R. began a two-month visit to the United States and Canada, beginning in New York and then spending time in Chicago before proceeding to Quebec, Montreal, and Ottawa. While there he made some guarded comments on the deteriorating international situation. He referred to the challenge of maintaining peace in a time of conflicting ideologies and talked about the relationship between atomic science and world security. He also warned an American audience of the dangers inherent in any two-power system in international affairs, and intimated that France and Britain must be included in any discussions with Russia that might impinge on Europe.[1] However, the main focus of the visit was to foster goodwill and to highlight opportunities for trade between North America and Socialist Britain. In successive addresses, mainly to the large Welsh expatriate community, he described the valiant efforts that were being made to revive Britain's industrial base, the developments in coal mining and the steel industry, the work to restore shipbuilding after decades of decline, and to rebuild manufacturing capacity after the dislocation of war. He took advantage of every opportunity to promote Wales as a tourist destination, and highlighted opportunities for investment and trade with the old country.[2]

By the time he returned home, the Labour Party was in the throes of preparing for the election due at the latest in the summer of 1950. From his own standpoint, the redistribution of parliamentary constituencies meant that the next election would be fought on very different boundaries. Those areas of Gower which had been included in the Swansea County Borough since 1918 were now transferred into the two Swansea constituencies: Llansamlet, Treboeth, Penderry and the outskirts of Morriston to Swansea East, while Fforestfach, Sketty, Killay and Mumbles were transferred to Swansea West. Meanwhile, Pontardawe Rural District was reunited with Gower, producing a much safer Labour seat, dominated by Welsh-speaking, working-class communities reliant on mining and steel and tinplate manufacturing. D. R.'s own view was that the changes should be postponed until new housing patterns were established, something which would not have impacted on his own position but would have helped Percy Morris in Swansea West in view of the large and growing Conservative vote in some of the wards transferred from Gower. Even so Chuter Ede, as Home Secretary, resolutely resisted such demands and insisted on allowing the redistribution to proceed, thus generating yet another obstacle to Labour's chances of a majority in Britain as a whole.

When the election was called D. R.'s opponent was the leading south Wales barrister, Rowe Harding, the son of the manager of Cae Duke Colliery in Loughor, a former Welsh rugby international who had played for both Llanelli and Swansea as well as Cambridge University. His political journey included an appearance on Sir Oswald Mosley's fascist platform in Swansea, a fact which Labour never allowed him to forget. However, by the time he faced D. R. in Gower he had morphed into a National Liberal and Conservative. D. R. was not complacent, but he had no need to be concerned. On a poll of nearly a 85 per cent turnout, he secured 32,661 votes, giving him a majority of 22,356 over Harding. Across the UK as a whole, Labour added 1.3 million to its tally of votes as compared to 1945 on a much increased turnout. But the outcome in terms of seats was disappointing, mainly because of the way the Labour vote was distributed. It produced 315 seats, and an overall majority of just five.

As far as D. R. was concerned the outcome, and in particular the weight of the Labour vote, meant the government had been given a mandate to build on what it had achieved since 1945. However more, much more, needed to be done. He supported the argument made by D. J. Williams, during the annual 'Welsh Day', of a renewed economic plan for Wales capable of sustaining a population of a least three million. It should be achieved on the basis of a significant expansion of coal, steel, and tinplate capacity, made possible by a relentless drive to increase exports.[3] As part of this strategy, D. R. called for the establishment of a Welsh Development Commission, 'consisting in the main of Welsh people on the spot doing the job which is necessary to save that small country,' which should have recourse to a budget of at least £200 million in recognition of the scale of the task it would face.[4]

Meanwhile, he devoted a great deal of his time scrutinising the details of the Coal Mining Subsidence Bill, introduced by the government in response to the Turner Committee, which had recommended limiting the NCB's liability only to cases that had become apparent since nationalisation. He challenged Philip Noel-Baker repeatedly on this issue but, while ministers were sympathetic, they could not be moved: any change would saddle the NCB with the burden of a potentially huge compensation bill and a liability for the outcomes of mining practices for which it had not been responsible. While the issue was not pressed to a division, D. R. was under no illusion that the decision would frustrate efforts to secure compensation throughout Britain's mining communities by excluding historic cases. Householders, particularly private individuals such as those which predominated in many parts of south Wales, would be forced to incur heavy costs to obtain compensation for damage caused to their properties.[5]

As the months passed it was clear that another election

would be held. The government struggled to pursue its legislative programme with such a slim majority. Internal divisions, highlighted by Aneurin Bevan's resignation over Hugh Gaitskell's imposition of charges in the NHS, was a cause of further instability.[6] Even so, this did not prevent Labour from obtaining its highest-ever level of support, polling 14 million votes – 230,000 more than the Tories and their allies. In Gower, D. R. again faced Rowe Harding and secured a result virtually identical to the previous contest, winning three-quarters of the votes on a turnout of over 84 per cent, with a majority of 22,310. For D. R., the national outcome was a bitter disappointment, and Labour had been robbed of the fruits of its endeavours over the previous six years due to the way the votes had been distributed in individual constituencies. Despite the endorsement of half of the electorate, Labour was in opposition, facing an overall Conservative majority of 17. The Tories might be unwilling to risk pursuing its objective of reversing what Labour had done since 1945, but progress towards a Socialist Britain had come to an end, a task unfinished and a dream unfulfilled.

Some personal respite came at the end of November when he joined a parliamentary delegation to the Antipodes, starting in Auckland before proceeding to Wellington and then to the Australian cities of Melbourne and Adelaide.[7] The climax of the tour was a visit to Canberra to present a mace to the Australian parliament, a gift of thanks for the country's contribution to the war effort.[8] Again, D. R. delighted in meeting Welsh expatriates, many of them men and women who had sought refuge from the ravages of the inter-war years. He spoke to Welsh societies and met with Labour leaders, including some from Wales, among them his old comrade from Gowerton, George Manning, by then a leading figure in the politics of Christchurch, New Zealand.[9]

Upon his return to the UK, D. R. was thrown into the atmosphere of bitter recrimination that followed the election defeat. Throughout the years of the Attlee governments, he had been a frequent critic of several aspects of government policy, even though his absolute loyalty to the Labour Party was never in question. Aneurin Bevan's resignation and his behaviour during the subsequent weeks exasperated him, though he was by no means unsympathetic to his basic argument.[10] D. R. had, of course, taken a prominent part in the opposition to the National Service Act and made no secret of his antipathy for the Labour government's foreign policy. Imposing token charges on the NHS to support an unsustainable rearmament programme made no political sense as far as D. R. was concerned, and represented yet another attempt to court American approval when Britain should be concentrating on its own Socialist vision. An indication of D. R.'s feelings was seen in March 1952, when the Conservative government presented its Statement on Defence to the Commons. Its content, and Winston Churchill's opening speech in particular, were calculated to highlight differences on the Labour benches rather than make the case for the government's policy. Labour MPs contradicted each other throughout the ensuing debate, especially over the extent to which a rearmament programme could be delivered, what would be the impact on domestic spending and on the country's standard of living, over what timeframe should it be delivered, and the consequences of its delay or failure on the thousands of conscripted personnel undertaking National Service.[11] The party leadership proposed an amendment approving the strategy outlined in the White Paper, but declaring it had no confidence in the government to deliver it. Labour MPs were also ordered to abstain when, inevitably, that amendment would be lost. D. R. did not speak in the debate but his position was made clear when he joined Aneurin Bevan and more than 50 other MPs in voting against the White Paper.[12]

Six months later, D. R. became the member with the longest continuous service and succeeded the Ulster Unionist Sir Hugh

O'Neill MP as Father of the House of Commons.[13] The position was largely honorary but brought a certain prominence on ceremonial occasions. One such event came on the eve of the Queen's Commonwealth tour when, by his own admission, D. R. made his 'most non-party speech' in his whole time in parliament.[14] He was also in a non-party mode when he was called upon to move a tribute to Winston Churchill on behalf of the Commons. This was the man whom D. R. a quarter of a century earlier had described as the most sinister figure in British politics, but he did not let a lifetime on the opposite side of the political divide affect him when he declared Winston Churchill to be 'This outstanding representative of the British parliament and the most celebrated statesmen of our time'. However, he could not resist adding, 'I learned to admire even when I could not approve.'[15]

A few months later he was made a Freeman of the Borough of Swansea, along with another ex-miner, Alderman Dan Williams of Fforestfach, himself a product of the ILP with whom he had worked closely throughout his years in parliament.[16] The same year saw D. R. honoured with the award of Chevalier de la Légion d'honneur for contribution to Anglo-French relations.[17] A dinner in his honour was organised by the Anglo-French Friendship Society in Swansea where Attlee joined him as guest of honour. The *Daily Herald* saw the heroic in his life:

A street-hawker and pit boy when 13, then an MP honoured by governments, kings and princes. That broadly is the life story, unfinished, of 73-year old David Grenfell, MP for Gower and Father of the House of Commons, whose many friends paid public tribute to his achievements at the week-end when he was guest of honour at the Anglo-French Friendship Society. Attlee was there, Churchill sent a congratulatory telegram. D. R. said, 'I have always been convinced it should be easy to live on terms of friendship with people of other countries. And I am not pessimistic now.'[18]

Later he gained recognition from two great Welsh institutions – the Gorsedd of Bards awarded him the status of *Derwydd, er anrhydedd* (honorary druid), and the University of Wales awarded him an honorary doctorate (it is not recorded if he ever chose to be referred to as Dr D. R. Grenfell).[19]

Such honours did not divert D. R. from dealing with the varied needs of his own constituency. One local controversy occurred when the Ministry of Supply announced its intention to take over a disused proof-range at Salthouse Point on the Gower peninsula. Representatives of the north Gower cockle industry warned that the proposal would destroy their livelihoods, and feared that the nuisance would blight communities across the peninsula. The Ministry found themselves facing the combined opposition of local authorities, public bodies, and the Gower Society who established the Gower Protection Fund and redoubled their efforts to secure the status of Area of Outstanding Natural Beauty (AONB).[20] The area had not been included among those originally designated as national parks in 1931. However, a review published in 1945 recommended that it be designated as 'other amenity area' (later the term conservation area was used before AONB was adopted) due to its unspoilt natural beauty and the impact of its complex geology, resulting in far more stringent regulation of development and land usage.

The people of the Gower constituency continued to experience uncertainty as the process of industrial restructuring continued apace. When production started at the cold-reduction plant at Trostre, doubts began to emerge about whether a second works would ever be built, especially now that the Conservative government was committed to reducing the role of the State in economic planning and commercial decisions. D. R. was particularly fearful that the whole question of where a third cold-reduction facility should be sited could be revisited, and continually demanded that ministers should honour the commitment to the Llangyfelach site. He therefore had cause for celebration when authorisation was given to proceed with the building of the cold-reduction plant at Velindre (as the Llangyfelach site had become known), with a capacity to produce eight million basic boxes each year. The *Western Mail* was quick to remind its readers of the part played by Gower's MP:

> Mr D. R. Grenfell, Socialist MP for Gower, should be a happy man to-day. For the announcement that a new cold-reduction mill is to be sited at Velindre has brought him a victory – albeit long delayed – in a desperate battle he waged in 1947. At that time it seemed settled that a cold-reduction plant to make tinplate from the strip produced at the Steel Company of Wales' Abbey Works would be sited at Llangyfelach.

Recalling the subsequent controversy over the decision to prioritise the development at Trostre, the paper's correspondent sought to exploit internal divisions within the Labour Party:

> None of his arguments were refuted. Sir Stafford Cripps, then President of the Board of Trade, admitted that tinplate produced at Trostre would cost 2d. a box more than that produced at Llangyfelach. But despite protest meetings and the fact that Mr Grenfell and other Welsh MPs raised the matter time and again in Parliament, the Government remained adamant... Behind this policy Mr Grenfell thought he could detect the hand of Mr James Griffiths, the Socialist MP for Llanelly. And Mr Griffiths was in the Cabinet; Mr Grenfell was not. Mr Grenfell accused Mr Griffiths of 'special pleading'. Mr Griffiths, not unnaturally, denied the accusation. The 'war' continued throughout the summer months.[21]

The new works was scheduled to open in 1956 and the existing works were to continue production. Several of those which had been closed were re-opened to meet increased

376

demand. However, this positive picture masked the fact that those works had no long-term future once production was started at Velindre, and the new plant would require a much smaller workforce. This message was presented starkly in January 1953 when an article in the *New Statesman*, entitled 'The shadow of Velindre', concluded that nearly 8,000 people in south-west Wales were likely to lose their livelihoods. For D. R., this created two distinct but related issues. Firstly, it meant an economic problem as capacity in the old works was affected because experienced, skilled men were leaving to work in Trostre, the Abbey Works, and in other industries, knowing that their existing jobs would be coming to an end at some point. Secondly, and even more seriously, the generation that was growing up and entering the workforce did not have the confidence that work would be available for them. South-west Wales was being robbed of the self-assurance that came with the certainty of full employment, and faced the prospect of returning to the dark days when Wales lost half a million of its people due to poverty and unemployment.

D. R. used the Welsh Day debate in January 1953 to highlight the social catastrophe that would follow unless an economic plan for the region was implemented. The Minister for Welsh Affairs, David Maxwell-Fyfe, sought to defuse the situation by announcing the appointment of a committee, under Lord Lloyd, to advise on the economic implications and to consider how new industries could be attracted to the region.[22] For local MPs, the answers were already known: road and rail communications needed to be improved, including a new road linking south-west Wales to the markets of the English Midlands; two new bridges were needed – one over the river Severn and the other at Briton Ferry to remove bottlenecks and get road haulage moving; and more shipping should be directed to ports in south Wales.[23] These arguments were echoed by several leading industrialists, in particular Capt

Leighton Davies of the Steel Company of Wales, who worked tirelessly to convince government ministers and officials of the need for action to address the situation. The Lloyd Committee's declaration, that transference should not be seen as the solution to the problem, represented a clear departure from the politics of the inter-war years. The committee declared that the closure of the old works should be planned so that those situated in areas where other jobs were available were decommissioned first. The government should provide funding to clear derelict sites and improve communications. At the same time, companies such as Morris Motors, Metal Box, and ICI should be approached to expand their operations in the region.

D. R. welcomed the report and many of the actions which followed it. But it was also clear, despite such warm words, no Conservative government would allow social needs to override business decisions as was made clear when RTB sought to relocate its galvanizing operation from Gorseinon to Ebbw Vale in 1954.[24] Despite the strong case presented by D. R., Robert Williams on behalf of the unions at the Bryngwyn works and Cllr Glyn Mathias on behalf of Llwchwr UDC, the Ministry of Supply struck a doctrinaire laissez faire attitude. Secretary of State Duncan Sandys was adamant that the decision had to be taken solely on commercial grounds. Although RTB remained a State-owned company, the government 'had decided to treat Richard Thomas and Baldwin and the other publicly owned firms in the industry as ordinary commercial undertakings.'[25] Whatever problems would be caused by unemployment in Gorseinon, the situation would be even worse if production was hampered by being located in the wrong place. The message from the Lloyd Committee that nationalised industries might look more favourably on south-west Wales had clearly not reached Duncan Sandys.

Meanwhile, D. R. was able to take pleasure when the Mines and Quarries Bill made its passage through parliament, the long-delayed outcome of the Royal Commission on Safety in the Mines. At committee stage, D. R. drew on his background knowledge to move amendments on specific aspects, working closely with Aneurin Bevan throughout the proceedings.[26] D. R. was particularly proud of one such amendment which gave managers legal authority to demand that they be given written instructions, and empowering them to refuse to carry them out if they believed they would prejudice the safety or health of the persons employed at a mine or quarry.[27] He also succeeded in clarifying the responsibility of deputies, strengthened the requirements to keep plans and report accidents, and established a legal responsibility to consult workmen on safety issues.[28] Speaking during the Bill's final reading, D. R. referred to the massive changes that had occurred in the industry since he had started work as a twelve year old in Gorseinon. Men were now working at far deeper levels, in much higher temperatures, and using technology unheard of when he had begun his working life. This called for different legislation to regulate how the work was conducted, and he commended ministers and their advisers for the consensual way in which they had progressed the Bill:

> When I first saw the Bill I confess to showing my impatience.
> I thought it was not good enough. Now I stand here and
> say that it is a very good Bill indeed. I thank the two Right
> Hon. gentlemen for what they have done. I thank also their
> advisers, the men who do the work in the department – as one
> who has been in the department I know how much is owed
> to those men – for the attempt made this time to produce a
> working and workable Bill to serve the desires of each and
> every one of us.[29]

He was also active on the question of the government of Wales, although on this occasion he was on the opposite side to those who had been among his disciples in the 1945 parliament. Winston Churchill's appointment of a nominal Minister for

Welsh Affairs had been calculated to maximise Labour's discomfort over the question of a Welsh Secretaryship without surrendering any measure of administrative autonomy. What was, in essence, a miniscule concession was seized upon by the Parliament for Wales campaign in support of its own argument that a far more radical policy was required that involved the creation of a wholly separate elected body for Wales. The campaign, chaired by Lady Megan Lloyd George, attracted the support of the Welsh Nationalists, several Welsh Liberals, and S. O. Davies, Goronwy Roberts, and Tudor Watkins along with Cledwyn Hughes and T. W. Jones from among the Welsh Labour MPs.[30] The campaign drew some support in the Gower constituency as shown by a meeting in Libanus chapel, Gorseinon (where the minister, the Rev. D. J. Odwyn Jones, introduced Megan Lloyd George as 'an expert on all things except marriage').[31]

Those advocating a Parliament for Wales within the Labour Party had hoped that D. R. could be persuaded to join them, and his previous declarations on the subject indicated those expectations were justified. At the very start of his parliamentary career he had written to the former Liberal and Labour MP, E. T. John, expressing strong support for the idea:

> Beth am Ymreolaeth i Gymru nawr. Credaf ein bod wedi clywed y gair ola amdani oddiar wefusau'r Rhyddfrydwyr, a bydd iddynt wrthwynebu pob ymgais er sicrhau ymreolaeth oherwydd ynfydrwydd y Bolsheviciaid o'r Deheudir. Ar y llaw arall, cawn weled mwy o ddiddordeb ymhlith Llafurwyr Cymru ac Ysgotland am fesur o lywodraeth gartrefol ar linellau Iwerddon.[32]

> [What about Home Rule for Wales now. I think we have heard the last word on the subject from Liberal lips, and they will oppose all efforts to secure self-government because of their fear of the Bolshevik menace from the South. On the other hand, we will see more interest within Labour in Wales

and in Scotland for some measure of home rule on Irish lines.]

Similar sentiments could be detected in his comments on a Secretaryship for Wales in 1938, when he pressed the Attlee government to establish such a post. He based his case as much on claims of Welsh nationality as on administrative efficiency. Moreover, throughout the inter-war years a strong sense of Welsh nationhood was evident in his trenchant criticism of the way the British State had abandoned Wales to its fate.

Even so, D. R. did not join S. O. Davies and his colleagues.[33] He remained committed to increasing administrative autonomy for Wales through a Secretary of State but, despite lengthy discussions with the Labour 'Home Rulers', Goronwy Roberts in particular, he could not be brought to support what he believed would be a replica of the kind of devolution settlement granted to Ulster. Welsh interests would not be served by creating another Stormont, with the consequent diminution of the role of Welsh MPs in Westminster. Welsh Labour MPs should be working for a Labour government that would use the power of the British State to bring about economic and social transformation, with a Secretary of State for Wales inside the cabinet. He expressed some irritation with the issue in a letter to Cliff Prothero. 'I do not feel called upon to spend my time discussing Home Rule in any form. I am a Socialist and not a Nationalist.'[34] Throughout his political career he had sought to overcome the economic and social consequences of the marginalisation of Wales on the fringes of the United Kingdom, not least in the mining industry where a British-wide policy, through a British National Coal Board with a British National Union of Mineworkers, championed those working in the industry. The same principles applied to a British system of National Insurance, a British National Health Service and a nationalisation programme on a British level.

His thoughts on the subject were reflected in a series of memoranda and letters written in 1952 and 1953, beginning when he was appointed to represent the Welsh Labour group on the WCL's Welsh Affairs Committee in June 1952. He advocated a Welsh national plan to deal with issues of low production and inadequate communication within the context of a British policy that recognised that these were not matters confined to Wales alone. Looking to the rural parts of Wales in particular, he believed a programme of new towns and building up agricultural interests, including forestry, should be part of any such 'comprehensive programme of levelling up', and Welsh MPs needed to become more effective in promoting such ideas.

> The mere stimulation of old regionalisation and petty political ambitions will not result in great prosperity and comfort for the Welsh rural areas. Home rule for Wales or a Parliament for Wales does not stand up as a substitute to good planning with ample resources to recreate the neglected and deserted countryside. There should be no suggestion of hostility towards the parliament at Westminster. All that is needed could be done by the ordinary process of legislation and of social reconstruction with the full support of the present parliament... The problems of Wales in these days are not so distinct from those submitted by Scottish political opinion... The greatest grievances of Wales arise from the failure to secure special relief and special measures to cope with the economic inequalities within Wales as shown by the White Paper.[35]

The following year, D. R. advocated a strengthened structure for the Labour Party in Wales. It would follow an approach similar to that in Scotland above and beyond the administrative machinery which existed in the WCL. 'The Secretary of State for Scotland has substantial powers, and Scotland does play, within the Labour Party, a similar part which we hope to play within the UK Labour Party... We are a Regional Council, but we must become the National Council of Labour by releasing the imagination and political fertility that existed in the Labour Party in Wales.'[36] Even so, he continued to express his opposition to 'political devolution'. Furthermore, he deplored the lack of clarity on issues related to Wales in the annual demonstrations organised by the WCL, and demanded a clear statement of policy worthy of Labour's strength in Wales. 'We are responsible for a Welsh Labour Party programme as the predominating political party in the industrial and rural areas.'[37]

D. R. touched briefly on the desirability of an all-Wales national council designed to address weaknesses within the system of local government responsible for those functions best performed on an all-Wales basis. This argument can be seen in the context of later models for an elected Council for Wales, but did not diminish the role of Westminster and Welsh MPs in any way. He did not elaborate on the theme either before or after the discussion of the Government of Wales Bill, and for D. R., at least, the question of a Council for Wales was distinct from that of a separate parliament.

The WCL, for its part, argued that a separate Welsh parliament would have to resort to inducements to attract industries into Wales, whereas the UK government could use the power of direction. Administering nationalised industries would be complicated if responsibility was divided among different parliaments. Local government would be weakened were they to lose Exchequer Equalisation grants under a Welsh parliament. The WCL's attitude was summarised in its conclusion that it would be difficult to see what useful function a parliament could fulfil. This was echoed in the message outlined in *Labour's Policy for Wales*, published March 1954. While it recognised that the problems confronting Wales had generated a demand for a separate parliament, it insisted that the real cause of the country's woes stemmed from two and a half years of Tory misrule, and constitutional change was not the remedy.[38] A Labour government under Attlee had given people the right to work in their own country, denied to hundreds of thousands in the inter-war years. New industries had been attracted to Wales, the old ones had been modernised and Welsh farming had prospered. Added to that were the benefits of National Insurance, the NHS, and better educational facilities, and the creation of Welsh administrative departments where the need was proven. The answer lay in the election of another Labour government, and Labour's attention should be focused firmly on that goal.

This was certainly the view taken by D. R. as he stood on the verge of an eleventh campaign in Gower.[39] Along with Jim Griffiths, he was dispatched to the annual conference of the south Wales area NUM to champion official Labour policy.[40] There, they were confronted by Cyril Parry of Pontarddulais (in D. R.'s constituency) moving a resolution in favour of a Parliament for Wales on behalf of the Morlais lodge (in Jim's Llanelli constituency). But D. R. did not mince his words in response. The Labour MPs, he insisted, were representing 'the democracy of Wales' and any separate institution would be nothing but a diversion.[41] He repeated the same message a few weeks later at the Welsh Council of Labour's annual conference, which overwhelmingly endorsed the argument that Welsh interests would be best served through economic planning on a British scale, and not a separate parliament.[42]

When S. O. Davies presented a Parliament for Wales Bill to the House of Commons the following year, D. R. warned of the danger of separation: 'The main point of objection which I have to this Bill, and I sustain it to this moment, is that it does not combine and amalgamate, but divides. It separates Wales from that for which we have spent a lifetime struggling in order to accomplish proper standards of life, namely, amalgamation and cooperation with our neighbour.'[43]

He joined the overwhelming majority of Welsh Labour MPs

(including others who championed administrative autonomy) in voting against the Bill. Not surprisingly, D. R. found himself the target of Welsh Nationalist attacks. Unexpectedly, perhaps, for a man as used to criticism as D. R., he entered into detailed correspondence with two leading Welsh Nationalists – D. J. Williams, before the debate on the Parliament for Wales Bill, and Gwynfor Evans, afterwards – in which he defended his position. He told Gwynfor Evans that he did not under any circumstances want to replicate in Wales the kind of violence seen in Ireland, and to impose an Ulster-style settlement on Wales would be the worst kind of outcome.[44] Closer to home, D. R. was at pains to reassure Goronwy Roberts, in particular, that he would cooperate fully in all future movements that would benefit Wales. Nevertheless, any opportunity that might have existed in the 1950s was over.[45]

Within weeks of the discussion on the Parliament for Wales Bill, Anthony Eden called an election in order to capitalise on his honeymoon period as Tory leader and to strengthen his party's parliamentary majority. D. R. faced two opponents, B. Gwyther Jones on behalf of the National Liberals and Conservatives, and Chris Rees, standing for Plaid Cymru while serving a prison sentence for his refusal to enlist for National Service. Gwyther Jones promised less government involvement in people's lives, while Chris Rees' campaign focused almost entirely on the issue of compulsory military service, carefully overlooking D. R.'s consistent opposition to it. In the event, their efforts made little impression on the voters in Gower, despite the energetic campaign waged by Plaid Cymru supporters in the constituency as D. R. was returned with a majority of over 18,000.

One consequence of Labour's defeat was that Clement Attlee's era as Labour leader was coming to an end. This threatened to expose the party's internal divisions as never before, as Herbert Morrison, Hugh Gaitskell and Aneurin Bevan made their case to succeed him. D. R. was certainly not part of the Bevanite circle, despite having voted with the left-wing rebels on some occasions during the 1951–55 parliament. There was a Bevanite presence within Gower CLP – as in Pontardawe where they sold *Tribune* outside party meetings – but none of those involved sought to undermine D. R.'s position as the local MP and he had nothing to fear from that quarter.[46]

D. R. had, of course, known Bevan since their days in the SWMF in the 1920s, and worked with him as a fellow miners' MP from south Wales for over 25 years. In their different ways, both men had played a crucial role in parliament and in the country as Labour sought to rebuild itself after the defeat of 1931, and both had been critics of the wartime coalition. D. R.'s high regard for Bevan, coupled with exasperation at some of his behaviour, was obvious. 'I admire his talents – I have admired them for years, even when he was rather a cheeky boy,' was one such comment.[47] Unfortunately, nothing for D. R. and many of his parliamentary colleagues could excuse some of Bevan's actions during the previous four or five years. Therefore, if the 'cheeky boy' was to fulfil his great potential, he needed time to rehabilitate himself within the PLP by devoting himself to some serious work on the opposition front bench, comparable to the detailed work D. R. had witnessed him undertake in discussion of the Mines and Quarries Bill. For that to happen, D. R. believed, both Bevan and Gaitskell needed to stand aside and allow Morrison to succeed Attlee. It did not escape his or anyone else's attention that Morrison was already 67 and an election was not due for at least another four years.

This led D. R. and other senior MPs to propose that Morrison be allowed to assume the mantle unopposed. 'Surprise move by nine MPs to avoid a vote for Attlee's successor,' was how the *Daily Mirror* reported the suggestion, helpfully adding their ages: E. Shinwell (aged 71), D. R. (aged 74), C. W. Key (aged 72), W. T. Paling (aged 63), Walter Monslow (aged 60), R. R. Stokes (aged 58), S. P. Viant (aged 73), Sir Frederick Messer (aged 69), and D. T. Jones (aged 56).[48] Derek Marks in the *Daily Express* insisted Aneurin Bevan was personally behind the plot, declaring 'Bevan Blows it Up: Let Morrison Lead… With many Socialist MPs seriously worried about the effects of a public fight for the leadership, Mr Bevan's move was cleverly timed.' Gaitskell, however, calculated correctly that he already had sufficient support to defeat both opponents, and do so convincingly.[49] Within months, Morrison had resigned the deputy leadership, making way for Jim Griffiths, and the infighting which had bedevilled the party since 1951 continued unabated.

D. R. understood that to win power Labour had to appeal to a broad range of voters, including those experiencing the joys of a consumer society by the mid-1950s. He also knew very well that his own constituents in Gower were by no means basking in any new prosperity. The prospect of redundancies arising from the changes in steel and tinplate manufacturting were mirrored in the coal industry. Garngoch No. 1, Ystalyfera, and later Cwmllynfell were among the collieries closed by the NCB either due to financial losses or spuriously due to the need for the manpower elsewhere. Such closures affected the supply chain, as was exemplified when BTC closed the Ystalyfera Wagon Repair depot because it was no longer needed.[50] D. R. demanded that colliery modernisation should always be explored as an alternative to closure and that, where that was not possible, the men affected should be given alternative work within the industry.[51] Meanwhile, he continued to look to the NCB to create a modern, technologically driven mining industry in which men would want to work.[52] This, he believed, should include a new colliery in the Gorseinon area to work at far deeper levels than before, which should provide modern facilities for its workforce. However, the preparation and exploratory work took far longer than he had ever envisaged.

Meanwhile, he lobbied government departments to encourage private firms to locate their plants in the area, continuing the policy of the Attlee government which had seen developments such as Teddington Bellows in Pontarddulais, Swears and Wells in Gorseinon, and several light manufacturing operations in areas bordering the constituency. He welcomed the arrival of the Minnesota Mining Company at Garngoch, and assisted them when prolonged planning delays threatened their plans to expand.[53] At the same time, he supported efforts by Swansea CBC to develop the former RAF base at Fairwood Common which, he believed, should be used for continental services.[54]

In the same way, the Iron and Steel Board's decision to proceed with the building of a fourth integrated strip mill was greeted warmly by representatives of the industry in south-west Wales, convinced that their region was the natural location for such a plant. Initially, the signs were promising, especially when the arguments of those who continued to maintain that any new works should be built in the East Midlands were rejected. Then, in response to strong intervention by Scottish interests, it was agreed that the additional capacity would be achieved by building two new steelworks, one of which would be in Scotland. This meant that a smaller site would be required, therefore increasing the possibility that a suitable location could be found in south-west Wales. For D. R., this represented a further opportunity to secure the industrial future of his own constituents and he was sympathetic to the case for the works to be sited on an area of Stafford Common, between Gorseinon and Gowerton, within easy reach by road and rail of several of the traditional works which could be used for ancillary purposes.

This option, along with several others, was discounted early in the process by the Steel Board, mainly due to concerns about the size of the area of land that would be available. The Elba Works site in Crymlyn Burrows was given more serious consideration, but it too was deemed to have too many disadvantages. This meant that the final choice lay between two locations, one between Pembrey and Kidwelly (referred to as the Kidwelly site), and the other at Newport (Llanwern). Llanelli's representatives saw the matter in simple terms. Kidwelly was the only option if the new works was to be built in the western half of south Wales, and this required a concerted effort throughout the region to bring the works to the west.[55] The scars of the dispute over the location of the cold-reduction plant still ran deep in some quarters, as was clear when Swansea CBC refused to endorse the case for Kidwelly (although it did not oppose it, either). Llwchwr UDC, on the other hand, resolved to throw its weight behind the Kidwelly option.[56]

Their view was not shared by their MP, who continued to harbour his decade-long resentment against Jim Griffiths. Kidwelly, D. R. maintained, would bring no benefit to the Llwchwr area or any other part of the Gower constituency. The Swansea and Llwchwr valleys would become mere 'reservoirs of labour' for the Trostre and Kidwelly plants. Instead of supporting Kidwelly, the Llwchwr UDC and local trade unionists should demand that the Steel Board reconsider a Swansea site. It was a position that made sense earlier in the process but, with Kidwelly the only possible option in south-west Wales, it was hardly a convincing argument. However, not even a public personal appeal by W. E. Heycock, a longstanding stalwart from Pontarddulais, could move him.[57] There was no way that D. R. could be brought round to any proposal that involved locating a steel producing plant on a site west of Loughor.

Prominent individuals within the Gower CLP, particularly those with a connection to the steel and tinplate industry, were increasingly exasperated by their MP's attitude. Matters came to a head when one of the most impetuous of them, Gwynne Thomas of Pontarddulais, made a public declaration calling on D. R. to forget his quarrel with Jim Griffiths and support the Kidwelly option.[58] Gwynne Thomas spoke for many, especially the unions in the steel and tinplate industries, and their concerns were not allayed when D. R. prepared a long, rambling statement on the issue containing much irrelevant detail about the region's geological features and its impact on industrial development (of great value to a historian but limited in its impact on the matter under discussion). He then compounded his own difficulties by making a brief and unhelpful contribution in the Commons:

> I am very much involved in this question, although I have
> not said much about it. I have very strong opinions about the
> suitability of sites in south Wales. I know them better than
> any man in this House and, I think, better than any man
> in the country, as I taught geology and mining in that area
> and know the ground very well indeed. I do not think justice
> will be done to Wales or to men like myself if we ignore the
> subject of the location.[59]

Given his performance, it was inevitable that D. R. would face further criticism from the Labour Party in the Gower constituency. At a meeting of the CLP Executive Committee, members demanded that their MP should retire at the next election. No-one denied that he had been a fine parliamentarian and no-one doubted his dedicated service to the Labour Party and to his constituency, but it was time to hand the baton to someone else. A special management committee meeting was called, with one item on the agenda – to receive the MP's resignation. D. R. insisted that they had acted improperly, arguing correctly that he had never agreed to retire. He remained defiant at the meeting, including when County Alderman Gwilym Thomas of Gowerton, who was not part of any conspiracy to oust D. R., suggested that a man of his age should be thinking of retirement. 'Why don't you retire then, you're older than me,' was D. R.'s combative reply. When approached by the NUM about the issue, D. R. replied that he intended to contest the next election and would be seeking their support in doing so, although he made it clear he would not be opposing the official Labour candidate.

The Labour Party National Executive authorised the CLP to begin the process of selecting its candidate for the next election – D. R. could be a candidate but other nominations could also be made. In the event, D. R. did not pursue the issue. The NUM nominated Dick Beamish of Abercrave, the steelworkers opted for County Alderman Richard Roberts of Pontardawe. Other nominees included Dil Jeremiah, also of Pontardawe, and Ken Griffin was nominated by the postal workers. However, the candidate with the strongest support among the ward parties in the Gower and Llwchwr areas was the CLP secretary, Ifor Davies, a county councillor and chapel deacon, and he was the eventual winner, defeating Dick Beamish in the final ballot by four votes.[60]

The Labour Party in Gower was ready to move on to the next chapter, but the circumstances in which it did so left a bitter taste in many mouths. Many still loyal to D. R. understood why the decision had been taken: he did not enjoy the physical and mental powers that had sustained his immense reputation in the constituency; he was prone to wander over the past and recall old faces when dealing with current issues; he would have been in his mid-80s by the time he had completed another full term as Gower's MP. Even so, the way certain elements in the CLP had behaved did not do justice to a man who had given his life to the Labour movement and whose name had been synonymous with the Gower constituency for so long.

D. R. kept his own counsel about the way in which he had been removed. In a letter to the *South Wales Evening Post* (quoted in other papers at the time), he stated, 'I had never heard a complaint against my work in Parliament or in the constituency. I would have been willing to discuss any grievance, but there has been no complaint, and I was pained to hear one of my colleagues say that he and his friends would vote unanimously against me if I were to be put up as a candidate for Parliament again. I do not know anything of the meetings held by my opponents.'[61]

'They do not want me' was his sad comment to the *Western Mail* reporter when asked about the decision.[62] He said he did not want a peerage, which all assumed he would have been offered as the retiring Father of the House. But the huge pile of correspondence which he received from old colleagues, constituents, political friends and foes, journalists, and international contacts, was testimony to the extent of his activities throughout his life. He valued above all the tribute he received when the miners' historian, 'Robin' Page Arnot, published *The Miners in Crisis and War*, the third volume of the history of the MFGB dealing with the years from 1930 to 1945.[63] In it he dealt at length with the issues faced by D. R. as Secretary for Mines in the wartime coalition, and gave a comprehensive account of the unprecedented difficulties he had encountered. Arnot's depiction – 'Dai Grenfell, on whom there had fallen the heavy burden of keeping chaos at bay in the coal industry during the first two years of the Churchill administration and whose sound policies for this purpose had been more than once rejected' – may well have brought him some justified comfort.

CHAPTER 17

A Man Not Easily Moved

D. R. LEFT the House of Commons a disappointed man, having given 37 years' service to the Gower constituency and with an unstinting record to the Labour Party. The nature of his departure generated conflicting emotions even among his most loyal followers, many of whom were appalled at the way he had been treated, while also acknowledging that he was no longer at the height of his powers. It may have been time to go, but the manner in which the decision was taken, and the part played by certain individuals within the Gower Labour Party, was of no credit to them.

He withdrew from public life, living at Ardwyn where Beatrice and Eileen provided the care he needed during his eight years of retirement as old age took its toll. His death, on 21 November 1968, was followed by an interment at Brynteg chapel in Gorseinon, appropriately where his father had been the head deacon. There were obituaries in the major newspapers. *The Times* published a 600-word obituary outlining his achievements. It stated that he had been Secretary of Mines at an 'extremely critical period' adding, tellingly, that, 'In a country which does not often appoint a technical expert to the control of an appropriate department, the placing of Grenfell in charge of Mines was recognized as a happy, imaginative gesture.' It referred to his quest for learning as a young miner, his acquisition of languages, his membership of the Forestry Commission and the Royal Commission on Mine Safety. It noted the conscientious ways he responded to parliamentary questions, skimmed over his departure from government, and mentioned the widespread surprise that he had not been included in the Attlee government. Along with Rhys Davies he was said to have given a 'sharp lesson' to government ministers over the Control of Engagement Order in November 1947.[1] A similar summary was given by *The Guardian*.[2]

Since then, D. R.'s role on the British stage has rarely been acknowledged. There are few references to D. R. in the biographies of the leading figures of the Labour movement in the 1930s and 1940s (one of those who acknowledges him commits the error of referring to him as Will Grenfell), although Michael Foot gives D. R. an honourable place in his works on Aneurin Bevan and, likewise, Kenneth O. Morgan refers to his importance in Welsh Labour politics in the 1930s and 1940s. It is, however, impossible to avoid the conclusion that he became one of Labour's forgotten figures, possibly because his heyday came before rather than during the Attlee government.

The tributes that were paid to him at the time of his death encapsulated one interpretation of D. R.'s life, the working-class hero whose life journey took him from very humble beginnings in Penyrheol, Gorseinon, as he moved from agitator to local leader, and thence via ministerial office to the embrace of the British Establishment as Father of the House of Commons. To take such a view is, however, to display a superficial understanding of the man's journey and the principles to which he adhered throughout his long career. D. R. Grenfell was a product of industrial south Wales at its most expansionist and confident, a man reared in the exporting, outward-looking society moulded by the coal and metal manufacturing industries. He witnessed the evolution of Gorseinon and Loughor into modern settlements whose social and community life was shaped by the influx of mainly young people from the area's hinterland, from Llanelli and rural

Carmarthenshire in particular. It was a neighbourhood where Welsh remained the main language and where a combination of communal endeavour, coupled with the philanthropy of individual industrialists, created powerful local institutions. A combination of that spirit of confidence and an appreciation of what an industrial community could achieve for itself, given the right circumstances and conditions, undoubtedly inspired D. R.'s belief both in himself and in the people among whom he had been nurtured. It also deepened his understanding, evident as a child, that the opportunities available in Edwardian working-class areas were sparse and inadequate. He himself had made the most of the available educational and training provision, but this fell far short of what was needed. Moreover, it was not enough to secure opportunities for his own advancement. D. R. was determined to build a platform for everyone and committed his life to that task.

As a young man he had developed strong views, to which he adhered. For example, he was a teetotaller and supported, at least in his early days, proposals to control the liquor trade. On several occasions he also joined efforts to restrict the gambling industry (including an occasion when he made an ill-advised comment disparaging the Chinese for their predilection towards gambling). In D. R.'s case, this cannot be attributed to a Welsh Nonconformist upbringing nor to the fact that he hailed from the cradle of the 1904–5 religious Revival. Unlike some of his parliamentary neighbours (Tudor Watkins, William Jenkins and Percy Morris prominent among them), he did not combine political and parliamentary work with active participation in Nonconformist circles. He was a product of the Brynteg Sunday school, and extremely thankful towards it, but that, it appears, was as far as he went. His predecessor, John Williams, was a lay preacher clearly more interested in the legal and civil position of Nonconformists than in any Socialist theory, and who valued the support of chapel leaders. Nonetheless, like him, D. R. was able to count on the unswerving loyalty of the numerically substantial congregations throughout the Gower constituency.

He was a product of the 1870 Education Act, the legislation that gave England and Wales the opportunity to create a system of schools to provide the rudiments of learning for all children. The Llandeilo Talybont School Board was typical of the majority of those established in Wales. It was keen to wrestle control of the schools from the Anglican Church, but less efficient at tackling the job which it had been entrusted to undertake. Crucially in D. R.'s case – and despite its inadequacies – Penyrheol Elementary School, under the leadership of a man like Alaw Defynog and his kindly female assistant teacher, provided a foundation of learning. This was put to the service of the community for D. R. as a political leader, while W. J. Grenfell became a public figure and social administrator, and Mansel was a respected adult educator. The generation of Labour MPs from south Wales with whom D. R. worked, as well those who rose to prominence in the trade union movement, were the products of the same system of schooling. It provided them with a solid, if rudimentary, basis on which they subsequently built. In some cases, it nurtured a love of learning that was to last for the rest of their lives.

For this generation, however, their experiences of the education system emphasised the limitations of the provision, and their journey into adulthood intensified their appreciation of what should be made available. This aspiration was reinforced by the work of the ILP branches, such as the one in Gorseinon to which D. R. devoted a great deal of his time in the years before and during the First World War. The importance of the ILP's missionary work and its contribution to developing Socialist thought was clearly reflected in D. R.'s experience, and throughout his life he acknowledged his debt to the way it had nurtured his political awakening. It was through the ILP, and the combination of talented people in his own branch of the party and those who it invited to speak in Gorseinon and the surrounding areas, that D. R. gained the intellectual training which formed the basis of his subsequent thinking and action. Economics and, in particular, Karl Marx's work was studied and debated in Gorseinon and Loughor as elsewhere in the coalfield. In D. R.'s case, this was part of a much broader curriculum that looked to develop an understanding of the whole human condition. Through its combination of adult education, fervent discussion, and tireless activity, the Gorseinon ILP sought an ethical framework that combined the notion of the State as the handmaiden of society with a central belief in the dignity and freedom of the individual, ideas that were at the heart of D. R.'s political thinking and those of countless others of its members in different walks of life over the following decades. In the case of the Grenfell family, this was reflected in Mansel's lifetime's contribution to the WEA and in D. R.'s own commitment in advancing adult learning.

In his early years as a miner, D. R. often worked in atrocious working conditions and, even in a modern mine like the Mountain Colliery, he saw at first hand the failure of capitalist companies to operate in ways that provided a safe environment and decent terms and conditions for those working there. Private enterprise could not develop and run the kind of mines that were needed in the early 20th century unless operating costs were kept to the bare minimum, which meant low wages and cutting corners in terms of working practices. Working for a colliery company that was struggling financially imperilled the livelihoods of hundreds of his fellow miners and, for D. R., this brought a realisation that the answer lay in a radically different economic structure. Whatever its rhetoric about Welsh radicalism in industrial south Wales, the Liberal Party was part and parcel of the economic system with which D. R. grappled in the Mountain Colliery. The doctrine of economic liberalism, that abhorred State 'interference' and professed a personal relationship between employer and employee in a shared endeavour, was a bankrupt idea for D. R. long before the days of faceless capitalism, represented by the combines, that took possession of the coal and metal industries as the 20th century progressed.

It may well have been a factor that determined the course of D. R.'s life, notably his deviation from what looked like an assured progression to mining engineer and potentially mine manager to becoming, instead, a miners' leader. That experience was also undoubtedly influenced by the behaviour of the State in relation to the people of Gorseinon, as testified both by the actions of the police during the tinplate strike of 1913 and the subsequent attitudes revealed by the judiciary when matters came to court. The people who D. R. knew, whose thrift, independence, and strength of character he applauded continuously, deserved better from the State and this would never happen without a fundamentally different balance of political power in the country.

Such a transformation could not be achieved through theoretical discussion alone, but needed a Labour and trade union movement that was as modern and efficient as the capitalist system which it sought to displace. By the end of the 1914–18 war, D. R. had become a central figure in the Labour movement in the western half of the south Wales coalfield, with an established record of fighting on the issues that were the basis of daily discontent both to the miners and the broader working class in the region. He was given a platform to address longstanding rank-and-file grievances and the way in which the Western District had been led. D. R. brought a new dynamism and a hardened attitude: dynamism in the way he reorganised the working practices of the Western District, creating a more professional and efficient organisation, and a hardened attitude in the leadership he provided on both political and industrial matters. This was evident in the part played by the Western District in the militant wing of the SWMF, the uncompromising approach adopted in local disputes throughout 1919–21, and the vigour with which D.

R., as Miners' Agent, sought to garner popular support for the nationalisation of the mining industry.

D. R. remained unwavering in his belief that Socialism in Britain could only be achieved through parliamentary means. This had been one of his constant themes during his time as Miners' Agent, especially in the discussions within the SWMF and MFGB in 1920 and 1921. He had fought a hard and difficult by-election that secured victory on the back of the efforts of the Socialist movement in the constituency that was determined to win the hearts and minds of voters and to secure the return of one of its own to parliament. The same political forces had, of course, been the ones responsible for returning John Williams in 1906 and twice in 1910 but, in 1922, they had a candidate whom they trusted to proclaim an unconstrained Socialist message.

D. R. was thus catapulted into a House of Commons that was witness to the death throes of the Lloyd George coalition and the unceremonious removal of the man who had dominated Welsh politics for much of the previous quarter of a century. D. R.'s second election victory, in a matter of six months, meant he was part of a much larger PLP and a first-hand participant in the uneasy struggle between those determined to demonstrate Labour's respectability and fitness to govern and those, such as the Clydesiders, who wanted to use the House of Commons as a platform for the Socialist revolution.

In their midst sat D. R., who was convinced of the role of parliament and the need for a Labour government that could enact legislation of benefit to working people. This was evident in the way he constantly drew attention to the deficiencies of existing legislation, especially as it affected the mining industry, that could be rectified by parliamentary means. He did not question the importance of industrial action in securing gains for working people, but he watched in despair as the ineptitude the MFGB leadership became increasingly apparent, especially from the summer of 1925. He warned that Red Friday had only bought time for the government to build up its own forces while awarding the employers a very generous interim settlement. Moreover, the miners and every other branch of the organised working class needed to be on their guard, lest they became tied to any agreement that the employers could later exploit to their detriment, a lesson that he had learned early on in his experiences within the SWMF

It is not surprising, therefore, that during his 37 years as an MP, D. R. used the House of Commons and its facilities to highlight the need to modernise the legislative structure governing the way mines were operated, and the impact that had on the health and wellbeing of those employed in the industry and their families. That, as much as the struggle for economic and industrial power within the industry, was arguably as much of a priority for D. R. As noted above, D. R. had first-hand experience of the human cost of mining during his time working in the small mines in Gorseinon and Loughor. The working class were paying the price of capitalist speculation. In addressing these concerns, he made full use of the excellent House of Commons library to assist in crafting parliamentary questions, and he thus accumulated an impressive body of evidence for the miners' case which he advanced in parliamentary committees and on the floor of the House of Commons, on subjects such as wages, working conditions, and safety in mines.

Progress in resolving these issues proved painfully slow. The battle to get silicosis recognised as an industrial disease, and then to secure acknowledgement of the true extent of the problem, was a continuous battle fought by D. R. for much of his time in parliament. Against him stood not only the mine owners but the constant procrastination of the Mines Inspectorate and the Department of Mines, who failed to grapple with the problem despite the evidence. Equally frustrating was the timidity of Labour ministers, especially between 1929 and 1931, who were far too ready to listen to official advice and lacked the determination or indeed expertise to introduce the robust measures that were required.

Like his colleagues from other mining constituencies, D. R. did not need to be reminded of the consequences of the way Britain's mines operated and its impact both in terms of accidents and on long-term health. But it took the Gresford disaster to put those issues on the front pages of Britain's papers, and even then only until something else came to dominate the headlines. Gresford encapsulated all that D. R. had warned about regarding the condition of the industry, the out-dated legal framework and the ineffectiveness of the inspectorate. Only then was a British government moved to appoint a Royal Commission on Mines Safety and, even after that had sat for two years, it took another 20 years before its findings were implemented.

He wanted a mining industry that was properly organised, operated safely with decent terms and conditions for those who worked in it, and a resource for Britain as a whole. State ownership was vital if this was to become a reality. It was a belief that D. R. was to take with him to the Department of Mines where he himself paid the price when this fell on the deaf ears of government colleagues.

More broadly, D. R. did not need to be reminded of the degradation of Wales in the inter-war period and the crisis that drove half a million people to leave the country during that period. Mass transfer of people from the locality and charity for those who remained were clearly no answer to such problems. While D. R. was happy to acknowledge the efforts of Tom Jones, Percy Watkins and others, not least the South Wales and Monmouthshire Council of Social Service, such efforts did not address the underlying problems in his view. Neither did the national government's effort to develop a 'less orthodox' policy provide any meaningful solution. In the event it stuck rigidly to its free market dogma. D. R.'s own analysis, published in time for the 1935 election, testified to his own experience and conviction that the salvation for Wales, as with other industrial areas of Britain, lay in economic planning and in measures to determine the location of its industrial base.

The inappropriateness of laissez faire was already apparent, and no-one realised that more than D. R. The days of individual enterprise and free competition had long disappeared in the coal, steel and tinplate manufacturing industries which, especially in south Wales, were now dominated by large-scale combines. Production in both those sectors was determined by pre-set quotas administered by cartels, introduced in order to shield them from the disastrous impact of a competitive free market. State intervention, legislative regulation, and government involvement on key decisions was a reality in the coal and steel industry in the 1930s, as was shown by the government's decision to nationalise mineral rights, and the experience of Richard Thomas and Co. in Ebbw Vale. For D. R. that principle was a given, and it was a matter of extending the realm of State responsibility.

The events of the summer of 1931 had reinforced his conviction of the need for a fundamental change in both the priorities and values of the British state. It was not merely a matter of rescuing the economy from the speculators or of ensuring that technology and mechanisation lightened the load on working people instead of compounding poverty. Nor was it merely a matter, as D. R. did on countless occasions, of responding to specific events or government announcements and demonstrating their inadequacy. Economic planning was needed, not merely on grounds of efficiency, but to secure a deeper moral purpose that freed people from their sense of foreboding about the future derived from the realities of life in a capitalist economy. The ideas that were central to the debates of the Gorseinon ILP applied to the context of inter-war Britain, were clearly articulated by D. R. in *Labour Calls for Power*, in published articles, and in speeches both inside and outside parliament.

These ideas were central to his thinking as he stepped up to the plate following Labour's defeat in the 1931 general election. For over a decade, as D. R. operated on British and international levels, the sheer physical and mental demands on him were immense. That he was able to undertake numerous onerous roles testified to his physical strength and endurance, as well as his commitment to the cause. Whether on the floor of the House of Commons, in press articles, or on public platforms throughout Britain, D. R.'s name was invariably to be seen at the forefront of efforts to rebuild the Labour Party as an effective force. More to the point, he acted as a tribune for the six million people who had supported the Labour cause in the 1931 election, whose voices were drowned by the overwhelming parliamentary majority of the 'national government'.

The man who had been rejected repeatedly by Ramsay MacDonald as unsuitable for ministerial office, and whose only formal education had finished when he left Penyrheol Elementary School barely more than twelve years old, had to master successive briefs on a range of complex technical matters affecting trade, industrial policy, and Britain's relationship with the rest of the world. In the days when MPs' support structures were limited, and with little secretarial support for the opposition, it fell to individual MPs to undertake the preparation and forge the links with policy experts in the different fields, a task which D. R. undoubtedly performed with great effectiveness throughout the 1930s.

Whatever advice might be proffered, D. R. was absolutely clear that the Labour movement and its parliamentary arm was the only means by which the internal problems of Britain and the challenges it faced overseas could be addressed effectively. A unification of the parties of the Left might be appropriate in France and Spain, but in Britain nothing would be gained by any accommodation between Labour and either the ILP or the Communist Party. Electoral arithmetic undoubtedly supported his position: 8.3 million people voted Labour in 1935, just over 27,000 voted Communist, and these figures reinforced D. R.'s view that other parties of the Left offered, at best, a distraction from Labour's work in securing the election of a majority Labour government.

During the early 1930s, he sat as one of 15 Welsh Labour MPs, a group that represented a quarter of the PLP at the time. The extent to which the PLP was dependent on its Welsh members is suggested by the columns of *Hansard* and countless memoranda that have survived from the period. Charles Edwards and Will John had key roles in the parliamentary machinery, dealing with day-to-day matters around whipping and organising MPs for parliamentary and committee appearances. George Daggar, D. L. Davies, and Tom Griffiths constantly led delegations to ministers, often on matters relating to south Wales as a whole, and their involvement was by no means limited to their own constituencies. W. G. Cove undertook detailed policy development work, especially relating to education and training. Sir William Jenkins and Dai Watts-Morgan divided their time between Westminster and their roles as aldermen on Glamorgan County Council, where they occupied positions as powerful committee chairs and often gave their priority to work there, where they were in a position to influence decisions. A similar impression is gleaned from the contribution of David Williams (another alderman as well as MP) in Swansea at this time, while Dr J. H. Williams' role was affected by ill-health. There were important contributions from G. H. Hall and Ted Williams, both of whom went on to become ministers in the Attlee government, and from S. O. Davies and W. H. Mainwaring after they joined the ranks of the Welsh MPs in by-elections during that parliament. But as far as Welsh MPs in parliament were concerned, the bulk of the work for most of those trying years fell to D. R., along with Aneurin Bevan and Morgan Jones.

A similar analysis can be applied more broadly to the PLP

and D. R.'s closest colleagues, a small group of determined Socialists who, like him, came to the fore in the debacle of 1931. They included Rhys Davies, Seymour Cocks and Tom Williams (the latter an unsung hero of the Attlee government, the effect of whose work as Minister of Agriculture deserves greater credit, especially in Wales), with whom D. R. collaborated effectively throughout these years. As noted above, D. R. venerated George Lansbury and was heartbroken at his departure from the Labour leadership. Already he had favoured Clement Attlee as the deputy leader, while working closely with Sir Stafford Cripps both on the front bench and at Gresford. D. R. was pivotal in his becoming Labour leader and he continually watched his back during his time as leader of the opposition from 1935, as Sir Stafford Cripps, Herbert Morrison and others indulged in various schemes to replace him.

Several of that group that had led the opposition to the national government were among the Labour colleagues who served in the wartime coalition government in which D. R. served two strenuous years as repeated crises affected Britain's coal industry. There was initial enthusiasm within the Labour Party for D. R.'s appointment as the first former miner to serve as Secretary for Mines, and he enjoyed the confidence of those of his colleagues who knew most about the industry. D. R. adopted a very different approach to that of previous Labour holders of the post, Emanuel Shinwell and Ben Turner, both of whom had opened themselves to criticism from the MFGB (and especially the SWMF) for being too even-handed in their dealings with the two sides of an industry where owners and employed had diametrically opposed views on its future direction.

This was an unprecedented time to hold the position of Secretary for Mines and, other ministers, notably Ernest Bevin, were behaving as none of their predecessors had done (a strength according to most conclusions). D. R. may well have failed to grasp the full extent of the special circumstances under which he fulfilled his responsibilities. He had 18 years' experience of the way ministers and their officials normally behaved and the departmental boundaries which they observed, matters that were not clear at all in his time at the Department for Mines, and which affected his own freedom of action. He also underestimated the malevolence of Hugh Dalton, despite having observed him at close quarters as colleagues in the PLP, and his reputation for undermining colleagues.

It may be said, in his defence, that his somewhat dismissive attitude towards structures set up during the war, notably the CPC, has to be considered in light of the way they and the local pit production committees were ignored by most mine owners and only played a significant part in boosting productivity where their work was promoted by particularly progressive managers. In any case, D. R.'s firm views on the need to protect wages and working conditions, miners' freedom to leave the industry, the State's role in relation to the industry, the danger of abandoning certain pits that were considered unproductive and, above all, the question of manpower in an industry dominated by an older workforce exhausted by physical labour, reflected long-held views based on a lifetime's experience of the coal mining industry. As noted above, support for his analysis of the mining industry was evident from others with a similar background, the mining group of Labour MPs in particular. But D. R. was the victim of the personification of the coal issue by his opponents – it became the 'Grenfell problem' – when fundamental problems already existed in the industry. Furthermore, Labour ministers in the government, Attlee included, failed to support a party colleague who was facing opposition from officials across government. The question arises of whether the fuel crisis which bedevilled Clement Attlee's government could have been averted had the kind of actions demanded by D. R. been taken, and taken earlier, as D. R. wanted. This was the view held by many in south Wales and was echoed by R. Page Arnot in his historical account.

But the reality was that D. R. left the government in the summer of 1942 having served as Secretary for Mines for two years. Thereafter, he was no longer constrained by the collective responsibility of the wartime coalition government, and for three years he operated in a grey area where his responsibility lay with the Labour opposition whose leaders were, in turn, members of a coalition government with its approval. For D. R., such an arrangement was the proof of how Britain differed from the dictatorships which it was fighting, and he revelled in opportunities to show that, even in wartime, disagreements were possible in an elected parliament. By this means, D. R. and his colleagues on the Labour benches were able to remind the public where the instincts of Tory ministers lay, and expose the inadequacies of their vision for the future. This was reflected in debates over workmen's compensation, the Beveridge Report, the imprisonment of Sir Oswald Mosley, and an array of other issues. As in 1931–35, Welsh MPs, notably Aneurin Bevan, Jim Griffiths and S. O. Davies, were prominent in setting out an alternative vision of Britain's future, and it was work which D. R. supported to the full, even if his own contribution was less prominent. The work, led by Labour members outside the government, was a key element in forging Labour's victory in 1945 but went further than the Labour government elected that year was able to go. For D. R., two themes in particular emerged. First, the Labour Party's international policy, and secondly, Wales' position within the British state. On more than one occasion, D. R. used the PLP's decision to suspend standing orders at the beginning of the 1945 parliament (therefore providing freedom for backbench criticism and scope for its creativity) to question the approach taken by Labour ministers.

Throughout his life, D. R. looked at the issues confronting society both in the context of industrial south Wales and as part of an international Socialist movement. Like many others with the same background in coal mining, D. R. considered himself part of an international industry that was itself part of a global working class. His loyalty was to workers in other countries. He regarded himself as a pacifist, and described himself as such throughout his life. Yet he was not one of the leaders of the anti-war movement in Gorseinon and the fact that it was Mansel, and not D. R., who came to prominence as a political opponent of the war is, in itself, significant. D. R. did not play in Gorseinon the kind of role which Jim Griffiths occupied, for instance, in Ammanford. The fact that he was already a Miners' Agent, with responsibilities to his members that included the delicate tasks that befell that role in the machinery of wartime, may be cited as an explanation of D. R.'s position. He was close to the leaders of the anti-war movement, attended their meetings, and by his presence and some of his utterances made his own anti-war views clear as a political opponent of that conflict.

In doing so, he could rely on the support of the Western District whose political opposition to the war and to the government's policies in pursuit of its aims became more and more apparent in 1917 and 1918. D. R. had, of course, attended the Leeds Conference and it is likely that he would have been at the disrupted conference at the Elysium in Swansea in July 1917, had he not been in Scotland at the MFGB conference. Whatever can be said about the extent of his own involvement in the anti-war movement, that experience moulded his subsequent beliefs on matters of individual conscience and the claims of the State on the individual. Repeatedly – in 1939, in 1944, and again during the days of the Attlee government and thereafter – D. R. opposed any notion of interference with the liberty of the individual by the State, even during a time of war. He defended the rights of conscientious objectors during both wars. He opposed the direction of labour. He believed that working people should be convinced to come to the aid of the State, rather than be compelled to do so by statute. He believed that it was the duty of the Labour movement to be the guardian of those principles.

He had experienced at first hand the notion of international brotherhood during his 18-month stint in Canada. This had inspired him to teach himself a range of European languages to an astonishing level of fluency at a time when he was also engaged in studies for mining qualifications and beginning his work as a trade unionist and political activist in Gorseinon. Again, as so often in D. R.'s life, theoretical contemplation was linked to practical action. The Union of Democratic Control – of which there was a branch in Gorseinon chaired by Mansel by 1914 – stood on a platform that proclaimed the end of secret diplomacy, a rejection of a balance of power and the arms race as a basis of international security, and the divestment of control of foreign affairs from the narrow social and economic elite responsible for the calamity that had engulfed Europe in 1914.

He put his faith in a collective peace system based on the democratic will of the people and driven by the international Socialist movement. He was appalled by Versailles and recognised the inadequacy of the League of Nations as it emerged in the 1920s.

In less than a decade he saw at first hand the failure of the peace settlement as he watched fascist oppression across swathes of Europe. He built connections with the Socialist movement across the Continent, especially with the German-speaking world whose leaders testified to the hopes that were being destroyed by the reactionary hysteria that had gripped Europe. The culmination of his thinking came when he witnessed the events in Spain and was driven to conclude that pacifism was no answer to such a calamity. The pacifist from Gorseinon faced the reality that discussions at the League of Nations and a policy of non-intervention did not resolve matters. He also understood that Soviet Russia did not offer an answer to Europe's plight: he blamed the British government and its underlying social attitudes for the failure to forge a tactical alliance with Soviet Russia against Germany in the 1930s, but this did not mean he was blind to the realities of life there nor the power politics in which Stalin was engaged.

Neither was the answer to be found in the United States of America, especially not in the post-war years. D. R. may have been well-disposed to many aspects of Roosevelt's New Deal America, but even that featured infrequently in his public pronouncements. He was never comfortable with a foreign policy that put Britain at the behest of America and its economic might, even at a time like 1945. His involvement with the SEG, however tentative, and his decision to sign the 'Stop the Coming War' manifesto were all signs of where D. R. stood, as was his decision to join successive backbench rebellions against the government's foreign policy during 1945–50. It might be possible to dismiss such criticisms of the government as personal retaliation towards Ernest Bevin following the events of 1940–42. But to do so would be to ignore the evidence of D. R.'s political testimony throughout his journey from his early days in the Gorseinon ILP.

The fact that D. R. did not develop a more public critique of the Labour government's foreign policy, other than a few statements such as those he made at Cwmllynfell in 1947, should not detract from the significance of his statements and his voting record in the lobbies. But it is striking that D. R. barely spoke in any of the parliamentary debates on international issues held during these years, and only discussed these themes in very general terms despite his deep involvement in international issues in the 1920s and 1930s. A combination of social background, age, and his place in the Labour family differentiated D. R. from Keep Left and similar groups, and the same can be said of the other Welsh and indeed Scottish Labour MPs. The same was true of many of his fellow rebels on international issues during the 1945–50 parliament: Tudor

Watkins and D. J. Williams, with their background in the ILP in Ystradgynlais and Gwaun-cae-gurwen respectively, Rhys Davies likewise in Llangennech, and Percy Morris' political moulding in Swansea.

Their position and that of several of their colleagues was indicative of a deep unease at aspects of the government's foreign policy, not least among those reared in the Welsh Labour movement and its internationalist traditions. Many of the same individuals continued to express doubts semi-privately about official Labour Party policy in the 1950s as the Bevanite controversy raged, but again they were rarely to be found at the centre of those arguments, at least not in public. Vociferous exceptions included Aneurin Bevan and S. O. Davies, but the presence of a much broader group from Wales clearly uneasy at the direction of Labour policy should not be overlooked, and is a subject which would benefit from further research.

During the Attlee government, D. R. was often the most senior Welsh Labour MP to raise questions about decisions taken by government ministers, free as he was from the collective responsibility which bound others, such as Aneurin Bevan and Jim Griffiths. There is no clear evidence about D. R.'s relationship with Aneurin Bevan, other than the public record that the two of them worked closely and effectively for 30 years as parliamentary colleagues. D. R. had been an MP for seven years when Aneurin Bevan – 16 years his junior – entered parliament, and both watched as the second Labour government disintegrated under Ramsay MacDonald. The two men played complementary roles in opposition, especially during 1931 to 1935, and privately both held similar views of the Spanish Civil War. They were on diametrically different sides of the argument about a United Front in Britain, but they worked closely during the war years (Aneurin Bevan defending D. R. as Secretary for Mines and D. R. supporting Aneurin Bevan over Section 1A(a) and other matters being notable

411

examples). To portray D. R. as a Bevanite (or even proto-Bevanite) would be to misrepresent his position, but the stance he took on foreign policy in particular from 1945 until he left the House of Commons is a reminder that not all Labour MPs could be categorised as either Bevanites or Gaitskellites in the 1950s. It was by no means a neat division, as was evident in D. R.'s case. He was guided by his own principles and beliefs and he stuck to that position irrespective of what others might have urged him to do.

From the outset, D. R. supported the notion of administrative devolution and the proposal for an appointment of a Secretary of State for Wales responsible for co-ordinating government business in Wales. This, he believed, would be an essential part of an effective response by Whitehall to the distinctive problems facing Wales in the inter-war years and beyond. This was a common view among most but not all Welsh Labour MPs at the time. It was certainly not a reaction to the rise of the Welsh Nationalist movement, which had little impact in the electoral battles being waged by Labour. Rather, D. R. was one of a minority of Welsh Labour MPs who were acutely conscious of Labour's responsibility to the Welsh electorate and the duties that this placed on the party's leaders. His analysis was sustained in his opposition to military service (a combination both of Welsh particularism and his strong anti-militarist record) and in his views on the use of military land in Wales for training purposes. The Labour Party would have been truer to its founding principles had his views been heeded. But the Labour Party was a long way from agreeing to a distinctive approach to Welsh issues in the immediate post-war years.

His change of heart on the question of a parliament for Wales, from his supportive comments in the early-1920s to his opposition to the measure proposed by S. O. Davies three decades later, raises many questions about his views on Welsh devolution. He was by no means an implacable opponent of an elected body serving the whole of Wales, and wanted a stronger and more autonomous Welsh Labour Party, but in the 1950s the idea of the Stormont model was something which he could not advocate. Short-term political calculations may well have influenced his view on the question of a parliament. So too, undoubtedly, was the bitter experience of local authorities and public bodies in Wales throughout the 1920s and 1930s, struggling to deliver vital public services when their resources were depleted at the time of greatest need. It took a Labour government, harnessing the power of the British state to address those issues, both of its own accord and by means of what Aneurin Bevan's transformation of local government finance enabled local councils to achieve. A parliament for Wales was an idea that would take a long time to become the settled will of Welsh Labour, let alone of those sent to Westminster in their name.

He was a proud Welshman who appreciated Welsh culture, celebrated the achievements of its literary figures, and had a gifted poet as his agent for many years. On the issue of the Welsh language he had no doubts: Welsh was the natural tongue of thousands of his fellow countrymen, even if the number of people who spoke it had fallen below two-fifths of the population of Wales by 1931 and was to fall again, to below a third of the population, by 1951. What D. R. did not seem to admit, as few did, was the sharp decline in the percentage of children and young people reported as being able to speak Wesh in the 1951 census, and nowhere was this more apparent than in parts of his own constituency. He was certainly no opponent of the Welsh language but he gave limited attention to the matter. His attitude reflected the complacency of many of his generation at a time when Welsh was spoken by many but enjoyed little status. He supported the limited provisions of the first Welsh language legislation, but in common with many others he regarded the matter of the language as largely outside the purview of the political struggle in which he was involved.

Jim Griffiths, nine years younger than D. R. and a native of Ammanford, a mere 14 miles from Gorseinon, had looked to D. R. for support as he sought to expand his role in the Labour movement both in Wales and in Britain as a whole. D. R. had supported his work in winning Llanelli for Labour, and he had subsequently been prominent in Labour activity in the constituency. Jim Griffiths' election to parliament had provided an important injection of energy into the PLP. He had taken forward aspects of work, such as on the silicosis issue, which D. R. had previously undertaken. The correspondence which exists between the two men indicates a warmth and rapport. Again, this was seen in Jim Griffiths' unstinting defence of D. R. (along with Aneurin Bevan) during 1940 to 1942. Subsequent events testify that it is not fanciful to suggest that D. R. was speaking for Jim Griffiths when he advanced the case for a Secretaryship of State, which Jim was unable to support as a government minister. The rift over the location of the cold-reduction works therefore assumes an almost tragic quality, for it divided the two most effective tribunes of the Labour Party in south-west Wales at the time when a united front was required to promote the region's economy after the ravages of depression and war.

There was now no possibility of D. R. and Jim Griffiths ever forming what could have been a powerful alliance, at the solid core of the party, as the Labour government sought to clarify its direction in 1948 and 1949 and in the difficult years that followed. Once again, D. R. had reached his own conclusion about the location of the cold-reduction works and Jim Griffiths' influence on the government's decision, and nothing would move him from what he believed.

Similarly with S. O. Davies, whose inspiring portrayal by Robert Griffiths focuses on his repeated rebellions, his clashes with Labour leaders and his eventual triumph over the Labour machine in his last election in Merthyr Tydfil. What should also not be ignored is the evidence contained in *S. O. Davies:*

A Socialist Faith about the continuous and determined work which he undertook both in parliament and in the country to rebuild the Labour Party in the 1930s, often at D. R.'s side. Both men also took on their party's leaders over various issues relating to Wales, as both were clearly frustrated by its failure to show greater urgency in addressing the extent of problems in Wales.

Even so, D. R. could not be persuaded to support S. O. Davies' proposals for home rule for Wales and, in doing so, he found himself on opposite sides of the argument to two of the 1945 intake with whom he had worked closely, Goronwy Roberts and Tudor Watkins. D. R. was impressed by their talents and in particular nurtured Goronwy Roberts. The mutual respect was clear and often to be reflected in the pages of *Y Cymro* edited by Goronwy Roberts' confidant, John Roberts Williams. There appears to have been some distance when Goronwy Robers supported the Parliament for Wales campaign, and subsequent correspondence between the two men suggests that matters were only restored after D. R. insisted they should work on 'measures of advantage to Wales'. By then, D. R. was in his final term as an MP and shortly was to become involved in the unseemly battle with members of his own CLP that distracted him in his last years as Gower's representative.

D. R. Grenfell's achievements were underpinned by the loyalty of thousands of men and women across the diverse communities which he represented. Many years after his death his name was revered by those who had come into contact with him, many of whom who could testify to the help they had received from him. Such feelings were by no means confined to the electors of Gower, and this volume will, hopefully, give David Rhys Grenfell the place he deserves both in the history of the Gower constituency and in the wider Labour movement.

Bibliography

1. Newspapers
The main newspapers consulted either in original or on-line versions were:

Cambria Daily Leader

Daily Herald

Daily Worker

Herald of Wales

Llais Llafur

Llanelly Mercury

New Leader

Reynolds News

South Wales Daily Post (later *South Wales Evening Post*)

South Wales Tribune

The Cambrian

Western Mail

Labour Monthly

Other papers were consulted on an ad-hoc basis, primarily through on-line access. References to those papers are presented as they arise in notes to individual chapters.

2. Manuscript collections
The main collection consulted was the D. R. Grenfell papers held at the West Glamorgan Archives in Swansea.

The other key collections consulted were:

Wales Labour Party papers, National Library of Wales

Gwynfor Evans papers, National Library of Wales

Goronwy Roberts papers, National Library of Wales

E. T. John papers, National Library of Wales

D. J. Williams papers, National Library of Wales

New Fabian Research Bureau papers, London School of Economics

John Parker papers, London School of Economics

Lord Elwyn Jones papers, National Library of Wales

James Griffiths papers, National Library of Wales

Clement Attlee papers, Bodleian Library, Oxford
Papers of William Gillies, Labour History Archive and Study Centre, Manchester
BBC Welsh Service papers, BBC Archives, Caversham
Hugh Dalton diaries (London School of Economics, on-line access)
Winston Churchill papers (Churchill College, Cambridge, on-line access)
Parliamentary Debates (Hansard), on-line access

3. Minutes and official records

Minutes of the Miners' Federation of Great Britain, South Wales Miners' Library
Minutes of the South Wales Miners' Federation, South Wales Miners' Library
Minutes of the Swansea Rural District Council, West Glamorgan Archives
Minutes of Llwchwr Urban District Council, West Glamorgan Archives
Annual Reports, Forestry Commission
Report of Royal Commission on Safety in Coal Mines

4. Books

Abel Smith, Edward, *Active Goodness* (London, 2017).

Addison, Paul, *The Road to 1945 British Politics and the Second World War* (London, 1977).

Agorti, Aldo, *Palmiro Togliatti, a biography* (London, 2008).

Arnot, R. Page, *A History of the Scottish Miners* (London, 1955).

Arnot, R. Page, *South Wales Miners, Glowyr De Cymru, 1898–1914* (London, 1967).

Arnot, R. Page, *South Wales Miners, Glowyr De Cymru, 1914–1921* (Cardiff, 1975).

Arnot, R. Page, *The Miners in Crisis and War* (London, 1961).

Arnot, R. Page, *The Miners, Years of Struggle* (London, 1953).

Ashworth, William, *The History of the British Coal Industry, Volume 5, 1946–1982, the nationalised industry* (Oxford, 1986).

Awberry, Stan, *Labour's Early Struggles in Swansea* (Swansea, 1949).

Bevan, Aneurin, *Why Not Trust the Tories* (London, 1944).

Bew, John, *Citizen Clem, A Biography of Attlee* (London, 2016).

Brennan, T., Cooney, E. W., and Pollins, H., *Social Change in South-West Wales* (London, 1954).

Brooke, E. H., *Chronology of the Tinplate Works of Great Britain* (Cardiff, 1944).

Bryant, Chris, *Stafford Cripps, the first modern Chancellor* (London, 1997).

Bullock Alan, *Ernest Bevin* (London, 2002).

Burgess, Simon, *Stafford Cripps, a Political Life* (London, 1999).

Burns, Duncan, *The Steel Industry, 1939–1959* (Cambridge, 1961).

Campbell, John, *Nye Bevan and the Mirage of British Socialism* (London, 1987).

Carlton, David, *MacDonald versus Henderson, the foreign policy of the second Labour government* (London, 1970).

Crossman, R. H. S., Foot, Michael, and Mikardo, Ian, *Keep Left* (London, 1947).

David, Wayne, *Remaining True, a Biography of Ness Edwards* (Caerphilly, 2006).

Davies, D. J., and Davies, Noelle, *Cymoedd Dan Gwmwl* (Denbigh, 1938).

Davies, Dewi Eirug, *Byddin y Brenin, Cymru a'i Chrefydd yn y Rhyfel Mawr* (Swansea, 1988).

Davies, Eric, *A Biography of Daniel Hopkin* (Carmarthen, 1991).

Davies, Gwilym Prys, *Cynhaeaf Hanner Canrif, Gwleidyddiaeth Cymru, 1945–2005* (Llandysul, 2006).

Davies, Gwilym Prys, *Llafur y Blynyddoedd* (Dinbych, 1991).

Davies, Ithel, *Bwrlwm Byw* (Llandysul, 1984).

Davies, John, *Broadcasting and the BBC in Wales* (Cardiff, 1994).

Davies, Rhys, *Seneddwr ar Dramp* (Liverpool, 1934).

Edwards, John, *Remembrance of a Riot, the History of the Llanelli Railway Strike of 1911* (Llanelli, 1988).

Eirug, Aled, *The Opposition to the Great War in Wales, 1914–1918* (Cardiff, 2018).

Ellis, E. L., *T. J., a Life of Thomas Jones C.H.* (Cardiff, 1992).

Evans, Eifion, *The Welsh Revival of 1904* (Port Talbot, 1969).

Fishman, Nina, *Arthur Horner, a Political Biography, Vol 1, 1894–1944; Vol II, 1944–1968* (London, 2010).

Foot, Michael, *Aneurin Bevan, a Biography, Vol I, 1897–1945* (London, 1962); *Vol II, 1945–1960* (London, 1973).

Francis, Hywel, and Smith, David, *The Fed, a history of the South Wales Miners in the twentieth century* (London, 1980).

Francis, Hywel, *Miners Against Fascism, Wales and the Spanish Civil War* (London, 1984).

Galbraith, Russell, *Without Quarter, A Biography of Tom Johnston* (Edinburgh, 1995).

Ginsborg, Paul, *A History of Contemporary Italy, 1943–1980* (London, 1990).

Gower Divisional Labour Party, *Brochure to Celebrate Anniversary of Mr D. R. Grenfell's 25 Years as Member of Parliament* (Gorseinon, 1947).

Grenfell, D. R. *Labour's Way to Plan Prosperity* (London, 1935).

Grenfell, D. R., *A Plea for Leasehold Enfranchisement* (Gorseinon, 1950).

Grenfell, D. R., *Coal* (London, 1947).

Griffiths, James, *Glo* (Liverpool, 1945).

Griffiths, Robert, *Killing No Murder, South Wales and the Railway Strike of 1911* (London, 2009).

Griffiths, Robert, *S. O. Davies, A Socialist Faith* (Llandysul, 1983).

Harris, Kenneth, *Attlee* (London, 1995).

Healey, Denis, *My Secret Planet* (London, 1992).

Herald Book of Labour Members (London, 1922).

Howell, David W., *Nicholas of Glais, the people's champion* (Clydach, 1991).

Jaksch, Wenzel and Kolarx, Walter, *England and the Last Free Germans* (London, 1941).

Jaksch Wenzel, *Europe's Road to Potsdam* (London, 1963).

Jaksch, *Sudeten Labour and the Sudeten Problem* (London, 1945).

Jenkins, Gwyn, *Prif Weinidog Answyddogol Cymru, Cofiant Huw T. Edwards* (Talybont, 2008).

Jenkins, Mark, *Bevanism, Labour's High Tide* (London, 1979).

Jenkins, Paul, *Twenty By Fourteen, A History of the South Wales Tinplate Industry, 1700–1961* (Llandysul, 1995).

Jones, Brynmor P., *Voices from the Welsh Revival* (Bridgend, 1995).

Jones, Elwyn, *In My Time* (London, 1983).

Jones, F. Elwyn, *The Battle for Peace* (London, 1938).

Jones, Gwynoro, and Gibbard, Alun, *Whose Wales, the politics of Welsh devolution and nationhood, 1880–2020* (Gorseinon, 2021).

Jones, Thomas, *A Diary with Letters, 1931–1950* (London, 1954).

Jones, Wyn, *A History of Gorseinon and its Environs* (Gorseinon, 1992).

Kendall, Walter, *The Revolutionary Movement in Britain, 1900–21: the origins of British Communism* (London, 1969).

Kirsti Bohata, Kirsti, Alexandra Jones, Mike Mantin, and Steven Thompson, *Disability in Industrial Britain: a cultural and literary history of impairment in the coal industry, 1880–1948* (2019).

Kushner, Tony and Knox, Katharine, *Refugees in an Age of Genocide: global, national and local perspectives during the twentieth century* (London, 1999).

Lansbury, Edgar, *George Lansbury, My Father* (London, nd).

Lawson, Jack, *A Man's Life* (London, 1932).

Leeworthy, Daryl, *Labour Country, Political Radicalism and Social Democracy in South Wales, 1831–1985* (Cardigan, 2018).

Lewis, Richard, *Leaders and Teachers, Adult Education and the Challenge of Labour in South Wales, 1906–1940* (Cardiff, 1993).

Marquand, Hilary, *South Wales Needs a Plan* (London, 1936).

McLeod, Robert R., *Markland or Nova Scotia: Its History, Natural Resources and Native Beauties* (Markland 1903).

Meehan, Eugene J., *The British Left Wing and Foreign Policy: a study of the influence of ideology* (New Brunswick, 1960).

MFGB, *The Claim for Legal Minimum Wages for Mineworkers.*

Middlemas, R. K., *The Clydesiders, A left wing struggle for parliamentary power* (London, 1965).

Mikardo, Ian, *Back-bencher* (London, 1988).

Morgan, J. Vyrnwy, *The Welsh Religious Revival, 1904–5, A Retrospect and a Criticism* (London, 1909).

Morgan, Kenneth and Jane, *Portrait of a Progressive, the political career of Christopher, Viscount Addison* (Oxford, 1980).

Morgan, Kenneth O., *Callaghan, a life* (Oxford, 1997).

Morgan, Kenneth O., *Consensus and Disunity: The Lloyd George Coalition Government, 1918–1922* (Oxford, 1979).

Morgan, Kenneth O., *Labour in Power, 1945–51* (Oxford, 1984).

Morgan, Kenneth O., *Labour People, Leaders and Lieutenants, Hardie to Kinnock* (Oxford, 1987).

Morgan, Kenneth O., *Rebirth of a Nation Wales, 1880–1980* (Oxford, 1981).

Morgan, Kenneth O., *Wales in British Politics, 1868–1922* (Oxford, 1963).

National Industrial Development Council for Wales and Monmouthshire, *Second Industrial Survey of South Wales* (Cardiff, 1937).

Pearce, Edward, *Denis Healy, a life in our times* (London, 2002).

Pimlott, Ben, *Harold Wilson* (London, 1992).

Pimlott, Ben, *Hugh Dalton* (London, 1985).

Pimlott, Ben, *Labour and the Left in the 1930s* (Cambridge, 1977).

Pollard, Sidney, *The Development of the British Economy, 1914–1967* (London, 1969).

Potts, Archie, *Zilliacus, a Life for Peace and Socialism* (London, 1999).

Rabinbach, Anson, *The Crisis of Austrian Socialism, from Red Vienna to Civil War, 1927–1934* (London, 1983).

Rees, D. Ben, *Jim Griffiths, Arwr Glew y Werin* (Talybont, 2014).

Rowlands, Ted, *Something Must Be Done, South Wales v Whitehall, 1921–1951* (Merthyr Tydfil, 2000).

Saville, John, *The Politics of Continuity, British Foreign Policy and the Labour Government, 1945–46* (London, 1993).

Schaffer, Gordon, *Baby in the Bathwater: memoirs of a political journalist* (Lewes, 1996).

Shepherd, John, Davis, Jonathan, and Wrigley, Chris (eds), *Britain's Second Labour Government, 1929–31, a reappraisal* (Manchester, 2012).

Shepherd, John and Laybourn, Keith, *Britain's First Labour Government* (Basingstoke, 2006).

Sherman, A. J., *Island Refuge, Britain and Refugees from the Third Reich, 1933–1939* (London, 1977).

Sissons, Michael, and French, Philip (eds), *Age of Austerity, 1945–51* (Harmondsworth, 1964).

Smith, J. Beverley, *James Griffiths and His Times* (Cardiff, 1977).

Smith, Robert, *Hanes Libanus Gorseinon* (Gorseinon, 2012).

Stratton, Harry, *To Anti Fascism By Taxi* (Port Talbot, 1984).

Symons, M. V., *Coal Mining in the Llanelli area, Vol. 2, 1830–1870* (Llanelli, 2013).

Tanner, Duncan, Williams, Chris, and Hopkin, Deian (eds) *The Labour Party in Wales, 1900–2000* (Cardiff, 2000).

Terrill, Ross, *R. H. Tawney and his times, Socialism and Fellowship* (London, 1974).

Thompson, Steven, *Unemployment, Poverty and Health in Interwar South Wales* (Cardiff, 2006).

Timmins, Nicholas, *The Five Giants a biography of the Welfare State* (London, 1995).

Unofficial Reform Committee, *The Miners' Next Step, being a suggested scheme for the reorganisation of the Federation* (Tonypandy, 1912).

Wainwright, David, *Men of Steel, The History of Richard Thomas and his Family* (London, 1986).

Ward, Paul, *Huw T. Edwards, British Labour and Welsh Socialism* (Cardiff, 2011).

Williams, D. J., *Capitalist Combination in the Coal Industry* (London, 1924).

Williams, Glanmor (ed), *Swansea, an illustrated history* (Llandybie, 1990).

Williams, J. Ceri and Davies, D. Tom, *Hanes Brynteg, Gorseinon* (Gorseinon, 1980).

Williams, John, *Was Wales Industrialised? Essays in Modern Welsh History* (Llandysul, 1995).

Williamson, Stanley, *Gresford, The Anatomy of a Disaster* (Liverpool, 1999).

Wyn, Hefin, *Ar Drywydd Niclas y Glais, Comiwnydd Rhonc a Christion Gloyw* (Talybont, 2017).

5. Articles, theses etc.

Alban, John R., 'Municipal Administration and Politics from the 1830s to 1974', in Glanmor Williams (ed), *Swansea: an illustrated history* (Swansea, 1990).

Cleaver, David, 'Labour and Liberals in the Gower Constituency, 1885–1910', *Welsh History Review*, Vol. 12 (1984).

Davies, D. K., 'The Influence of Syndicalism and Industrial Unionism on the South Wales Coalfield 1898–1921: a study in ideology and practice' (Unpublished PhD thesis, Cardiff University, 1991).

Edward May, 'A Question of Control: Social and Industrial Relations in the South Wales Coalfield and the Crisis of Post-war Reconstruction'

(Unpublished PhD thesis Cardiff University, 1994).

Davies, John, 'Y Gydwybod Gymdeithasol yng Nghymru rhwng y Ddau Ryfel Byd', in G. H. Jenkins (ed.), *Cof Cenedl*, IV (Llandysul, 1989).

Egan, David, 'The Swansea Conference of the British Council of Soldiers' and Workers' Delegates 1917', *Llafur*, Vol. 1, No. 4, 1975.

Evans, Neil, 'South Wales has been roused as never before: marching against the Means Test, 1934–36', in K. O. Morgan and D. W. Howell (eds), *Crime, Protest and Police in Modern British Society: Essays in Memory of David J. V. Jones* (Cardiff, 1999)

Green, Andrew, 'A Czech refugee artist in Mumbles', https://gwallter.com, accessed 20 November 2023.

Jones, Howard C., 'The Labour Party in Cardiganshire', *Ceredigion*, Vol. 9 (1981).

Smith, Robert, *In the Direct and Homely Speech of the Workers: Llais Llafur, 1898–1915*, Centre for Advanced Welsh and Celtic Studies, Aberystwyth, occasional paper, 2000.

Talbot, Kathy, 'The Painter and the Politician: Ernest Neuschul and D. R. Grenfell MP', *Journal of the Gower Society*, 53 (2002).

Thompson, Steven, 'The South Wales Miners' Federation as a Disability Organisation', *Llafur*, Vol. 12 (2013).

Thompson, Steven, 'The living dead of the mining industry: Deindustrialisation, sheltered workplaces and the re-employment of disabled miners in post-war Wales', *Welsh History Review*, Vol. 31 (2023).

Williams, L. J., 'The Road to Tonypandy', *Llafur*, Vol. 1 (1973).

Williams, Sian Rhiannon, 'The Bedwellty Board of Guardians and the Default Act of 1927', *Llafur*, 2, No. 4 (1979).

Endnotes

Chapter 1: A Boy from Penrheol

1 West Glamorgan Archives, D. R. Grenfell Papers, Box 9, notes towards autobiography.
2 Glanmor Williams (ed.), *Swansea an illustrated history* (Llandybie, 1990). M. V. Symons, *Coal Mining in the Llanelli area, Vol. 2, 1830–1870* (Llanelli, 2013). Wyn Jones, *A History of Gorseinon and its Environs* (Gorseinon, 1992). E. H. Brooke, *Chronology of the Tinplate Works of Great Britain* (Cardiff, 1944). Paul Jenkins, *Twenty By Fourteen, A History of the South Wales Tinplate Industry, 1700–1961* (Llandysul, 1995). J. Ceri Williams and D. Tom Davies, *Hanes Brynteg, Gorseinon* (Gorseinon, 1980).
3 E. H. Brooke, *Chronology of the Tinplate Works of Great Britain* (Cardiff, 1944).
4 This was reflected in the very limited clearance work that had to be undertaken by the Llwchwr Urban District Council in the post-war years.
5 David Cleaver, 'Labour and Liberals in the Gower Constituency, 1885–1910', *Welsh History Review*, Vol. 12 (1984).
6 *Parliamentary Debates*, 8 June 1937.
7 Care needs to be exercised with the use of the word evangelical in this context. An evangelical preacher was defined as someone who based a sermon on the contents of the word of the Bible rather than on the approved teachings of a clerical hierarchy, as distinct from its 20th-century American-influenced connotations.
8 Notes to the author by Brynmor Grenfell.
9 *Western Mail*, 7 April 1922, 28 June 1922.

Chapter 2: The Makings of a Miners' Leader

1 West Glamorgan Archives, D. R. Grenfell Papers 1, Box 9, autobiographical notes.
2 J. Vyrnwy Morgan, *The Welsh Religious Revival, 1904–5, A Retrospect and a Criticism*. Eifion Evans, *The Welsh Revival of 1904* (Port Talbot, 1969). Brynmor P. Jones, *Voices from the Welsh Revival* (Bridgend, 1995).
3 West Glamorgan Archives, D. R. Grenfell Papers 1, Box 9, autobiographical notes.

4   Ibid.

5   Ibid.

6   Robert R. McLeod, *Markland or Nova Scotia, Its History, Natural Resources and Native Beauties* (Markland, 1903).

7   *Weekly Mail*, 2 September 1905.

8   *Cambrian*, 5 December 1906, 5 July 1907.

9   *Cambrian*, 5 July 1907.

10 *Llais Llafur*, 11 July 1914, 8 August 1914. David Cleaver, 'Labour and Liberals in the Gower Constituency 1885–1910', *Welsh History Review*, Vol. 12 (1984).

11 *Llais Llafur*, 7 January 1911. Robert Smith, *In the Direct and Homely Speech of the Workers: Llais Llafur, 1898*–1915, Centre for Advanced Welsh and Celtic Studies, Aberystwyth, occasional paper, 2000.

12 Thomas George and Ben Matthews. Gorseinon Trades and Labour Council included representatives from the Dockers Union, the Tin and Sheet Millmen's Association, the gas workers and SWMF, representing a total of 750 affiliated members.

13 A dispute at the Mardy Works in March 1913 (*Cambrian*, 29 March 1913) provided further impetus for the local Labour cause as the local tinplate workers' branches and SWMF lodges became galvanised behind the Labour Party.

14 *Llais Llafur*, 21 February 1914. Edgar Chappell, the housing reformer from Ystalyfera, established the Swansea Valley Public Health and Housing Association. It acted as a prototype for later all-Wales organisations.

15 *Llais Llafur*, 22 June 1912, 28 June 1913.

16 Papers of William Evans, Llanerch, private possession. I am grateful to Mr and Mrs Walters, Brynteg Road, Gorseinon, for allowing me to access these papers.

17 *Llais Llafur*, 4 November 1911, 3 December 1912. *Labour Leader*, 9 February 1912.

18 *Llais Llafur*, 11 July 1914.

19 *Evening Express*, 5 February 1909.

20 E. H. Brooke, *Chronology of the Tinplate Works of Great Britain* (Cardiff, 1944).

21 *Evening Express*, 28 May 1907.

22 *Cambrian*, 16 August 1907.

23 *Evening Express*, 9 November 1909. *South Wales Daily Post*, 13 April 1910. *Llanelly Mercury*, 1 April 1910, 3 October 1910.

24 *South Wales Daily Post*, 31 January 1910, 7 April 1910. R. Page Arnot, *South Wales Miners, Glowyr De Cymru, 1898–1914* (London, 1967).

25 *South Wales Daily Post*, 13 April 1910.

26 Unofficial Reform Committee, *The Miners' Next Step, being a suggested scheme for the reorganisation of the Federation* (Tonypandy, 1912). All four of those named were to play key roles in the SWMF and local

Labour politics as checkweighers, county councillors and leaders in their respective communities. See L. J. Williams, 'The Road to Tonypandy', *Llafur*, Vol. 1 (1973). Gwilym Bedw served as D. R.'s agent throughout the 1920s and 1930s.

27   *Llais Llafur*, 29 March 1913.
28   *Western Mail*, 12 June 1913.
29   *Cambria Daily Leader*, 11 June 1913, 13 June 1913.
30   *Cambria Daily Leader*, 2 July 1913.
31   *Cambria Daily Leader*, 14 July 1913.
32   *Cambria Daily Leader*, 29 July 1913.
33   *Llais Llafur*, 1 February 1913. The international unity of the working-class movement was also recognised in the same month when a resolution was passed demanding the release of the Irish trade union leader Jim Larkin, and a collection was made for the Dublin Sufferers (*Llais Llafur*, 8 November 1913, 22 November 1913). A meeting later in the same year heard R. Neft and S. O. Davies champion the cause of international brotherhood.
34   *Llais Llafur*, 8 August 1914.
35   Ibid.
36   *Llanelly Mercury*, 20 July 1916. *Merthyr Pioneer*, 12 September 1914, 26 September 1914, 3 October 1914.
37   *Llanelly Mercury*, 4 May 1916. *Herald of Wales*, 6 November 1915.
38   *Llanelly Mercury*, 20 July 1916. *Herald of Wales*, 7 November 1914, 13 March 1915.
39   *Llanelly Mercury*, 11 May 1915.
40   *Herald of Wales*, 17 April 1915. Dewi Eirug Davies, *Byddin y Brenin, Cymru a'i Chrefydd yn y Rhyfel Mawr* (Swansea, 1988).
41   Robert Smith, *Hanes Libanus, Gorseinon* (Gorseinon, 2012).
42   *Merthyr Pioneer*, 1 July 1916.
43   The Great War resulted in some calls for restrictions on public entertainment in the area to be relaxed. For example, there were demands that the cinemas should be allowed to open on Sundays, something which was resisted forcefully by local chapels (West Glamorgan Archives, Minutes of Swansea RDC, 13 April 1915, 11 May 1915). The council took the view that some activities should be allowed, such as benefit concerts, provided that all such performances were within the realms of what it considered to be appropriate activities for a Sunday (West Glamorgan Archives, Minutes of Swansea RDC, 20 July 1915). *Llanelly Mercury*, 13 January 1916, 4 May 1916. *Herald of Wales*, 23 January 1915, 19 August 1915. *Herald of Wales*, 22 May 1915.
44   *Llais Llafur*, 5 September 1914.
45   Ibid.
46   Ibid.
47   *Llais Llafur*, 3 October 1914.

48 *Glamorgan Gazette*, 31 March 1916.

49 *Merthyr Pioneer*, 18 June 1916, 18 August 1916. 'Rebels' from Gorseinon marched to Llanelli in August 1917 to show their support for Dan Griffiths at a meeting convened by the Rev. John Evans, and addressed by Bob Williams and S. O. Davies.

50 David W. Howell, *Nicholas of Glais, the people's champion* (Clydach, 1991). Hefin Wyn, *Ar Drywydd Niclas y Glais. Comiwnydd Rhonc a Christion Gloyw* (Talybont, 2017). Robert Griffiths, *S. O. Davies, a Socialist Faith* (Llandysul, 1983). T. Gibbon Davies was a brother of S. O. Davies.

51 *Merthyr Pioneer*, 8 December 1917. *Herald of Wales*, 25 December 1915.

52 *Merthyr Pioneer*, 24 June 1916. For W. I. Thomas, see *Merthyr Pioneer*, 16 December 1916.

53 *Merthyr Pioneer*, 8 July 1916.

Chapter 3: The Miners' Agent

1 *Cambria Daily Leader*, 21 February 1916.

2 *Llais Llafur*, 19 February 1916. 4 March 1916.

3 Ibid.

4 *Herald of Wales*, 26 March 1916.

5 *Cambria Daily Leader*, 15 March 1916.

6 *Cambria Daily Leader*, 23 March 1916.

7 *Llais Llafur*, 15 April 1916.

8 *Cambria Daily Leader*, 15 April 1916.

9 *Merthyr Pioneer*, 22 April 1916.

10 *Merthyr Pioneer*, 20 May 1916.

11 *Llais Llafur*, 13 May 1916.

12 Ibid.

13 *Llais Llafur*, 13 January 1917. D. R. would spend the next five years sitting alongside John James, George Daggar, D. L. Davies, Oliver Harris, Arthur Jenkins, George Barker, A. J. Cook, Vernon Hartshorn, Noah Rees, S. O. Davies and Noah Abblett and others.

14 *Cambria Daily Leader*, 13 May 1916, 23 September 1916, 30 June 1917, 25 August 1917, 13 September 1917, 17 September 1917, 31 October 1917, 3 September 1919. *Llais Llafur*, 25 August 1917, 6 October 1917.

15 This was confirmed by the audit of company accounts undertaken as part of the government's measure of control. R. Page Arnot, *South Wales Miners, Glowyr De Cymru, 1914–1921* (Cardiff, 1975); *The Miners, Years of Struggle* (London, 1953). Anthony Môr O'Brien, 'Patriotism on Trial: the strike of the south Wales miners, 1915', *Welsh History Review*, Vol. 12, 1984.

16 *Llais Llafur*, 10 June 1916.

17 *Cambria Daily Leader*, 5 May 1917.

18 *Llais Llafur*, 10 June 1916, 21 July 1917. *Cambria Daily Leader*, 16 July

1917, 8 March 1918, 26 August 1918, 28 August 1918. *South Wales Weekly Post*, 14 July 1917, 8 September 1917.

19 *Cambria Daily Leader*, 21 July 1917.

20 *Llais Llafur*, 5 August 1916. *Merthyr Pioneer*, 16 September 1916.

21 *Llais Llafur*, 15 January 1916, 13 May 1916. *Merthyr Pioneer*, 27 May 1916. R. Page Arnot, *The Miners: Years of Struggle* (London, 1953).

22 *Cambria Daily Leader*, 12 March 1918.

23 *Cambria Daily Leader*, 27 January 1917.

24 *Cambria Daily Leader*, 19 March 1917, 12 April 1917, 16 April 1917, 30 June 1917, 15 August 1917, 25 August 1917.

25 *Cambria Daily Leader*, 13 January 1917, 27 February 1917. *Llais Llafur*, 23 December 1916.

26 *Cambria Daily Leader*, 27 February 1917, 10 November 1917.

27 *Cambria Daily Leader*, 10 November 1917.

28 *Western Mail*, 26 June 1917.

29 *Merthyr Pioneer*, 12 May 1917. *Herald of Wales*, 11 December 1915.

30 *Merthyr Pioneer*, 20 October 1917.

31 *Merthyr Pioneer*, 2 June 1917.

32 He admitted having endeavoured to convince the people of the futility of war, and had organised an anti-militarist demonstration before the outbreak of the war, while acting as secretary of the ILP. Martin was fined £5 and handed over to the military authorities.

33 Aled Eirug, *The Opposition to the Great War in Wales, 1914–1918* (Cardiff, 2018). D. K. Davies, 'The Influence of Syndicalism and Industrial Unionism on the South Wales Coalfield 1898–1921: a study in ideology and practice' (Unpublished PhD thesis, Cardiff University, 1991). Edward May, 'A Question of Control: Social and Industrial Relations in the South Wales Coalfield and the Crisis of Post-war Reconstruction (Unpublished PhD thesis, Cardiff University, 1994).

34 Aled Eirug, *The Opposition to the Great War in Wales, 1914–1918* (Cardiff, 2018).

35 Ibid.

36 David Egan, 'The Swansea Conference of the British Council of Soldiers' and Workers' Delegates 1917', *Llafur*, Vol. 1, No. 4, 1975.

37 Wesh Glamorgan Archives, D. R. Grenfell Papers 2, Diary of D. R. Grenfell, 1917. D. J. Williams later returned to Gwaun-cae-gurwen and was returned as the Labour MP for Neath in a by-election in 1945.

38 *Cambria Daily Leader*, 11 June 1917, 25 August 1917.

39 *Cambria Daily Leader*, 15 May 1916, 9 February 1918, 9 March 1918.

40 John R. Alban, 'Municipal Administration and Politics from the 1830s to 1974' in Glanmor Williams (ed.) *Swansea: an illustrated history* (Swansea, 1990).

41 *Cambria Daily Leader*, 9 March 1918.

42 *Cambria Daily Leader*, 25 November 1918, 3 December 1918.

43 *Cambria Daily Leader*, 25 November 1918.
44 *Cambria Daily Leader*, 3 December 1918.
45 Ibid.
46 *Western Mail*, 21 June 1922.
47 West Glamorgan Archives, D. R. Grenfell Papers 1, Box 9, file of correspondence re Gower Constituency.
48 Kenneth O. Morgan, *Consensus and Disunity: The Lloyd George Coalition Government, 1918–1922* (Oxford, 1979); *Wales in British Politics, 1868–1922* (Oxford, 1963).
49 *Llais Llafur*, 12 November 1919, 27 December 1919.
50 *The Spot*, 25 October 1935.
51 Robert Griffiths, *S. O. Davies, A Socialist Faith* (Llandysul, 1983).
52 *New Leader*, 14 March 1924, 16 May 1924, 31 May 1924, 13 June 1924, 3 October 1924. *Herald of Wales*, 22 September 1923.
53 Walter Kendall, *The Revolutionary Movement in Britain, 1900–21: the origins of British Communism* (London, 1969), p 27. *Labour Leader*, 21 April 1921.
54 R. Page Arnot, *The Miners: Years of Struggle* (London, 1953); *South Wales Miners, Glowyr De Cymru: A History of the South Wales Miners' Federation* (Cardiff, 1975). Hywel Francis and David Smith, *The Fed, a History of the South Wales Miners in the Twentieth Century* (London, 1980).
55 *Daily Herald*, 5 May 1919.
56 R. Page Arnot, *The Miners: Years of Struggle* (London, 1953).
57 South Wales Miners' Library, MFGB Conference Minutes, 21 and 26 March 1919. *Daily Herald*, 5 May 1919.
58 *Cambria Daily Leader*, 11 October 1919.
59 *South Wales Daily Post*, 15 February 1919.
60 *South Wales Daily Post*, 10 May 1919.
61 *Cambria Daily Leader*, 30 January 1919, 5 February 1919, 19 March 1919.
62 *Cambria Daily Leader*, 6 May 1919.
63 South Wales Miners' Library, Minutes of MFGB Conference, 1 March 1920.
64 *Western Mail*, 27 January 1920.
65 *Nottingham Evening Post*, 25 March 1920. *Lancashire Evening Post*, 3 April 1920. *Western Mail*, 5 April 1920.
66 R. Page Arnot, *The Miners: Years of Struggle* (London, 1953).
67 Ibid.
68 *Western Mail*, 7 March 1921.
69 South Wales Miners' Library, Minutes of MFGB Conference, 18 March 1921.
70 *Western Mail*, 18 April 1921.
71 West Glamorgan Archives, D. R. Grenfell Papers 2, Diary 1921.
72 *Daily Herald*, 16 May 1921.

73 *Llanelly Mercury*, 24 March 1921, 31 March 1921, 9 June 1921, 16 June 1921.

74 *Llanelly Mercury*, 28 April 1921, 23 June 1921, 27 June 1921. West Glamorgan Archives, Minutes of Swansea RDC, 27 June 1921.

75 *Herald of Wales*, 18 June 1921.

76 *Western Mail*, 1 August 1920.

77 *Western Mail*, 13 July 1921, 19 July 1921. *Herald of Wales*, 16 April 1920, 29 November 1920. Further evidence of the extent to which matters at Tirdonkin and the Garngoch collieries took up much of D. R.'s time is given in his diary entries, West Glamorgan Archives, D. R. Grenfell Papers 2, Dairies 1919 and 1920.

78 An excellent analysis of the process is provided in D. J. Williams *Capitalist Combination in the Coal Industry* (London, 1924). This process was mirrored in the steel and tinplate industry. Lewis Bros was purchased by the Grovesend Steel and Tinplate Co., which itself became part of Richard Thomas & Co. in 1923, making that firm one of the dominant industrial concerns in south-west Wales. Baldwin's, who already owned the Elba works in Gowerton, purchased the neighbouring Fairwood works from the Davies family. *Western Mail*, 21 October 1918, 27 February 1920, 7 May 1920.

79 *Llanelly Mercury*, 14 July 1921.

80 *Llanelly Mercury*, 14 July 1921. Personal information on W. J. Roberts.

81 West Glamorgan Archives, D. R. Grenfell Papers 2, Diary, 6 July 1921.

82 *Western Mail*, 8 July 1921. *Western Daily Press*, 8 July 1921.

83 For police reinforcements see *Western Mail*, 16 July 1921. For subsequent court case, see *Western Mail*, 19 July 1921, 26 February 1924.

84 *Western Mail*, 4 August 1921, 6 August 1921, 22 August 1921, 23 August 1921. *Northern Whig*, 18 August 1921.

85 *Western Mail*, 20 January 1922, 25 September 1923, 26 September 1923, 25 January 1924, 5 January 1925, 10 August 1925. *Citizen*, 26 August 1921.

86 *Western Mail*, 14 November 1921, 9 January 1922.

87 *Western Mail*, 27 July 1920. *Daily Herald*, 20 July 1920.

Chapter 4: A Man of Extreme Views

1 *Western Mail*, 12 December 1921, 22 June 1922.

2 *Western Mail*, 7 July 1922.

3 Ibid.

4 Ibid.

5 *Western Mail*, 7 July 1922, 11 July 1922.

6 *Western Mail*, 12 July 1922, 13 July 1922.

7 *Western Mail*, 14 July 1922.

8 *Western Mail*, 14 July 1922, 17 July 1922.

9 South Wales Miners' Library, Minutes of MFGB, 6 July 1922. *Western Mail*, 7 April 1922, 28 June 1922.

10 *Western Mail*, 7 July 1922, 10 July 1922.

11 *Daily Herald*, 12 July 1922.

12 *Western Mail*, 10 July 1922, 11 July 1922, 12 July 1922.

13 *Daily Herald*, 15 July 1922.

14 *Western Mail*, 11 July 1922.

15 *Western Mail*, 12 July 1922.

16 *Daily Herald*, 10 July 1922, 12 July 1922, 17 July 1922.

17 *Daily Herald*, 17 July 1922.

18 *Western Mail*, 12 July 1922.

19 *South Wales Daily Post*, 20 July 1922.

20 *Western Mail*, 15 July 1922.

21 *Western Mail*, 20 July 1922.

22 *Daily Herald*, 13 July 1922, 22 July 1922.

23 *Western Mail*, 22 July 1922.

24 *Daily Herald*, 22 July 1922, 24 July 1922.

25 *Daily Herald*, 16 July 1922.

26 *Daily Herald*, 24 July 1922.

27 Kenneth O. Morgan, *Consensus and Disunity: the Lloyd George coalition government, 1918–1922* (Oxford, 1979).

28 *Cambrian*, 10 November 1922.

29 The Tories and their allies secured 5.5 million, the Liberals 2.6 million, and Lloyd George's 'National' Liberals 1.3 million.

30 *Herald Book of Labour Members* (London, 1922).

31 *Daily Herald*, 21 April 1923. The Welsh MPs concerned were R. T. Jones (Caernarfon), Morgan Jones (Caerphilly), Robert Richards (Wrexham), J. H. Williams (Llanelli) and D. R. himself. Russel Galbraith, *Without Quarter, A Biography of Tom Johnston* (Edinburgh, 1995). R. K. Middlemas, *The Clydesiders, A left wing struggle for parliamentary power* (London, 1965).

32 *Daily Herald*, 7 June 1923. *Parliamentary Debates*, 15 June 1925, 11 March 1926, 15 March 1926, 18 March 1926, 22 March 1926, 25 March 1926, 29 April 1926.

33 9s. 6d. per shift by the close of 1922.

34 *Parliamentary Debates*, 13 December 1922.

35 *Herald of Wales*, 3 December 1923. *Cambrian*, 6 February 1925.

36 *Cambrian*, 27 June 1924.

37 *Cambrian*, 30 November 1923.

38 The election expenses in Gower for the 1923 contest were slightly short of £950, all of which were paid by the MFGB.

39 John Shepherd and Keith Laybourn, *Britain's First Labour Government* (Basingstoke, 2006).

40 Rhys Davies, *Seneddwr ar Dramp* (Liverpool, 1934).

41 South Wales Miners' Library, Minutes of MFGB Executive, 9 May 1924.

42 R. K. Middlemas, *The Clydesiders: A left wing struggle for parliamentary*

power (London, 1965). Russell Galbraith, *Without Quarter, A Biography of Tom Johnston* (Edinburgh, 1995).

43 R. Page Arnot, *The Miners: Years of Struggle* (London, 1953).

44 John Shepherd and Keith Laybourn, *Britain's First Labour Government* (Basingstoke, 2006).

45 *Herald of Wales*, 11 October 1924. His appeal was typified by the loyalty of voters in Garden Village, Gorseinon, where stalwarts were assisted by a horse, appropriately named Ramsay, who would be draped in red and yellow ribbons to transport the populace to the polling station at Pontybrenin School in a cart. Ramsay would be gently coaxed by his owner, Wat Jenkins, to climb the hill towards the school. However, he would only do so on condition that his owner walked at his side. (Recollections of Hilda Richards, Mary M. Howells, Beryl Roberts, Betty Edwards, Bessie M. Thomas, and Eiddwen Jenkins in discussions with the author.)

46 *Herald of Wales*, 25 October 1924.

47 Ibid.

48 Ibid.

49 *Herald of Wales*, 10 January 1925.

50 Ibid.

51 *Herald of Wales*, 24 February 1925.

52 *Herald of Wales*, 24 February 1925. *Daily Herald*, 21 January 1925.

53 Further bitterness was injected by Edward Harris who, upon hearing of the verdict, alleged that one of the jurors was related to a man who had been killed. *Cambrian*, 13 March 1925.

54 *Parliamentary Debates*, 28 July 1925.

55 *Parliamentary Debates*, 7 July 1925, 3 May 1928.

56 R. Page Arnot, *The Miners: Years of Struggle* (London, 1953).

57 *Daily Herald*, 3 August 1925.

58 South Wales Miners' Library, MFGB Conference, 19 August 1925. Cited in R. Page Arnot, *The Miners: Years of Struggle* (London, 1953), p.384.

59 *Daily Herald*, 16 September 1925.

60 *Daily Herald*, 19 October 1925.

61 Ibid.

62 Ibid.

63 *Daily Herald*, 20 October 1925.

64 *Daily Herald*, 19 October 1925.

65 *Parliamentary Debates*, 1 March 1926.

66 Ibid.

67 *Parliamentary Debates*, 14 March 1928.

Chapter 5: The People in the Villages were Wonderful

1 Hywel Francis, 'The Anthracite Strike and Disturbances of 1925', *Llafur*, Vol. 1, 1973.

2 *Daily Herald*, 3 March 1926.

3 *Western Mail*, 10 February 1926.

4 On 10 February 1926 he seconded an amendment to a backbench motion on the need to increase industrial production.

5 *Parliamentary Debates*, 10 February 1926.

6 West Glamorgan Archives, D. R. Grenfell papers 2, Diary, 1926.

7 *South Wales Daily Post*, 3 March 1926.

8 Ibid.

9 West Glamorgan Archives, D. R. Grenfell Papers 1, Box 2, D. R. Grenfell to Mansel Grenfell, June 1926.

10 *South Wales Daily Post*, 3 May 1926.

11 *Parliamentary Debates*, 6 May 1926.

12 Ibid.

13 West Glamorgan Archives, D. R. Grenfell papers, Diary, 1926.

14 West Glamorgan Archives, D. R. Grenfell Papers 1, Box 2, D. R. Grenfell to Mansel Grenfell, June 1926.

15 Ibid.

16 Ibid.

17 *South Wales Daily Post*, 13 May 1926.

18 *Herald of Wales*, 15 May 1926.

19 *Herald of Wales*, 26 June 1926.

20 South Wales Miners' Library, Minutes of MFGB Conference, 14 May 1926. R. Page Arnot, *The Miners: Years of Struggle* (London, 1953).

21 *South Wales Daily Post*, 4 June 1926, 5 June 1926.

22 *Parliamentary Debates*, 1 July 1926.

23 *Daily Herald*, 4 August 1926.

24 *Llanelly Mercury*, 17 June 1926, 24 June 1926, 22 July 1926, 26 August 1926, 7 October 1926, 4 November 1926, 11 November 1926. At the same time, members of public bodies sought to use their powers to best effect. In particular, Glamorgan County Council which provided school meals.

25 South Wales Miners' Library, Minutes of MFGB Conference, 2 September 1926.

26 R. Page Arnot, *The Miners, Years of Struggle* (London, 1953).

27 *South Wales Daily Post*, 2 September 1926. *Cambrian*, 2 September 1926.

28 *Parliamentary Debates*, 26 October 1926.

29 *Daily Herald*, 4 October 1926.

30 South Wales Miners' Library, Minutes of MFGB Conference, 7 October 1926.

31 South Wales Miners' Library, Minutes of MFGB Conference, 4–5 November 1926.

32 *Cambrian*, 20 May 1927.

33 Steven Thompson, 'The South Wales Miners' Federation as a Disability Organisation', *Llafur*, Vol. 12 (2013). Kirsti Bohata, Alexandra Jones,

Mike Mantin, and Steven Thompson, *Disability in Industrial Britain: a cultural and literary history of impairment in the coal industry, 1880–1948* (2019).

34 *Parliamentary Debates*, 1 March 1927: The level of detail included issues such as the number of men suffering from nystagmus in collieries worked using oil lamps compared with those using electric ones. *Parliamentary Debates*, 28 June 1927: The number of men aged over 60 working in the industry and the use of safety detonators, and accidents during the process of shot-firing. *Parliamentary Debates*, 20 March 1928: The use of pit ponies and their treatment underground. *Parliamentary Debates*, 5 April 1927, 22 May 1928.

35 *Parliamentary Debates*, 5 June 1928.

36 *Parliamentary Debates*, 21 June 1928, 28 September 1928.

37 *Parliamentary Debates*, 21 June 1928.

38 *Parliamentary Debates*, 11 May 1927, 11 May 1926.

39 *Parliamentary Debates*, 2 March 1927, 5 April 1927, 21 June 1927, 13 March 1928, 20 March 1928, 3 April 1928, 28 November 1928, 29 January 1929, 13 March 1929, 14 March 1929, 18 March 1929, 10 May 1929.

40 *Parliamentary Debates*, 12 July 1927.

41 Ibid.

42 *Parliamentary Debates*, 12 July 1927, 20 March 1928, 3 April 1928.

43 *Parliamentary Debates*, 21 June 1928.

44 *Parliamentary Debates*, 18 May 1927.

45 *Parliamentary Debates*, 1 December 1927.

46 *Parliamentary Debates*, 1 December 1927, 10 September 1928.

47 *Parliamentary Debates*, 6 December 1927, 22 December 1927.

48 NLW, Thomas Jones MSS, H7.20, *Second Annual Report of the Council of Social Service for South Wales and Monmouthshire*.

49 *Western Mail*, 17 January 1928. NLW, Thomas Jones MSS, H7.24, H7.25, H7.41. Their activities included distributing items of clothing, boots and blankets and the development of an infrastructure by which that could be done. E. L. Ellis, *T. J., a Life of Thomas Jones C.H.* (Cardiff, 1992).

50 *Western Mail*, 13 December 1928. *Cambrian*, 14 December 1928.

51 Labour Party, *The Distress in South Wales, report of the Labour Party committee of inquiry* (London, 1928).

52 *Parliamentary Debates*, 8 November 1928.

53 *Parliamentary Debates*, 25 March 1929.

54 *Parliamentary Debates*, 8 November 1928.

55 *Parliamentary Debates*, 24 February 1926, 8 November 1928.

56 *Parliamentary Debates*, 8 November 1928.

57 *Daily Herald*, 7 February 1927.

58 *Daily Herald*, 28 October 1928. See also reports on 10 January 1925, 14 March 1925, 20 April 1925.

59 *Daily Herald*, 10 March 1927.

60 *Daily Herald*, 20 April 1927, 10 March 1927.

61 *Daily Herald*, 8 April 1927, 20 April 1927.

62 *Daily Herald*, 8 April 1927. *Cambrian*, 22 April 1927.

63 *Parliamentary Debates*, 2 August 1926, 14 March 1927, 28 March 1927, 12 December 1927.

64 *Parliamentary Debates*, 14 March 1927, 28 July 1927. When the Indian Navy Act was passed to create an Indian navy, he elicited the startling revelation that not one of the 131 officers commissioned into the Royal Indian Marine were of Indian birth, as all the commissioned offers were Europeans. He blamed the situation on the fact that the 1927 Act did not put the navy under the control of the Indian Legislative assembly and denounced the result as a British navy imposed on the Indians.

65 *Parliamentary Debates*, 25 March 1929.

66 *Parliamentary Debates*, 22 March 1929, 25 March 1929.

67 Ross Terrill, *R. H. Tawney and his times, Socialism and Fellowship* (London, 1974).

68 *Cambrian*, 25 January 1929.

69 *South Wales Daily Post*, 22 May 1929, 29 May 1929.

70 *South Wales Daily Post*, 29 May 1929.

71 For example Welwyn, *Daily Herald*, 1 May 1928; and Bath, *Daily Herald*, 4 February 1929.

72 *South Wales Daily Post*, 10 May 1929, 22 May 1929, 24 May 1929.

73 John Shepherd, Jonathan Davis, and Chris Wrigley (eds), *Britain's Second Labour Government, 1929–31, a reappraisal* (Manchester, 2012).

74 *Western Mail*, 31 March 1934.

75 *Western Mail*, 21 February 1930, 24 February 1930, 16 May 1930.

76 *Parliamentary Debates*, 17 December 1929.

77 R. Page Arnot, *The Miners in Crisis and War* (London, 1961).

78 South Wales Miners' Library, Minutes of MGFB Executive, 16 July 1930, 17 July 1930.

79 South Wales Miners' Library, Minutes of SWMF Executive, 29 November 1930.

80 South Wales Miners' Library, Minutes of SWMF Executive, 1 December 1930, 2 December 1930.

81 South Wales Miners' Library, Minutes of SWMF Executive, 5 December 1930. Minutes of SWMF Special Conference, 13 December 1930.

82 On 17 January 1931, the agreement was accepted by 169 to 72. South Wales Miners' Library, Minutes of SWMF Executive, 30 December 1930, 5 January 1931, 7 January 1931, 8 January 1931, 9 January 1931, 10 January 1931, 17 January 1931.

83 This was produced by a committee consisting of Aneurin Bevan, Tom Cope, Duncan Graham, Gordon Macdonald and Tom Williams.

84 *Daily Herald*, 15 June 1931.
85 Russell Galbraith, *Without Quarter, A Biography of Tom Johnston* (Edinburgh, 1995).
86 *South Wales Daily Post*, 24 August 1931.
87 Ibid.

Chapter 6: The Statesmen are Criminals Themselves
1   *South Wales Daily Post*, 7 October 1931, 12 October 1931, 14 October 1931, 20 October 1931, 22 October 1931.
2   Ibid.
3   *South Wales Daily Post*, 7 October 1931, 12 October 1931, 14 October 1931, 20 October 1931, 22 October 1931. Miss Dillwyn, moving his adoption, warned the electors not to put the country at the mercy of the TUC and the ILP.
4   *South Wales Daily Post*, 22 October 1931.
5   *South Wales Daily Post*, 22 October 1931.
6   *South Wales Daily Post*, 15 October 1931.
7   *South Wales Daily Post*, 17 October 1931.
8   *South Wales Daily Post*, 15 October 1931.
9   Ibid.
10 Chris Bryant, *Stafford Cripps the first modern Chancellor* (London, 1997). Simon Burgess, *Stafford Cripps a Political Life* (London, 1999).
11 *South Wales Daily Post*, 16 October 1931, 17 October 1931.
12 *South Wales Daily Post*, 16 October 1931.
13 Ibid.
14 Eric Davies, *A Biography of Daniel Hopkin* (Carmarthen, 1991).
15 *Cambrian*, 31 October 1931.
16 *Daily Herald*, 21 November 1925. Edgar Lansbury, *George Lansbury, My Father* (London, 1934). Kenneth O. Morgan, *Labour People, Leaders and Lieutenants, Hardie to Kinnock* (Oxford, 1987).
17 Ben Pimlott, *Labour and the Left in the 1930s* (Cambridge, 1977).
18 *Labour Party Annual Conference Report*, 1932.
19 This was reconstituted to bring together representatives of the Labour Party NEC, the PLP Executive and the TUC General Council. D. R. was to serve on the body for much of the ensuing decade. Alan Bullock, *Ernest Bevin* (London, 2002). Kenneth O. Morgan, *Labour People Leaders and Lieutenants Hardie to Kinnock* (Oxford, 1987).
20 *Parliamentary Debates*, 12 November 1931, 19 November 1931, 30 November 1931, 1 December 1931.
21 *Parliamentary Debates*, 1 December 1931, 8 December 1931, 26 February 1932, 2 March 1932, 3 March 1932, 9 March 1932. 16 March 1932, 17 March 1932, 18 March 1932, 21 March 1932, 6 April 1932, 28 October 1932, 1 November 1932. He later led for the opposition in the debate over subsidies for agricultural labourers' wages, 17 November 1931. *Daily Worker*, 21 November 1931.

22 *Parliamentary Debates*, 4 December 1931.
23 *Parliamentary Debates*, 4 December 1931, 10 December 1931, 7 July 1932. John Williams, *Was Wales Industrialised? Essays in Modern Welsh History* (Llandysul, 1995). Sidney Pollard, *The Development of the British Economy, 1914–1967* (London, 1969).
24 *Parliamentary Debates*, 5 February, 1932, 16 February 1932. *Daily Herald*, 25 February 1932. *Daily Worker*, 27 February 1932.
25 *Parliamentary Debates*, 5 February 1932.
26 *Daily Herald*, 16 June 1932, 28 September 1932, 3 November 1932. See also *Parliamentary Debates*, 4 May 1932, 13 May 1932, 23 May 1932.
27 *Parliamentary Debates*, 28 October 1932, 3 November 1932.
28 *Parliamentary Debates*, 3 November 1932. D. R. put similar arguments in debates over import duties, the Exchange Equalisation Act, reduction of certain duties in 1933 and the World Economic Conference, 1933.
29 Kenneth and Jane Morgan, *Portrait of a Progressive, the political career of Christopher, Viscount Addison* (Oxford, 1980).
30 *Parliamentary Debates*, 13 March 1933. Although in the final division Liberals, like Isaac Foot, his son Dingle, Geoffrey Mander, Francis Acland, and D. O. Evans, voted with the PLP, the Bill went through with a large majority for the government.
31 *Parliamentary Debates*, 23 November 1933.
32 Ibid.
33 *Parliamentary Debates*, 4 February 1932.
34 *Parliamentary Debates*, 25 February 1932, 7 March 1932, 9 March 1932, 12 April 1932.
35 *Parliamentary Debates*, 18 October 1932, 26 October 1932.
36 *Parliamentary Debates*, 12 November 1931. *Daily Herald*, 26 May 1932, 22 June 1933, 9 April 1934.
37 *Western Mail*, 24 September 1932.
38 This resulted in closer working over issues such as the UAB regulations and policy in the Special Areas. *Parliamentary Debates*, 7 December 1931, 8 December 1931, 9 February 1932, 16 November 1933.
39 West Glamorgan Archives, D. R. Grenfell Papers 1, Box 1, file of correspondence and notes.
40 Ibid.
41 J. Beverley Smith, *James Griffiths and His Times* (Cardiff, 1977). D. Ben Rees, *Jim Griffiths, Arwr Glew y Werin* (Talybont, 2014).
42 The Coal Miners Minimum Wage Act, 1912, had established a minimum wage for all underground workers, other than those specifically omitted under district rules or other provisions. This resulted in a 'levelling-up' of wages in several districts, and it guaranteed a minimum wage in case of abnormal working conditions. The average annual wage of men employed in the industry was £82 in 1913, rising £105 in 1932, an increase of 19 per cent However, during the same period, the cost of living was estimated to

have risen by 42 per cent, with the result that the miners' representatives estimated that an addition of £11 would be required to restore wages to the pre-war level. This loss of earnings was despite an increase in the average output per person.

43 Coal Mines Minimum Wage Amendment, 1933. *Parliamentary Debates*, 3 March 1933.

44 Order dated 16th day of October, 1931, made by the Minister of Labour under Section 35 of the Unemployment Insurance Act, 1920.

45 *Parliamentary Debates*, 26 November 1931.

46 Ibid.

47 *Parliamentary Debates*, 26 November 1931. John Campbell, *Nye Bevan and the Mirage of British Socialism* (London, 1987). Michael Foot, *Aneurin Bevan, a Biography, Vol. I, 1897–1945* (London, 1962); *Vol. II, 1945–1960* (London, 1973).

48 *Parliamentary Debates*, 11 April 1932, 26 May 1932.

49 The Transitional Payments Prolongation (Unemployed Persons) Bill.

50 *Parliamentary Debates*, 11 April 1932.

51 *Parliamentary Debates*, 11 April 1932, 14 November 1932. *Western Mail*, 12 November 1932, 15 November 1932.

52 *Parliamentary Debates*, 14 November 1932.

53 Ibid.

54 *Western Mail*, 26 February 1932, 14 March 1932, 4 April 1932.

55 *Western Mail*, 26 February 1932, 12 March 1932.

56 *Western Mail*, 12 March 1932.

57 Sian Rhiannon Williams, 'The Bedwellty Board of Guardians and the Default Act of 1927', *Llafur*, 2, No. 4 (1979).

58 *Western Mail*, 2 April 1932, 3 Janaury 1933.

59 *Western Mail*, 10 January 1933. *Western Mail*, 23 January 1933.

60 Kenneth Harris, *Attlee* (London, 1995). John Bew, *Citizen Clem, A Biography of Attlee* (London, 2016).

61 *Parliamentary Debates*, 7 December 1931, 2 February 1932, 8 February 1932, 9 February 1932, 7 March 1932, 25 April 1932, 24 October 1932, 12 December 1932, 7 January 1933, 13 February 1933. *Daily Herald*, 8 February 1932, 15 February 1932, 7 March 1932, 23 May 1932, 30 May 1932, 27 June 1932, 26 November 1932, 28 November 1932.

62 *Parliamentary Debates*, 24 March 1932. *Daily Herald*, 8 May 1932.

63 *Parliamentary Debates*, 27 March 1933.

64 *Parliamentary Debates*, 28 March 1933.

65 *The Scotsman*, 18 September 1934.

66 *Daily Express*, 27 February 1932.

67 Ibid.

68 *Daily Herald*, 6 June 1932, 28 January 1937. Duncan Tanner, Chris Williams, and Deian Hopkin (eds) *The Labour Party in Wales, 1900–2000* (Cardiff, 2000).

69 *Daily Herald*, 28 January 1937.

70 *Daily Herald*, 17 March 1932. Russell Galbraith, *Without Quarter, a biography of Tom Johnston* (Edinburgh, 1995).

71 *Daily Herald*, 22 September 1932. West Glamorgan Archives, D. R. Grenfell papers 2, Diaries. Howard C. Jones, 'The Labour Party in Cardiganshire', *Ceredigion*, Vol. 9 (1981).

72 *South Wales Tribune*, 10 June 1933, 17 June 1933. These issues included articles by D. Graham Pole on India and Ithel Davies on the menace of war and why workers should say no. D. R. was one of its most frequent contributors, along with fellow MPs Morgan Jones and Ted Williams, and prominent campaigners like the Rev. Daniel Hughes of Machen.

73 *South Wales Tribune*, 26 May 1933.

74 *South Wales Tribune*, 3 June 1933, 10 June 1933, 24 June 1933.

75 John R. Alban, 'Municipal Administration and Politics from the 1830s to 1974' in Glanmor Williams (ed.), *Swansea: an illustrated history* (Swansea, 1990).

76 *The Spot*, 15 February 1935, 15 May 1935, 17 July 1935.

77 *South Wales Evening Post*, 1 June 1936. *Western Mail*, 1 June 1936.

78 *South Wales Evening Post*, 16 November 1937.

79 *Western Mail*, 30 October 1933.

80 *Herald of Wales*, 3 June 1933.

81 *Daily Herald*, 24 November 1931.

82 *Daily Herald*, 13 December 1932. West Glamorgan Archives, D. R. Grenfell papers, Box 1, file of correspondence and notes.

83 *Western Mail*, 29 July 1933.

84 London School of Economics, Papers of the Fabian Society, J/23/3.

85 National Library of Wales, Forestry Commission Annual Report, 1937, 1938, 1939.

Chapter 7: Labour Calls for Power

1 *Daily Herald*, 24 September 1934.

2 *Daily Herald*, 8 October 1934.

3 West Glamorgan Archives, D. R. Grenfell Papers, Box 8, files on Gresford disaster.

4 *Daily Worker*, 16 April 1936.

5 Ibid.

6 *Liverpool Echo*, 5 February 1935.

7 *News Chronicle*, 8 July 1935.

8 *Northern Daily Mail*, 6 July 1935.

9 *Daily Worker*, 21 September 1935.

10 *Daily Worker*, 12 September 1936.

11 *Llwchwr Gazette*, 9 March 1934.

12 South Wales Miners' Library, Minutes of SWMF Executive, 4 January 1934, 13 April 1934, 14 April 1934.

13 *Western Mail*, 27 August 1934.

14 Neil Evans, 'South Wales has been roused as never before: marching against the means test, 1934–36', in K. O. Morgan and D. W. Howell (eds), *Crime, Protest and Police in Modern British Society: Essays in Memory of David J. V. Jones* (Cardiff, 1999).

15 South Wales Miners' Library, Minutes of the SWMF Executive, 5 January 1935. The date for the conference was set for 26 January 1935. *Western Mail*, 28 January 1935, 13 February 1935.

16 *Llais Llafur*, 9 February 1935.

17 *South Wales Evening Post*, 19 January 1935.

18 *Western Mail*, 1 February 1935, 3 February 1935.

19 *Llais Llafur*, 9 February 1935.

20 *South Wales Evening Post*, 18 February 1935. *Daily Herald*, 18 February 1935.

21 *South Wales Evening Post*, 18 February 1935.

22 *South Wales Evening Post*, 6 February 1935.

23 *Sheffield Independent*, 17 May 1935.

24 *Parliamentary Papers*, 1933–34, XIII.

25 *Parliamentary Papers*, 1933–34, XIII. The report on West Cumberland and Haltwhistle was undertaken by the Rt Hon. L.C.C. Davidson, Chancellor of the Duchy of Lancaster; Durham and Tyneside by Captain D. Euan Wallace, Civil Lord of the Admiralty; South Wales and Monmouth by Lt Col. Sir William Portal, and Scotland by Lt Col. Sir Arthur Rose.

26 According to Portal, the plight of the area was worse when it was realised that the official unemployment figure of 53,000 did not include those who had changed jobs on a temporary basis. Therefore, he estimated that the total deficiency of jobs in south Wales could be placed at 81,000.

27 The report recommended that ICI should be encouraged to investigate the possibility of developing hydrogenation plants. It supported undertaking experimental work in relation to gas road vehicles and it also suggested examining coal-exporting agreements with Italy on the lines of the recent agreement with Scandinavia which had benefited the North-East at the expense of south Wales.

28 *Parliamentary Papers*, 1934–35, X.

29 *Parliamentary Debates*, 14 November 1934.

30 *Parliamentary Papers*, 1934–35, X.

31 The government introduced legislation which compelled every person under the age of 18, who was not in full-time employment, to attend some form of education or training.

32 More than a third, 28,490 (35.3%), of the unemployed had been out of work for more than three years, 44,250 for more than two years, and 9,384 for more than five years. For example, in Blaina and Merthyr Tydfil, those unemployed for over four years accounted for 21.2% and 23.1% respectively, and the problem of finding employment was

particularly present among men over the age of 46. *Parliamentary Papers*, 1934–35, X.

33 *Parliamentary Debates*, 12 November 1936, 9 March 1937.

34 *Western Mail*, 26 February 1932, 13 May 1932. Hilary Marquand, *South Wales Needs a Plan* (London, 1936); also his work as Director of *Second Industrial Survey of South Wales* (Cardiff, 1937). Ted Rowlands, *Something Must Be Done, South Wales v Whitehall, 1921–1951* (Merthyr Tydfil, 2000).

35 West Glamorgan Archives, D. R. Grenfell papers 1, Box 6, file on reconstruction and unemployment. These files contain references to the way certain information had been withheld from Marquand.

36 *Western Mail*, 2 August 1935.

37 West Glamorgan Archives, D. R. Grenfell papers 1, Box 7, file of articles by D. R.

38 *Llwchwr Gazette*, 9 March 1934.

39 David Grenfell, *Labour's Way to Plan Prosperity* (London, 1935). He had emphasised these themes continually since 1931 at public gatherings across Britain. On May Day 1934, he was in Coventry at the annual gathering of the Warwickshire Federation of Labour Parties where he dealt with the potential of production and the problems caused by under-consumption. *Daily Herald*, 7 May 1934.

40 *Daily Herald*, 4 January 1935.

41 *Daily Herald*, 15 June 1931.

42 *Western Mail*, 17 July 1935. David Wainwright, *Men of Steel, The History of Richard Thomas and his Family* (London, 1986).

43 *Hull Daily Mail*, 17 July 1935.

44 *Daily Herald*, 26 July 1935.

45 *Parliamentary Debates*, 18 July 1935.

46 *Western Mail*, 23 October 1935, 24 October 1935.

47 *Western Mail*, 14 November 1935. *South Wales Evening Post*, 6 November 1935.

48 *Western Mail*, 27 March 1936, 6 April 1936.

49 *Western Mail*, 9 April 1936. On 4 April 1936 the Mayor of Swansea, Cllr A. R. Ball, convened a conference of local authorities to discuss the issue.

50 *Western Mail*, 23 April 1936, 24 April 1936.

51 *Daily Herald*, 30 May 1936.

52 *Western Mail*, 27 May 1936.

53 *Western Mail*, 28 May 1936.

54 *Western Mail*, 11 January 1937, 26 January 1937.

55 Richard Lewis, *Leaders and Teachers, Adult Education and the Challenge of Labour in South Wales, 1906–1940* (Cardiff, 1993).

56 *Daily Herald*, 26 July 1935.

57 *Western Mail*, 30 November 1933.

58 *Daily Herald*, 3 June 1935, 13 June 1935.

59 *Parliamentary Debates*, 22 November 1934.
60 *Daily Herald*, 23 November 1934.
61 *Parliamentary Debates*, 23 March 1933.
62 Ibid.
63 Ibid.
64 *Parliamentary Debates*, 7 November 1933.
65 *Parliamentary Debates*, 7 November 1933, 29 January 1934.
66 *Parliamentary Debates*, 19 March 1935. *Daily Herald*, 20 March 1935. Parliamentary Labour Party, Executive Minutes, 28 March 1935.
67 *Daily Herald*, 23 October 1935.
68 West Glamorgan Archives, D. R. Grenfell Papers 1, Box 9, notes for autobiography.
69 Kenneth Harris, *Attlee* (London, 1995). John Bew, *Citizen Clem, A Biography of Attlee* (London, 2016).
70 *South Wales Evening Post*, 6 November 1935.
71 *Western Mail*, 5 November 1935. *South Wales Evening Post*, 7 November 1935.
72 *South Wales Evening Post*, 2 November 1935.
73 Ibid.
74 *South Wales Evening Post*, 7 November 1935.
75 *South Wales Evening Post*, 5 November 1935.
76 *Herald of Wales*, 5 November 1935. *South Wales Evening Post*, 6 November 1935.
77 *Daily Herald*, 7 November 1935.

Chapter 8: A Remarkable and Gifted Man

1 West Glamorgan Archives, D. R. Grenfell Papers 2, Diaries, especially entry for 26 November 1935.
2 Kenneth Harris, *Attlee* (London, 1995). John Bew, *Citizen Clem, A Biography of Attlee* (London, 2016).
3 A. J. Sherman, *Island Refuge Britain and Refugees from the Third Reich, 1933–1939* (London, 1977). Elwyn Jones, *In My Time* (London, 1983); *The Battle for Peace* (London, 1938).
4 Anson Rabinbach, *The Crisis of Austrian Socialism, from Red Vienna to Civil War, 1927–1934* (London, 1983).
5 *Daily Herald*, 20 March 1934.
6 *Daily Worker*, 23 March 1934. His findings confirmed the dilemma in which the NCL was placed. The Society of Friends were permitted to operate in Austria because they did not take political allegiances into account when distributing relief, but this meant that money raised by the Labour movement in Britain could be used to relieve those who were part of pro-government paramilitary organisations as well as those on the Left.
7 *Daily Herald*, 27 December 1935. *Daily Worker*, 5 March 1936.
8 *Llwchwr Gazette*, 20 January 1936.

9   *Llwchwr Gazette*, 10 July 1936.
10 *Herald of Wales*, 12 October 1935.
11 *Parliamentary Debates*, 6 December 1935. *Daily Worker*, 7 December 1935.
12 R. Page Arnot, *The Miners in Crisis and War* (London, 1961). Hywel Francis and David Smith, *The Fed, a history of the South Wales Miners in the twentieth century* (London, 1980).
13 *Western Mail*, 9 October 1935.
14 *Parliamentary Debates*, 6 December 1935.
15 *Daily Worker*, 7 January 1936.
16 *Labour*, March 1936.
17 Report of Royal Commission on Safety in Coal Mines.
18 Witnesses were examined in 52 sessions held between 10 February 1936 and 27 April 1937, running to 1,500 pages of evidence. There were 36,954 questions and answers, including a compendium of legislation affecting coal mining in other countries produced by the ILO.
19 *Daily Worker*, 26 February 1936, 11 March 1936, 19 May 1936, 20 May 1936, 1 July 1936, 28 July 1936, 20 October 1936, 24 March 1937. *Daily Herald*, 11 February 1936.
20 *Daily Worker*, 21 April 1936, 19 May 1936. *Daily Herald*, 10 March 1936, 24 March 1936.
21 *Daily Worker*, 3 November 1936.
22 *Daily Worker*, 7 April 1936.
23 Ibid.
24 *Daily Worker*, 8 April 1936.
25 *Daily Herald*, 21 April 1936.
26 *Daily Worker*, 11 February 1936.
27 *Daily Worker*, 22 April 1936. *Daily Herald*, 4 November 1936.
28 *Daily Worker*, 27 January 1937.
29 *Western Mail*, 16 June 1936.
30 *Belfast Newsletter*, 7 February 1936.
31 West Glamorgan Archives, D. R. Grenfell papers 1, Box 8. D. R. had annotated comments to a transcript of the hearing now held among the D. R. Grenfell Papers.
32 *Parliamentary Debates*, 9 April 1936.
33 Ibid.
34 Ibid.
35 *Daily Worker*, 13 May 1936.
36 South Wales Miners' Library, Minutes of SWMF Executive, 11 July 1936.
37 *Daily Worker*, 29 August 1936. *Daily Herald*, 31 August 1936.
38 *South Wales Evening Post*, 19 January 1935.
39 *Parliamentary Debates*, 9 November 1936.
40 Ibid.

41 Ibid.

42 Ibid.

43 Kenneth Harris, *Attlee* (London, 1995). John Bew, *Citizen Clem, A Biography of Attlee* (London, 2016).

44 *Daily Herald*, 20 July 1935, 25 July 1935.

45 Labour History Archive and Study Centre, Papers of William Gillies, LP/WG/IND/277.

46 *Daily Worker*, 5 February 1936. *Daily Herald*, 4 February 1936.

47 *Daily Herald*, 4 January 1936.

48 *Daily Herald*, 6 February 1936, 7 February 1936.

49 *Parliamentary Debates*, 21 November 1938.

50 *Daily Herald*, 24 March 1936. *Daily Worker*, 24 March 1936, 7 November 1936.

51 *Daily Worker*, 26 June 1936.

52 *Daily Herald*, 29 June 1936.

53 This committee consisted of representatives of the various signatories, including Britain, France, Portugal, Spain and Germany. Tony Kushner and Katharine Knox, *Refugees in an Age of Genocide, global, national and local perspectives during the twentieth century* (London, 1999).

54 Hywel Francis, *Miners Against Fascism, Wales and the Spanish Civil War* (London, 1984).

55 *Daily Mirror*, 6 October 1936.

56 Report of Labour Party Annual Conference, 1936.

57 *Daily Mirror*, 6 October 1936.

58 Daryl Leeworthy, *Labour Country, Political Radicalism and Social Democracy in South Wales, 1831–1985* (Cardigan, 2018). I am grateful to him for drawing my attention to these comments in the NCL Minutes.

59 South Wales Miners' Library, Minutes of MFGB Executive, 11 December 1936.

60 *Daily Herald*, 19 October 1936. Consequently, as far as the public was concerned, there was little to differentiate his comments from those of Greenwood, Wedgewood Benn and A. V. Alexander.

61 *Daily Herald*, 19 November 1936. Its members included Seymour Cocks, W. P. Crawford Greene, Lt Col. D. W. James, Captain J. R. J. McNamara and Wilfred Roberts.

62 *Daily Worker*, 20 November 1936.

63 *Daily Worker*, 26 November 1936.

64 Ibid.

65 *Daily Worker*, 18 December 1936.

66 Ibid.

67 Ibid.

68 *Daily Herald*, 18 December 1936. *Parliamentary Debates*, 19 January 1937.

69 *Daily Herald*, 8 December 1936, 17 December 1936.

70 *Daily Herald*, 17 December 1936.

71 *Daily Worker*, 18 December 1936.

Chapter 9: A Man of Real Ability

1   Thomas Jones' note of observations by Lloyd George about Labour front bench, June 1937, in Thomas Jones, *A Diary with Letters 1931–1950* (Oxford, 1954), p.351.

2   *Daily Worker*, 12 December 1936.

3   *Daily Herald*, 21 December 1936, 22 December 1936, 7 January 1937.

4   *Daily Worker*, 22 December 1936, 14 January 1937. *Daily Herald*, 12 January 1937.

5   *Daily Worker*, 18 February 1937, 20 February 1937.

6   *Labour*, January 1937.

7   *Parliamentary Debates*, 19 January 1937.

8   Ibid.

9   Ibid.

10 *Parliamentary Debates*, 17 March 1937.

11 *Labour*, March 1937.

12 *Parliamentary Debates*, 20 April 1937. Hywel Francis, *Miners Against Fascism, Wales and the Spanish Civil War* (London, 1984).

13 *Parliamentary Debates*, 20 April 1937.

14 Ibid.

15 *Parliamentary Debates*, 6 May 1937.

16 Ibid.

17 *Daily Herald*, 9 August, 1937.

18 *Daily Worker*, 24 August 1937. The signatories included Vyvyan Adams MP, Katharine Atholl MP, C. S. Bristol, Henry Carter CBE, F. Seymour Cocks MP, Hugh Dalton MP, T. E. Harvey MP, Walter Layton CBE, Gilbert Murray LittD, FRSL, Eleanor Rathbone MP, Wilfrid Roberts MP, Francis Underhill DD, Dean of Rochester, Violet Bonham-Carter, J. Scott Lidgett CH, and Julian S. Huxley.

19 Tony Kushner and Katharine Knox, *Refugees in an Age of Genocide: Global, National and Local Perspectives during the Twentieth Century* (London, 1999).

20 Born in Barry in 1904, Betty Morgan was a graduate of the University of Wales and the Sorbonne. She had worked for Lloyd George's propaganda department and was herself a Liberal parliamentary candidate for seats in England and had worked as a special correspondent, mainly for the *News Chronicle*, specialising in articles on social conditions in Britain and the role of women in business and industry.

21 *Herald of Wales*, 10 July 1937, 2 October 1937. Harry Stratton, *To Anti Fascism By Taxi* (Port Talbot, 1984).

22 *Herald of Wales*, 31 July 1937.

23 *Herald of Wales*, 31 July 1937, 2 October 1937, 4 December 1937.
24 *Daily Herald*, 1 July 1937. D. R. was present at the conference on Spain organised by the Birmingham Labour Party in July 1937 which passed a resolution denouncing non-intervention as a 'crime against democracy'.
25 *Daily Herald*, 8 October 1937.
26 *Labour Party Annual Conference Report*, 1937.
27 *Daily Herald*, 23 October 1937, 28 October 1937.
28 *Daily Worker*, 18 November 1937, 26 November 1937. Earlier that day, D. R. had also addressed a meeting at the Lyceum Theatre in Newport. For the Bristol meeting, see *Daily Worker*, 11 December 1937. *Herald of Wales*, 4 December 1937.
29 *Parliamentary Debates*, 2 February 1938, 4 April 1938, 18 May 1938.
30 *Daily Herald*, 2 February 1938.
31 *Parliamentary Debates*, 21 February 1938.
32 *Daily Herald*, 21 February 1938.
33 *Parliamentary Debates*, 21 June 1938. *Daily Herald*, 22 June 1938.
34 *Western Mail*, 24 May 1937, 21 June 1937.
35 *Daily Herald*, 5 September 1935.
36 *Daily Worker*, 6 July 1936.
37 *Daily Worker*, 11 July 1936.
38 *Daily Worker*, 11 July 1936. For Frank Roper, see *Neath Guardian*, 17 December 1948.
39 *Daily Worker*, 19 April 1937.
40 Ibid.
41 Ithel Davies, *Bwrlwm Byw* (Llandysul, 1984), pp.166–7.
42 *Parliamentary Debates*, 23 February 1937.
43 *Daily Worker*, 24 February 1937.
44 *Parliamentary Debates*, 23 February 1937.
45 Ibid.
46 Ibid.
47 Ibid.
48 *Daily Herald*, 10 February 1937.
49 *Daily Worker*, 23 February 1937. *Daily Herald*, 24 February 1937, 23 March 1937.
50 *Western Mail*, 8 June 1937, 11 June 1937, 12 June 1937, 14 June 1937.
51 *Parliamentary Debates*, 25 July 1938. *Daily Worker*, 26 July 1938, 27 July 1938. *Daily Herald*, 25 July 1938.
52 *Daily Herald*, 26 July 1938. D. R. had attended the inquiry into the explosion at Markham No. 1 Colliery, near Chesterfield in Derbyshire, where 79 men had lost their lives on 10 May 1938. Along with Jim Griffiths, he drew comparison between the high rate of accidents in Britain and the situation in other countries, the new perils created by mechanisation, and the effects of working at ever-greater depths.
53 *Report of the Royal Commission on Safety in Mines* (London, 1938).

54 *Parliamentary Debates*, 27 July 1938. *Daily Herald*, 28 July 1938.

55 *Parliamentary Debates*, 1 February 1939.

56 This was undertaken in stages and the Coal (Registration of Ownership) Act, 1937, began the process of establishing a register of ownership of mineral interests.

57 *Parliamentary Debates*, 22 November 1937.

58 *Parliamentary Debates*, 13 December 1937.

59 Ibid.

60 *Parliamentary Debates*, 3 February 1938.

61 *Parliamentary Debates*, 25 July 1938.

62 Ibid.

63 Ibid.

64 *Daily Herald*, 26 July 1938.

65 *Parliamentary Papers*, 1936–37, XII. Kenneth O. Morgan, *Rebirth of a Nation, Wales 1880–1980* (Oxford, 1981). Ted Rowlands, *Something Must Be Done, South Wales v Whitehall, 1921–1951* (Merthyr Tydfil, 2000).

66 *Parliamentary Papers*, 1936–37, XII.

67 *Parliamentary Papers*, 1940, X.

68 *Parliamentary Papers*, 1936–37, XII. *Parliamentary Papers*, 1937–38, XII. *Parliamentary Papers*, 1938–39, XII.

69 *Parliamentary Papers*, 1937–38, XII. *Parliamentary Papers*, 1938–39, XII. The Commissioner provided assistance with the development of trading estates, most notably the development at Treforest and smaller sites at Dowlais, Llantrisant and Cyfarthfa. *Parliamentary Papers*, 1936–37, XII. *Parliamentary Papers*, 1937–38, XII.

70 *Parliamentary Debates*, 26 April 1937.

71 Ibid.

72 *Parliamentary Debates*, 26 April 1937. Steven Thompson, *Unemployment, Poverty and Health in Interwar South Wales* (Cardiff, 2006). John Davies, 'Y Gydwybod Gymdeithasol yng Nghymru rhwng y Ddau Ryfel Byd', in G. H. Jenkins (ed.), *Cof Cenedl IV* (Llandysul, 1989).

73 *Parliamentary Debates*, 29 April 1937.

74 *Parliamentary Debates*, 8 June 1937.

75 Ibid.

76 Ibid.

77 Ibid.

78 *Llwchwr Gazette*, 17 January 1936.

79 Kenneth O. Morgan, *Rebirth of a Nation, Wales 1880–1980* (Oxford, 1981). Gwilym Prys Davies, *Cynhaeaf Hanner Canrif, Gwleidyddiaeth Cymru 1945–2005* (Llandysul, 2006). Gwilym Prys Davies, *Llafur y Blynyddoedd* (Dinbych, 1991). Gwynoro Jones, *Whose Wales? The battle for Welsh devolution and nationhood, 1880–2020* (Gorseinon, 2021).

80 *Western Mail*, 1 July 1938.
81 *Western Mail*, 28 July 1938.
82 Ibid.

Chapter 10: Freiheit!
1 Freiheit was the battlecry of the Left-wing opposition to Hitler in the Sudetenland.
2 F. Elwyn Jones, *The Battle for Peace* (London, 1938). Wenzel Jaksch, *Sudeten Labour and the Sudeten Problem*. Anson Rabinbach, *The Crisis of Austrian Socialism, from Red Vienna to Civil War, 1927–1934* (London, 1983).
3 Wenzel Jaksch, *Sudeten Labour and the Sudeten Problem*, p.40.
4 *Daily Worker*, 18 February 1938.
5 *Daily Herald*, 8 March 1938.
6 The National Archives, CO 323 1607/9, Emigration from Czechoslovakia and Sudetenland. Wenzel Jaksch, *Europe's Road to Potsdam* (London, 1963).
7 A few days later, following reports sent by Jaksch to the Labour Party NEC, Lord Snell and George Latham MP were sent to meet other members of the Socialist International, which they did, as they gathered at the funeral of J. Lonquet in Paris on 27 September. Later the same month, Dalton met the leaders of the French Socialist Party and the CGT to discuss the situation. *Labour Party Annual Conference Report*, 1939.
8 *Parliamentary Debates*, 28 September 1938.
9 *Daily Herald*, 30 September 1938.
10 R. Page Arnot, *The Miners in Crisis and War* (London, 1961). For reports of the views within the SWMF, see *The Scotsman*, 3 October 1938. Likewise, the LSI denounced the Munich Agreement for augmenting the strength of the dictators, militarily, economically and morally, and for weakening European democracy. National Archives, CO 323 1607/9, Emigration from Czechoslovakia and Sudetenland.
11 *Labour Party Annual Conference Report*, 1939. Labour convened a large demonstration at Earl's Court stadium which was addressed by Attlee, Dalton, Charles Dukes, and Barbara Ayrton-Gould, and a broadcast message was sent to the German people in an attempt to succour the Socialist opposition to the Nazis. *Daily Herald*, 27 September 1938.
12 *Parliamentary Debates*, 5 October 1938.
13 Ibid.
14 This enabled more than 15,000 refugees to be brought to Britain in the following six months, of whom 2,500 were Sudeten Germans and 1,000 were Reich Germans or Austrians. This was in addition to thousands more who were helped to travel directly to destinations in the Dominions, through a government gift of £4million.

15 West Glamorgan Archives, D. R. Grenfell Papers 2, Diaries.

16 Telegram No. 944 from British Embassy, Prague, to Foreign Office, 12 October 1938. The National Archives, CO 323 1607/9, Emigration from Czechoslovakia and Sudetenland.

17 Telegram No. 947 from British Embassy, Prague, to Foreign Office, 12 October 1938. The National Archives, CO 323 1607/9, Emigration from Czechoslovakia and Sudetenland.

18 The National Archives, CO 323 1607/9, Emigration from Czechoslovakia and Sudetenland. Edward Abel Smith, *Active Goodness* (London, 2017).

19 Wenzel Jaksch and Walter Kolarx in *England and the Last Free Germans* (London, 1941).

20 *Daily Herald*, 25 October 1938.

21 Wenzel Jaksch and Walter, Kolarx, *England and the Last Free Germans* (London, 1941).

22 Edward Abel Smith, *Active Goodness* (London, 2017). At that point it was unclear to the Foreign Office how the refugees would be taken out of Czechoslovakia: a route through Poland to Warsaw was one possibility; another involved various routes through Romania, Hungary and Yugoslavia. Telegram to Sir M. Palaired, Bucharest, Sir H. Kennard, Warsaw, Sir G. Knox, Budapest, and Sir Campbell, Belgrade, from the Foreign Office on 18 October. The National Archives, CO 323 1607/9, Emigration from Czechoslovakia and Sudetenland.

23 The National Archives, CO 323 1607/9, Emigration from Czechoslovakia and Sudetenland.

24 Interview with Brynmor Grenfell.

25 Wenzel Jaksch and Walter, Kolarx, *England and the Last Free Germans* (London, 1941), p.49.

26 The National Archives, CO 323 1607/9, Emigration from Czechoslovakia and Sudetenland.

27 Telegram No. 999 from British Embassy, Prague, to Foreign Office, 26 October 1938, The National Archives, CO 323 1607/9, Emigration from Czechoslovakia and Sudetenland.

28 *Parliamentary Debates*, 21 November 1938.

29 *Daily Herald*, 22 November 1938.

30 *Parliamentary Debates*, 7 February 1939.

31 Ibid.

32 Ibid.

33 Wenzel Jaksch, *Sudeten Labour and the Sudeten Problem* (London, 1945), p.40.

34 *Parliamentary Debates*, 15 March 1939.

35 Ibid.

36 Ibid.

37 Ibid.

38 Ibid.
39 Ibid.
40 Ibid.
41 *Daily Herald*, 16 March 1939.
42 *Daily Express*, 16 March 1939.
43 Ibid.
44 *Daily Herald*, 17 June 1939. Kathy Talbot, 'The Painter and the Politician: Ernest Neuschul and D. R. Grenfell MP', *Journal of the Gower Society*, 53 (2002). Andrew Green, 'A Czech refugee artist in Mumbles', https://gwallter.com, accessed 20 November 2023.
45 *Western Mail*, 6 May 1940.
46 *Parliamentary Debates*, 4 May 1939.
47 *Parliamentary Debates*, 11 May 1939.
48 Ibid.
49 Ibid.
50 *Parliamentary Debates*, 5 September 1939, 14 September 1939.
51 *Parliamentary Debates*, 14 September 1939, 15 September 1939.
52 *Daily Mirror*, 14 September 1939.
53 *Daily Herald*, 4 October 1939.
54 *Daily Herald*, 31 October 1939, 2 November 1939.
55 *Daily Herald*, 13 December 1939. *Western Mail*, 4 December 1939. *Llwchwr Gazette*, 12 January 1940.
56 *Llwchwr Gazette*, 12 January 1940.
57 *Llwchwr Gazette*, 5 July 1940.
58 *Welsh Gazette*, 31 October 1940.
59 *Western Mail*, 26 January 1940.
60 *Western Mail*, 29 February 1940.
61 Ibid.
62 *Western Mail*, 21 March 1940, 26 March 1940.

Chapter 11: Let Your Work Proclain Your Worth
1   R. Page Arnot, *The Miners in Crisis and War* (London, 1961). Report of Labour Party NEC, 10 May 1940. *Daily Express*, 27 June 1940. Notwithstanding such misgivings, the NCL agreed that Labour MPs should be allowed to enter the government, subject to their being answerable to the party.
2   Kenneth O. Morgan, *Labour People, Leaders and Lieutenants Hardie to Kinnock* (Oxford, 1987). Alan Bullock, *Ernest Bevin* (London, 2002).
3   *Western Mail*, 20 May 1940. Previous Secretaries of Mines had also been responsible for petroleum but, at the creation of the new government, the roles were separated, and the Tory Geoffrey Lloyd became Parliamentary Secretary with responsibility for petroleum.
4   *Western Mail*, 16 May 1940.
5   *The Scotsman*, 16 May 1940. *Liverpool Echo*, 16 May 1940. *Yorkshire Post*, 16 May 1940.

6   *Western Daily Press*, 20 May 1940, *Western Mail*, 22 May 1940.

7   *Glamorgan Gazette*, 21 June 1940.

8   *Western Mail*, 17 June 1940. R. Page Arnot, *The Miners in Crisis and War* (London, 1961).

9   *Western Mail*, 21 May 1940, 23 May 1940.

10 *Western Mail*, 20 May 1940.

11 Ibid.

12 R. Page Arnot, *The Miners in Crisis and War* (London, 1961).

13 The MFGB had demanded a new standard that took account of the increase in the cost of living since 1914, as well as a bonus for disabled men. R. Page Arnot, *The Miners in Crisis and War* (London, 1961).

14 R. Page Arnot, *The Miners in Crisis and War* (London, 1961).

15 The National Archives, POWE 20/52.

16 *Western Mail*, 27 May 1940, 24 June 1940.

17 *Western Mail*, 30 May 1940.

18 Cited in R. Page Arnot, *The Miners in Crisis and War* (London, 1961), p.303.

19 R. Page Arnot, *The Miners in Crisis and War* (London, 1961), p.304.

20 *Daily Worker*, 26 June 1940, 16 July 1940, 23 July 1940.

21 Alan Bullock, *Ernest Bevin* (London, 2002).

22 The National Archives, LAB 8/1473, History of labour supply from May 1940.

23 Ibid.

24 *Daily Worker*, 17 July 1940. Wayne David, *Remaining True, a Biography of Ness Edwards* (Caerphilly, 2006).

25 *Daily Worker*, 8 July 1940, 12 July 1940, 17 July 1940.

26 South Wales Miners' Library, MFGB, Minutes of Annual Conference, 1940.

27 *Daily Worker*, 17 July 1940. A subsidy scheme was introduced to enable collieries affected by loss of export markets to continue production, *Daily Worker*, 12 December 1940.

28 The National Archives, LAB 8/1473, History of labour supply from May 1940.

29 *Daily Worker*, 24 August 1940.

30 The National Archives, LAB 8/1473, History of labour supply from May 1940. West Glamorgan Archives, D. R. Grenfell Papers 1, Box 6, D. R. to Bevin, 27 June 1940.

31 West Glamorgan Archives, D. R. Grenfell Papers 1, Box 6, Bevin to Grenfell, 9 July 1940.

32 The National Archives, LAB 8/1473, History of labour supply from May 1940. These included 1,500 Durham miners and 2,100 men from south Wales (mainly to West and South Yorkshire) However, a far greater number (more than 15,000) were placed in other industries.

33 The National Archives, LAB 8/1473 History of labour supply from May 1940.

34 Ibid.
35 *Parliamentary Debates*, 5 September 1940.
36 Ibid.
37 Ibid.
38 Ibid.
39 Ibid.
40 Ibid.
41 The National Archives, LAB 8/1473, History of labour supply from May 1940.
42 Ibid.
43 South Wales Miners' Library, Minutes of MFGB Executive. *Daily Mirror*, 26 September 1940.
44 South Wales Miners' Library, Minutes of MFGB Executive, September 1940. R. Page Arnot, *The Miners in Crisis and War* (London, 1961).
45 R. Page Arnot, *The Miners in Crisis and War* (London, 1961). South Wales Miners' Library, Minutes of MFGB Executive, September 1940.
46 South Wales Miners' Library, Minutes of MFGB Executive, October 1940.
47 The National Archives, LAB 8/1473, History of labour supply from May 1940.
48 West Glamorgan Archives, D. R. Grenfell Papers 1, Box 6.
49 *Daily Mirror*, 22 June 1940. *Daily Worker*, 10 December 1940.
50 South Wales Miners' Library, Minutes of SWMF Executive, 9 November 1940. The National Archives, LAB 8/1473, History of labour supply from May 1940. I am grateful to Douglas Davies (Saron), Benny Williams (Ammanford), Bill Murphy (Garnant), and Ken Williams (Cwmgwili) for considerable information on the situation in the Anthracite Area during this period.
51 The National Archives, LAB 8/1473, History of labour supply from May 1940. *Daily Worker*, 20 November 1940.
52 *Daily Express*, 6 November 1940. *Daily Worker*, 12 November 1940. The National Archives, LAB 8/1473, History of labour supply from May 1940.
53 The National Archives, LAB 8/1473, History of labour supply from May 1940.
54 *Daily Express*, 4 November 1940.
55 Ibid.
56 Ibid.
57 The National Archives, LAB 8/1473, History of labour supply from May 1940.
58 Ibid.
59 West Glamorgan Archives, D. R. Grenfell papers, Box 7, file re Mines Department. Particular reference is made to speeches in Rowenstall, Lancs; Mansfield, Notts, and to the SWMF. *Daily Worker*, 25 May 1940.

60 *Daily Record*, 19 March 1941. *The Scotsman*, 20 March 1941. R. Page Arnot, *A History of the Scottish Miners* (London, 1955).

61 *Daily Worker*, 16 October 1940. West Glamorgan Archives, D. R. Grenfell papers 1, Box 6.

62 *Daily Herald*, 9 April 1941.

63 *Daily Herald*, 20 February 1941, 25 March 1941.

64 *Parliamentary Debates*, 19 February 1941.

65 South Wales Miners' Library, Minutes of MFGB Executive, 17 January 1941. The National Archives, LAB 8/1473, History of labour supply from May 1940.

66 *Daily Express*, 1 February 1941.

Chapter 12: I Am Glad I Trusted My Own Judgement

1 The National Archives, PREM 4/9/5, Memorandum from D. R., 8 April 1941.

2 R. Page Arnot, *The Miners in Crisis and War* (London, 1961). Hywel Francis and David Smith, *The Fed, a history of the South Wales Miners in the twentieth century* (London, 1980).

3 *Daily Herald*, 4 April 1941.

4 South Wales Miners' Library, Minutes of MFGB Executive, 10 April 1941. R. Page Arnot, *The Miners in Crisis and War* (London, 1961).

5 Ibid.

6 South Wales Miners' Library, Minutes of MFGB Executive, 10 April 1941.

7 Ibid.

8 *Daily Herald*, 22 May 1941, 23 May 1941. National Archives, LAB 8/1473, History of labour supply from May 1940.

9 The National Archives, LAB 8/1473, History of labour supply from May 1940.

10 South Wales Miners' Library, Minutes of MFGB Executive, 1 May 1941. Minutes of MFGB Special Conference, 8–9 May 1941.

11 Ibid.

12 Ibid.

13 The National Archives, LAB 8/413. Horner's key role is outlined in Nina Fishman, *Arthur Horner, a political biography* (London, 2010), pp.449–52.

14 *Parliamentary Debates*, 28 May 1941.

15 Ibid.

16 South Wales Miners' Library, Minutes of the National Joint Standing Consultative Committee, 21 May 1941, printed with MFGB Executive Committee Minutes, The National Archives, LAB 8/413.

17 R. Page Arnot, *The Miners in Crisis and War* (London, 1961).

18 The National Archives, LAB 8/413.

19 Ibid.

20 Ibid.

21 The National Archives, LAB 8/413. Once again, he cited evidence that there were 16,000 miners who were classified as 'temporarily stopped', especially in the Anthracite Area, who could be deployed to other mines. Former miners, deemed unfit through injury, could be re-employed in the industry, he argued.

22 The National Archives, LAB 8/413.

23 Ibid.

24 Ibid.

25 Ibid.

26 *Daily Express*, 24 June 1941.

27 *Daily Herald*, 29 July 1941. H. R. S. Phillpott, on behalf of the *Daily Herald*, called for men to be brought back to the industry as the only way to counter the prodution crisis. 'The pits have been stripped of men. These men – the coal producers – must be sent back.'

28 The National Archives, LAB 8/1473, History of labour supply from May 1940.

29 *Daily Herald*, 18 June 1941.

30 Churchill College Cambridge, Churchill Archive, Char/20/34/9, Clement Attlee to Churchill, 18 July 1941.

31 The National Archives, LAB 8/1473, History of labour supply from May 1940. Regulations dated 16 June 1941.

32 The National Archives, LAB 8/1473, History of labour supply from May 1940. I am grateful to Douglas Davies, Saron, Ammanford, for his insights into this issue and the men's subsequent experiences while working in England.

33 South Wales Miners' Library, Minutes of MFGB Annual Conference, 14 July 1941.

34 The National Archives, LAB 8/1473.

35 South Wales Miners' Library, Minutes of MFGB Executive, 11 September 1941.

36 Ibid.

37 R. Page Arnot, *The Miners in Crisis and War* (London, 1961).

38 The National Archives, LAB 8/1473.

39 South Wales Miners' Library, Minutes of MFGB Executive, 25 February 1942.

40 Nina Fishman, *Arthur Horner, a political biography* (London, 2010), pp.453–4.

41 The National Archives, CAB 75/14/32.

42 West Glamorgan Archives, D. R. Grenfell Papers 1, Box 6, memorandum to Ernest Gowers, dated 22 January 1942.

43 When the memorandum was passed on by Gowers to Capt Leighton Davies, the latter expressed considerable sympathy with its contents.

44 West Glamorgan Archives, D. R. Grenfell Papers 1, Box 6, memorandum to Ernest Gowers, dated 22 January 1942.

45 South Wales Miners' Library, Minutes of MFGB Executive, 8 January 1942, 22 May 1942.
46 South Wales Miners' Library, Minutes of MFGB Executive, 12 March 1942. Underground workers were provided with some additional rations, but this did not apply to surface workers.
47 *Daily Herald*, 13 May 1942.
48 *Daily Express*, 29 January 1942. *Daily Mirror*, 28 January 1942. *Daily Herald*, 28 January 1942.
49 *Daily Herald*, 30 January 1942, 3 February 1942.
50 *Daily Herald*, 7 May 1942.
51 The National Archives, LAB 8/461, Absenteeism and Amendment of EWO.
52 *Daily Herald*, 1 June 1942.
53 The National Archives, LAB 8/461, Absenteeism and Amendment of EWO.
54 *Newcastle Evening Chronicle*, 30 April 1942.
55 *Daily Herald*, 15 May 1942.
56 *Daily Mirror*, 30 May 1942.
57 The National Archives, LAB 8/1473, History of labour supply from May 1940.
58 Ibid.
59 Ibid.
60 Ibid.
61 The National Archives, PREM 4/9/5.
62 *Daily Herald*, 22 April 1942.
63 The National Archives, LAB 8/1473 History of labour supply from May 1940.
64 Ibid.
65 South Wales Miners' Library, Minutes of MFGB Executive, 8 January 1942. The wider dissatisfaction with the White Paper was reflected by Arthur Horner who summarised the men's grievances in the summer of 1942: the miners were being treated unfairly in comparison with other workers, the number of men employed in the industry was insufficient for the task expected of them, the mood of the men would never be improved while the mine owners continued to profit at their expense.
66 Ben Pimlott, *Hugh Dalton* (London, 1985), p.352.
67 LSE Archives, Hugh Dalton's Diaries available on-line https://lse-atom.arkivum.net/uklse-dl1hd01, entry for 2 March 1942.
68 Ibid.
69 Ben Pimlott, Hugh Hugh Dalton (London, 1985), p.352.
70 LSE Archives, Hugh Dalton's Diaries available on-line https://lse-atom.arkivum.net/uklse-dl1hd01, entry for 4 March 1942.
71 LSE Archives, Hugh Dalton's Diaries available on-line https://lse-atom.arkivum.net/uklse-dl1hd01, entry for 19 March 1942.

72 Ibid.
73 LSE Archives, Hugh Dalton's Diaries available on-line https://lse-atom. arkivum.net/uklse-dl1hd01, entry for 20 March 1942.
74 LSE Archives, Hugh Dalton's Diaries available on-line https://lse-atom. arkivum.net/uklse-dl1hd01, entry for 25 March 1942.
75 LSE Archives, Hugh Dalton's Diaries available on-line https://lse-atom. arkivum.net/uklse-dl1hd01, entry for 30 March 1942.
76 LSE Archives, Hugh Dalton's Diaries available on-line https://lse-atom. arkivum.net/uklse-dl1hd01, entry for 10 April 1942.
77 LSE Archives, Hugh Dalton's Diaries available on-line https://lse-atom. arkivum.net/uklse-dl1hd01, entry for 6 May 1942.
78 *Daily Express*, 27 February 1942.
79 Nina Fishman, *Arthur Horner, a political biography* (London, 2010), p.457.
80 Ibid., p.437.
81 Ibid., p.448.
82 Ibid, pp.453, 457.
83 David Carlton, *MacDonald versus Henderson, the foreign policy of the second Labour government* (London, 1970).
84 LSE Archives, Hugh Dalton's Diaries available on-line https://lse-atom. arkivum.net/uklse-dl1hd01, entry for 1 July 1940, 10 July 1940, 25 November 1940, 21 January 1942.
85 LSE Archives, Hugh Dalton's Diaries available on-line https://lse-atom. arkivum.net/uklse-dl1hd01, entry for 11 March 1942.
86 Ben Pimlott, *Hugh Dalton* (London, 1985).
87 Nina Fishman, *Arthur Horner, a political biography* (London, 2010).
88 Bodleian Library Archives and Manuscripts, Papers of Clement Richard Attlee, Dep 51/96, letter from D. R. Grenfell.
89 South Wales Miners' Library, Minutes of MFGB Annual Conference, 20 July 1942.
90 *Daily Express*, 25 July 1942.
91 West Glamorgan Archives, D. R. Grenfell papers 1, Box 6, D. R. to Clement Attlee, 13 November 1942.
92 West Glamorgan Archives, D. R. Grenfell Papers, Box 9, file of broadcast materials.

Chapter 13: The Labour Movement Stands for Liberty

1 *Daily Herald*, 3 May 1943. BBC Written Archives Centre, Caversham, Welsh Miscellaneous Contributor Files. D. R. contributed to at least one instalment of *The Week at Westminster* produced by Guy Burgess who concluded, 'what an obliging and vey nice fellow he is', before adding that he was, 'too heavy in the hand for the kind of commentary we have come to expect in this series'.
2 *Western Mail*, 19 April 1943.
3 West Glamorgan Archives, D. R. Grenfell Papers 1, Box 6. This

included a plan which D. R. had endorsed, to work the Ilston seam more effectively. Minutes of MFGB Executive, 8 August 1941.

4   West Glamorgan Archives, D. R. Grenfell Papers 1, Box 6, Memorandum on post-war reconstruction.

5   West Glamorgan Archives, D. R. Grenfell Papers 1, Box 9, Material re Gower Constituency.

6   Ibid.

7   The National Archives, LAB 8/1473, History of labour supply from May 1940.

8   *Parliamentary Debates*, 1 October 1942.

9   *Parliamentary Debates*, 6 October 1942.

10 *Parliamentary Debates*, 9 December 1942.

11 *Daily Herald*, 2 December 1942, 20 February 1943. *Western Mail*, 2 December 1942, 15 December 1942. Paul Addison, *The Road to 1945, British Politics and the Second World War* (London, 1977). Nicholas Timmins, *The Five Giants, a biography of the Welfare State* (London, 1995).

12 *Parliamentary Debates*, 18 February 1943.

13 Others involved in the rebellion included Jim Griffiths, Aneurin Bevan, W. G. Cove, S. O. Davies, Charles Edwards, W. H. Mainwaring, Ted Williams, and D. L. Mort, along with W. J. Gruffydd, Clement Davies, D. O. Evans, and Megan Lloyd George from the Liberal benches.

14 *Parliamentary Debates*, 20 May 1943.

15 Michael Foot, *Aneurin Bevan, a Biography, Vol. I, 1897–1945* (London, 1962). Other rebels included D. L. Mort, Charles Edwards, Ness Edwards, Aneurin Bevan, Sir William Jenkins, W. G. Clyne, George Daggar, Clement Davies, S. O. Davies, and W. H. Mainwaring from the Welsh Labour benches.

16 *Parliamentary Debates*, 19 May 1943.

17 Ibid.

18 Ibid.

19 Ibid.

20 A request from Wenzel Jaksch that a separate fund be set up specifically for the benefit of the Sudeten refugees had been rejected by Runciman.

21 Those accused included Yvonne Kapp (a biographer of Eleanor Marx), Margaret Mynath, George Musgrave, Binford Hale, Elizabeth Allan, Dennis Donson, Mrs Pennning Rowsell, Kate Thornycroft, Herman Field, and Vincent Duncan-Jones.

22 He told a rally organised by the Ministry of Fuel and Power at Ardwick, 'When I was Minister of Mines, I placed before the Government a complete scheme for the nationalisation of the mines, and drafted a miners' charter... I still feel that nationalisation is the solution of our mining problem.' *Daily Worker*, 11 October 1943, 12 October 1943.

23 *Parliamentary Debates*, 12 October 1943.

24 *Parliamentary Debates*, 13 October 1943.

25 *Daily Worker*, 14 October 1943.

26 *Parliamentary Debates*, 13 October 1943.

27 Ibid.

28 Ibid.

29 Ibid.

30 *Parliamentary Debates*, 27 October 1943. *Daily Worker*, 28 October 1943.

31 *Parliamentary Debates*, 27 October 1943. *Daily Herald*, 28 October 1943.

32 *Parliamentary Debates*, 27 October 1943. *Daily Worker*, 28 October 1943. The rebel MPs from Wales included Aneurin Bevan, W. G. Cove, George Dagger, Charles Edwards, Ness Edwards, W. H. Mainwaring and D. L. Mort, along with the expatriate Rhys Davies.

33 *Parliamentary Debates*, 1 December 1943.

34 *Parliamentary Debates*, 1 December 1943. *Daily Worker*, 2 December 1943.

35 *Parliamentary Debates*, 28 April 1944.

36 Ibid.

37 *Daily Mirror*, 29 April 1944. *Daily Herald*, 3 May 1944.

38 *Reynolds News*, 21 May 1944.

39 *Daily Worker*, 3 May 1944, 17 May 1944.

40 Paul Addison, *The Road to 1945, British Politics and the Second World War* (London, 1977).

41 *Parliamentary Debates*, 11 October 1944. *Daily Worker*, 12 October 1944.

42 *Labour Party Annual Conference Report*, 1944. *Daily Worker*, 15 December 1944.

43 *Daily Herald*, 24 February 1945.

44 *Western Mail*, 23 January 1945.

45 *Parliamentary Debates*, 29 May 1945. The committee was chaired by Sir Charles Reid, formerly of the Fife Colliery Co.

46 *Parliamentary Debates*, 29 May 1945.

47 *Daily Mirror*, 29 July 1944. *Daily Herald*, 29 July 1944. *Daily Worker*, 29 July 1944. These included Lord Farringdon, Seymour Cocks, George Daggar, Philip Price, Reg Sorensen, and George Strauss. D. R. had also joined 45 MPs calling for the creation of an international police force to settle disputes between countries.

48 *Parliamentary Debates*, 18 January 1945.

49 *Western Mail*, 31 May 1945, 5 June 1945.

50 *Western Mail*, 19 February 1945, 13 March 1945, 2 June 1945, 21 June 1945, 23 June 1945, 30 June 1945.

51 *Western Mail*, 11 June 1945, 12 June 1945.

52 Iwan Morgan was a member of a well-known Cardiganshire family and had connections in Gorseinon where he had lived when his father, J. J. Morgan, taught at Penyrheol school before becoming headteacher

of the higher grade school at Pontycymmer. For D. R.'s involvement in the campaign, see *Welsh Gazette*, 2 November 1944, 22 February 1945.

Chapter 14: You, As Our Leader
1 Aneurin Bevan, *Why Not Trust the Tories* (London, 1944).
2 West Glamorgan Archives, D. R. Grenfell Papers 1, Box 9, broadcasts.
3 *Aberdeen Press and Journal*, 1 November 1946.
4 West Glamorgan Archives, D. R. Grenfell papers 1, Box 9, correspondence.
5 *Daily Herald*, 28 December 1946. *The Scotsman*, 19 October 1945.
6 The National Archives, LAB 21/244, Training and Resettlement of Disabled Persons: Grenfell Factories. Steven Thompson, 'The living dead of the mining industry: Deindustrialisation, sheltered workplaces and the re-employment of disabled miners in post-war Wales', *Welsh History Review*, Vol. 31, No. 3, 2023.
7 The National Archives, LAB 21/244, Training and Resettlement of Disabled Persons: Grenfell Factories.
8 Steven Thompson, 'The living dead of the mining industry: Deindustrialisation, sheltered workplaces and the re-employment of disabled miners in post-war Wales', *Welsh History Review*, Vol. 31, No. 3, 2023.
9 *The Scotsman*, 19 October 1945.
10 Wenzel Jaksch, *Europe's Road to Potsdam* (London, 1963).
11 *Parliamentary Debates*, 26 October 1945. Kenneth O. Morgan, *Labour in Power, 1945–1951* (Oxford, 1984). Denis Healey, *My Secret Planet* (London, 1992). Edward Pearce, *Denis Healy, a life in our times* (London, 2002). Archie Potts, *Zilliacus, a Life for Peace and Socialism* (London, 1999). Robert Griffiths, *S. O. Davies: a Socialist faith* (Llandysul, 1983).
12 *Nottingham Journal*, 1 November 1945.
13 Kenneth O. Morgan, *Labour in Power, 1945–1951* (Oxford, 1984).
14 *Parliamentary Debates*, 13 December 1945.
15 Kenneth O. Morgan, *Labour in Power 1945–1951* (Oxford, 1984). Nicholas Timmins, *The Five Giants, a biography of the Welfare State* (London, 1995). Michael Sissons and Philip French (eds), *Age of Austerity, 1945–51* (Harmondsworth, 1964).
16 James Griffiths, *Glo* (Liverpool, 1945). William Ashworth, *The History of the British Coal Industry, Volume 5, 1946–1982, the nationalised industry* (Oxford, 1986).
17 D. R. Grenfell, *Coal* (London, 1947).
18 *Daily Herald*, 2 November 1948.
19 *Parliamentary Debates*, 23 March 1945. Under the Act, the Board of Trade was given responsibility for issuing Industrial Development Certificates, without which factory construction could not begin.
20 *Western Mail*, 7 September 1945, 30 October 1945, 29 January 1946.

21 *Western Mail*, 12 January 1946, 1 October 1946, 12 October 1946.

22 *Western Mail*, 2 February 1946.

23 *Daily Herald*, 8 December 1948.

24 *Parliamentary Debates*, 12 July 1946. Strauss said that the problems confronting the docks could be attributed directly to the iron and steel situation and that as much shipping as possible would be directed to south Wales.

25 *Daily Herald*, 8 December 1948.

26 *Western Mail*, 8 May 1946.

27 *Western Mail*, 23 May 1945, 8 November 1945, 10 May 1946, 17 July 1946.

28 *Western Mail*, 29 October 1946. The transfer scheme for people who had indicated they wanted to return to south Wales was designed to enable them to have a claim upon a job as soon as one became available. *Western Mail*, 13 April 1946.

29 *Y Cymro*, 26 October 1946. This was quoted by Ritchie Calder in a report in the *Daily Herald* during a tour of the Valleys in February 1941. *Daily Herald*, 18 February 1941. Kenneth O. Morgan, *Rebirth of a Nation, Wales 1880–1980* (Oxford, 1981).

30 *Y Cymro*, 1 March 1946. West Glamorgan Archives, D. R. Grenfell papers 1, Box 9, file re Secretary of State for Wales.

31 *Reynolds News*, 4 August 1946.

32 *Y Cymro*, 12 April 1946, 19 April 1946, 7 June 1946. Goronwy Roberts refused a post in government while Robert Richards refused the post of Governor of Malta over the issue.

33 *Y Cymro*, 17 May 1946. *Reynolds News*, 26 May 1946.

34 West Glamorgan Archives, D. R. Grenfell papers 1, Box 9 file re Secretary of State for Wales.

35 Ibid.

36 *Western Mail*, 15 February 1946.

37 West Glamorgan Archives, D. R. Grenfell papers 1, Box 9, letter from Clement Attlee, 31 May 1946.

38 *Western Mail*, 3 August 1946. *The Scotsman*, 15 August 1946.

39 *Y Cymro*, 9 August 1946.

40 *Y Cymro*, 23 August 1946.

41 West Glamorgan Archives, D. R. Grenfell papers 1, Box 9, file re Secretary of State for Wales.

42 West Glamorgan Archives, D. R. Grenfell Papers, Box 9, file re Secretary of State for Wales, Goronwy Roberts to D. R., October 1946.

43 *Daily Herald*, 11 October 1946. *Y Cymro*, 4 October 1946.

44 *Reynolds News*, 6 October 1946, 20 October 1946.

45 *Reynolds News*, 6 October 1946.

46 *Reynolds News*, 13 October 1946.

47 Ibid.

48 *Parliamentary Debates*, 28 October 1946. *Daily Herald*, 29 October 1946.

49 *Parliamentary Debates*, 28 October 1946.

50 *Reynolds News*, 1 November 1946.

51 *Western Mail*, 5 November 1946, 19 November 1946, 15 March 1947. *Daily Herald*, 9 December 1946. The proposals included taking 500 acres at Aberporth, 290 at Carew, 330 at Templeton, 450 at Dale, 370 at Tabenny, 430 at Brawdy, 181 at St Davids, and 42 at Withybush. A total of 16,000 acres was to be included at Mynydd Preseli. This was in addition to further parks at Aberaeron, Fforest Fawr (Carmarthenshire), Pembrey, Pendinam, Merthyr-Hirwaun, Abergavenny, Tredegar, Ebbw Vale and Radnor Forest.

52 *Y Cymro*, 31 January 1947.

53 *Western Mail*, 16 May 1947, 14 July 1947.

54 *Western Mail*, 31 January 1947, 22 February 1947, 3 June 1947, 6 June 1947, 17 October 1947. *Y Cymro*, 7 February 1947.

55 *Y Cymro*, 21 March 1947.

56 *Western Mail*, 24 March 1947. Gwyn Jenkins, *Prif Weinidog Answyddogol Cymru, Cofiant Huw T. Edwards* (Talybont, 2008).

57 West Glamorgan Archives, D. R. Grenfell papers 1, Box 9, file of correspondence.

58 *Western Mail*, 9 April 1947.

59 *Western Mail*, 14 November 1947.

60 *Western Mail*, 27 November 1947, 19 January 1948, 23 January 1948. *Y Cymro*, 30 January 1948.

61 *Western Mail*, 23 January 1948.

62 *Western Mail*, 24 March 1948, 10 April 1948, 5 June 1948, 3 January 1949, 5 April 1949, 9 May 1949, 30 May 1949.

63 *Western Mail*, 15 February 1949, 11 August 1949, 5 March 1950, 21 June 1950.

64 *Western Mail*, 1 April 1947.

65 *Daily Herald*, 19 March 1947.

66 *Parliamentary Debates*, 1 April 1947. Others included W. G. Cove, George Daggar, Will John, Percy Morris, Robert Richards, Goronwy Roberts, Emlyn Thomas, George Thomas, Tudor Watkins, and D. J Williams, several of their Scottish colleagues and others who were prominent in Keep Left and various other left-wing groups in the 1950s.

67 *Y Cymro*, 4 April 1947. He was not among those who voted against the third reading of the National Service Bill, May 1947, as he was not present.

68 *Y Cymro*, 11 April 1947.

69 *Parliamentary Debates*, 6 May 1947. Twenty-one MPs voted in favour of excluding Wales, including D. R. The other 20 were W. H. Ayles, Roderic Bowen, James Carmichael, W. G. Cove, Clement Davies, S. O. Davies, Rhys Davies, Lady Megan Lloyd George, W. J. Gruffydd, J. Hudson, Gordon Lang, F. Longden, H. McGee, John McGovern,

Percy Morris, Rhys Hopkin Morris, Emrys Roberts, Goronwy Roberts, Campbell Stephen, and D. J. Williams. *The Scotsman*, 7 May 1947.
70 Cited in Alan Bullock, *Ernest Bevin* (London, 2002), p.536.

Chapter 15: D. R. and the New Jerusalem

1   Duncan Burn, *The Steel Industry, 1939–1959, A study in competition and planning* (Cambridge, 1961).
2   Paul Jenkins, *Twenty By Fourteen, A History of the South Wales Tinplate Industry, 1700–1961* (Llandysul, 1995).
3   National Library of Wales, James Griffiths papers, file on Trostre. National Library of Wales, W. Douglas Hughes papers, letter from Jim Griffiths. *Western Mail*, 15 July 1947.
4   *Parliamentary Debates*, 19 June 1947.
5   *Western Mail*, 20 June 1947.
6   National Library of Wales, W. Douglas Hughes papers, letter from Jim Griffiths.
7   *Western Mail*, 14 July 1947.
8   Ibid.
9   *Western Mail*, 7 July 1947.
10 *Western Mail*, 27 June 1947.
11 *South Wales Evening Post*, 28 June 1947.
12 *Western Mail*, 7 July 1947.
13 *South Wales Evening Post*, 7 July 1947.
14 *South Wales Evening Post*, 28 June 1947.
15 *South Wales Evening Post*, 30 June 1947.
16 West Glamorgan Archives, D. R. Grenfell Papers 1, Box 3. *Western Mail*, 28 June 1947, 26 July 1947.
17 *Daily Mirror*, 7 July 1947.
18 *Parliamentary Debates*, 7 August 1947.
19 *Daily Herald*, 12 August 1947.
20 West Glamorgan Archives, D. R. Grenfell Papers 1, Box 3, Text of radio broadcast, 'Llangyfelach or Trostre', 9 September 1947.
21 Ibid.
22 *Parliamentary Debates*, 26 January 1948.
23 *Western Mail*, 1 December 1952.
24 *Y Cymro*, 18 November 1949.
25 Kenneth O. Morgan, *Labour in Power, 1945–1951* (Oxford, 1984). *South Wales Evening Post*, 3 September 1947, 8 September 1947.
26 *South Wales Evening Post*, 11 December 1947.
27 *South Wales Evening Post*, 12 September 1947.
28 *Western Mail*, 29 September 1947. *South Wales Evening Post*, 15 September 1947, 3 October 1947, 11 October 1947. He also addressed a public meeting at the Albert Hall on 30 September 1947.
29 *South Wales Evening Post*, 20 October 1947. *Parliamentary Debates*, 3 November 1947.

30 *South Wales Evening Post*, 8 December 1947.

31 Gower Divisional Labour Party, *Brochure to Celebrate Anniversary of Mr D. R. Grenfell's 25 Years as Member of Parliament* (Gorseinon, 1947). *Daily Herald*, 8 December 1947.

32 *Parliamentary Debates*, 28 May 1946.

33 West Glamorgan Archives, D. R. Grenfell papers 1, Box 1, file on Gower; Box 9, file of correspondence. *Parliamentary Debates*, 25 February 1943.

34 West Glamorgan Archives, D. R. Grenfell Papers 1, especially files in Box 1, Box 3, Box 7 and Box 9.

35 *Parliamentary Debates*, 3 November 1947. *Daily Herald*, 4 November 1947. This represented an extension of the Essential Works Order against which D. R. had rebelled, along with Bevan, in 1944 and had been criticised by Labour backbenchers in August 1945. Shinwell had agreed then that prosecution measures had not prompted attendance but, instead, undermined the goodwill that had prevailed in the industry. He agreed to consider the possible removal of the penal clause within the EWO.

36 *Daily Herald*, 4 November 1947.

37 *Parliamentary Debates*, 3 November 1947.

38 Ibid.

39 Ibid.

40 Ibid.

41 *Parliamentary Debates*, 3 November 1947. *Daily Herald*, 4 November 1947.

42 The National Archives, KV2/2048, Communists and Suspected Communists, including Russian and Communist Sympathisers.

43 *Daily Herald*, 26 April 1948. Aldo Agorti, *Palmiro Togliatti a biography* (London, 2008). Paul Ginsborg, *A History of Contemporary Italy, 1943–1980* (London, 1990).

44 *Neath Guardian*, 7 May 1948. W. G. Cove declared that he would comply with the NEC decision at the end of April. S. O. Davies was also threatened with disciplinary action. Robert Griffiths, *S. O. Davies, a Socialist Faith* (Llandysul, 1983).

45 Bodleian Library Archives and Manuscripts, Papers of Clement Richard Attlee, Dep 70/108, letter from D. R. Grenfell. Kenneth O. Morgan, *Callaghan, a life* (Oxford, 1997).

46 Ibid.

47 *Gloucestershire Echo*, 7 May 1948. *Northern Whig*, 30 June 1948.

48 Gordon Schaffer, *Baby in the Bathwater: memoirs of a political journalist* (Lewes, 1996). John Saville, *The Politics of Continuity, British Foreign Policy and the Labour Government, 1945–46* (London, 1993). R. H. S. Crossman, Michael Foot, and Ian Mikardo, *Keep Left* (London, 1947). Archie Potts, *Zilliacus, a Life for Peace and Socialism* (London, 1999). Eugene J. Meehan, *The British Left Wing and Foreign*

Policy: a study of the influence of ideology (New Brunswick, 1960). Ian Mikardo, *Back-bencher* (London, 1988).

49 *Llais Llafur*, 10 April 1948.
50 West Glamorgan Archives, D. R. Grenfell Papers 1, Box 3, WCL memorandum.
51 *Daily Herald*, 25 November 1948. Gwyn Jenkins, *Prif Weinidog Answyddogol Cymru, Cofiant Huw T. Edwards* (Talybont, 2008).
52 *Western Mail*, 30 November 1948.
53 *Western Mail*, 17 October 1948, 27 November 1948, 3 January 1949.
54 West Glamorgan Archives, D. R. Grenfell Papers 1, Box 9.
55 *Western Mail*, 6 January 1949, 30 March 1949, 4 April 1949.
56 In south Wales, in particular, a pattern of ownership had evolved whereby individual householders leased land on which to build private dwellings as owner-occupiers. The prevalence of 99-year leases meant that many of those whose houses had been built during the Victorian era would soon be at the mercy of the system.
57 *Parliamentary Debates*, 11 February 1938, Leasehold Property (Repairs) Bill.
58 *Parliamentary Debates*, 11 February 1938.
59 West Glamorgan Archives, D. R. Grenfell Papers 1, Box 4, materials on leasehold reform.
60 Ibid.
61 West Glamorgan Archives, D. R. Grenfell Papers 1, Box 6, materials on leasehold reform.
62 D. R. Grenfell, *A Plea for Leasehold Enfranchisement* (Gorseinon, 1950).
63 A conclusion that one of its members, Roderic Bowen, the Welsh Liberal MP for Cardiganshire, was never allowed to forget by his Labour opponents in the county.
64 West Glamorgan Archives, D. R. Grenfell Papers 1, Box 5, broadcasts.
65 BBC Archives, Llandaff, Minutes of the Welsh Advisory Committee.
66 John Davies, *Broadcasting and the BBC in Wales* (Cardiff, 1994).
67 *Liverpool Echo*, 16 June 1948. Ben Pimlott, *Harold Wilson* (London, 1992).
68 *Western Mail*, 18 September 1943, 9 December 1943, 19 April 1945, 28 October 1947.
69 *Liverpool Daily Post*, 14 August 1945, 12 November 1945.
70 *Western Mail*, 7 May 1946, 9 May 1946, 23 October 1947, 30 October 1947.
71 *Western Mail*, 2 December 1946, 13 May 1947, 17 September 1947, 27 October 1947.
72 *Western Mail*, 4 December 1947, 15 January 1948.
73 *Western Mail*, 24 February 1948, 20 March 1948.
74 *Western Mail*, 20 March 1948.

75 West Glamorgan Archives, D. R. Grenfell Papers 1, Box 7, Welsh Tourist Board. *Western Mail*, 11 May 1948, 3 July 1948.

76 *Western Mail*, 17 July 1948.

77 *Western Mail*, 15 July 1948, 29 July 1948, 10 August 1948, 12 August 1948, 7 September 1948.

78 *Western Mail*, 17 July 1948, 7 September 1948, 7 May 1949. *Hull Daily Mail*, 12 September 1949.

79 *Western Mail*, 3 January 1950, 22 April 1950, 31 August 1950, 27 October 1950, 17 April 1951, 6 June 1951.

80 *Western Mail*, 7 September 1949.

81 *Western Mail*, 25 January 1949, 26 January 1949.

82 *Western Mail*, 4 March 1949, 30 October 1950.

83 *Western Mail*, 19 December 1949.

84 *Western Mail*, 18 March 1950, 5 August 1950.

85 *Western Mail*, 23 September 1950.

86 *Western Mail*, 16 November 1950.

Chapter 16: Father of the House

1 West Glamorgan Archives, D. R. Grenfell Papers 1, Box 5, visit to Canada and the United States.

2 *Western Mail*, 30 March 1949, West Glamorgan Archives, D. R. Grenfell papers 1, Box 5.

3 *Parliamentary Debates*, 5 December 1950.

4 *Parliamentary Debates*, 21 March 1951.

5 *Parliamentary Debates*, 17 May 1950.

6 Kenneth O. Morgan, *Labour in Power, 1945–51* (Oxford, 1984).

7 West Glamorgan Archives, D. R. Grenfell Papers, Box 5, visits to Australia and New Zealand.

8 West Glamorgan Archives, D. R. Grenfell papers, Box 5.

9 I am grateful to twin brothers, the late Cllr Harry Thomas, Gowerton, and the late Cllr Morlais Thomas, Gorseinon, for background information on George Manning.

10 Michael Foot, *Aneurin Bevan, a Biography, Vol II, 1945–1960* (London, 1973). Mark Jenkins, *Bevanism, Labour's High Tide* (London, 1979).

11 Mark Jenkins, *Bevanism, Labour's High Tide* (London, 1979).

12 *Daily Herald*, 7 March 1952.

13 *Daily Herald*, 5 July 1952.

14 *Daily Herald*, 20 November 1953.

15 West Glamorgan Archives, D. R. Grenfell Papers 1, Box 1, broadcasts. The tribute to Churchill was dated 30 January 1954. The comment on Churchill was reported 4 May 1925.

16 *Daily Herald*, 17 April 1953, 23 November 1953.

17 *Daily Herald*, 23 November 1953.

18 Ibid.

19 West Glamorgan Archives, D. R. Grenfell Papers 1, Box 1.

20 West Glamorgan Archives, D. R. Grenfell Papers, Box 1, circular by Gwent Jones, 22 July 1953.

21 *Western Mail*, 1 December 1952.

22 *Parliamentary Debates*, 22 January 1953. The impact of industrial changes is discussed in T. Brennan, E. W. Cooney, and H. Pollins, *Social Change in South-West Wales* (London, 1954).

23 *Parliamentary Debates*, 22 January 1953.

24 *Llwchwr Gazette*, 21 May 1954.

25 West Glamorgan Archives, D. R. Grenfell Papers, Box 7, file of correspondence.

26 *Parliamentary Debates*, 30 June 1954.

27 This arose from the Knockshinnock disaster in Scotland. *Parliamentary Debates*, 30 June 1954.

28 *Parliamentary Debates*, 1 July 1954.

29 *Parliamentary Debates*, 2 July 1954.

30 Gwilym Prys Davies, *Cynhaeaf Hanner Canrif, Gwleidyddiaeth Cymru, 1945–2005* (Llandysul, 2006); *Llafur y Blynyddoedd* (Dinbych, 1991). Gwynoro Jones and Alun Gibbard, *Whose Wales, the politics of Welsh devolution and nationhood, 1880–2020* (Gorseinon, 2021). Robert Griffiths, *S. O. Davies, A Socialist Faith* (Llandysul, 1983).

31 Robert Smith, *Hanes Libanus, Gorseinon* (Gorseinon, 2012).

32 National Library of Wales, E. T. John papers, 4074, letter from D. R. Grenfell to E. T. John.

33 *Western Mail*, 23 September 1952. Robert Griffiths, *S. O. Davies, A Socialist Faith* (Llandysul, 1983).

34 National Library of Wales, Labour Party Wales archive, File 28.

35 Ibid.

36 Ibid.

37 Ibid.

38 *Western Mail*, 3 March 1954.

39 National Library of Wales, Labour Party Wales papers, File 28.

40 *Western Mail*, 12 May 1954.

41 *South Wales News*, 14 May 1954.

42 *Western Mail*, 31 May 1954.

43 *Parliamentary Debates*, 4 March 1955.

44 National Library of Wales, Gwynfor Evans papers, G1/18, letter from D. R. Grenfell to Gwynfor Evans.

45 National Library of Wales, Goronwy Roberts papers, C 1/4, letter from D. R. Grenfell.

46 I am grateful to Roy Harris, Glanaman, previously of Pontardawe, for sharing his recollections of this period when he was active in the Labour Party in the Swansea Valley. T. R. Lloyd, Les Higgon, Vernon Davies, Phil Davies, E. James Thomas, D. Raymond James, and Eric Davies also provided valuable information about the context of Labour politics in the Llwchwr area in this period.

47 *Parliamentary Debates*, 28 October 1946.
48 *Daily Mirror*, 9 December 1955.
49 *Daily Express*, 9 December 1955.
50 West Glamorgan Archives, D. R. Grenfell Papers 1, Box 9, constituency correspondence.
51 West Glamorgan Archives, D. R. Grenfell Papers 1, Box 1, constituency correspondence. The men employed there had been redeployed to Abecrave (110), Varteg (30), and Ynyscedwyn (58).
52 West Glamorgan Archives, D. R. Grenfell Papers 1, Box 5, correspondence.
53 West Glamorgan Archives, D. R. Grenfell Papers 1, Box 1.
54 West Glamorgan Archives, D. R. Grenfell Papers 1, Box 1, Box 9.
55 *Llwchwr Star*, 31 May 1958.
56 *Llwchwr Star*, 14 March 1957.
57 *Llwchwr Star*, 1 April 1957.
58 I am grateful to T. R. Lloyd, Kingsbridge, Gorseinon, for his insight into these events.
59 *Parliamentary Debates*, 31 July 1958.
60 *Western Mail*, 21 March 1959.
61 *Manchester Guardian*, 24 June 1959.
62 *Western Mail*, 21 September 1959.
63 West Glamorgan Archives, D. R. Grenfell Papers 1, Box 5. *South Wales Evening Post*, 20 July 1961.

Chapter 17: A Man Not Easily Moved
1 *The Times*, 26 November 1968.
2 *Manchester Guardian*, 27 November 1968.

Index

Morris, Rhys Hopkin 143, 332, 347
Morrison, Herbert 128, 176, 199, 226, 243, 277, 289, 299–300, 302, 307, 324, 328, 358, 385–7, 405
Mort, D. L. 332, 341, 343, 347, 350
Mosley, Sir Oswald 121, 300–2, 370, 407
Mountain Colliery 21, 32, 37, 40–1, 44, 54–5, 66, 70, 319, 348, 397
Murray, Andrew 99
Mussolini, Benito 104, 171–2, 177, 203, 206

N
National Coal Board (NCB) 318–19, 358, 371, 387
National Council of Labour (NCL) 128, 190, 195, 205, 229, 289
National Industrial Development Council for Wales and Monmouthshire 219–20, 368
National Joint Committee for Spanish Relief 198, 203
National Service Bill (1947) 337, 373
National Union of Railwaymen (NUR) 67, 102
Nehru, Jawaharlal 190–1
Nenni, Pietro 353
Nethercoat, E. T. 88, 114
Neuschul, Ernest 236
New Fabian Research Bureau 146, 176
New Zealand 110, 240–2, 271–2, 353, 372
Newbolt, Walton 64
News Chronicle 228–30
Newton, Sir Basil 229
Nicholas, Rev. T. E. (Niclas y Glais) 48, 75
Nicholas, Sir Walter 90
No Conscription Fellowship (NCF) 48–9, 59, 79
Non-intervention Committee 206
North Wales Coalfield 148, 212, 277–8
North Wales Mineworkers' Union (NWMU) 148, 212
North Wales Resorts Association 367
Nova Scotia 34–7

O
Ormerod, Mary 294
Ormond, John 363

Ottawa 369
Ottawa Agreement 128–9

P
Paling, Wilfred 248, 386
Parker, John 176–9, 301
Parry, Cyril 384
Pearson, Colonel 54–5
Pearson, J. 267
Pensions and Determination of Needs Bill (1943) 292
Penuel Chapel, Loughor 24
Phillips, Evan 311
Phillips, G. Tracey (Ammanford) 311
Philpott, H. R. S. 218
Pimlott, Ben 127, 281
Platts-Mills, John 352
Pollitt, Harry 206
Pontarddulais 19–24, 31, 38, 41–2, 45–6, 48, 64, 69, 104,115, 144–5, 193, 212, 289, 341, 345, 384, 387–9
Pontardulais Co–operative Society 27
Pontypridd Divisional Labour Party 336–7
Popular Front (France) 194, 201
Popular Front (Spain) 193, 196
Portal, Sir Wyndham 156, 166, 244, 247
Prague 177, 225–6, 229–232, 235, 294–5
Prieto, Indalecio 196
Pritchard Hughes, Rev. Joshua 109
Prohibition Bill 82
Prothero, Cliff 357, 381

Q
Quebec 369

R
Randall, David 26
Redbourn 163–8
Rees, E. Chris 385
Regulation 1a(a) 302–3
Reid, Sir Charles 305
Religious Revival 1904–05 33–4
Reynolds News 303, 321–2, 325, 328, 330, 334, 352
Richard Thomas & Co. 163–6, 221, 340
Richards, Robert 127, 175, 211, 321, 328, 336, 355
Richards, Tom 50, 97, 120

Also from Y Lolfa:

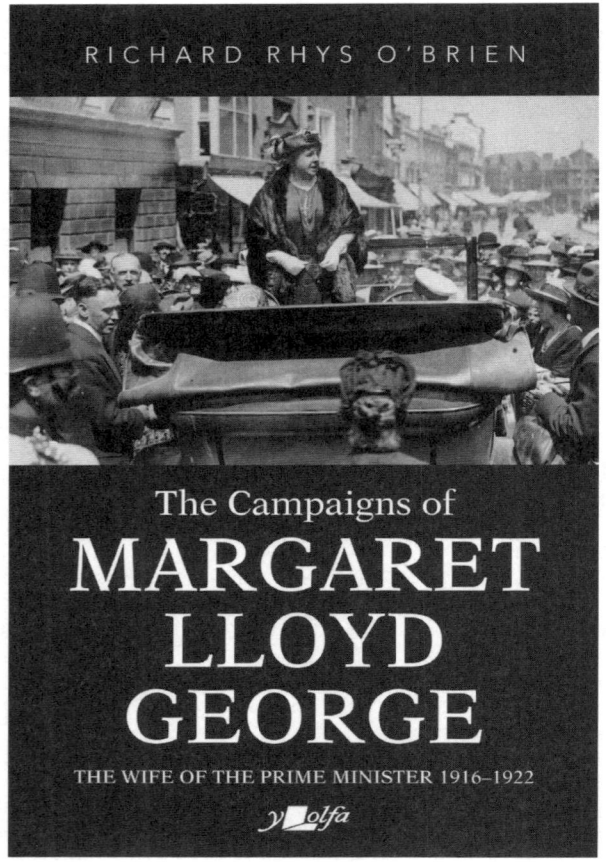

£14.99

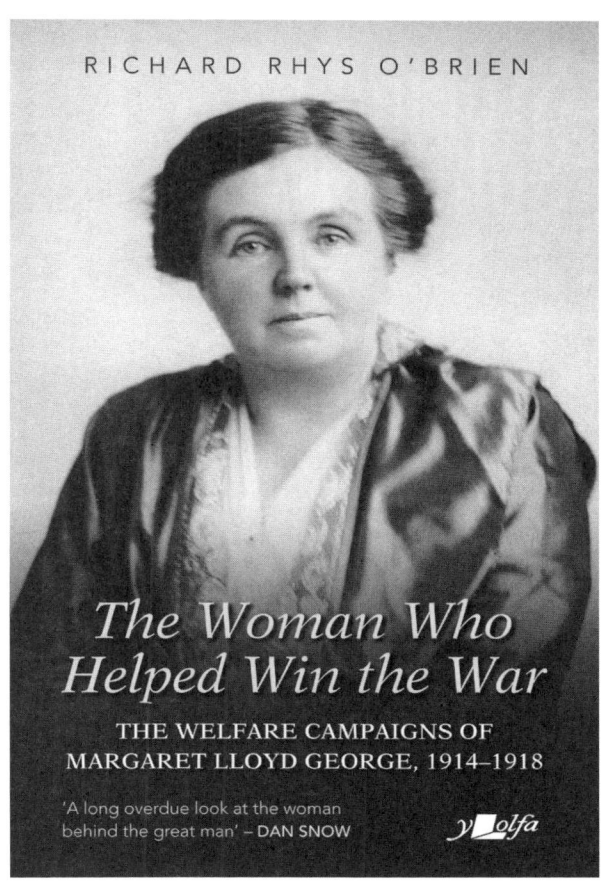

RICHARD RHYS O'BRIEN

The Woman Who
Helped Win the War

THE WELFARE CAMPAIGNS OF
MARGARET LLOYD GEORGE, 1914–1918

'A long overdue look at the woman
behind the great man' – **DAN SNOW**

y*lolfa*

£19.99

Stories of Solidarity

HYWEL FRANCIS

y Lolfa

£9.99

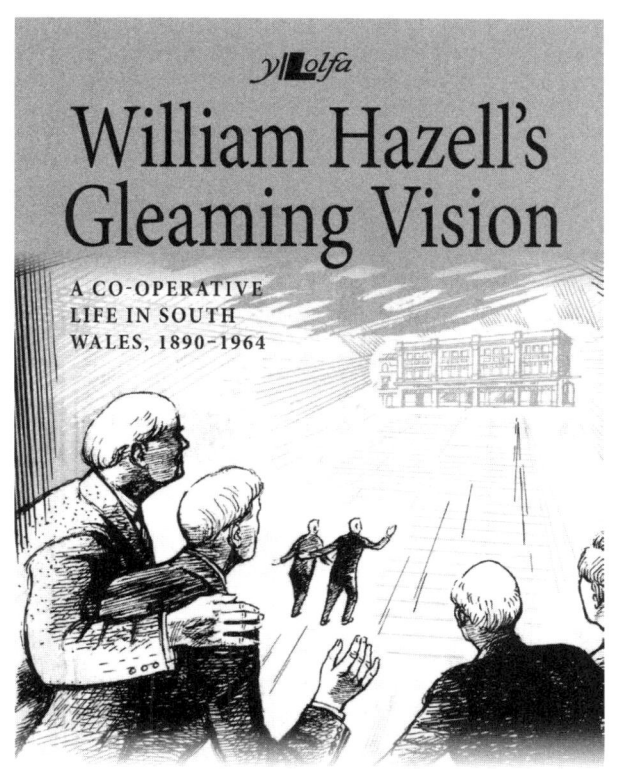

William Hazell's
Gleaming Vision

A CO-OPERATIVE
LIFE IN SOUTH
WALES, 1890–1964

y Lolfa

A L U N   B U R G E

£9.95